Democratic Futures

Democracy promotion has been an influential policy agenda for many Western states and international organisations, and amongst many NGO actors. But what kinds of models of democracy do democracy promoters promote or support? This book examines in detail the conceptual orders that underpin such activity, and the conceptions of democracy that democracy promoters, consciously or inadvertently, work with. Such an examination is not only timely but much-needed in today's context of multiple democratic and financial crises. Contestation over democracy's meaning is returning, but how is this contestation reflected, if at all, in democracy promotion policies and practices?

Seeking to open up debate on multiple models of democracy, this text provides the reader not only with the outlines of various possible politico-economic models of democracy, but also with a close empirical engagement with democracy promoters' discourses and practices. Drawing on a broad spectrum of examples, it exposes the challenges faced by Western governments and international organisations in trying to reshape the political and economic landscape across the world and tentatively advances a set of concrete policy provocations which may enable a more pluralist and flexible democracy promotion practice to emerge.

This innovative new work will be essential reading for all students of democratisation, democracy promotion and international relations.

Milja Kurki is a professor at Aberystwyth University and the Principal Investigator of a European Research Council funded project, 'Political Economics of Democratisation' (2008–2012).

Interventions

Edited by:
Jenny Edkins, Aberystwyth University and
Nick Vaughan-Williams, University of Warwick

'As Michel Foucault has famously stated, "knowledge is not made for understanding; it is made for cutting". In this spirit the Edkins–Vaughan-Williams Interventions series solicits cutting-edge, critical works that challenge mainstream understandings in international relations. It is the best place to contribute post-disciplinary works that think rather than merely recognize and affirm the world recycled in IR's traditional geopolitical imaginary.'
Michael J. Shapiro, University of Hawai'i at Mãnoa, USA

The series aims to advance understanding of the key areas in which scholars working within broad critical, post-structural and post-colonial traditions have chosen to make their interventions, and to present innovative analyses of important topics.

Titles in the series engage with critical thinkers in philosophy, sociology, politics and other disciplines and provide situated historical, empirical and textual studies in international politics.

Critical Theorists and International Relations
Edited by Jenny Edkins and Nick Vaughan-Williams

Ethics as Foreign Policy
Britain, the EU and the other
Dan Bulley

Universality, Ethics and International Relations
A grammatical reading
Véronique Pin-Fat

The Time of the City
Politics, philosophy, and genre
Michael J. Shapiro

Governing Sustainable Development
Partnership, protest and power at the world summit
Carl Death

Insuring Security
Biopolitics, security and risk
Luis Lobo-Guerrero

Foucault and International Relations
New critical engagements
Edited by Nicholas J. Kiersey and Doug Stokes

International Relations and Non-Western Thought
Imperialism, colonialism and investigations of global modernity
Edited by Robbie Shilliam

Autobiographical International Relations
I, IR
Edited by Naeem Inayatullah

War and Rape
Law, memory and justice
Nicola Henry

Madness in International Relations
Psychology, security and the global governance of mental health
Alison Howell

Spatiality, Sovereignty and Carl Schmitt
Geographies of the nomos
Edited by Stephen Legg

Politics of Urbanism
Seeing like a city
Warren Magnusson

Beyond Biopolitics
Theory, violence and horror in world politics
François Debrix and Alexander D. Barder

The Politics of Speed
Capitalism, the state and war in an accelerating world
Simon Glezos

Cosmopolitan Government in Europe
Citizens and entrepreneurs in postnational politics
Owen Parker

Studies in the Trans-Disciplinary Method
After the aesthetic turn
Michael J. Shapiro

Alternative Accountabilities in Global Politics
The scars of violence
Brent J. Steele

Celebrity Humanitarianism
The ideology of global charity
Ilan Kapoor

Deconstructing International Politics
Michael Dillon

The Politics of Exile
Elizabeth Dauphinee

Democratic Futures
Revisioning democracy promotion
Milja Kurki

Postcolonial Theory
A critical introduction
Edited by Sanjay Seth

Democratic Futures

Revisioning democracy promotion

Milja Kurki

LONDON AND NEW YORK

First published 2013
by Routledge
2 Park Square, Milton Park, Abingdon, Oxon OX14 4RN

Simultaneously published in the USA and Canada
by Routledge
711 Third Avenue, New York, NY 10017

Routledge is an imprint of the Taylor & Francis Group, an informa business

British Library Cataloguing in Publication Data
A catalogue record for this book is available from the British Library

Library of Congress Cataloging in Publication Data
Kurki, Milja.
  Democratic futures : revisioning democracy promotion / Milja Kurki.
  p. cm. — (Interventions)
  Summary: "This text explains the different models of democracy and the
  varied approaches taken by a number of international actors to promote
  (or impose) democratic and economic reform"— Provided by publisher.
  Includes bibliographical references and index.
  1. Democratization—Case studies. I. Title.
  JC423.K855 2012
  321.8—dc23
                                                        2012027473

ISBN: 978–0–415–69032–4 (hbk)
ISBN: 978–0–415–69034–8 (pbk)
ISBN: 978–0–203–07313–1 (ebk)

Typeset in Times New Roman
by Swales & Willis Ltd, Exeter, Devon

Printed and bound in Great Britain by the MPG Books Group

Contents

Tables

Preface

Democracy promotion, assistance and support have been key foreign and development policy agendas for most Western governments and international organisations since the 1990s. Yet, not only has democracy promotion been surprisingly unsuccessful in many contexts in the last few decades, it has also been increasingly challenged by many political actors for breaching the right of populations to 'freely' determine the shape of their own political and economic governance structures. Democracy promotion is a curious policy agenda – not least in involving advocacy of an idea which in and of itself has been declared 'contested' in nature.

The aim here is to call attention to an often noted but rarely tackled problem in democracy promotion; namely, that when we talk of democracies or promote democracies, we tend to have in mind particular conceptions of the idea 'democracy', rather than a plurality of possible meanings that this contested concept can take. This book addresses three inter-related questions about democracy promotion (or support as this agenda is now known in some circles) today. First, what kinds of 'politico-economic' visions of democracy are currently promoted by key democracy promotion actors, how and why? Second, how do the models of democracy promoted today reflect and shape the dynamics of a developing international order? Third, more normatively, what kinds of alternative visions of democracy, besides those practised, exist, and how might democracy promotion take account of visions of alternative democratic futures?

It is argued here that, at present, the dominant conception of democracy in democracy promotion is broadly 'liberal democratic' and ties its promotion to a liberal economic agenda. Despite many attempts to grapple with 'alternative' conceptions of democracy – American explorations of 'reform liberal' ideas, the European Union's exploration of 'social democratic' ideas, the International Financial Institution's leanings to 'embedded neoliberal' ideals of democracy – engagements with the idea of democracy have so far exposed democracy supporters to a rather limited range of democratic visions. Indeed, their efforts to escape the confines of the 'liberal democratic paradigm' have been constrained, even as various different traditions of liberal democratic thinking now proliferate, unnoted by most practitioners, in democracy support. The inability to move beyond 'liberal democratic' ideals is caused, as will be seen, by the curious and shifting nature of liberal assumptions in democracy support today. Increasingly 'implicit' liberal assumptions, I argue, provide the backdrop for democracy promotion, support and assistance, and delimit the nature and extent of 'debates' that can be had over democracy's meaning in democracy promotion.

Of course, this is no disaster as such: liberalism is a powerful, pluralistic and adjustable emancipation ideology. Throughout the years, its core ideas have been used and modified in diverse ways in the cause of multiple struggles for rights, recognition and equality around the globe. Yet, it is also important to note the strong, and increasingly hidden, nature of the liberal vision in today's world-ordering practices. This is because the implicit, and thus often un-noted, liberal principles structure views, actions and preferences of donors, and thereby also the real political structures, struggles and alternatives available to recipients of democracy support. We need to be aware of how 'implicitly liberal' dynamics, and paradoxes, play themselves out in the world order. This book seeks, through a detailed study of the conceptual foundations of democracy support, to contribute towards better understandings of the conceptual and ideological parameters of democracy promotion today.

I examine the parameters of democracy promotion's 'conceptual orders' in the context of a variety of democracy promotion and support actors: the United States, the European Union, non-governmental organisations and international financial institutions. I identify the distinct, and yet surprisingly shared, conceptual and ideological orientations in the practices and discourses of these actors in the democracy support community. Focusing primarily on the donors and key deliverers of democracy aid, I seek to make sense of the 'conceptual politics' of democracy support in the context of a changing world order.

The study here is not only empirical, however. I also seek to ask whether and how debate on alternative models of democracy can be incorporated into democracy promotion – nowadays a stated, but elusive, aim in democracy support. Such a normative and praxeological line of inquiry may seem strange to some 'objectivist' researchers. Yet, I argue that such types of inquiry should play a role in serious scientific analysis of democracy support which is currently confined too readily to 'problem-solving' positivist research agendas. Social science need not be purely empirical but involves, inevitably, questions of a normative kind. Acknowledging rather than denying this in the analysis of democracy support today, I argue, helps rather than hinders our ability to make sense of our research.

But is it really practical or, indeed, legitimate to look for alternatives to liberal capitalism and liberal democracy today? Is it, even in the context of multiple crises of democracy support and the liberal capitalist order, really viable to ask whether alternative models of democracy should be considered? Liberal (capitalist) democracy is after all almost synonymous with the idea of democracy today, and provides a robust defence against totalitarian systems and, some would argue, inequalities. Does opening up pluralism on democracy dangerously relativise conceptions of democracy, and hence legitimate authoritarian or developmentally laggard social and political systems in the global scene?

As serious as these worries are, the paradox at the centre of all democratic life is that, in debating the meaning of democracy, we should not avoid pluralistic debate. There is, almost by definition, a plurality of views to be had on democracy and its meaning, and these views need to be aired for the idea to gain hold in any democracy-aspiring society. Moreover, it is important to remember that the pluralisation and politicisation of debates on democracy is not synonymous with the relativisation of debates on democracy. We can still judge a democracy's content even if the criteria for it are under some debate: in fact, we may through such debate be led to more rigorous and dialogical debate on democracy's content, not just in target countries, but also in the 'West' among the supposed high achievers of democratic development. It is, then, not to the undermining of democracy or democracy support that this book looks to contribute, but rather to their revitalisation through conceptual inquiry. Taking seriously the conceptual politics of democracy promotion is crucial, I argue, for our ability to understand the power politics of today's democracy promotion, as well as the scope for considering and envisioning alternative democratic futures.

Acknowledgements

This book has been in the making since the summer of 2008, when the start of the European Research Council's (ERC's) generous Starting Grant allowed me to focus on developing this analysis of democracy promotion. I wish to then thank the ERC for its financial assistance to this book undertaken as part of the 'Political Economies of Democratisation' project based at Aberystwyth University. I also wish to formally acknowledge that the research leading to these results has been funded by the European Research Council under the European Community's Framework Programme Seven (2007–2013) ERC grant agreement number 202 596. All views expressed here are mine and do not necessarily reflect those of the European Community or its representatives.

Second, I wish to warmly thank the team that has worked with me on the 'Political Economies of Democratisation' project since 2008. They have helped, stimulated and contributed to the outcome of the project immeasurably, as well as having had to cope with my sometimes frustrated efforts to get to the heart of the democracy promotion's complex conceptual foundations. Chris Hobson has been an invaluable instructor and friend during this process, despite having left the project to take up a new life in Tokyo in 2010. Stepping into Chris's shoes, Jeff Bridoux has, since April 2010, provided both excellent academic contributions and organisational assistance to the project. The reader should also note that Chapter 7 on US democracy support here is co-authored with Jeff. Anja Gebel has not only contributed her own independent research input to the project in the form of her PhD work on politico-economic models in the international anti-corruption agenda, but also has added excellent provocations – both theoretical and empirical – to the analysis of the conceptual orders of democracy promotion. Marcel Van Der Stroom's research assistance in the final few months of the project has also been invaluable.

I also wish to thank various readers of sections of the manuscript: Heikki Patomäki, Rita Abrahamsen, Bill Robinson, Jessica Schmidt and Jonathan Joseph. Discussions with these colleagues have been very helpful indeed. I especially wish to thank Heikki, also a Visiting Professor within the ERC project. He read and commented on the manuscript in its entirety, as well as on various other outputs of the team over the last four years. His contributions have improved the output of the project, including this book, significantly.

I should also thank a few excellent audiences to whom this work has been presented. While many conference papers have been given on the themes of this book, I wish to thank the audiences at three particularly productive events: at the Kings College, London in February 2010; at Aberystwyth University in October 2011; and at the London School of Economics in October 2011. These events and the close interaction of the participants with the material have provided invaluable food for thought in the work leading up to this manuscript. When presented with occasions such as these, one still holds out hope for an academia which stands for freedom of thought, challenges conformist thinking and invests in critical interrogation of self-evident truths. I also wish to acknowledge that some material, especially in Chapters 2 and 3, appears in adopted form in the article: Milja Kurki (forthcoming 2012), 'Revisiting Politico-economic Models in Democracy Promotion', *International Studies Perspectives*, © International Studies Association.

Finally, on a more personal note, I'd like to thank Peter: first, for having to indirectly endure some of the stresses and strains arising from the project; second, for the many (cynical but provocative) commentaries on the future of democracy and the global financial order; and, finally, for providing a forest in mid-Wales as a welcome safe haven to escape to when necessary.

1 Introduction

Democracy, crises and contestation: revisiting conceptual foundations of democracy promotion

> The rights and liberties which were such vital factors in the origins and earlier stages of industrial society . . . are losing their traditional rationale and content. Freedom of thought, speech, and conscience were – just as free enterprise, which they served to promote and protect – essentially *critical* ideas, designed to replace an obsolescent material and intellectual culture by a more productive and rational one. Once institutionalized, these rights and liberties shared the fate of the society of which they had become an integral part . . . Independence of thought, autonomy and the right to political opposition are being deprived of their basic critical function.
>
> (Marcuse, 1964: 19, italics in original)

As this book was being prepared, the Western nations were dithering over whether to get involved in Syria, having intervened in Libya in the previous year in defence of democracy. These cases demonstrated to many people that Western democracy promotion suffers from inconsistencies and defects: democracy promoters, whatever their rhetoric, seem to be unable consistently to stand by democratic forces against authoritarian leaders.

While inconsistencies in 'high politics' of democracy promotion surely persist, it would be a mistake to view democracy promotion as insignificant, as something to be seen as mere rhetorical claptrap. This is because not only is the advancement of democracy one of the most powerful international policy dynamics in the post-Cold War era, it is also now a broad-ranging, relatively well-funded and firmly institutionalised policy field. Note that democracy promotion is today often discussed in terms of 'democracy support'. While shifts in democracy advocacy have taken place, here the terms 'promotion' and 'support' are used interchangably for democracy support is seen as the continuation of the generic democracy promotion agenda.[1]

Democracy promotion enjoyed a particularly prosperous context in the early 1990s. In the post-Cold War years not only was there agreement on the importance and universality of democracy as a principle of organising social life and 'modernising' post-communist states, there was also a consensus on the view that democracy could be promoted, or supported, by multiple actors, states, international organisations and non-governmental organisations (NGOs) (Sen, 1999; McFaul,

2004/5). At the same time as a side effect, if you like, of the rise to prominence of democracy promotion of Western states, democratic countries in the West became hailed as the 'high achievers' of democratic content and substance, and as such both legitimate role models and promoters of democratic values.

Yet, not only is Western democracy – as Marcuse above reminds us – far from unproblematically 'democratic' or conducive to fostering a real sense of democratic criticism, but also the role of democracy promotion can be rather 'undemocratic' in democratising societies where it can facilitate some power factions over others in far from egalitarian and dialogical ways. This is not only because democracy is often advanced in the interest of democracy-promoting states or societies themselves, a fact pointed to by many realist and critical observers, but also because it is often advanced according to their preferred 'models' of democratic governance, which are not necessarily reflective of the democratic thought and practice in target countries or the kinds of democratic visions that inform the multiplicity of actors who have a stake in the advance of democracy on the ground (Abrahamsen, 2000; Carothers and Ottaway, 2000).

Unfortunately, much of the current literature on democracy promotion, and importantly current policy practice, is ill-equipped to inform an in-depth debate about the visions of governance that Western democratisers and development actors promote. In part this is because a consensus has come to reign in the discourses and practices of democracy support: there is now a consensus on the need for democracy support in global politics and, perhaps even more significantly, a consensus on what democracy broadly means (see also Smith, 1994; Burnell, 2000; Gershman and Allen, 2006; Kurki, 2010). Thus, even when Western actors accept that they do not always promote democracy, or do everything they can in defence of democracy, they agree broadly on *what should be promoted* when democracy is promoted. Curiously, despite an increasing interest in facilitating local variations in democratic paths and the need for ownership of democracy aid, the democracy promotion paradigm comes with a consensual discourse that specifies the confines within which realistic and reasonable debate on democracy's meaning should be accommodated. Below a 'diversity-appreciating surface', a surprisingly agreed-upon idea of democracy emerges.

This is partly because there has been a distinct lack of interest among democracy promoters, and democracy promotion scholars, to seriously interrogate, reflect on and debate the various conceptual meanings that democracy can take. While liberal democracy is seen as the core ideal to be promoted, the contested meanings this concept can take are not systematically tackled. As a result, few practitioners or scholars have a good sense of what participatory democracy, social democracy and cosmopolitan visions of democracy actually entail; just as advocates of these visions have argued that realistic democratic practice needs to recognise the inadequacy of the traditional 'liberal democratic' paradigm.

This lack of interest in reflecting on democracy's multiple potential meanings itself reflects in part the dominance of what might be called an 'instrumental' 'problem-solving' attitude in the study and practice of democracy promotion. Democracy promotion practitioners have been primarily interested in instrumental questions of implementation – that is, how to deliver democracy promotion more successfully – and as a result have been concerned with practicalities which trouble democracy promotion, rather than exploration of the underlying visions of democracy, which condition its practice (Chandler, 2006b: 5). Many scholars too have preferred to stick to 'problem-solving' theorising and analysis. This is well evidenced in a forum on 'meanings of democracy' which appeared recently in the prominent *Journal of Democracy* (Diamond, 2010). While attempting to accommodate and reflect on the differences in meanings attached to the idea of 'democracy' globally, the forum's key concern was, in fact, how to measure support for 'liberal democracy' – a specific understanding of democracy's meaning – in non-Western states. *Contestation* over democracy's meaning between political actors was not discussed.

This book is informed by the belief that the failure to probe the conceptual underpinnings of democracy support is an important, and a consequential, weakness of current democracy support scholarship and practice. This is because instrumental approaches which ignore conceptual contestation over democracy's meaning come to delimit democratic debate over democracy and, thus, frank discussion over what is at stake in adopting one interpretation of the idea of democracy over another. Such approaches depoliticise democracy support practice – a practice once conceived (rightly) as deeply normative and ideological in nature!

To counter such instrumentalist tendencies, this work is informed explicitly by a critical theoretical impetus, which contrasts sharply with the problem-solving approach that is dominant at present in both study and practice of democracy support (Cox, 1981; see also Hobson and Kurki, 2011). Instead of seeking merely better implementation of democracy support, I focus on analysis of the hidden conceptual contours of existing practices, and their hidden ideological assumptions, power relations, conformities and contradictions. I study, from a broad critical theory perspective, the current conceptual foundations in democracy promotion, and notably the models of democracy that are promoted by core democracy promotion actors today. I seek to understand which models are promoted exactly by which actors. My focus is on understanding the 'high philosophies' of democracy promotion, but also the way in which they play themselves out in democracy promotion 'common sense' – implicitly or explicitly, systematically or unsystematically.

The aim here, then, is to go 'behind the appearances' of democracy support. I am not just interested in what is done or not done in democracy support and how 'effective' it is, but also in how patterns of thinking, social relations, power and room for political alternatives are structured through this policy agenda. Thus, I challenge here the more positivist approaches to democracy support, which conceive the policy area as normatively pre-given and thus primarily technical in nature. Instead I explicitly explore – and invite the reader to explore – the multiple diverse traditions of thought on democracy which motivate many democratic activists and agitators in the West as well as in the many target countries of democracy assistance. While I cannot explore all possible meanings which democracy can take in the multiplicity of local and global contexts, I seek to put forward some possible alternatives and examine how they are, and can be, engaged with in democracy promotion.

I challenge the assumption that democracy promotion, or even democracy *per se*, is inherently progressive or emancipatory: critical theory reminds us that easy conclusions about the emancipatory edge of specific processes (e.g. democracy under capitalist hegemony) tend to hide rather more complex, and rather darker, truths. Often, forms of conformism, lack of critical thought and thus 'hidden' forms of oppression of both thought and action can lie behind seemingly emancipatory ideals. Yet, being more attuned to the positive critical theory of early Horkheimer rather than late Adorno, I am *not merely sceptical* of limits of emancipatory practices.

Perhaps, rather controversially for many critical theorists, I too seek, in my own way, to construct room for better democratic and democracy support practice. I seek room for revitalisation of alternative modes of thought within the existing policy agenda. There are then not only negative critical insights offered here, but also praxaelogical proposals for reformulation, revitalisation and re-empowering of critical thought, and through it, the practice of democracy promotion. Indeed, critical theory as conceived here necessitates that we open up the possibility of engagement, rather than mere critique, with those who formulate policies, practices and programmes of democracy support (see Kurki, 2011b).

This means that liberalism and liberal democracy promotion – identified as key conceptual shapers of current practice, albeit in somewhat varied and sometimes disguised forms – are not merely critiqued but engaged in a constructive fashion. Thus, I do not mean to suggest, for example, that liberal democratic assumptions and hence practices – elections, rights discourses or rule of law – cannot be progressive and emancipatory. Surely, in Syria or Libya, liberal democratic rights are crucial in defence of the interests of people of various classes and political affinities. These rights and even their promotion, then, are surely preferable to support for authoritarian rule.

However, I argue for a revitalisation of democratic principles even within the 'liberal democratic' paradigm. Equality, pluralism and rights are contested values and thus liberal democracy itself is something that should be recognised to be ideological and contested rather than 'fixed' and 'technical' in nature. Indeed, opening up debate on the meaning of liberal democracy as well as democracy more broadly is a key aim of this work. This is crucial today, for not only is debate on democracy's meaning returning to political practices with a vengeance, but also most democratic theorists and practitioners remind us that liberal democratic practices may now be dangerously 'behind the curve': in rapidly changing structures of political and economic power, and with new forms of democratic agitation arising, classical liberal democratic ideals may be quite incapable of meeting the requirements of meaningful democratisation today (see e.g. Held, 1995; Crouch, 2004; Keane, 2009).

Crises of democracy support

I analyse the conceptual contours of democracy support in a context of a dual crisis of democracy promotion (Kurki, 2012b). The dual crisis is partly a crisis of democracy promotion itself. Democracy promotion, as many commentators have noted, has experienced an intense backlash in the years following the Iraq War (Gershman and Allen 2006; Whitehead, 2009, 2010). As Carothers (2006b) argues, this war, more than anything else, delegitimised democracy support in the eyes of many political actors and target states, which had already started to question the ability and the legitimacy of Western democracy promoters to transform other societies.

This is not all. A deeper, systematic, and I would argue a more substantial, challenge now threatens democracy and democracy support. The repeated financial crises of the last 10 to 15 years have demonstrated the fallibility of Western economic and political models of governance. The changing power structures in world politics – the relative decline of US power, resurgence of the BRIC countries (Brazil, Russia, India, China) and the increasing confidence of non-liberal states – are all placing some pressure on Western democracy promotion policy. To what extent should Western liberal countries and their development organisations lead in structuring the societies elsewhere when their own political, social and politico-economic structures are failing, both in terms of effectiveness and legitimacy?

Indeed, in the context of today's crises, no longer is democracy promotion a straightforwardly uncontested agenda (if it ever was). Not only are democracy promoters today more circumspect, if not apologetic, about their policies and practices, but also recipient states and populations too have demonstrated significant scepticism of the West's agenda (see e.g. Sadiki, 2000, 2004; International IDEA 2009a). Moreover, some commentators have explicitly called for greater awareness of the problems of Western democratic governance models in the context of democratisation (Armony and Schamis, 2005; O'Donnell, 2007; Rupnik, 2010).

Yet, the democracy support industry has not relinquished its power, and shows little sign of disappearing from Western policy agendas. Whether it be developments in Libya, or Syria, or North Korea, it is still predominantly in the name of democracy 'promotion' – or the 'rebranded' somewhat less pushy notion of 'democracy support' – that such countries are engaged by Western actors. The instruments and projects of Western development agencies and NGOs show little sign of losing interest in democratisation of third countries. What is interesting to note is that the democracy support agenda rolls on, despite the challenges facing democracy promotion in the context of the crisis of the legitimacy of Western foreign policy interventions and the crisis of Western models of democracy and economics. (For arguments in defence, see e.g. Diamond, 2008a; Mandelbaum, 2007; McFaul, 2010.)

However, what is not often noted is that the agenda today rolls on in *very interesting new ways*. The last 10 to 15 years have brought about interesting conceptual as well as practical shifts in democracy support, and their nature and significance are in part what I am interesting in examining in my analysis of the conceptual basis of democracy support. What does the move to local ownership, civil society aid, and language of diverse paths to democracy mean for democracy support? The conceptual approach adopted here speaks not only to current debates on what kind of democracy should be promoted, and the power relations of democracy support, but also to debates about the capacity of democracy support to shift their practices and ideals in an arguably shifting liberal world order.

These dynamics are not, it would seem, fully addressed or appreciated in contemporary studies of democracy support. Why?

Literature – state of the art

Current studies can be divided into roughly two camps. In academia, the mainstream literature on democracy promotion that is relevant to policy has been getting more substantial and detailed. Much has been written on democracy support, its actors, its targets and its instruments. However, the so-called 'mainstream democracy promotion literature' also has very specific interests. Almost exclusively, it focuses on analysis of one of three things.

For many, the core puzzle involves analysis of why democracy promotion should be engaged in and what its relevance and impact are in international politics (see e.g. Carothers, 2005; Diamond, 2008a; Mandelbaum, 2007; McFaul, 2010; Youngs, 2010). Others analyse the motivations which specific kinds actors have to engage in specific types of democracy promotion (see e.g. Smith, 1994; Cox et al., 2000; Carothers and Ottaway, 2000, 2005; Carothers 2005, 2006a, 2009a; Youngs, 2001, 2010; Pridham, 2005; Hyde-Price, 2008; Magen, Risse and McFaul, 2009; Lavenex and Schimmelfennig, 2010) or analysis of why democracy promotion unfolds as it does today (Burnell, 2000; Kumar, 2005; Zeeuw, 2005; Barany and Moser, 2009; Burnell and Youngs 2010; Texeira, 2009; Barkan 2011). A third group of analysts focus on interrogating the specific successes and failures of democracy support, in specific cases or across cases (Teixeira, 2008; Youngs 2010; Burnell, 2011; Wolff, 2009). There is much interest also in working out when and where democracy support succeeds and under what conditions. Further, more and more work today is focused on analysing the different modes of operation of democracy support: problems of electoral support vis-à-vis civil society support, or development aid vis-à-vis military intervention (Burnell, 2000; Carothers, 2006a; Huber 2008).

Studies such as these are both systematic and evidence-based and cover more and more ground in terms of cases and regions. They are then very welcome additions to the academic study of democracy promotion, which some decades ago was rather meagre. Yet, such studies are also problematic, or rather incomplete, in two ways. First, as already mentioned, they tend to focus on analysis of concrete implementation problems on the ground and their interests are, in the language of critical theory, 'problem-solving' (Cox, 1981). They tend to want to identify what goes wrong in democracy support and how to make it better. Second, there is little reflection in the literature on the conceptual assumptions on which democracy promotion, support, and assistance are based. Most studies work within a paradigm which sees democracy as an uncontested good, and crucially as a concept, the meaning of which is self-evidently captured by Western liberal democratic understanding of democracy (Burnell, 2000; Whitehead, 2002). Democracy entails elections, civil and political rights and rule of law, and – crucially – is assumed to go together with a capitalist market economy (see Kurki, 2010 for detailed analysis).

Even those who note the historical contingency of such conceptual leanings acknowledge that these conceptual decisions are necessary in today's context, given that liberal ideals seem to dominate (Burnell, 2000; Whitehead, 2002). As a result, the literature does not engage with the differences of views over democracy among target populations or the donors (Abrahamsen, 2000; Sadiki, 2004; Bell, 2006), nor the power relations involved in the promotion of specific concepts of democracy (Robinson, 1996; Gills et al., 1993).

This is the case, despite the fact that recently some more reflective 'conceptually oriented' studies have emerged from the mainstream. Collier and Levitsky's (1997) conceptual study initiated some conceptual reflexivity, for example. They discussed the various options political scientists have to speak of 'democracy with adjectives' and noted various ways to proceed as well as various dangers involved in 'conceptual stretching'. Yet, this effort did not involve dealing with normative visions of democracy beyond an essentially liberal paradigm, nor exploration of the ideological debate that is attached to definitions of democracy. In not touching on these aspects of conceptual decision-making Collier and Levinski bracketed out the 'conceptual politics' (Hobson and Kurki, 2011) involved in debating democracy's meaning in democracy support.

The *Journal of Democracy*'s (2010) forum on the meaning of democracy promised another possible way forward. In it, four sets of authors examined the poll data on the meaning of democracy generated from Africa, Asia, China and the Arab world, and aimed to come to some view on how to 'anchor the D-word' in the context of globally diverse understandings of democracy. The approach adopted, however, was 'objectivist' rather than 'interpretivist'. Thus, on the basis of poll data, objective evaluation of 'understandings' of democracy took place. Thus, Chu and Huang (2010), for example, categorised views of democracy in Korea as 'consistent', 'critical', 'superficial' and 'non'-democratic. Significantly, all categories assumed that liberal democracy constituted the 'end point' of any adequate understanding of democracy. Indeed, throughout this forum authors struggled to deal with the 'failure' of target populations to understand democracy 'correctly' according to liberal democratic ideals. Interestingly, no conceptual reflection or shifting of views on democracy's core meaning was required from the Western actors, despite the finding that Africans, Arabs and Asians tended to prioritise somewhat different value systems and institutions vis-à-vis Western actors.

Another, more sophisticated, effort to deal with conceptual matters in democracy promotion specifically has come through Thomas Carothers' (2009b) engagement with 'political' and 'developmental' approaches to democracy support. Carothers points out that in the Western democracy promotion paradigm singular understandings of the relationship between democracy and its context do not exist. Instead he argues that two paradigms – political and developmental – dominate in the development and democracy promotion communities. While those preferring a political approach prioritise purely institutional–procedural understanding of democracy and thus political levels of intervention in democracy support, the developmental approach involves taking into account the socio-economic development of states. Carothers records the sometimes tense relationships between these perspectives, although he suggests that no simple logic can be derived from the analysis. For example, it is false, he suggests, to consider the United States as a political actor and the European Union (EU) as a developmental actor in democracy support; both actors have both perspectives represented.

Carothers' argument is significant in accepting that different understandings of democracy, and what its promotion entails, may exist in democracy support. It raises the question of contestation within current democracy support as well as opening up room for overt debate over different approaches to democracy's meaning. Yet, it is not a perspective that aims to delve directly or deeply into different conceptual or ideological models of democracy or the political debate between them. Thus, the role of liberal democratic (or any other ideological) background assumptions in the 'debate' between political and development perspectives, for example, is not explicitly discussed.

These perspectives have been limited in their ability to deal with conceptual questions. Yet, to portray the academic scholarship on democracy support as purely unreflective or uncritical with regard to the conceptual foundations, ideologies or power relations of democracy support would be unkind to some important – if often poorly appreciated – 'critical' studies of democracy promotion within which its problematic conceptual foundations have been highlighted.

William Robinson's (1996) *Promoting Polyarchy* was a crucial intervention to the field in that he placed emphasis squarely on analysis of some of the core conceptual leanings of American democracy support. He argued that the democracy promotion agenda, driven by the United States, was tied to the promotion of a very specific procedural liberal democratic understanding of democracy, which by its very conceptual exclusions denied the possibility of more radical socialist or leftist understandings of democracy in target countries. This model, Robinson argues, directly benefits American capital interests. Democracy promotion, then, is but a tool of de-radicalising target states and stunting anti-capitalist politico-economic forces within them. Crucially, Robinson sought to understand the historical and socio-economic as well as political contexts from within which the promotion of democracy emerged as a key strategic shift in US foreign policy – but also the conceptually structured nature of the strategic shift.

Rita Abrahamsen (2000), in her study of good governance projects of the international financial institutions (IFIs), extended a conceptual critique to analysis of international organisations' work. Through a Foucauldian approach she sought to show how a liberal democratic 'Western' conceptualisation of democracy dominated the IFIs' good governance agenda, in such a way as to disenable calls for more social democratic practices on the ground in African states. The tying down of African states through development aid dependency, she argues, has resulted in a situation where African elites have to adopt the choices presented to them by the IFIs with regard to good governance, which in turn pushes them towards electoral democratisation without any real sense of popular democratisation on the ground.

An elitist conservative dynamic is embedded in the procedural liberal democratic notion of democracy in the good governance agenda.

Julie Hearn's (2000) and Alison Ayers' (2006) studies are also of relevance here. Hearn (2000) traces the way in which civil society actors are funded and supported by democracy promoters. She shows how stability of social order remains a key goal of democracy promoters, with the result that democratisation becomes more about fostering stable liberal democratic orders than about 'democratising' target countries. Crucially, echoing Abrahamsen, she argues that social democracy is becoming impossible in 'democratising' states where Western democracy promoters structure the field of action (Hearn, 2000: 818).

Alison Ayers (2006), on the other hand, records the way in which neoliberal understandings of the state, the civil society and individuals come through in democracy support. She argues that while (neo)liberal ideals on democracy – elections, universal franchise, constitutionalism, rule of law, human rights, good governance, minimal neutral accountable participatory government with effective bureaucracy and independent pluralist civil society (2006: 323) – seem natural, they are in fact highly ideological aims in Western actors' activities. The state, for example, is conceived as a tool in moulding society into the image of market society. Civil society support, too, carves out room for 'corporate society': it facilitates organisations and individuals with pro-liberal pro-market viewpoints (2006: 332). Bowen (2011), Gills et al. (1993) and Moyo (2001), too, show how elites and civil society can be co-opted to the cause of multi-cultural market democracy.

David Chandler's analyses (2000, 2006b) are concerned with the lack of room provided for indigenous determination of democracy's meaning, or indeed room given for democratic space at all by the eagerness of international organisations to govern for others. He examines the case of Bosnia as an example where democracy promotion is but 'tutelage': technical solutions on rule of law, good governance, and human rights result in a situation which 'leaves little room for the autonomy or self-determination of those to whom democracy is brought. Democracy is often presented as a solution to the problems of the political sphere rather than as a process of determining and giving content to the 'good life' (Chandler, 2006b: 483). Similar critiques by Sadiki (2004) and Teivainen (2009) make reference to the 'pedagogy of power' which pervades democracy support and its Western-centric conceptions of democracy incapable of grasping the meaning of democratic governance or related concepts in 'target' countries. Here liberal democracy becomes a form of rule, not a concept of liberation. As Rosanvallon (2008: 3) states:

> the problem lies . . . in the conception of democracy that has been exported and promoted. The fact of the matter is that a combination of western arrogance and a blindness to the nature of democracy have together produced disastrous results . . . multiple meanings are part and parcel of a regime that always resisted efforts to categorise it.

These studies provide an important context for this work, and it is such studies that I seek to build upon here in a distinct way.

The strength of the existing conceptual or critical accounts is that they highlight the significance of *conceptual decisions* made on democracy *by key democracy promotion actors* for the power relations between target states and donors, within target states, and in the ideological structuring of world order in accordance with liberal capitalist vision. It is to this literature I seek to contribute by analysing in detail the key shapers of democracy's meaning with respect to democracy promotion activity.

Even so, these accounts are not unproblematic. First, they can be overly theory-driven. The neo-Gramscian interventions (Robinson, 1996), for example, tend to *assume* an interest-driven and capital-driven function for democracy support, without being able to provide adequate empirical evidence for how democracy support is exactly tied to specific politico-economic interests. As a result, as Richard Youngs (2011a) argues, such critical analyses of democracy support can miss the nuances in actual practices, discourses and interest-formations present in democracy support.

Second, critical accounts also – surprisingly – seem to assume an overly singular understanding of the ideology of democracy support. Ayers and Hearn, Robinson (1996) and Gills et al. (1993) for example, suggest that liberalism or liberal proceduralism dominates in democracy support and argue that it is their dominance which closes down room for different conceptions of democracy. Yet, the meaning of liberal democracy is not, it seems, as clear to donors today as it is for their critics: close analysis shows movement on what liberal democracy actually means today in democracy promotion.

The language of 'extra-liberal' models of democracy now seems to pepper democracy support practice of the key donors – something not allowed for, nor seriously studied by critical commentators. Important rhetoric as well as methodological movements have taken place in democracy support and the ensuing pluralism (or fuzziness) of the conceptual approaches has not been analysed in detail. What is the consequence of the change of perspective on democracy of the Obama administration or the impact of the EU's move to promotion of the social model? What does the shift to post-Washington consensus mean for the International Financial Institutions' (IFI's) advocacy of democracy? The existing critical literature has not grappled with the full richness of (liberal) democratic variations of thought and practice, nor the possibility that alternative models of democracy may now make up a part of democracy support practice.

Third, many of the critical theory accounts mentioned above are dated. Having been written in late 1990s and early 2000s many of these interventions cannot fully take into account the key shifts in democracy support and development policy in the last 5 to 10 years. Key shifts include the move away from 'one-size-fits-all' democracy promotion to local ownership and participation-led practice of democracy support. The current democracy promotion scene is much more complex than it was 10 years ago. As will be argued here, the liberal hegemony in democracy support, if present at all, has changed its stripes. Not only is Washington consensus and its structural adjustment policies long gone from development practice, but so is the 'liberal-procedural' focus of democracy promotion practice of the 1990s. These shifts are important to theorise and to empirically appreciate (cf. Youngs, 2011a).

Fourth, it should also be noted that many critical accounts, while detailed in the analysis of singular actors, tend to be focused on the analysis of the democracy support of specific actors: key states, such as the United States, or key organisations such as the World Bank. This is a focus which, while understandable, also obscures the increasingly global nature of the democracy support practice. My focus, although primarily on key donor and delivery actors rather than 'local NGOs', encompasses analysis of a wide array of actors: the United States, the EU, NGOs and IFIs. This wide focus will of course narrow down the level of detail with which we can analyse each type of actor (and necessitates that we do not analyse 'local' democracy promotion activities in any detail), but is considered essential in analysis of the conceptual foundations of democracy support today. Not only is it important to understand the discourses of these 'democracy shapers' because they structure engagements with democracy in target countries, but also we must appreciate the global rather than merely 'national' context within which democracy support discourses function today.

Analytical orientations adopted here

As mentioned, I turn here to critical theoretical scholarship as an alternative to the problem-solving scholarship of the mainstream. An interpretive, reflective and normative-theory attuned approach is necessary, it is argued, to fully appreciate the contested nature of democracy's meaning – theoretically and empirically. We need to go beyond poll data (Diamond, 2010), and delineation of different policy paradigms (Carothers, 2009b), and systematically appreciate the role of conceptual assumptions about democracy in shaping and structuring democracy promotion discourses.

The analytical orientations informing this conceptual study originate from broadly critical theoretical background, but, crucially, are *intentionally much looser* in nature than those of many critical scholars, whether they be Marxists, neo-Gramscians or Foucauldians. Rather than interpreting democracy promotion's conceptual orders through specific theoretical frames, I think it is fruitful to draw from various schools of thought and concepts in making sense of the complex reality of conceptual dynamics in democracy promotion. Much like Tania Murray Li (2007) who, in her analysis of development policy in Indonesia, refuses to opt for a singular or fixed theoretical starting point, I too seek to start the analysis from a rather broad theoretical perspective, to keep multiple perspectives open in the empirical analysis that follows.[2] The broadness of perspective adopted here is also partly motivated by the realisation that critical theory, in its obsession with specific theoretical schools, is failing precisely because it has become too fragmented and abstract (Kurki, 2011a; see also Joseph, 2012).

Just three broad analytical starting points, then, are adopted as the guide for the analysis:

1. *Conceptual analysis.* I draw from the critical theoretical paradigm in that the starting point is explicitly conceptual in nature. Instead of starting from what is done or asking whether and how democracy promotion succeeds, I argue that it is interesting to analyse how conceptions of democracy, and hence specific ideological currents of thought, play out in democracy support in complex ways. Conceptual decisions structure in important ways who is funded, and how, and define what correct democratic values, institutions and social relationships should be in target countries, and between targets and donors. Conceptual considerations are far from insignificant, even if they do not explain everything. Conceptual understandings of democracy are not merely of abstract interest but are closely tied to the political struggles and projects of different political actors, representing different societal interests, classes or values (Gray, 1977; Kurki 2010; Hobson and Kurki, 2011).

2. *Essential contestability.* Again, in reflection of critical theoretical orientation, instead of assuming that democracy is an uncontested concept and has a singular meaning, I focus on how the contestability of the idea of democracy is taken into account. Political and democratic theory has for a long time highlighted the essentially contested nature of the idea of democracy (Gray, 1977; see also Kurki, 2010). My puzzle is: What is the relevance of this for democracy support? Given that in democratic theory, and even in democratic practice, democracy is a highly contested and politically charged concept – that liberal democrats, social democrats, participatory democrats, radical democrats, deliberative democrats, cosmopolitan democrats, all have different views on power relations in societies we live and hence of what core democratic values should be and what the key structures of democratic practice in society should be – it is important to ask what relevance this basic insight has for democracy support, especially today, as democracy promoters increasingly contend that they do take account of the contestability, or pluralistic nature, of the idea of democracy.

3. *Politico-economic models of democracy.* The third assumption that guides the project is the idea that democracy is always a politico-economic system or idea. This is often ignored in the core literature, and in practice, where democracy is curiously seen as something narrowly 'political' – a 'political' system of governance. Against the mainstream liberal perspective which separates the economic from the political, and hence the democratic from economic structures, I argue that all models of democracy are, in fact, politico-economic models of democracy (see Chapters 1–5; see also Kurki, 2012a). What this means is that different models of democracy conceive of and structure the relationship between the economic sphere and the 'political arena' in different ways. Even (and especially!) the liberal model, by separating the economic and the political, structures the relationship between democracy and the economy. The role of the 'democratic' in economy and vice versa then must not be left unexamined. If it is, we come to misunderstand the role, scope, and functions of democracy and democracy promotion in international politics. We will also miss the role of key actors in democracy promotion: the role of IFIs, for example.

The core research puzzle that emanates from these three very basic theoretical moves, and my analysis of the weaknesses of current literature, amounts to the following fairly simple one:

- What kind of politico-economic models do the democracy promoters advance today, how and why?

This core puzzle reflects an interest in a number of other related puzzles such as:

- To what extent do democracy promoters take account of the contestability of the idea of democracy?
- Are there specific conceptual models of democracy that emanate from their work or are their models undefined or unclear in their conceptual orientations?
- What do conceptual orientations of democracy promotion tell us of this policy agenda's role in the international political scene?
- What kind of alternative models can be delineated and what are their implications for democracy support today?

I also ask some more 'diachronic' questions, such as:

- How have conceptual foundations shifted in the last 10–15 years?
- How do such shifts sit within developments in democracy support and the liberal world order?

My view is that a new detailed critical theoretical reading that focuses on these questions is necessary given that existing literature is weak on detailed analysis of conceptual foundations. It is interesting to ask these questions in the current context because, while much has been written about the fortunes of democracy promotion, relatively little interest has been shown so far in detailed analysis of the conceptual confines which this agenda brings with it and how these contours have developed in recent times.

Comment on politico-economic approach, method and scope of this study

Before we proceed with this study, some introductory notes on methods and scope are necessary. Let me start by clarifying what is meant by the idea of 'politico-economic models' of democracy. I will then set out how I seek to trace them.

As mentioned above, a key theoretical orientation of this study is that democracy is understood as a contested as well as a politico-economic concept. That is, models of democracy are seen to be multiple and are seen to relate not only to the 'political realm', but also to structure relationships between the political and the economic. This starting point reflects the fact that this study starts from the assumption that there is nothing natural or obvious about the conjoining of capitalism and liberal democracy in the conceptual foundations of democracy support. This study does not accept the 'there is no alternative' (TINA) position, characteristic of much of economic and political science, which argues that liberal capitalism is the only viable economic paradigm today and is self-evidently attached to the promotion of liberal democracy. I seek to challenge this approach by re-examining the connection between democracy and the economy. I do so in two stages.

First, in Chapters 2–5, I explore in detail alternative 'politico-economic models of democracy': liberal democracy in its various contested forms and 'extra-liberal' social democratic, radical democratic, participatory and cosmopolitan visions of democracy. These models are often misunderstood and poorly engaged with in democracy promotion literature and practice; I argue that they need to be better engaged with and grasped by democracy promotion scholarship and practice. I then invite the reader, especially the non-scholarly reader, perhaps – to pay careful attention to these chapters in order to gain an understanding of why liberal democracy is *not* a singular or uncontested idea and why radical democracy or cosmopolitan visions deserve to be considered today.

Second, in Chapters 6–10, I examine how and whether such visions actually inform democracy promotion policies, assumptions and discourses. I trace empirically the characteristics of the ideal-type politico-economic visions in democracy promotion practices, with the aim of discerning value- and concept-hierarchies and hence models of democracy, or democracy ideologies, embedded – even if implicitly – in the practices of democracy promoters today.

Such a study of multiple politico-economic models of democracy – in democratic theory and democracy promotion practice – may be surprising to many democracy support practitioners and scholars if they have assumed that democracy and liberal capitalism simply 'go together' in a self-evident manner. Yet, the complications of this relationship were evident to Robert Dahl, one of the leading lights of liberal democratic thought:

> The relationship between a country's democratic political system and its non-democratic economic system has presented a formidable and persistent challenge to democratic goals and practices through the twentieth century. That challenge will surely continue in the twenty-first century.
>
> (Dahl, 2000: 179)

He is not alone. Neither Adam Smith (1970), nor the Marxist critics (Marx, 1978), have taken the relationship between democracy and the economy for granted but have explicitly advocated specific understandings of their inter-relationship. Thus, while liberals sought to safeguard the economic from democratic controls, the Marxist critics of liberal democracy and participatory democrats, for example, sought to do the opposite: to institute democratic controls over the functions of the economy. Even in twentieth century, political science scholars have – albeit mostly from a 'positivist' perspective, which reduces study of the economy–democracy relationship to measurement of economic and democratic variables against each other – paid attention to the relationship between democracy and economics, trying to understand how one conditions the other (Lipset, 1960; Haggard and Kaufman, 1995; Przeworski, 1991, Przeworski, Cheibub and Limongi, 2000).

The focus on politico-economic dynamics of democratic models is not new, then. Yet, the focus of this study is certainly different from the focus of classical positivist studies of the economy–democracy relationship. The focus here is on analysis of the *conceptual* tying together of economics and democracy: how do specific understandings of democracy condition understandings of the economic, and vice versa. The focus here is not the study of economics and democracy as empirical variables, but as conceptual frameworks.

This kind of approach has its limitations. For example, since I do not study here political economies of democratisation 'on the ground' but rather political economies of democratisation 'in the minds' of actors, there is only so much we can do in terms of elucidating specific transitional problems, say in Bulgaria or China. Yet, I will be argue here that understanding the models in the minds of actors (specifically democracy promotion actors) does assist in understanding concrete problems on the ground. It does so, first, in attuning us to the kinds of orientations and biases that might prevail in our efforts to understand the social world, but also it allows us to understand conceptual disagreements between actors, for example, donors and recipients. Crucially, then, a conceptual approach forces us to re-interpret, with a critical eye, the kinds of empirical analyses that are conducted 'out there' and how they are framed with and embedded in specific discursive frameworks themselves.

It should also be noted that the approach taken here cannot in a sense 'solve' the problem of what the relationship between economics and politics of democracy 'really' is or should be. Rather than seeking to find out the universal truth about how economics underpins democracy and vice versa, *the focus here is on exploring a plurality of models on how the inter-linkage can be thought about* – and crucially – on investigation of the *political consequences that arise from these differences*. Since the emphasis here is on conceptual and discursive systems within which knowledge about democratisation and democracy promotion policies is formulated, the focus is in essence on challenging frameworks of knowledge and, in fact, on re-politicising knowledge related to 'politico-economic models of democracy'. As the post-positivist turn in philosophy of science and social theory has taught us, where we speak from and how we deal with differences of viewpoints are crucial questions of power and politics, not issues to be siphoned off from analysis of political dynamics. Refocusing on conceptual questions, and exploration of a plurality of different conceptions of the relationship between economics and democracy, are then important moves in analysing the power relations embedded in democracy promotion. Indeed, as will be seen, I will argue that economic discourses have a crucially important role to play in delimiting and shaping the nature of our normative assumptions about democracy, even if they often do so quite unbeknown to analysts (they do so as 'formal causes'; see Kurki, 2008, ch. 6).

But how then do I seek to trace politico-economic models or understandings of the economy–democracy relationship in democracy support? In the empirical

Chapters 7–10 I try to find evidence of which conceptual set ups, or politico-economic models, are embedded in actors' accounts, through analysis of which values or concepts are seen as essential to 'democracy' in the discourses.

As is discussed in more detail in Chapter 6, this empirical analysis is informed by post-positivist philosophy of science, an interpretive 'hermeneutic' approach, and within it an analytical orientation to conceptual ideology analysis, which draws loosely in the first instance on some of the ideas of Michael Freeden. But what do I focus on analysing?

Given the 'conceptual' objects of study in this research, the data analysed is that which gives us indications of the conceptual contours and discursive trends in democracy promotion. The data used here is qualitative in nature and consists of textual and documentary and interview material. I conduct much of the empirical analysis through reading various core texts, policy papers, and guidance manuals, which shape democracy promotion practice of various different actors. Besides analysis of conceptual models in texts, a number of interviews have been conducted with relevant people in the practitioner field, in order to gain a sense of whether the conceptual patterns and contradictions identified in documents actually play themselves out in how practitioners think and practice democracy support. These interviews have targeted officials, desk officers, and private or NGO practitioners.

The texts and the interviews cover primarily the period of the last 15 years in democracy support, although I also, in each empirical chapter, refer to the history of democracy support beyond this timespan. The focus is on the last 15 years for a reason: I wish to examine the current state of play in democracy support but also to what extent shifts have taken place in democracy support since the late 1990s, the Bush years and the financial crises, which are the key 'shapers' of 'new' democracy support referred to earlier. Indeed, while essentially a synchronic study of conceptual orientations of current democracy support, I also do wish to make some comments on 'trends' and 'shifts' in democracy support.

In this context a brief comment on the scope and nature of the analysis is also in order. It is important to note that I do not seek here to cover every democracy promotion actor or instrument, although I still aim to cover a significant range of them: the United States, the EU, NGOs and IFIs.

In the case of each type of actor, with the exception of the analysis of NGO actors which is focused on careful study of individual NGO actors, the analyses in Chapters 7–10 have a two-fold structure. First, I analyse both the historical origins and a number of the core documents which guide the overall discourses of democracy promotion of the organisation. Second, I examine a selection of three to four concrete 'case studies' of the democracy support of each organisation. These cases do not seek to be representative, nor comparative. Rather, I have chosen to focus on areas of work in democracy support of each actor, which is unique to them. Thus, in the case of US democracy promotion, I examine the role of democracy support in its reconstruction policies, its civil society work, and its conditionality mechanism, the Millennium Challenge Account. In the case of the EU, I examine its specialism in electoral and parliamentary work, its civil society funding through the European Instrument for Democracy and Human Rights (EIDHR), its unique neighbourhood policy, and its democracy promotion through trade. In the case of IFIs, I examine 'good governance' work, anti-corruption programmes and the Poverty Reduction Strategy process.

The empirical analyses of actors, despite including wide-ranging documentary analyses as well as case studies, inevitably provide snippets only of the full range of democracy support conducted by the actors. Nevertheless, while not representative of the 'actors' *per se* – as we will see, most actors' democracy promotion is itself disparate and conceptually far from consistent across different areas of activity – the chapters seek to reflect the specific interests and specialisms of the different actors in democracy support, and hence arguably will be able to provide a 'flavour' not only of their conceptualisations of democracy, but also how these conceptualisations unfold in practice. But what does the book argue about democracy support today, and what is the significance of this argument?

The argument

I argue that the detailed conceptual study of the understandings of democracy played out in democracy promotion activities reveals that, while practices and conceptions of democracy are now more multifaceted than in the 1990s, still, a liberal democratic and a liberal economic paradigm continues to play an important role in democracy promotion activities. Even though the liberal democratic model may be *passé* as a descriptor of the reality of democratic practice 'out there' – as many critics have said, democratic practice even in the West has moved beyond liberal democratic governance (Crouch, 2004; Keane, 2009) – the conceptual assumptions continue to motivate actors working in the democracy promotion field. It is primarily liberal democratic politics that they envisage in target states.

Yet, I also argue that the liberal democratic orientation in democracy promotion is much more varied and diverse today than many critics of 'liberal democracy promotion' have suggested. Critics often imply that a narrow procedural idea of liberal democracy dominates. This is not true. Not only are civil society engagement and participatory consultations now part of 'liberal democracy promotion', but also, crucially, we find that important debates between various different liberal democratic traditions of thought can be seen to be present in current democracy support. Thus, classical liberal understandings of democracy are inter-mingled with neoliberal ideals as well as, today, some calls for reform liberal democracy, where the state's role in liberal democracy and social welfare provision is seen as much wider than for classical or neoliberal democrats.

There is, we observe, a complex interplay of liberal democratic models in current democracy support, even if this interplay is often rather un-systematised and poorly conceptualised in practice, and as a result, tends to be rather inconsistently applied or implemented. Practitioners, nor scholars, seem to be aware of the fact that, while liberal democratic ideals may be dominant, liberal democracy's meaning is now far from clear-cut in democracy support. Oscillation and confusion exist *within* the liberal democratic discourse itself.

While noting the conceptual divergences in current practices, I also note that despite the partial undoing of a clear (and narrow) liberal democratic ideal, and the resultant proliferation of meanings of liberal democracy in democracy promotion discourses, there is still a liberal hegemonic consensus at the heart of democracy promotion. Understanding its role, I argue, is crucial, for it is only with adequate theoretical tools to understand the contours and functions of this conceptual hegemony that we can understand whether room exists for alternative politico-economic models in democracy support.

I argue that it is almost exclusively within the liberal democratic set of conceptual parameters that democracy's meaning today is explored, debated or discussed in democracy promotion. While some debate on democracy's meaning can be held, this debate is confined to liberal democratic markers. This means, crucially, that accommodation of 'extra-liberal' models of democracy of interest to many democratic agitators today – models such as social democracy, participatory democracy, radical democracy or cosmopolitan democracy – is stunted at best. Interestingly, in rhetoric, the essential contestability of democracy, or at least diversity of the meanings of democracy, is now taken into account by democracy supporters. Yet, this insight, which now appears in almost all democracy support documents and guidance, has remained rather poorly followed up in interrogation of concrete political possibilities, visions and struggles over democracy's meaning. No consistent exploration of the implications of social or participatory democracy, let alone radical or global democracy, is present in democracy promotion today. While the language of social and participatory ideals is sometimes incorporated into the democracy promotion discourses, it is, in fact, liberal democratic re-interpretations of these ideals that emerge from such engagements, not a debate on alternative visions of democracy, or even adequate exploration of the meaning and content of such alternative visions. A liberal democratic background discourse has been dominant in much of academic study as well as practice of democracy and democratisation and, as a result, contestedness of the nature of democracy has received rather a formal and limited recognition only. Why is this?

One of the key contentions here is that liberal politico-economic visions of democracy, while still influential, have 'gone into hiding' in the democracy promotion paradigm. Liberalism in democracy support today manifests itself increasingly in an 'implicitly liberal' manner. What this means is that instead of sticking up for 'Big-L Liberal' principles, democracy supporters increasingly hide liberal conceptual underpinnings deep within the discursive and practical paradigms they work in. The managerial tools, guidance manuals, technical standards and rules of best practice become the source of liberalism in democracy support. Democracy support is simultaneously depoliticised and 'small-l liberalised'.

This development goes hand in hand with the other key trends, notably the movement towards diversity-accommodating consensus across actors. Curiously, even as liberal democratic ideas are actually proliferating and the language of alternative models of democracy are also accommodated, debate on contested-ness of models of democracy is becoming stunted, precisely through the spreading of a depoliticised 'consensus' on 'broadly' liberal democratic ideals. There is a fundamental paradox at the heart of the democracy project's conceptual foundations: they are seemingly pluralist, yet are constrained and consensus-oriented.

This paradox, while puzzling, can be understood and grappled with through a selection of Gramscian and Foucauldian ideas explored in Chapter 11. A synthesis of Gramscian and Foucauldian theoretical ideas can account for, I argue, many of the seeming contradictions of current conceptual orders in democracy support. These theoretical tools both point us in the direction of considering the conceptual orders of democracy support in the context of a politico-economic system of liberal governance and its 'governmentality' techniques. They also explain two further trends recognised in this study.

First, I also note here the prioritisation of role of NGOs and civil society organisations (CSOs) in democracy support delivery. No longer is it state institutions or bureaucracies that are democratised. One of the key dynamics that has emerged as a result of the move towards local ownership of development aid is that democracy support is about facilitation of the right kind of 'democratic civil society'. This also means that today the management and delivery of democracy assistance is in large part in the hands of 'autonomous' NGOs, civil society organisations, or private companies.

This has, crucially, entailed a key shift among donors towards development of detailed technical management guidance for democracy aid, and it is in these bureaucratic regulations that the 'conduct' of democracy-facilitating NGOs is 'conducted', where they are regulated and 'written in' as the right kinds of NGO actors, acting in defence of the right kind of civil society forces. Appreciating the subtle trends towards 'governing' of actors through 'techniques' is, I argue, essential today in understanding the way in which 'implicit liberalism' works in democracy support. It is central to understanding how specific models of democracy can emerge into democracy support practice even when policy practitioners argue that they do not work with a 'specific model'. Indeed, as I argue in Chapter 9, the work of even openly politicised or ideological NGO democracy supporters (e.g. political foundations) is now increasingly managed, depoliticised and regulated through donors' management practices.

A further finding pertains to the role of a 'strong stable active liberal state' as a key assumption structuring democracy promotion, support and assistance. Despite the moves towards civil society support and 'action at a distance' in democracy, it is also crucial to note that the heart of the agenda still involves – and perhaps involves more than ever – an interest in facilitating the right kinds of states. These, today, are not 'minimal' states or even 'procedurally democratic' states, but rather strong stable liberal democratic states. They should have the right kinds of tax systems, legal frameworks, economic policies and governmental structures, hence the interest of 'democracy promoters' – the EU and the IFIs, for example – in regulating their technical governance frameworks in minute detail. When democracy promotion functions in the context of such assumptions, as I suggest here, room for thinking or debating alternative politico-economic models of democracy becomes immediately restricted. Whatever the language of partnership, participation or dialogue, if the 'ideal' towards which actors on the ground are to work is already 'set' by the technical, economic and legal regulations which define what a stable strong liberal state looks like, room for democratic debate on democracy's meaning will be limited.

These findings, elaborated on in the empirical Chapters 7–10 and in Chapter 11, are important in pointing to often un-noted trends in democracy support. They also, as I argue in Chapter 11, give us clues about important shifts in global governance agendas more widely. Indeed, it is not necessarily the conceptual orders of democracy support alone which are shifting today; so are world ordering practices in the liberal world order more widely. Trends towards 'small-l liberalism' in democracy support may be reflective of trends in liberal world order more generally towards more depoliticised, locally-owned and diversity-accommodating forms of liberal hegemony.

Crucially, what we find is that Marcuse's warnings about the potential failures of liberal democracy in the West, ring true also in relation to democracy promotion. The potentially radical and critical edge of democratic development – and the role of alternative politico-economic projects in re-visioning democratic futures – are being de-politicised and de-radicalised *within* the democracy promotion paradigm and its 'implicitly' liberal agenda. The EU, it is argued, is a leader in this fudging of agendas, although the United States too has taken a shift towards such agendas. Interestingly, democracy promotion NGOs too, while seemingly the bastions of politicised and radical democracy promotion, have found a role within the new 'implicitly' liberal superficially diversity-accommodating agenda.

These developments would be far from significant if they did not have real effects on the power relations of democracy promotion and the future of global order. Conceptual decisions and commitments, even when (and especially when) implicit, can play an important role in structuring states and societies of target countries, and increasingly also the 'attitudes' of the public and civil societies of these states, even though those effects may not be universal or constant across contexts (see Joseph, 2012). They also can, and often do, structure relations between the 'West and the rest' and crucially are reflected (if do not deterministically follow) politico-economic interests and power relations. It is then important to pay attention to them, even if these conceptual dynamics do not on their own account for all developments in democracy support (see Chapter 11).

The line of argument developed here on the 'politico-economic models of democracy in democracy promotion' re-enforces, but also challenges, the views of some key commentators, such as Youngs (2010), who have recently argued that liberalism is on the wane in democracy promotion. The problem, according to Youngs (2010), is not the excess but rather the lack of consistent liberal practice in democracy promotion and foreign policy more generally (in his work the focus is on the case of the EU). This judgement is persuasive: few democracy promoters now openly accept that they engage in an ideological enforcement of a liberal politico-economic model and accept the contestability of the idea of democracy, the contextual nature of democracy, and the need for participatory and bottom-up approaches in supporting democratic developments. While this is the case, I argue that liberalism still plays an important role – albeit often an implicit one – in the conceptual premises of democracy and market promotion. Behind pluralistic language and practice and diversity-accepting discourses can lie also hard edges of very specific (neo)liberal ideals. Certainly, it seems that the apparent plurality of models of democracy in democracy support discourse does not translate to true recognition of political contestability of the idea of democracy or a broad range of alternative politico-economic visions.

This has important consequences for how we understand the role of democracy support in world politics. Have we moved away from hegemonic single-size fits all approaches in democracy promotion as a result of the many adjustments that have taken place in the agenda in the last decades? How significant are those shifts? I argue that, yes, there have been crucial shifts, but these have not resulted in substantive shifts in models advocated, prescriptions applied to target states, or power-dynamics between donors and recipients. Conceptual foundations of democracy support are more complex and nuanced, but also still far from maximally 'pluralist'. Reliance on local actors, deliverers and democratically competitive methods of delivery in the context of a seemingly pluralistic discourse is useful and pragmatic for democracy promoters: much more so than commitment to Big-L Liberal ideas, which target states in current context can too easily contest as 'pushy' and 'Western'. New conceptual tools and shapes are in place, then, in democracy support and these play foundational roles in facilitation of a still-existing hegemony of liberal economic thought and practice.

It is the reshaping of these conceptual foundations that Chapter 12 tackles. In the praxaelogical frame of reference adopted here I wish to make recommendations for how different types of policy actors can seek to advance, from their differential positions, the cause of more open debate on democracy's meaning in democracy support today. Such redirections of debate are important ethically, I argue, for democratic debate on democracy's meaning is a crucial demand for any democracy-aspiring community but also, practically, for re-invigoration of democracy support in the context of the re-emerging contestation over democracy's meaning.

Part I

Democracy as a contested concept

Surveying politico-economic visions of democracy

Introductory notes on 'models' of democracy

The essential contestability of the notion of democracy has been a key theme in democratic theory (Gray, 1977). But what kinds of meanings can the idea of democracy take? Specifically, what kinds of politico-economic visions do democratic theory and democratic practice contain? These are difficult questions, not only because of the difficulty of drawing clear lines between different ideas about democracy, but also because of the endlessly plural meanings that may be attached to the idea. Some brief introductory comments then are necessary on what is meant by politico-economic 'models' of democracy in this study.

Why the language of 'models' in relation to the idea of democracy?

On the most basic level the concept of 'model' refers to specific set of assumptions which a person, or a group of people, has about a given object. A model implies an abstract idea of an object. In the social sciences most 'social objects' – the state, law, economy, globalisation – are objects which have to be captured through some kind of 'abstraction'. Democracy too, while a lived practice, is also a social object that can be, and in some regards has to be, captured in 'abstract' terms. It does not simply 'exist out there' but acquires meaning and content through specific assumptions and ideas held about the notion and its relationship to other concepts and ideas.

This abstract nature of the idea of democracy is neatly captured in the idea of 'models of democracy'. This notion was developed by David Held (1996), who in turn drew on the ideas of C.B. Macpherson (1977). For David Held (1996: 7), 'model of democracy' is a notion which refers 'to a theoretical construction designed to reveal and explain the chief elements of a democratic form and its underlying structure of relations . . . Models are . . . complex "networks" of concepts and generalizations about aspects of the political realm and its key conditions of entrenchment, including economic and social conditions'. He argues that in examining models of democracy 'it is important to inquire into their key features, their recommendations, their assumptions about the nature of society in which democracy is or might be embedded, their fundamental conceptions of the political capabilities of human beings and how they justify their views and preferences' (Held, 1996: 8).

Held's idea captures neatly the idea that there is no one object called 'democracy' but various ways of giving the concept, and its practice, meaning. Thus model language emphasises that a single concept can acquire different meanings – assemblages of ideals, forms and values – and that these can be structured differently into various 'ideal types', or 'models', which in turn can be used to both understand democratic orders and come to guide democratic practice.

With regard to the kinds of views of democracy that we are concerned with here, the focus is specifically on those models of democracy where an economic theory or a discourse is closely interlinked with and influential on the understandings people have of the nature of democracy. 'Politico-economic models of democracy', then, are seen here as models of democracy linked to specific politico-economic discourses.

There are aspects which different 'politico-economic models of democracy' entail and aspects on which they differ. In my approach to examining ideal types of models of democracy, I focus analysis on how models:

- hold specific (and in relation to compating models, different) conceptions of the *balance of values* that democracy protects and embodies;
- hold specific (and different) conceptions of the *relation that should exist between democratic publics and economic processes/policies/sphere*; and
- work with specific (and different) conceptions of *how democracy should function* or work institutionally.

The considerations listed above constitute core aspects of different 'politico-economic models of democracy'. Such models work, in sum, with different analyses of the nature of man and society, of power relations in society, of core democratic values, and of concrete institutions and functions of democratic processes. While this may seem clear enough, there are a couple of complications we have to note in using the idea of 'models'.

First, it is important to note that the idea of 'model' of democracy used here is meant in an abstract 'ideal type' sense. That is, by the liberal democratic model, for example, I do not make reference here to, say, the concrete French or Italian models of democracy, but rather the core values and institutional forms that the idea 'liberal democracy' is associated with on a more abstract level. I work then with the term model in the broad sense; 'model' here has a meaning akin to 'conception' of democracy.

Second, it is also important to note, again following Held, that the approach taken here recognises that 'models of democracy involve necessarily . . . a shifting balance between descriptive-explanatory and normative statements; that is, between statements about how things are and why they are so, and statements about how things ought to or should be' (Held, 1996: 8). This again echoes Macpherson's perspective which emphasised that models of democracy:

> have been both explanatory and justificatory or advocatory. They are, in different proportions, statements about what a political system or a political

society is, how it does work or could work, and statements about why it is a good thing, or why it would be good thing to have it or to have more of it (Macpherson, 1977: 4).

Macpherson (1977: 4) and Held (1996: 8) both warn us that, while some democratic theorists openly recognise the close interrelations between values and explanatory claims, many modern democratic theorists pretend – misleadingly – to be value-neutral in their descriptions of models of democracy. Here the approach is to openly recognise the *inherent normativity of models of democracy*. As democratic theorists – and democratic practitioners – we must recognise both empirical and normative content in our preferred visions.

Yet, it should be noted that values attached to views on democracy or conditions of democracy, may sometimes be only implicitly decipherable in theorists' (or practitioners') accounts. Many empirical democratic theorists, and democracy support practitioners dealing with democratic processes, for example, tend not to openly discuss the values they attach to democracy. However, through careful study, values can be delineated in various accounts despite theorists' or practitioners' unwillingness to talk about them. They can be deciphered within the texts through either unintended phrasings or omissions (Freeden, 1998; see also Chapter 6 for detail).

But how systematic can such ideas be? Corcoran (1983: 20) argues against the very language of 'models' because it implies that people hold 'systematic' views on democracy, an assumption he thinks is misleading. Rosanvallon (2008) also shares scepticism of model language: for him, democracy is a concept which is fundamentally dialogical and dynamic in nature.

These are important points. However, it is not my aim to argue that the models of democracy identified in the first part of this book are adopted in systematic ways in democracy support – indeed, as I will argue, the adoption of models is *increasingly unconscious and implicit* in democracy support! Yet, by appreciating the outlines of ideal type politico-economic models, we can, I argue, identify key patterns of values (Freeden, 1998) which we can use as bases for study of empirical reality of democracy support discourses.

The 'models' set out in Part I, then, are 'ideal typical' reconstructions or visions of democracy. Whether they play themselves out in democracy support is (here) a secondary question. Yet, as ideal types they do provide a 'road map' through which we can start to decipher the broad outlines of what we may be faced with in messy policy contexts (see Chapter 6). Thus, while individual policy-makers or documents may not display coherence of thought on ideal type democratic models, they may display value hierarchies, omissions, and understandings of relations between concepts that may betray conceptions of democracy associated with one or another tradition of thought, more or less closely.

What of the choice of models adopted as 'ideal types' here?

Defining the scope of what is to be considered is the most challenging question within a project such as this, for any interpretive decision on what to include also entails decisions on what to leave out. Such decisions of course are always not only acts that privilege some perspectives over others, but also moves that act against the very normative drive of the project to 'pluralise' perspectives. While I recognise these limitations, I have decided, for the sake of structuring the discussion and the analysis that follows, to choose a specific set of perspectives on democracy as my guiding visions.

The models I have chosen to discuss here are the following:

(1) The liberal democratic model, and its variants
(2) The socialist 'delegative' model and the social democratic model
(3) The participatory democracy model and the radical democracy model
(4) The cosmopolitan and global democratic model(s)

Two important criticisms of the choice of models here need to be addressed. First is the claim that these models are 'Western' in nature and ignore the different 'cultural' experiences with the idea of democracy, such as the Arabic, Chinese or African models of democracy. As important contributions such as Bell's (2006), Sadiki's (2004) and Sklar's (1987) have shown, many areas globally have their own indigenous debates on democracy and understandings of the concept (or related concepts).

The interest in this book (for better, for worse) is specifically on the study of politico-economic models of democracy, and it is for this reason that I focus primarily on setting out the above politico-economic ideal types. These models are arguably the most relevant for the analytical purpose of this study, even if they would not do for a book which sought to record different cultural experiences of democracy.

Second is that these models, while not by any means universally valid or representative of all global ideas on democracy, do also speak to the concerns of democratic practitioners beyond the 'West' (in itself a problematic notion). In a globe drawn together discursively as well as politico-economically, these models may, in different ways, provide an orientation point for many Middle Eastern and African actors too. Thus, while certainly contextually different and indigenous ideas about democracy also exist – I do not argue that they do not or should not – these ideas have also politico-economic qualities which can in important ways resemble those of the models set out here. Thus, these models provide an interesting orientation point in understanding cultural responses to democracy, even though they do not necessarily capture (nor would I claim they do) everything that is relevant about democratic thought and practice in different cultural contexts.

Are these models outdated?

John Keane (2009) argues that we have moved to the era of a qualitatively different type of democracy, namely 'monitory democracy'. Colin Crouch (2004) contends that we live today in a 'post-democracy', and Sheldon Wolin (2008) holds that democracy today is more akin to 'inverted authoritarianism'. These analyses are important. Yet, whatever the reality of 'democracy' on the ground, what is of interest to us is that discursively specific democratic models still play a central role in democracy promotion discourse. This is why analysing their role is important.

The selection of models here is partially arbitrary and selective; yet it can also be defended on analytical grounds. I am trying to portray the plurality of democratic thought on politico-economic models while also restraining the range of models considered to one which is realistic and empirically interesting for the actors and practices we study. The choices here may not convince all, but this should re-invigorate debate on models of democracy further – a key aim of this book, which, with its selection of models, provides but an opening gambit to pluralisation of thought on democracy in relation to democracy support.

2 The contested liberal democratic model

Its multiple variants

The idea of liberal democracy has been dominant in democratic theory, economic theory and social life more widely, during the twentieth century. It is thus a key notion of democracy for us to get to grips with. Dealing with this 'model', however, is far from straightforward. This is because democracy is a contested concept, not just between advocates of different models of democracy, but also among 'liberal democrats'.

The cluster concept 'liberal democracy', I will argue here, can take varied sets of meanings and hence there are (at least) four variants of a liberal 'politico-economic model of democracy' that we must consider. We will observe here that the meaning of the term 'liberal democracy' is subject to particularly pernicious pulls in meaning: while some emphasise 'liberal', others emphasis 'democratic' aspects of the term. There is no singular balance to be struck between liberalism and democracy in liberal democratic thought – although the oscillation of the term's meaning is, as we will see in later chapters, often ignored in analysis and practice of democracy promotion.

I examine here the evolution of meaning of the term liberal democracy. Four key models of liberal democracy are identified: classical liberal, reform liberal, neoliberal, and 'embedded' neoliberal. They all differ on crucial value-determinations, and thus in their understandings of how exactly liberal democracy should function. Nevertheless, we should not forget that there is also some ground of agreement between these variants of liberal democratic thought: generally all liberal democrats advocate a distinctly liberal conception of man and society; values of freedom and liberty as key democratic values; a representative parliamentary system as the key site and institution of democratic politics; and a liberal capitalist model of economics as a crucial underpinning of liberal democracy.

I will start with a brief introduction to the rise of liberal thought, followed by a detailed analysis of history of liberal democratic thought and, specifically, the role of different traditions of democratic thought within this venerable tradition. Echoing C.B. Macpherson, I argue here that we need to recognise 'how deeply the market assumptions about the nature of man and society have penetrated liberal democratic theory' (Macpherson, 1977: 21). This is despite the fact that the liberal arguments on the link between economics and democracy are not uni-linear.

Liberalism and liberal democracy

Liberalism,[1] as a political and economic tradition of thought – or as some would say, an ideology – arose at a very particular time in the development of modern society. It was a reaction to the religious doctrine, unlimited monarchies, and feudal modes of economic governance, and was primarily associated with, and expounded by, the rising bourgeois and middle classes in the seventeenth, eighteenth and nineteenth centuries. These groups or classes were gaining confidence and status in society but their power was threatened, in the first instance by the Church, which claimed monopoly over decisions over the 'good' life, and, second, by the arbitrary use of power by absolute monarchs, who through mercantilist policies unfairly restricted trade and commerce. Liberalism, in opposition to these forces, constituted a radical movement that sought to liberate the(se) people from arbitrary power and restrictions of the Church and the monarchs. It sought to do so by tackling simultaneously both economic and political constraints on the freedom of subjects. It had at its core a number of distinct assumptions about the nature of man, the natural patterns of interaction between men, and of the legitimacy of rule. Let us review some of these core assumptions of liberalism.

At the core of liberal thought is the idea of the *individual*. For liberalism, an 'individual is that being who, because he is human, is naturally entitled to 'rights' that can be enumerated, rights that are attributed to him independently of his function or place in society and that make him the equal of any other man' (Manent, 1996: xvi). Crucially, the individual at the centre of liberalism is one who is entitled to protection from arbitrary powers of the state. Thomas Hobbes had argued in the Leviathan that the absolute state is one that is premised on the basic human need for security. Drawing on this idea, the early liberals, such as Locke and Montesquieu, came to argue that individuals had a right to object to the absolute power of the state if the state actively harmed individuals' security or interests.

This is the origin of the idea of *a limited state*. Men could know their own good, liberals insisted. This meant that grounds should exist for involving men themselves in governance, in controlling the monarch. John Locke (1960) was among the first to introduce the right of rebellion within states. He also put emphasis on the need for a legislative body that was to control the executive government. Montesquieu, on the other hand, introduced the idea that power should check power, and hence the separation of power – between the legislative body, the executive and the judiciary – should form the cornerstone of a limited liberal state. These ideas were expanded upon by others: from Constant's emphasis on critical opposition to J.S. Mill's emphasis on representation. Developing limitations to state power was at the heart of the liberals' efforts.

A key such limitation was set by the idea of *representative government*. While democracy was a 'dirty word' among many liberals in the eighteenth and nineteenth centuries and up until the early twentieth century, it is crucial to note that most liberals, in thinking about the limited state, had in their minds a 'representative' form of government. This was considered to be the best mode of governance to accommodate government to the wishes of the bourgeois classes, if not 'the people'. It is for this reason that we can argue that some form of democracy seems to have been relevant to liberalism from the start. However, it is important to note that liberal thought has advanced a very particular set of ideas on democratic govern-ance. In fact, liberals tend to argue for very particular, and rather limited, notions of democracy, defined by representation of (some) people, separation of powers and emphasis on rights. Liberal values guide engagements with the idea of democracy.

Simultaneously to their political demands for a limited state, the liberals called for *opening up of restrictions on trade, and for the protection of property rights*. Indeed, property rights, and defence thereof, constituted a core demand of liber-alism: it is from property rights that the entire edifice of liberal rights emerges. Freedom to trade and exchange in 'civil society' (conceived as a market) was also seen as central to liberty.

Indeed, even though economic and political strands of liberalism are often treated separately in social theory today, not only did challenges to absolute state originally entail simultaneously both economic and political liberalisation, but cru-cially, the two forms of liberalisation were seen as interlinked. Yet, interestingly, the ways in which liberals have seen the relationship between the liberal capitalist economic system and liberal democratic representative governance differ and, for this reason, liberals with different orientations have come to hold rather distinct ideas about the meaning, core values and institutions of 'liberal democracy'.

In what follows I will examine, first, the key assumptions of classical liberal ideas of democracy. In the later sections, I move on to consider how reform lib-eral and neoliberal models of liberal democracy have extended and shifted liberal democratic thought beyond the classical liberal premises. Noting these variations in liberal democratic thought and practice is crucial to appreciating how the mean-ing of this term 'liberal democracy' can be determined in rather different ways, even by liberal democrats.

Classical liberals

Classical liberalism is known for its call for the values of rights and freedoms of the individual as a key underpinning of social life. Both political rights and economic rights are called for by classical liberals. The two systems of rights are seen as inextricably bound together, even if they have also been separated because of the tendency in classical liberalism to separate the 'economic sphere' from the 'political sphere'.

To gain a sense of how classical liberal thought developed, I examine here some exemplars of 'classical liberal' thought on democracy – from Locke's eighteenth century thinking to the very different twentieth century 'Dahlian' notion of liberal democracy.

Locke on origins of political rights

John Locke makes for a common starting point in discussions of liberalism, and is also pertinent for us in analysis of 'politico-economic' thought on democracy within the liberal tradition.

Locke famously argued for limitations to absolute sovereignty and for a semblance of representative governance as a check on monarchy's power. The starting point for his liberalism was that humans have certain natural rights: 'that moral rights and duties are intrinsic and prior to law' (Sabine, 1951: 526). The core assumption, which became central to liberal thought, was the idea that a human has a natural right to 'property', when he has 'mixed his Labour' with it (Locke, 1960 [1689]: 288). To combat hunger, men approached the natural world around them with the aim of appropriating from it a means of subsistence. By so doing, by exertion of their labour, men came to have the right to appropriate goods or land. Property then was a natural right (see Locke, 1960 [1689]: 287–91; Sabine, 1961: 527).

But what of the fact that most men exerting their power do not actually own the land or the product they exert themselves on or for? Locke argued that with the rise of the institution of money an ingenious way was found to preserve the value of labour exerted on a product, which could then be transferred (Locke, 1960 [1689]: 300–1). It followed that property needed not to follow labour but could be separated from it. As long as exchange of goods and labour was kept open and unrestricted, there was no problem in the transfer of the value of labour in the form of money. This in turn justified the maintenance of a property system whereby not all owned property. Free exchange of goods then, the assumption of free markets, was an assumption that followed, and justified, the previously established right of property and right of exchange through money.

What is interesting about this argument is that Locke's very idea of individual rights is deeply embedded in this *politico-economic argument*. A quite curious fact, which is often missed by commentators, is that for Locke the rights of the individuals, who were conceived as fundamentally egotistical (Sabine, 1961: 29), were dependent on a particular notion of political economy. Indeed, as Manent (1996: 46) powerfully argues, Locke 'made it possible to understand how the liberal philosophy of natural right spontaneously transformed itself into an entirely different type of thought: political economy'.

But what is the significance of Locke's politico-economic analysis for understanding representative government, if any? The key significance for us is that politico-economic concerns play a crucial role in Locke's conception of the role of the state. Locke saw protection of individual rights as the key role of the state. The role of the state is ultimately to defend property rights and the freedom of exchange, which justifies the existing property relations. It follows that the emphasis on legislative control on the executive or absolute sovereign was ultimately necessary in order to ensure that this defence of property was conducted in such a way that it did not infringe, in disruptive ways, on security of property and freedom of the market. In a sense, one could say that the limited form of representative government was needed to protect the efficient working of the 'moral' system Locke had set forth. Crucially, the absolute form of government was unpredictable in guaranteeing this, for it endangered individuals, and the system, to the whims of the lion, the absolute monarch. Importantly, for Locke, political institutions are necessary for the functioning of the economy in the 'civil society': he did not argue for the economic system on its own, but rather emphasised the role that political institutions had in 'guaranteeing its existence' (Manent, 1996: 47).

This politico-economic basing of classical liberalism is also evident in the foundational Scottish Enlightenment thought of the eighteenth century. A key concern for the Scottish Enlightenment thinkers was, as Chris Berry (1997) has pointed out, the concern with development of 'commercial society' as the basic premise of enlightened civilised social and moral order. Adam Smith was a key character in representing the so-called Scottish Enlightenment thought on commercial society.

Adam Smith

Adam Smith's theories are nowadays associated most closely with 'economic theory', because of the foundational influence that his *Wealth of Nations* (1970 [1776]) has had on the discipline of economics. Yet, it is important to note that Adam Smith, like most of the individuals associated with the Scottish Enlightenment, was a much more rounded thinker and by no means 'simply' an economist. Not only did he consider his own discipline to be one of 'political economy', but also his system of thought sought to advance a technical reading or explanation of liberal market system, as well as a deeply moral system of thought for a civilised modern society. This means that his work is not just 'scientific' and 'value-neutral', as it is often taken to be, but also deeply normative. Interestingly, his system of thought has built within it a deep, albeit often un-noted, theory, or at least 'proto-theory', of democracy (Kurki, 2012b).

What drove the Scottish Enlightenment thinkers, and Smith, was an interest in the rise of economic interdependence in society: they wanted to understand as well as morally evaluate this development. Economic interdependence was seen to lead to increasing freedom of individuals and 'civilisation' of society. Also, rule of law, legal equality and security arose out of economic interdependence (Berry, 1997: 124–125). How?

Adam Smith famously pointed to the invisible hand of the market as a key driver of societal life. Smith powerfully argued that our interactions, especially economic interactions, in society are not, and need not, be based on 'love for others', but rather on 'self-interested' aims. For Smith, a workable society arose automatically, or spontaneously, out of the self-interested actions of individuals (Smith, 1970 [1776]: 119). A basic driver of an economy was 'a certain propensity in human nature . . . to truck, barter and exchange' (Smith 1970 [1776]: 117). When individuals searched for profit through specialisation in production of specific goods, the whole society, through the free exchange of these goods, would gain in wealth and opulence. The invisible hand of the market ensured efficient allocation of resources, the balance of demand and output, the appropriate pricing of goods, resources and labour. It followed that there was no need for state or higher authorities to intervene in significant ways in the workings of the market. The market in important senses was self-regulating. The state, as much as it was to have a role, had three main functions: protection from external foes, maintenance of public goods (education especially) and administration of justice. But how did this view of the market link to the idea of liberal representational form of government and the idea of rule of law?

Crucially, a key argument at the heart of the economic and moral thought of the Scottish Enlightenment was, as Berry notes, the assumption that 'Commerce requires stability or consistency and security because it rests on a set of expectations and beliefs' (Berry, 1997: 125). Specialisation into specific aspects of economy is made in the expectation of a return on investment and this requires a set of systems to be in place, concerning stability of the value of money, enforcement of contracts, and guaranteeing of property rights. At the centre of the economic system and its efficient functioning is a rule of law that is an 'impartial administration of justice'. Ensuring such a system of justice is the primary function of the state. There is a need for impartial and equality-based rule of law and political governance *because* this is functionally necessary for the efficient functioning of the market, and hence for the maintenance of a civilised commercial society.

This is an interesting assumption, for what is clear is that for Smith and other Scottish Enlightenment thinkers, rule of law and the representative systems of government arise from the needs of the market, from specifically the need to ensure efficient grounds for economic interaction. Equality before law, and also representative government itself, is required – not because it has inherent moral value, but because such a system of governance and law allows for the efficient working of the market. Such systems ensure a 'stability of expectations' by merchants and producers, and if needs be, the feeding into the system of their interests in economic freedom, thus ensuring the stability of the system. Hence, representative government, even if not in any full form (in terms of suffrage), was good for stability and efficiency of the workings of the market.

It followed that most Scottish Enlightenment thinkers were adamant that the rise of commercial society and economic interdependence would lead to the ability of people to challenge their masters. Interdependence creates freedom of individuals: not from each other (because of interdependence), but from specific local masters.

It should be noted that Smith's views of economics and politics rely on a prioritisation of *economic* concerns. Indeed, his whole system has important but paradoxical consequences for the idea of 'politics'. Since the public sphere, for him, is now characterised by individuals interacting for the common good, there is nothing distinctly 'political' about the public sphere any more. The emphasis on similarity and conformity of thinking and obedience to law not only seems to imply the movement away from antagonistic form of interaction in the political sphere for the benefit of stable consensus, but also, more fundamentally, means *the displacement of politics as prior to economics* (Berry, 1997: 137).

This does not mean, it should be noted, that Smith's citizens are unconcerned with the welfare of their peers. For him, a good citizen must be concerned for the welfare of others and respect and obey the laws. It is just that the way of promoting their welfare is now considered in different light. By following one's own interest, one can now promote the welfare of others.

Outside of this too, Smith saw an important role for the state in caring for those that suffer negatively from the workings of the system. Smith was very concerned about the stupefying effect of simple manual labour for individuals, which is why he saw an important role for education as a responsibility of the state (Smith, 1970 [1776]).

In sum, then, the Scottish Enlightenment thought, and especially Smith's contribution within it, must be recognised as not just narrowly economic, without contribution or consequence to thinking about politics and specifically representative government. A representative model of governance, with an important focus on impartiality of rule of law and administration of justice, was *a key aspect* of Smith's thought. It follows that far from being merely interested in the economic sphere, as if it were neatly to be separated from the political, Smith and his compatriot David Hume clearly saw modern civilised commercial society to be constituted by a 'distinctive interlocking set of institutions behaviours and values' (Berry, 1997: 151). They also clearly recognised that values of representativeness and legal equality arose from and were crucial to the workings of an efficient liberal economic system. This is why political rights must be valued alongside economic rights.

Jeremy Bentham and James Mill

Many of the early liberals discussed here did not explicitly speak of democracy and could not really be referred to as 'democrats'. What they spoke about was legislative or 'representative government'. The idea of 'liberal democracy', however, is an invention that is, in many ways, distinct from both liberal views on representative government of the early liberals and prior (Greek) thought on democracy. Liberal democratic thought is a unique line of thought that only really took off in the nineteenth century.[2] I want to focus here on two key 'liberal democratic' authors – 'fathers', if you like, of the idea of liberal democracy. What is distinctive about each of them is that they very clearly highlight the deep interconnection between economic liberalism and liberal democratic thought.

Jeremy Bentham and James Mill 'deduced' democratic franchise, so the story goes, from the general theory of utilitarianism (Macpherson, 1977: 25), the principle that society should seek to follow policies that guarantee to deliver the 'greatest happiness of the greatest number'. What is distinctive about this deduction, however, is the extent to which it was premised firmly and fundamentally on the model of man and society derived from the classical political economists, Adam Smith and especially David Ricardo. They worked with a model of man, which saw man as a maximiser of utilities and a model of society, which saw society as a collection of individuals with conflicting interests (Macpherson: 1977, 24). Indeed, utilitarian thought was deeply embedded in not just egalitarian principles, but also 'market thinking'. This had deep impact on its understanding of 'liberal democracy'.

Indeed, Macpherson (1977) argues that Bentham and Mill actually came to the political system of liberal representative democracy through the backdoor

– because they saw it as productive and efficient for a functional capitalist economic system. A political system should 'both produce governments that would establish and nurture a free market society and protect citizens from rapacious governments' (Macpherson, 1977: 34).

Given that some form of representative government was what was envisaged, the key question became: what should be the extent of the suffrage so that the free market would not be jeopardised by the electoral processes? Bentham first excluded women, the poor, uneducated and their dependents, but later advocated more universal suffrage, convinced that it would be 'safe' for market society. Arguably, 'he moved to the principle of the democratic franchise only when he had become persuaded that the poor would not use their votes to level or destroy property' (Macpherson, 1977: 37).

James Mill also put forward a case for universal franchise but a case equally representative of a liberal market world-view, namely that each individual, to have power in society, needed to have the right to vote, for self-protection. Yet, he seemed to brush off those whose 'interests shared in those of others' (women, children, younger men/sons), and even later on was not entirely supportive of universal suffrage for political reasons (it would scare off key constituents in the middle classes that he wanted behind his reforms against the landed and moneyed class). His final view was that the rich were destined to rule and if they did so through representative means then that was all that could reasonably be required for a good government (Macpherson, 1977: 42).

Such a view of democracy is, as Macpherson puts it, neither inspiring nor inspired; it is 'protective democracy for a market man' (1977: 42). Democracy in this model is 'nothing but a logical requirement for the governance of inherently self-interested conflicting individuals who are assumed to be infinite desirers of their own private benefits' (Macpherson 1977: 43). A classical liberal view of democracy in the mid-nineteenth century, then, was hardly ambitious, because it was in many ways conceived of as a tool of class power. Yet, this is not the end of the line in the development of the idea of liberal democracy.

J.S. Mill

J.S. Mill's view of democracy is associated with the idea of 'developmental' liberal democracy (Macpherson, 1977; Held, 1996), a view of democracy that does not start from self-evidence of and priority of market competition and values, but rather from the need to consider and develop individuals' capacities and liberties within society. Representative democracy, as for his forebears, constituted the core of liberal democracy for Mill too, as did liberal rights against an over-bearing state. Yet, Mill extended the early liberal democrats' ideas in a crucial way and thus set the standards for a very different kind of classical liberal practice.

Here too both political and economic rights constituted the bedrock of liberal democratic governance. Yet, Mill developed a far less market-driven approach to liberal democratic governance. In fact, from a young age Mill was concerned with the cold-hearted and egotistical emphasis of his utilitarian father, James Mill, and

Bentham. He rebelled against this by developing a new version of philosophical radicalism: 'a new radicalism that retains what was 'permanently valuable' in the 'old' Benthamic school but at the same time made more adequate provision for cultivation of the higher feelings and for ideal social arrangements founded upon them' (Riley, 1994: xiv).

Mill was wary of the capitalism in nineteenth-century society and specifically was concerned about the nature of democratic representation in a capitalist society. He came to believe that both economic success of a nation and, importantly, its democratic credentials, depended on the ability of society to foster the development and education of individuals in such a manner that allowed them to use their reason to deal with social problems in a reasonable and co-operative manner. Economically, he envisaged a system where constant growth at the expense of individual development should be checked. He instead argued for a better 'co-operative' form of capitalism, remaining open even to the development of a kind of market socialism.

In terms of democracy he envisaged that citizens should be cultivated in terms of their attitude to society: indeed, for him 'the efficacy of democratic institutions depends on mass cultivation of certain moral feelings of co-operation and trust as well as on general intellectual improvement' (Riley, 1994: xv). Democracy, for Mill, was not conceived as a tool of protection of wealthy individuals against the government but as a potential vehicle for human development of those that suffered within the system. Democracy – conceived as liberal democracy – was seen as a superior system because it was morally and intellectually the most able to advance society and individuals within it (Macpherson, 1977: 47).

This is a very different understanding of liberal democracy from the utilitarians: Mill was deeply concerned with class inequalities in political power and wealth and saw that incompatibilities existed between inequality and developmental democracy. Crucially, and in contrast to Locke, James Mill or the utilitarians, Mill argued that not only consistent defences of liberal political rights of representation were required, but so was better capitalism. A more sympathetic economic system was necessary for liberal democracy to work to its full potential and this entailed a model of economy consistent with some level of basic subsistence redistribution and social insurance in order to safeguard the development of individuals' skills and moral judgements. Mill even allowed for the possibility of socialism: a form of decentralised market socialism where individual co-operatives would be jointly owned but would function in competitive struggle with each other for customers.

Yet, to clarify, he was a classical liberal democrat at heart. A representative system of 'political' democracy was what democracy entailed and, crucially, he did not call for 'the subversion of the system of individual property, but the improvement of it, and the full participation of every member of the community in its benefits' (Mill quoted in Riley, 1994). Further, liberal capitalist market assumptions seemed to underpin his very frames of reference. The kind of liberal man he envisaged was in fact by and large a self-interested rational market man, albeit with some added qualities for moral progression. In society too, competition between producers in a market was a natural state of affairs. Further, as did many liberal capitalist reformers at the time, he belittled in many ways the kinds of problem that capitalism creates. He failed, critics argue, to grasp the full consequences and limitations that a liberal economic system placed on democracy. He did not fully explore the kinds of alternative, non-liberal systems of democracy, which are examined in the following chapters.

Also, Mill's liberal representative democracy itself was far from fully representative. He put forward the idea of plural voting, for members of the lower classes – all were equal, but some were more equal than others. This plural voting went with class-based exclusions of those receiving welfare help, those bankrupt and those who did not pay direct taxes – for these did not contribute to the market society, to which the idea of representative democracy was inherently attached (Macpherson, 1977: 57). This voting ensured that those that were better educated and knew better would have more of say and, in fact, were viewed as morally crucial for a 'developmental democracy' (Macpherson, 1977: 59).

It follows, then, that despite his qualified critique of the market-driven utilitarian perspectives on democracy, J.S. Mill's idea of developmental liberal democracy was still deeply indebted to classical liberal thought as developed by his liberal forebears. While Mill did not start from the market values, he accepted the market understanding of society as a self-evident premise to the functioning of liberal democracy.

Classical liberalism and democracy in twentieth-century thought

Classical liberal democratic thought has a venerable tradition as we have seen. It has had at its heart the simultaneous promotion of liberal political rights and liberal economic rights: two sets of rights, which, while seen to defend individuals in two separate spheres of social life, were nevertheless tied together in 'holistic' defence of liberal society. Yet, the liberal tradition also underwent interesting shifts in the twentieth century. A key development that took place was the turn towards 'realistic' and 'procedural' understandings of liberal democracy.

While for classical liberals such as Locke and the Mill, liberal rights formed the cornerstone of thought on representative government or democracy, for twentieth-century theorists and political scientists the meaning of democracy has become solidified and thereby also narrowed down. The focus has become the study of democracy as procedures and as 'it is'. From Schumpeter to Dahl and Downs, a tradition of liberal democratic proceduralism has overtaken 'value-based' liberal treatments of liberal democracy. It has also given rise to a new kind of link between the economic and the political: a vision of market and democracy as separated but as 'analogical' in their functions.

The so-called elite competition model of liberal democracy, developed initially by Joseph Schumpeter, is classical liberal in that liberal rights, political representation and market society still form the crucial reference points of thinking on democracy. Yet, this is a very different version of a classically liberal model: it makes an analytical separation between markets and democracy and provides liberal democracy with narrow but clear procedural determinants. The key assumption of liberal democracy here is the idea that competition between individuals forms the core of the electoral system *in the same sense* as competition between individual firms and entrepreneurs forms the core of the market; hence, the term 'competitive model of democracy' as a descriptor for this line of thought.

Joseph Schumpeter was a political conservative but by no means fearful of radical arguments. Indeed, his most famous argument pertained to the inherent weaknesses of the capitalist system: the seeds of the decline of the capitalist system lay, he argued, within the very system itself. He was, however, sceptical of socialist agendas identifying many contradictions and problems within them. He was also remarkably sceptical in his thought on democracy. Doubtful of big normative visions of democracy, easily used to justify many radical agendas, he developed a narrowed down theory of democracy.

First, Schumpeter wanted to separate clearly and distinctly between the economic and the political. Unlike the classical political economists, Schumpeter drew a sharp distinction between positive factual 'science' and 'normative theory'. He wanted to approach democracy not as an ideal-theoretical 'utopian' normative system, but rather 'realistically'. To assume that democracy entails 'rule' or 'people' for some 'common good' was, for Schumpeter, foolish. There was no common good, for people inevitably disagreed. Also, people in democracies did not 'rule', they merely *elected leaders*.

Democracy, for Schumpeter, is not a value in itself; it is 'a political method, that is to say a certain type of institutional arrangement for arriving at political – legislative and administrative – decisions and hence incapable of being an end in itself' (Schumpeter, 1976 [1943]: 242).

Schumpeter famously argued that democracy should be considered in a much more narrow sense than allowed by the classical theorists, liberal or otherwise. Schumpeter defined democratic method as 'that institutional arrangement for arriving at political decisions in which individuals acquire the power to decide by means of a competitive struggle for the people's vote' (Schumpeter, 1976 [1943]: 269). A key here is that democracy was not about the general good or betterment of society, or indeed about the betterment of individuals, as it was for J.S. Mill. It had no normative content: it was quite simply a political system where people periodically voted in order for elected governments to be formed. Crucially, emphasis here, then, was on leadership. All political systems required leadership and democracy quite simply was one way, among many, of electing leaders.

How do we 'democratically' choose leaders then? Elections and competition of candidates in them became the core focus of Schumpeter's idea of democracy. Importantly, the role of democracy is not even to 'represent' the views of individuals, as earlier classical liberals had argued. In Macpherson's (1977: 78) words, for Schumpeter, '[t]he voters' role is not to decide political issues and then choose representatives who will carry out those decisions: it is rather to choose the men who will do the deciding'.

The core protection against tyranny in this model lies in the fact that elections are regular: the procedural institutionalisation of regular elections is what makes the system 'democratic' and in a sense 'liberal' (anti-absolutist). In both senses, one might say, however, the terms can only be interpreted in the minimal sense – for this model is not 'maximally democratic' in looking for active democratic participation, nor is it maximally liberal, for the focus is on elections (a procedure) as defence against enemies of liberty, not on guaranteeing greater amount of individual freedom (Schumpeter, 1976 [1943]: 271). There is no inherent value attached here to participation or moral values of any kind.

What is noteworthy, however, is the deep role that market assumptions play in this model, notably the emphasis on competition. 'Democracy seems to imply a recognised method by which to conduct a competitive struggle', Schumpeter argues (Schumpeter, 1976 [1943]: 271). What makes Schumpeter's approach to democracy distinctive is that it is premised upon and reproductive of a view of democracy as a form of competition akin to competition in the market sphere (Schumpeter, 1976 [1943]: 271). Like firms and individuals compete in the market; in exactly the same way, politicians compete for votes: they are professionals of a specific kind who 'deal in votes' (Schumpeter, 1976 [1943]: 285). Schumpeter recognises that the kind of competition that takes place in democracy is not always perfect – as it is not in any market system – but nevertheless democracy is essentially about 'competition for leadership' in the condition of 'free competition for free vote' (Schumpeter, 1976 [1943]: 271). It follows, crucially, that parties for example are not really about ideological values, they are simply groups of individuals who have come together in order to win power, to gain leadership. Their sole purpose then is not to represent people or values but 'to prevail over others in order to get into power or to stay in it' (Schumpeter, 1976 [1943]: 279). Parties 'constitute an attempt to regulate political competition exactly similar to the corresponding practices of a trade association' (Schumpeter, 1976 [1943]: 283).

Democracy, for Schumpeter, is reduced in meaning to be literally a synonym of the market. 'Democracy is simply a market mechanism: the voters are the consumers; the politicians the entrepreneurs' (Macpherson, 1977: 79). A market *analogy*, then, is crucial to this variant of thought. Just as economic man follows his self-interest and operates as a rational actor in the system, so do the voters and the politicians in the democratic system. Democratic systems can be analysed as akin to the liberal economic system. Yet, this does not mean, paradoxically, that this model of democracy is necessarily attached to the capitalist economic system. Importantly, but often ignored by commentators, Schumpeter discusses the possibility that capitalist system, from within which the competition model of democracy has arisen, is not the only system that it is compatible with. He actually raises the possibility that democracy in his sense is also possible within a socialist model, not just a capitalist one (Schumpeter, 1976 [1943]: 284).

Schumpeter, then, is a curious person to analyse as part of a liberal-democratic politico-economic model. While separating the political from the economic, there is an intertwining in Schumpeter's thinking on democracy and liberal capitalism. Although gone are the days of worrying about the effects of markets on democracy or democracy on the markets (as for the nineteenth century liberals) *democracy nevertheless is conceived to work akin to competition in the liberal capitalist market system*. Liberal economic 'competitive' thinking is a key condition for Schumpeter's system and the rational action of democratic consumers. Indeed, as Macpherson (1977: 79) poignantly argues, the market model of economics seems not only to correspond and explain the actual political behaviour of people in the political system (hence its perceived realism), but also seems to justify that behaviour and hence the whole system. On a deep level, then, the use of the economic analogy does place Schumpeter's logic deeply within the liberal politico-economic model.

This is also evident in the influential extension of Schumpeterian ideas, in the so-called economic theory of democracy (Downs, 1957). This approach, which has emphasised the importance of taking into account the 'economic realities' of political action (poorly appreciated by political theorists, Downs, 1957: 149), has proved a very powerful and dominant way of analysing party politics and democratic functions in the late twentieth century. It has entailed the expansion of rational choice and quantitative methods to the analysis of political behaviour, but crucially for us, the extension of 'analogic' thought about the nature of democracy and markets. On the one hand the two spheres, economic and political, are again separated. On the other hand, they are seen as united by a logic of behaviour and structural shapers: the availability of goods, the needs of demand and the logic of competition. The liberal capitalist economic system is assumed, or if you like, built within this theory of democracy.

Robert Dahl

Another key contributor to the empirical line of thought on liberal democracy was Robert Dahl, who in the context of political science elaborated on and systematised Schumpeter's competitive elitist approach to democracy. Dahl was in the 1960s a famous advocate or a theorist of this pluralist or elitist model, in arguing that the idea of polyarchy now corresponded well to the kind of liberal democracy that characterised the West. This model, which came to be seen as synonomous with the idea of liberal democracy by most of the late twentieth-century political theorists (and indeed democratisation researchers), consisted of seven criteria: constitutionally elected officials in government; frequent and fairly conducted elections; voting rights for practically all adults and the right to stand for elections for practically all adults; almost universal right to express oneself without the threat of violence; the right to seek alternative sources of information; freedom to form associations and organisations, including parties; and inclusive citizenship (Dahl, 2000: 85–6).

Dahl, like Schumpeter, clearly recognised the limitations of the system that he was explaining (and inadvertently perhaps also justifying). Notably, he recognised that this model was only to a fairly limited extent responsive to the views of the people – groups will not always, though at least some of the time, make their views heard to the government. The key to the system was not that it was directly representative or participatory, but rather that over a whole range of issues and issue areas and given the complex room for interests and negotiations that the pluralist political system leaves, some sort of an 'equilibrium' would be achieved on political interests and wishes, in such a manner that would allow the system to provide room for stable political interaction.

A key aspect of Dahl's conception of democracy is that it is, like Schumpeter's, a model of *political* democracy. What does that mean for the relationship between economics and democracy? This is interesting, and Dahl dedicates a number of chapters to exploring this relationship (Dahl, 2000). For Dahl, polyarchic liberal democracy is fundamentally linked to capitalist economics and a liberal market. This is because '[h]istorically experience shows pretty conclusively that a system in which countless economic decisions are made by innumerable independent but competing actors, each acting from rather narrow self-regarding interests and guided by the information supplied by the markets, produces goods and services more efficiently than any known alternative' (Dahl, 2000: ch. 13). Market capitalism leads to growth, and growth, he points out, leads to furtherance of democracy by reducing potential for conflict in societies, by decentralising decision-making away from central government and by co-ordinating interactions in complex societies (Dahl, 2000: 167–8). Polyarchic democracies, he argued, are fostered by economically liberal forces and the other way around, although he does recognise that economic growth is not unique to democracies, that market capitalism can exist without democracy, and that capitalism need not entail modern industrial capitalism (Dahl, 2000: 169).

Also, interestingly, Dahl's take on the link between economics and democracy recognises the clash between economic liberalism in a hard sense and democracy. Much like de Tocqueville, while seeing a close mutually reinforcing relationship between these systems, at the same time Dahl is very aware of the need for us to pay attention to the potential for clashes and contradictions that may arise from economic liberalism for democracy, especially in the form of rising inequalities (Dahl, 2000: 173–4). This is why, for Dahl, capitalism needs to be regulated. Absolutely crucially, this is why capitalism is only favourable to a 'polyarchic' form of government but does not favour development of a 'democracy' in any wider terms (Dahl, 2000: 178).

It is for this reason that Dahl, in fact, seems to have in his later thinking turned towards taking into account economic affairs far more seriously and has come to be interested in the idea of economic democracy. In his *Preface of Economic Democracy* (1986) Dahl argued that to obtain real democracy we must extend democratic principles from the political to the economic. Indeed, he argued that this must entail extension of principles of workplace democracy to the economic realm, despite the seeming contradictions with liberal ideals on property. This represents a sharp turn in Dahl's thinking which positions him closer to the welfare liberal democratic traditions.

Let us now turn to examine such a reform liberal tradition. Despite having been ignored by many classical liberals, this is an extremely important variant of liberal thought, which crucially reconfigures the meaning of 'liberal democracy' away from classical liberal principles which are focused single-mindedly on individual liberties, separation of the economic and the political, and competitive 'political' representative democracy.

A liberal democracy: towards reform liberalism

> With the apparent demise of Soviet communism and the Marxist version of socialism, many claim that liberal-democracy, and perhaps capitalism, won the Cold War. But the crucial question is, about which liberalism, which democracy and which capitalism is this claim made?
>
> (Waligorski, 1997: 1)

J.S. Mill's thought gave rise to an often-sidestepped but very important tradition of liberal thought on democracy and markets, and one that, while drawing and bolstering some classical liberal values, challenged the more extreme 'liberal' conceptions of the linkage between democracy and economy. This model consists of a rethinking not only of the mechanisms that connect democracy and the market, but also the very conception of economics and politics in liberalism, the role of political and normative assumptions in the economy, conceptions of individualism and community, and consequently of democracy. Thinkers associated with reform liberalism include both economists and political thinkers: figures such as John Hobson, T.H. Green, L.T. Hobhouse, Louis Brandeis, John Dewey, John Maynard Keynes, John Kenneth Galbraith, Lester Thurow, Robert Reich and John Rawls.

This is a significant tradition of thought to examine for a number of reasons. First, it is often sidestepped, even among liberal scholars. Second, it is very rich and practically powerful and, in fact, is historically much more consequential than often thought. Third, it is important because these lines of thought are arguably highly topical today as alternatives to libertarian and economistic liberalism are sought.

Reform liberalism differs radically in its focus from earlier forms of 'classical' liberalism. It takes the liberal value of individualism as its starting point but develops a very different view of individualism, and its relationship to community. The reform liberals recognise the role of the economic markets and liberalism in bettering society, yet they perceive and seek to tackle inequalities of wealth and power in society. They oppose 'ideological' fixity of much of classical liberal thought and emphasise instead the flexible needs of social and economic policy in the modern era.

Yet, reform liberals speak about social and political conditions from somewhat different angles. Hobson and Hobhouse, for example, elaborated their social liberalism in the context of early twentieth century British politics, whereas Brandeis and Dewey were responding to the ills of hyper-liberalism within the United States during the 1920s and 1930s. Keynes's thought was specifically tied to the economic crisis of the 1930s and beyond, whereas Galbraith commented on social policy in the post-Second World War era. To gain a better sense of what these authors have to contribute to rethinking of the relationship between democracy and liberalism, let's examine some of their ideas in more detail.

Reform liberalism and democracy

The reform liberals of the early twentieth century started from the recognition of the harsh consequences of economic *laissez-faire* for many individuals within states, both economically and politically. Importantly, these liberals interpreted liberty, not as an 'unfettered individual choice of action' but as 'welfare': 'welfare enabled a social actor to exercise meaningful free choice' (Freeden, 1998: 447; see also Freeden, 2008). These 'welfare liberals' recognised that there was an urgent need to address the economic inequalities that arise in capitalist liberal systems in order to achieve the political equality of individuals in society and in representative institutions within democratic states. Equality of opportunity, not merely of rights, was a key commitment.

One key welfare liberal whom we must consider is J.A. Hobson. Writing in the early part of the twentieth century, Hobson was a keen critic of *laissez-faire* liberal capitalism. Hobson had a firm commitment to tackling social ills and to 'interdisciplinary' study of social problems (Freeden, 1998: 442–3). At the centre of his thought were still liberal values: 'human flourishing, rational progress, individual choice and the encouragement of variety' (Freeden, 1998: 443). While classical liberals had premised their thought on protection of individual rights to privacy and property, for Hobson, rights were linked to 'securing of human well-being based on an appreciation of human needs' (Freeden, 1998: 443). Rights were seen as attached not just to individuals but rather as something with a dual role – rights protected individuals as persons and also as members of a community. This was because community's health was seen as dependent on the health of its parts. The individual and the community were not to be separated as in classical liberalism. Nor did Hobson see socialism and liberalism as necessarily conflictual ideologies: they could in his view be merged into a view that was more sympathetic and humanist.

Hobson thus came to envisage an active and in many ways extensive role for the state. This is because the state's role was to ensure the 'enlargement of personal liberty' (Hobson, 1909: 94). This meant that that the state should be involved in regulating capitalism and in redistributing wealth so as to counter the unfairness and brutality arising from 'pure' capitalism. Redistribution was to be based on existence of surplus – instead of allowing the leading capitalist power centres to appropriate this surplus, this surplus could and should be used to ensure the welfare of each and every person in a society. Welfare was, for Hobson, a value and a goal prior to wealth-making (Freeden, 1998: 447).

Much like Hobson, Hobhouse, Brandeis and Dewey also emphasised the need for the individual to be understood as part of a community, and for the gaps and problems of market capitalism to be recognised and tackled. Crucially, all saw economic relations as closely tied to politics – and thus the economic harm done by markets as something to be corrected by political society. Indeed, all rejected any notion of economic determinism, liberal or Marxist, emphasising instead the role of human and state intervention in social and economic life. Concentration of power had to be tackled, rather than being accepted as a 'natural law' leading to spontaneous order.

Reform liberals saw the pure economic science of neoclassical economists as a way of justifying a particular kind of normative order, within which specific power relations were legitimised and hidden. For them 'the laissez-faire vision was not scientific, nor was it morally, socially or politically acceptable' (Waligorski, 1997: 31). Right to fight overwhelming power within the economic system and society in general was needed: this included the right of trade unions to organise and take on powerful corporate interests, as well as public regulation of the power of corporations. This meant according the government a central role in economic affairs. Yet, none of these authors was 'revolutionary' in their approach to social and economic order (Waligorski, 1997: 35). This is portrayed well in their approach to democracy.

The reform liberals were not radical or participatory democrats (see Chapter 4). They tended to perceive the core of democracy as lying in representative parliamentary institutions and steered clear from socialist arguments for direct or delegative democracy (see Chapter 3). Yet, they did advocate an extension of the idea of democracy beyond the narrow classical liberal or elitist Schumpeterian forms of proceduralism. Democracy was not just about election of political leaders, nor was democratic decision-making capacity to be entirely removed from the economic sphere in defence of economic liberty. Quite to the contrary, democratic controls over economic decisions and processes became seen as necessary because of the understanding of power that the new liberals worked with: for them '[d]emocracy is endangered by inequality and by concentration of power' (Waligorski, 1997: 26). Democracy for them did not merely imply choice of leaders every few years, but had to exist on multiple levels and in multiple spheres in order to tackle the persistent power hierarchies in society. Indeed, democracy on the level of the 'political' and narrowly conceived was considered to be inadequate. As Brandeis powerfully put it: 'we cannot successfully grapple with the problem of democracy, if we confine ourselves to political democracy' (quoted in Waligorski, 1997: 26). The challenge for these democrats was then to come up with policies – employment policies, welfare policies, party political restrictions – which controlled the ability of affluent forces in society to hijack the liberal representative political process.

Crucially, the value of democracy for reform liberals lay not just merely in 'representation' of individual interests: 'democracy has goals that include social justice, development of individuality, and solving of public problems' (Waligorski, 1997: 26). This is because the functioning of a good democracy was dependent on the fostering of capable individuality and decision-making. Mere elections in a slave-society would not constitute democracy. Democracy entailed fostering of a fully developed individual, who was able to exercise choice autonomously and to fully participate in public affairs.

Recognition of this politico-economic conditioning of democratic life meant not only active socio-economic policies in support of individuals hard-done by the existing power relations, but also extending principles of democracy to social life more widely, including the economic sphere. Indeed, Dewey, for example, advocated a form of work-place or industrial democracy where individuals could exercise their democratic rights actively and hence 'liberate' their minds. Active ability to decide on matters of concern to one was seen as a crucial aspect of a democratic society. Such a society would be more deeply democratic, and more attuned to questions of social justice. The emphasis of the new liberals, then, was on extending the workings of democracy in their societies, of extending it to 'all areas and ways of living' (Dewey quoted in Waligorski, 1997: 28). While such principles did not arguably build a system of 'participatory' democracy as described in Chapter 4, and while focus of democratic representation still remained the liberal representative parliament, significant extensions and modifications to the working of liberal democracy, vis-à-vis the classical liberals, could be developed. Notably, active welfare policies, control of affluent sectors of society and emphasis on egalitarian education policies were seen as crucial aspects of effective liberal democratic governance. A more democratic and less liberal interpretation of democracy was advocated. While reform liberalism did not challenge the liberal democratic state or capitalism *per se*, it did require that the state should take on a responsibility to act as a facilitator of human flourishing. This emphasis was also central to Keynes's thought.

John Maynard Keynes

Keynes was one of the most crucial economic thinkers of the twentieth century. His thoughts on the state's role in the economy, as well as on stable international financial regulation and institutionalisation, have been very influential indeed in modern times. While Keynes was far less radical in orientation than either Hobson, Hobhouse, Dewey or Brandeis, his thought was very different from that of classical liberal economists or political theorists. Indeed, as Paul Krugman points out in his introduction to a new edition of Keynes's *General Theory of Employment, Interest and Wages*, the right-wing conservative scholars voted it in 2005 as one of the most dangerous books of the twentieth century, over and above those of Lenin and Frantz Fanon (Krugman, 2007: xxv).

His famous thesis and the Keynesian economic policies, which became hugely influential in the post-Second World War environment, were written in the context of the crisis of 1929 and the challenge of recession that it presented. Keynes is famous for having been one of the first to sharply critique, albeit with deep commitment and understanding, the liberal economic orthodoxy and the problems that it created in dealing with the particular context of economic downturn. Far from solving the crisis, the existing economic orthodoxy made it worse, Keynes argued.

Keynes's solution involved rethinking the very premises of wage and employment policy. He argued that the state should have a key role in generating demand within an economy, especially in a crisis situation. The state, instead of being pushed out of the sphere of economics, should be seen as an important growth-inducing player within it. By instigating large public works and public sector spending in general, the state could create employment at a time of crisis and also, in so doing, generate liquidity in the market with the hope of thus restoring economic confidence.

The key upshot and the most shocking aspect of Keynes's thought was that it argued that state action was necessary within the economy, that economic forces should not be allowed to play themselves out freely. If the state did not intervene in the economy, Keynes suggested, the very existence of capitalism and indeed democracy could be in doubt. As a defender of capitalism and democracy, Keynes then wanted to ensure that capitalism would not be allowed to destroy itself, which might lead us to either communism or fascism, alternatives he did not think were particularly attractive. The state's fiscal policy could be used to generate demand and stability in the economy without – crucially – having to go down the socialist route of nationalisation of ownership. Tinkering with employment policy and wages, Keynes thought, would be a far more modest and also efficient way of dealing with the inherent problems capitalism had created. But is there a distinctive view of democracy within Keynes's thought?

Keynes was primarily an economist and did not then take on the task of elaborating in detail a theory of democracy. Yet, Keynes was not disinterested in democracy. Key aspects of Keynes's thinking were (1) belief in democracy, understood as parliamentary democracy, and (2) commitment to capitalism. Yet, Keynes did not seem to argue for a traditional Schumpeterian liberal politicoeconomic model. Why? First, because of his belief in the importance of political control over markets, an aspect distinctly lacking in the earlier classically liberal models. Economic interaction was not driven by an invisible hand only, but rather by human decisions and values. Control over the economy was necessary: one that would foster a stable and efficient economy.

Yet, was this control to be democratic? Not necessarily. It is interesting to note that Keynes arguably considered economic policy to be the terrain of the economists. While important political and democratic goals could be furthered through his economic policies, his ideas were essentially technocratic – economics was the terrain of the experts like himself. While Keynes would have seen himself as a defender of political control of markets for social good, he *was not a radical democrat* in actually believing in popular (people's) control over markets. In this respect, as well as in many other respects, Keynes was fairly conservative. However, the key thing to note about Keynes is that it was his thought which enabled the consideration of the idea of an interventionist state, the notion of the state as a moral and political actor in the capitalist economy, and the sentiment that inequalities in society were not normal but in fact inefficient as well as morally problematic.

It was on such principles that other post-Second World War critics of liberal economic orthodoxy, such as Galbraith and Rawls, built their arguments. Galbraith, for example, argued that there was a desperate need for Western states to tackle the 'unequal power relations' embedded in the formally equal economic and political systems of the West. For him, this entailed curtailing the power of the dominant actors, such as corporations, as well as criticism of their ideological power in society. It also included critiquing the value-neutrality of economic science. Economic science for Galbraith was a crucial cog in the wheel of a capitalist system which favoured some over the others: 'economics has not been a science but a conservatively useful system of belief defending that belief as a science' (Galbraith quoted in Waligorski, 1997: 69).

John Rawls's system of thought was different: it emanated from political theory, notably his key work *Theory of Justice* (1971), and was elaborated on and defended in a number of later works (Rawls, 1993, 2004). Rawls evoked from within the liberal social contract tradition a justification for a distributive form of social justice within liberal democratic systems. He provided an argument for why we should all agree on a set of welfare liberal assumptions regarding distributive justice. His approach was premised on postulating the 'original position', which entailed imagining that we all make decisions about the nature of society we wish to live in 'behind the veil of ignorance'. Rawls surmised that in the original position, behind the veil of ignorance, self-interested actors – without knowledge of their ultimate place in society – would choose to back some kind of re-distributive policy.

All these interventions shared an interest in extending the classical liberal ideals of democracy in significantly new directions. The state's role was expanded, and liberal democracy was seen as something to be actively enabled through social policies. Separation of the economic and the political was not accepted. So what can we learn from reform liberals about thinking on democracy?

Reform liberal principles

Waligorski (1997) has usefully summarised the core precepts of new liberalism and it is these points which we need to pay heed to in understanding the impact of reform liberalism on thought about democracy.

1. *Critique of laissez-faire economics.* Reform liberals all agree that liberalism in its *laissez-faire* emphasis is deeply problematic and dangerous. Refusing to separate the political from the economic, these authors argue that the political and social effects – the 'social detail' of capitalist markets – cannot be ignored but should be taken seriously and adjusted to. Economics 'laws' should not be allowed to run their own course, rather economic policy should be reined in by higher political values. Markets, while useful and productive for societies 'cannot justify themselves' (Waligorski, 1997: 11) and do not necessarily entail a productive or morally acceptable 'equilibrium'.
2. *Freedom.* All new liberals emphasise the importance of freedom as a key liberal value, but reject a 'negative' conception of freedom. Hindrances to exercise of freedom are taken seriously, and include things like 'laissez-faire policy, concentrated economic power, discrimination, poverty, ignorance, and . . . . market failure and economic instability' (Waligorski, 1997: 12).
3. *Equality.* New liberals also value equality, and reject neoclassical economists' justifications of inequality. Instead, inequality is seen as inefficient economically and as politically and socially disruptive (Waligorski, 1997: 13). Hence, new liberals make a concerted effort to tackle inequalities in society, even if they accept that doing away with inequality altogether may be impossible within a market system (which they still favour).
4. *Democracy.* These authors challenge the neoclassical libertarian views that see a small role for democracy in society, and notably in economics. While new

liberals do not necessarily put forward a unique and clearly worked out theory of democracy, certain key characteristics can be identified in their thought on democracy. These authors are not radical or participatory democrats, yet all are interested in 'the impact of economics on democracy' (Waligorski, 1997: 13), and vice versa. They are concerned to make sure that markets are tamed to the workings of democracy. Their focus in this regard is rejection of libertarian views on markets necessarily promoting democracy, or on democracy consisting of 'market-like' competition. Instead, democracy has a deeper meaning that is related to the autonomy of citizens and also governments to intervene in and counteract the workings of the economy. Adjustments to markets and democracy are perceived as necessary for liberal democracy to function as it should, notaby in defence of the individual's rights and interests.

5. *Individualism.* The reform liberals are individualists to the core, yet they conceive individualism not as negative but as something that governments have to foster. For individuals to realise themselves fully, they must be in a position to do so: they must have adequate capacity and power in society.

6. *Power.* This entails that we must understand how power relations are embedded in society and in the economy, and often in ways un-noted by the classical liberals for whom all are essentially equal in the market and indeed procedural democracy. New liberals trace, instead, the multiple power hierarchies and relations embedded in society and the economy and attempt to battle these – for moral reasons, but also for reasons of efficiency.

7. *Public and private.* The new liberals reject an ideologically entrenched separation of the public and the private and emphasise the importance of the public sphere, both as a key focus of social action and as a site of encouragement of fuller senses of individuality. Certainly the reform liberals 'emphatically reject the notion that the economy constitutes a realm of private behaviour' (Waligorski, 1997: 15), nor do they accept the idea that 'natural laws' direct the spontaneous workings of the market towards a just and productive equilibrium.

8. *Positive role of government.* It follows that the role of the government is seen as active in society and the economic sphere. The new liberals, crucially, do not necessarily call for big government, but rather efficient and active government. The government, they argue, can have a positive role in solving problems of market distribution: from regulation of markets and working conditions to welfare problems. Yet, they do not 'love' big government but remain, as all liberals, 'mistrusting' of the government too (Waligorski, 1997: 17).

Key to all reform liberal thought has been the need for societies to respond to evils that arise to threaten the communities, and the individuals living within them. They are all policy-oriented and pragmatic thinkers emphasising the need to reform, in a consensual rather than revolutionary manner, the workings of liberal society. They are the reformers 'within the system' then, but nevertheless make possible and envision extensions to the classical and procedural understandings of liberal democracy.

A neoliberal reinstatement of economic freedom and the consequent mode of political liberty

Friedman, Hayek and 'embedded neoliberalism'

Milton Friedman and Friedrich Hayek stand for yet another formulation of liberal democratic thought. In the context of the rise of socialism, they were wary of the socialist ideals and their ability to maintain political freedoms. These authors were seeking to make the claim, at the time rather radical and unpopular, that economic freedom preserves and encourages political freedom and hence liberal democracy. Their thought has been influential – first with right-wing liberals and more recently in formulating and embedding neoliberal pro-market policies in societies.

Liberty first, democracy second

Friedrich Hayek made his core argument in his famous polemic *The Road to Serfdom* and in various texts that followed, perhaps most notably in the book *Constitution of Liberty*. The key concern of Hayek was to enforce upon liberal society in the West that the atrocities of the German and the Soviet systems were not committed by strange and vicious people, but rather arose out of the common European intellectual heritage. The enemy-within that concerned Hayek was the widespread belief in socialism and collectivist planning economy. 'Few', he argued, 'are ready to recognise that the rise of Fascism and Nazism was not a reaction against the socialist trends of the preceding period but a necessary outcome of those tendencies' (Hayek, 2001 [1944]: 4).

The problem with the increasing acceptance of seemingly socialist and social democratic ideals as common sense in the 1950s (see Chapter 3) was that this necessitated the willy-nilly abandonment of the liberal ideals that had been the cornerstone of Western societies' success, both economically and politically. 'We have progressively abandoned that freedom in economic affairs without which personal and political freedoms have never existed in the past ... Notably we have abandoned individualism and all the goods that recognition of man as supreme in his own personal sphere can provide' (Hayek, 2001 [1944]: 13–14). All this for the sake of idealistic and, ultimately totalitarian, collectivism.

The cornerstone of Hayek's response is a restatement of individual freedom, especially and most significantly in economic affairs. The kind of competitive society that Hayek envisages encapsulates law and the political system. Yet, at its base it is a system based upon prioritisation of economic freedom. Indeed, both the value of democracy and rule of law *arise from* their ability to protect the individual and his economic freedom against the arbitrary power of the state. Economic freedom is a primary value from which political freedoms arise.

> Parties in the market should be free to sell and buy at any price at which they can find a partner to the transaction, and that anybody should be free to produce, sell and buy anything that may be produced, or sold at all ... [I]t

is essential that entry into the different trades should be open to all on equal terms, and that the law should not tolerate any attempts by individuals or groups to restrict this entry by open or concealed force.

(Hayek, 2001 [1944]: 38)

Importantly, this does not mean that there should be no regulation where markets do not effectively allocate resources or that the rights of labour should be ignored. However, he recognises that 'the fundamental principle, that in the ordering of our affairs we should make as much use as possible of the spontaneous forces of society and resort as little as possible to coercion, is capable of an infinite variety of applications' (Hayek, 2001 [1944]: 17).

What is most interesting about his account for us is that it is premised on a very interesting take on democracy, and indeed a fascinating 'politico-economic' conception of democracy. For Hayek, first of all, democracy is not the 'end value': it is a potential means for protection of individual liberty. But neither is it necessarily successful in this, nor should we focus on it as the key value to be protected in modern society. Ultimately, Hayek is a liberal concerned with protection of freedom, conceived especially to arise out of economic freedom. Given that this is the case, Hayek is actually far more interested in the role of rule of law in society. This is because 'the rule of law', much like for Adam Smith, 'enables us to predict other people's behaviour correctly' and that is why it is so important that it applies equally to all cases (Hayek, 2001 [1944]: 83).

As much as he sees a role for 'liberal democracy', which he perceives in procedural terms akin to Schumpeter, he values it as one mechanism in protecting against arbitrary power of collectives to 'plan' for others.

> The fault [in descent to totalitarianism in democracies with economic planning] is neither with the individual representatives nor with the parliamentary institutions as such, but with the contradictions inherent in the task with which they are charged. They are not asked to act where they agree, but to produce agreement on everything – the whole direction of the resources of the nation. For such a task the system of majority decisions is, however, not suited.
>
> (Hayek, 2001 [1944]: 67)

This is a crucial argument for in it we see that quite simply as much as democracy can exist, for Hayek, it can only exist within a capitalist system. 'Representative democracy' of the right liberal kind is not suited to exist in the context of economic planning. This leads Hayek to conclude that contrary to the common belief that democracy is incompatible with capitalism, 'if "capitalism" means here a competitive system based on free disposal over private property, it is far more important to realise that only within this system is democracy possible. When it becomes dominated by collectivist creed, democracy will inevitably destroy itself' (Hayek, 2001[1944]: 73).

Although Hayek is less of a democrat than many would think, he is strongly of the view that if democracy matters for us it should be conceived of in utilitarian procedural manner (with defence of individual rights embedded in rule of law) and can only exist in capitalist society. Capitalist society in a sense provides the very basis for democracy, and perhaps more so, provides society with the ultimate values that democracy should proceed to protect.

In his *Constitution of Liberty* Hayek puts forward his particular form of constitutionalism, often referred to as the 'legal democracy' model (see Gabardi, 2001: 548). Here he argues that 'the predominant model of liberal democratic institutions, in which the representative body lays down the rules of just conduct and directs government, necessarily leads to a gradual transformation of the spontaneous order of a free society into a totalitarian system conducted in the service of some coalition of organized interest' (Hayek, vol 1, 1973: 2). This is the consequence not of democracy but 'that particular form of unlimited government with which democracy has come to be identified' (Hayek, vol 1, 1973: 2–3). He argues, then, for a restatement of liberal democratic constitutionalism that defends the ideal of individual liberty in the face of calls for 'unlimited democracy'. Hayek is a defender first and foremost of economic freedom and individual liberty, and in so far as he defends democracy he defends a particular kind of limited constitutional model of democracy which constrains welfare state functions and concentrates on the essential, the legal and constitutional defence of individuals against excessive social interference. His thought has been at the forefront of challenging tendencies towards extended forms of state intervention. Although liberal democracy is his focus and advocated system, he is sceptical of the scope of liberal democratic states in trying to design and regulate spontaneous order of society.

Friedman's work is associated with a somewhat similar argument. His *Free to Choose* (1980) and *Capitalism and Freedom* (2002 [1962]) argue that 'by relying primarily on voluntary co-operation and private enterprise, in both economic and other activities, we can insure that the private sector is a check on the powers of the governmental sector and an effective protection of freedom of speech, or religion and thought' (Friedman, 2002 [1962]: 3). Indeed, for Friedman, economic freedom itself is a value to be appreciated on its own merit, not in relation to higher aims. He then mounts two-fold arguments on the issue of economic freedom. Not only is it a value in and of itself but also, beyond this, it is also a 'necessary condition for political freedom' (Friedman 2002 [1962]: 4). 'The kind of economic organization that provides economic freedom directly, namely, competitive capitalism, also promotes political freedom because it separates economic power from political power and in this way enables the one to offset the other' (Friedman 2002 [1962]: 9).

Friedman (2002 [1962]: 12) specifies the 'indirect relation between market arrangements and political freedom'. Economic freedom is an important aspect of freedom because in a society one of the key concerns should be protection of individuals, both from bad people and good people (which often 'may be the same people' [Friedman 2002 [1962]: 12]). In managing economic interactions in complex modern societies, the capitalist system is by far the most efficient in making use of resources available. In a free, private enterprise exchange economy, Friedman (2002 [1962]: 14) insists that:

'so long as effective freedom of exchange is maintained . . . the consumer is protected from coercion by the seller because of the presence of other sellers with whom he can deal [and the] seller is protected from coercion by the consumer because of other consumers to which he can sell. Government is needed of course but only to determine the rules of the game.'

These are interesting and important arguments. Yet for our purposes even more interesting are arguments that link economic freedom to political freedom. Friedman (2002 [1962]: 15) defines political freedom as 'absence of coercion of man by his fellow man' and argues that while political power is difficult to disperse, economic power is not. It is precisely this form of dispersal that explains why there tend to be a plurality of views expressed and publicised in a capitalist system. For example, radical movements can more easily gain support in a capitalist system, because of the wide variety of patrons that they can turn to, whereas this would be far more difficult in a socialist system for example. In a capitalist society 'It is only necessary to persuade [people] that the propagation [of particular ideas] can be financially successful (Friedman, 2002 [1962]: 17). After all, 'an impersonal market separates economic activities from political views and protects men from being discriminated against in their own economic activities for reasons that are irrelevant to their productivity – whether these reasons are associated with their views or their color' (Friedman, 2002 [1962]: 21). Hence, unlike with reform liberals or classical liberals, it is the market forces specifically which come to the protection of a wide variety of political freedoms.

Shifts in neoliberalism: active market intervention and embedded neoliberalism

Hayek's and Friedman's ideas have been extremely important and influential in late twentieth-century political thought, economic science and political practice. They have underpinned important political and economic revolutions in the West and elsewhere. However, they have also moulded and shifted with time. Crucially, the idea of pro-market interventions – allowed for by Hayek but against the core gist of the idea of 'spontaneous order' – have become more and more important in neoliberal thought and practice.

David Harvey's (2005) examination of neoliberal thought and practice brings this to light well. He notes that while the neoliberal school arose in Chicago's economic science circles in the 1950s and 1960s, it was by and large ignored in the practice of international politics and economics until the 1970s, when the stagflation and the oil crisis precipitated Western states to look for new solutions. Then neoliberal ideas emerged on the agenda as one possible solution to macroeconomic crisis and were taken up step by step, first in New York, then more widely in the United States and in the United Kingdom, as well as being passed over to a number of Latin American countries through the increasing dominance of neoliberal thinking in think-tanks and major universities.

What is crucial to note about the shifting practices of neoliberalism, however, is that they have changed neoliberal principles in important ways. Crucially, the aim of neoliberalism today, Harvey argues, is not so much to defend negative freedoms, an emphasis still strong in Hayek, but to ensure that the state and civil society are *harnessed* for the purpose of reproducing the prominence of the market logic.

David Harvey then notes the rise of the *neoliberal state*, a particular form of a state that seeks to *actively* enforce market thinking through its structures and activities. While Hayek's aim was to defend freedoms, the aim of today's neoliberal thought and practice is, Harvey argues, to facilitate a market-led state and society. A business-friendly state with privatised services and utilities and with competition-friendly citizens and legal structures is what should be actively facilitated in the era of 'globalisation'.

This active neoliberal statism is a contradictory exercise in many ways, perhaps most fundamentally in that it relies on people 'wanting' such a pro-market state. The liberals believe in freedom to choose, but in a neoliberal state they should be free to choose in pro-market ways specifically. To guard against people thinking 'wrongly', the neoliberals tend to have an adverse attitude to democracy and instead put their faith in expert rule, especially rule by 'independent' economic authorities like central banks. This creates a paradox: 'of intense state interventions and government by elites and 'experts' in a world where the state is not supposed to be interventionist' (Harvey, 2005: 69). To create a good business culture then, the state and international organisations actively intervene and regulate the economy, rule of law and the state, in ways that are highly interventionist. At the same time they educate people to be good market actors and train the civil society to play along to the beat of the market drum. Neoliberalism has shifted from non-interventionist defence of economic freedoms to interventionist defence of the said freedoms.

Some theorists call this the 'embedded neoliberal' model, for it entails neoliberalism becoming embedded deeply within the structures of the state and society, and even in our personal lives (see e.g. Apeldoorn, 2001; Apeldoorn, Drahokoupil and Horn 2009; Hurt, Knio and Ryner, 2009). In such formulations, importantly, the neoliberal state can also accommodate 'flanking measures': various adjustments to welfare services and even redistribution of goods, which facilitate stability of this market society (Knio and Ryner, 2009). Indeed, unlike 'utopian' neoliberals such as Hayek advocated, most neoliberal practices today rely on stabilisation of market society through welfare measures and labour rights of a basic kind. A coming together of social welfare ideals and neoliberalism has been the name of the game over the last decades (Giddens, 1998).

This curious tendency was also noted by Michel Foucault. In his lectures on biopolitics (2008), for example, he documented how shifts have unfolded towards what he called a 'governmental' neoliberal logic (see also Brown, 2003; Vasquez-Arroyo, 2008). The idea he floated was that economic science and practice increasingly relied on self-regulation of actors, citizens and market actors, in accordance to the logic of the market, but at the same time with respect to the local peculiarities of social life. Thus, while neoliberalism both in the United States and Europe 'conducted the conduct' of individuals in ways which moulded the desires and thinking towards perceiving market thinking as self-evident, they did so in different ways. In Europe 'Ordo-liberal' welfare logic was attached to this neoliberal project, while in the United States a more direct market logic dominated. In either case both the state and civil society, he argued, were now governmental sites for the facilitation of the right kind of market freedoms: for the facilitation of the *homo oeconomicus*.

Conclusion

This chapter has sought to understand the complex nature of the liberal democratic model and how it can be grounded. The crucial thing we have noted is that there is no single argument that justifies the linkage between liberal capitalist system and liberal democracy. Instead a variety of arguments have been made.

Some classical liberals argue that economic and political rights are separate but go together. Whether in classical liberal formulations or in Schumpeterian forms, these classical liberals highlight both economic and political freedoms as essential for democracy, and democracy itself becomes associated with the idea of representational democracy.

Neoliberals, in contrast to these classical liberals, insist on the normative priority of economic rights and freedoms for democracy, conceived as procedural democracy, to be possible. Democracy, as much as it has value, derives its value from its ability to prop up and defend, and to make efficient, the liberal capitalist economic model. As these ideas have gained ground, some have come to believe that market values are so important that they – paradoxically – have to be actively defended and propped up in 'stable' viable forms. As a result embedded neoliberalism involves more active roles to be taken by the state, citizens and civil society in defence of these freedoms.

Yet, liberal or neoliberal thought does not encapsulate all of liberal democratic thinking. Indeed, there are those that argue for democracy as a prior value, where liberal capitalism is seen as useful for the sake of enabling us to make the most of the democratic rights. Reform liberals challenge the core values of other liberal democratic thinkers placing the onus of their thought on defence of individuals in a community against power centres. This entails concrete adjustments to the functioning liberal democracy: active defence of welfare rights, employment opportunities and educational facilities.

These arguments constitute different variants of the liberal politico-economic model. Yet they all share something too: all liberal democrats examined here advocate, in different forms, a distinctly liberal conception of man and society, values of freedom and liberty as key democratic values, representative parliamentary system as the key site and institution of democratic politics and liberal capitalist model of economics as a crucial underpinning of liberal democracy. Despite the variations in liberal democratic thought, a liberal core still remains to all the authors examined here. It is these liberal core assumptions that other models of democracy directly challenge.

3 Challenges to liberal democracy

Socialist critics and social democracy

> Instead of deciding once in three or six years which member of the ruling class was to misrepresent the people in Parliament, universal suffrage was to serve the people constituted in the Communes.
>
> (Marx, 1978: 633)

> [I]n actual life democracy will never be 'taken separately'; it will be 'taken together' with other things, it will exert its influence on economic life, stimulating its reorganisation; it will be subjected in its turn to the influence of economic development and so on.
>
> (Lenin, 1933: 61)

These reflections of Marx and Lenin on democracy suggest important things about their uncompromising critique of liberal democracy, notably their distrust of representational parliamentary democracy. The parliamentary liberal democratic model, celebrated by the thinkers reviewed in Chapter 2, was perceived by Marx and many of his followers as little more than a new form of class rule. Representative democracy failed to tackle the deep sources of economic and political inequality in society and, hence, by advancing an illusion of equality, actually perpetuated and deepened societal inequalities. As Joseph Femia powerfully summarises (Femia, 1993: 18), for Marx 'the fictitious equality and fellowship [promised by liberal democracy] . . . serve[s] to conceal the inequality and strife' experienced by workers in their everyday life. Marx and socialists then have famously provided a sharp critique of the failings of the liberal democratic model of democracy and have done so precisely on *politico-economic* grounds: it is the restrictions that capitalist economy places on the workings of democracy that result in the, for them, bastardised form of democracy that is liberal democracy.

But what is there to put in liberal democracy's place? This has been a far trickier question for the Marxists, first, because communism, when in place, was supposed to entail the withering away of the state and hence the very idea of state-based democracy; but, second, because it has proved incredibly difficult indeed to obtain agreement on the kind of democracy that Marxists should advocate in the move towards communism. Marx himself only made a few fairly fragmentary comments on what he understood democracy to entail in a proletarian society. In liberal democracy's place Marx suggested a form of delegative democracy where people would directly elect delegates who would be accountable to them on immediate basis. Yet, Marxist followers became torn about the adequacy of Marx's thinking on democracy. Lenin eventually veered towards the so-called vanguard party approach where democracy came to entail little more than the dictatorship of the proletariat. Kautsky, and many Eurocommunists, however, turned to a reformist parliamentary approach: parliamentary democracy, when used properly to contest the power of the bourgeoisie, could in fact serve the purposes of a socialist democratic strategy. Thus, while being critical of liberal democracy's failures, these critics developed an extended parliamentary strategy for democratic social revolution.

Whether Marxists, Leninist or Kautskyan in approach, socialist thinking has tended to place an emphasis on the increased participation by the people in decision-making. Some form of delegative democracy, and at least extension of liberal ideals to contestation over economic inequality in society, plays a role in the various strands of socialist thought. Yet, much like for the liberal democrats examined in Chapter 2, it has been difficult for socialist critics to reach an agreement on the exact mix that should exist between 'liberal' democratic vision of the rule *by* the people and the 'socialist' vision of democracy *for* the people.

A much more successful mix between these models has been developed by the so-called 'social democrats'. Indeed, the social democrats of the Swedish model in many ways perfected the union of 'liberal democratic' thinking and 'socialist' criticism, which is why they are examined here in detail. The second part of this chapter will examine the unique, but at the same time pragmatic and well-developed, social democratic 'ideal type' developed in the 1940s and 1950s as an alternative to the liberal and the socialist understandings of democracy.

The social democratic model deserves close attention, for not only has it been considerably successful during the twentieth century, but also its unique formulations and methods are rarely adequately appreciated in today's democracy promotion. (Most states often described as 'liberal democracies' today are, some contend, in fact 'social democratic' in key respects [Berman, 2006]). As we will see, when appreciated in its details, the social democratic model offers an important counter-proposition to both the liberal democratic and socialist visions of democracy.

Marx on democracy

The liberal democratic model has been dominant in the twentieth century. Yet, it was never self-evidently superior in the eyes of all political groups. From the nineteenth century onwards it has been criticised by social agitators of various persuasions: socialists as well as many women's and slaves' liberation movements. The socialist that developed the most famous and perhaps the sharpest, yet in many ways ill-defined, critique of the liberal democracy, was Karl Marx. Liberal democracy was famously dismissed by Marx not only as a 'petty bourgeois' ideal, but also as a dangerous sham responsible for reproducing the alienation and oppression of workers in modern industrial society. Critique of liberal democracy was a long-running theme in Marx's thought.

Femia (1993: 15) argues that Marx provides two sets of grounds for critique of liberal democracy, philosophical and sociological. Marx's more philosophical grounds for critique were based in his early writings on Hegel. Young Marx critiqued Hegel's conception of the civil society and state. Hegel had argued that the public sphere of the state is where the clashes between egoistical individuals in the 'civil society' can be overcome by the fostering of public-spirited and impartial interaction. For Marx, politics within the state was not a 'neutral arbiter' (Femia, 1993: 18). In a capitalist system politicians were spokesmen for particular economic interests. It follows that citizenship and rights accorded to individuals by the state were illusionary. Individuals in a capitalist society were alienated from each other and the products of their labour, and hence could never live up to ideals of equality that bourgeois democracy seemed to advocate. On the contrary, for Marx, liberal democracy manifested man's alienation from his full self in three senses: (1) it severs man from society by making him an 'imaginary' member of a supposedly equal society; (2) it sanctions struggle between men in civil society; and (3) it fosters a split in human consciousness between private interests and communal obligations (Femia, 1993: 20). Liberal democracy, then, corrupts the idea of man and society as envisioned in the Greek ideals. Here, man was a member of political society and community first and foremost, not simply an egotistical individual pursuing his own interests.

Differences were also seen in the idea of rights. For Marx, 'republics' and 'bourgeois democracies', as practiced in the capitalist West, were not much better than absolutist monarchies, for at their root they were premised, like monarchy, on private property and class rule. A republican political system, despite political equality, was still underpinned in practice by material inequality (see e.g. Harrington, 1981). This meant also that for Marx the 'limited' individuals fostered by liberal democracy and capitalism were not liberated by bourgeois 'rights'. For Marx, these rights, in fact, 'perfected' people's slavery. Even when political rights were conceded as having some positive roles for workers' causes (see e.g. Miliband, 1977: 77), rights in a bourgeois society did not extend far enough: they did not address positive economic rights (Mayo, 1955: 291). Against republican bourgeois democracy, Marx suggested that a 'real' democracy would entail addressing the origins of inequality in society, and that would involve challenging the capitalist economic system. Democracy then, crucially, cannot exist independently in the political realm without the correct adjustments on the economic front.

What does Marx's critique mean exactly for how we should view the parliamentary representative systems of liberal democracy? For Marx, the parliamentary system allowed legitimate distortions to democracy by allowing rich sectors of society to gain undue control of the state and the electoral process. Representatives were, after all, by and large from rich educated sectors of society and represented their own interests. As such parliamentary democracy encouraged an inherently corrupt kind democracy that enslaved the common working people. It followed that there was nothing to be gained from parliamentary democracy for the sake of the revolution: 'The political instrument of [workers'] enslavement cannot serve as the political instrument of their emancipation' (Engels quoted in Femia, 1993: 47; see also Marx, 1978: 635).

As will be discussed later on, this critique is rather general in nature and, I think it is also fair to say, overstated, empirically speaking. It would be hard to prove the claim that liberal democratic systems are nothing but talking shops and merely serve the rich (see Mayo, 1955: 292). Indeed, as we will see, even most twentieth-century Marxists have rejected these claims (see e.g. Miliband, 1977).

But what, for Marx, would an alternative to liberal democracy look like? Marx was reluctant to set out the details of an alternative system of govern-ance, because he thought it unscientific to speculate ahead of time what forms of governance social and political struggles would lead to in specific contexts. Also, his reflections on the issue of democracy were complicated by the fact that his thought implied that democracy would become non-existent within a truly communist system. Yet, Marx did have some conception of what a socialist 'transitional' democracy might look like. He developed his views on alterna-tives to liberal democracy in his essay *Civil War in France*. This entailed an analysis of incipient socialist regimes, notably the Paris Commune of 1870–1. This experiment, while short-lived, embodied many key principles of Marx's ideal of democracy.

Central to this was a *delegative model of democracy*. This would entail as much 'immediate participation' in deliberations and decisions as a mass-scale industrial system allowed. Marx recognised that nineteenth-century society would not allow for a Greek *polis* or for the Rousseaun general will. But it allowed for a far more participative system than existed. Instead of choosing representatives every few years to make decisions for them, as in liberal democracy, the Marxist democracy was to be premised on choosing of delegates to all levels of societal decision-mak-ing. These delegates were to be directly and immediately accountable and 'revo-cable at short terms' (Marx, 1978: 632) to those that delegated them. Thus, to elec-tions was added the idea of 'instant recall' (Lenin, 1933: 84). As for the delegates, they were to be paid workers' wages and were to be workers themselves. Workers would take over all positions including bureaucratic and managerial roles: 'so that *all* become bureaucrats for a time and *no one*, therefore, can become a "bureau-crat"' (Lenin, 1933: 85).

Crucially, the delegates were to be *driven by the defence of the interests of the community as a whole*, not by their personal or sectional interests. Thus, contrary to the liberal model, the Marxist delegates would not 'compete' for the votes of the electors by prioritising particular class interests as their 'policy pitch', but rather would consider and advance as much as possible the good of the community as a whole, as they did in the Paris Commune.

Another distinctive aspect of this vision of democracy was the *unification of legislative and executive power*. 'The commune would be a working, not a par-liamentary, body, executive and legislative at the same time' (Marx, 1978: 632). Instead of separating these powers, Marx sought to bring them together, in order to facilitate direct control by delegates over state policy. There would be no higher echelon of executors outside the delegates of the people.

This was to be government by the workers, hence the centrality of workers' coun-cils from which delegates would be chosen. The democracy would be premised on workers' control over their own work places and from there extended out to wider spheres. Indeed, as Lenin (1933: 34) emphasises, here 'democracy, introduced as fully and consistently as is generally thinkable, is transformed from capitalist democracy into proletarian democracy; from the state (i.e. a special force for the suppression of particular class) into something which is no longer really the state in the accepted sense of the word'. The power vestiges of class rule in the state would be broken up. The police and the army would be broken up and 'judicial functionaries divested of [their] sham independence' (Marx quoted in Lenin, 1933: 34).

This does not mean that the Commune ignored relations with non-factory and non-urban people. In fact, the Commune encouraged similar communes in the provinces and integrated these to the Commune through inviting delegates to meetings together. Thus the plan was to integrate rural communities with the Paris commune, to reach beyond the urban/rural divide. They also extended the commune beyond the state – it was seen as a *global commune*. The Commune welcomed and claimed to represent the workers of the world. It made no distinction of citizenship on national grounds as long as participants were willing to serve the commune and its egalitarian principles of workers' democracy (Marx, 1978: 638).

The practical experience with commune democracy was considered impressive by Marx, despite the short-lived nature of the experiment. While the Commune fell in the face of the deceit of Thiers and Bismarck, within the walls of Paris social life was much bettered by the experience of workers' rule. For example, he pointed out that crime all but disappeared from Paris during the 1870–1 interlude (Marx, 1978: 640).

Even though his interpretation of the Paris Commune could be considered somewhat overly optimistic, Marx's reflections on democracy have some attractive qualities. First of all, he is historically and sociologically correct in emphasising the class origins of liberal democracy as we know it (Moore, 1966; Macpherson, 1977; Rueschemeyer, Huber and Stephens, 1992). Also, recognition of the contradiction between formal equality in liberal democracy and the real delimitations suffered by people in their exercise of their rights is an important contribution to our understanding of the constraints on democratic practice. It may well be the case that some get more out of this form of democracy than others and that some interests are indeed 'in-built' into this form of democracy over those of others.

But how does the purported control of capital actually work? Lenin argued that 'the more highly democracy is developed, the more the bourgeois parliaments are subjected by the stock exchange and bankers' (Lenin, 1918: 4). Marx implied the same. But is this really the case? Arguably the relationship between capital and democracy is more complex than allowed here, and indeed, many modern Marxists have come to recognise this by arguing that the state is, in fact, 'relatively autonomous' from capital.

There is another problem with Marx's thought and this has to do with the idea of workers' councils. These councils, Femia argues, would not in practice be able to make allocative decisions of the kind that were necessary: this would in actuality necessitate central control (Femia, 1993: 87). A contradiction seemed to exist within the kind of democracy Marx envisaged and the social conditions within which it was to be practiced. These contradictions came out powerfully in the debates that followed within the Marxist tradition in the twentieth century.

Marxists debate democracy

Not all have accepted Marx's reflections on democracy as unproblematic, even within the socialist tradition. Thus, many argue that his thinking on democracy is inconsistent and fragmentary (Bobbio, 1976; Femia, 1993). Others highlight that the kind of authoritarian tendencies that existed within the Soviet system and the 'people's parties' around the world are a direct heritage of the core principles of Marx's thought on capitalism and democracy (Femia, 1993). Partially because of its incompleteness, Marx's thought on democracy has led to the development of quite diverse lines of socialist and Left thought democracy. Indeed, some of the fiercest 'in-fights' in the Marxist and socialist camps have been over the role and nature of the democratic process. Perhaps the most famous fight took place between Lenin and Kautsky.

Karl Kautsky, initially known as an authoritative interpreter of Marx and Engels, became a highly contested figure from 1918 onwards when he attacked the Bolshevik line on revolutionary activity and suggested a way forward for a parliamentary socialism. Kautsky argues that it was a valid strategy for proletarians to try to 'take over the state', rather than simply seek its downfall. This stance was developed as Kautsky's doubts grew over the ability of working classes to deal with the complications of governing. Expertise was necessary and direct democracy of the Greek kind was *passé* in the new era of industrial economy (see Femia, 1993: 97). Direct democracy, on its own, was an overly utopian and potentially dangerously ideal to aim for.

Also, the unity of legislative and executive powers sounded dangerous to Kautsky. While more workers' control was certainly advisable, this should not mean the destruction of the liberal parliamentary system and its controls over power centres. Kautsky came to see a liberal democratic political system as an 'indispensable political foundation of the new collective order' (Kautsky, quoted in Femia, 1993: 99). What angered his critics even more was that Kautsky also argued that bourgeois rights, dismissed by Marx, were not a sham but *could actually be used* in the struggle for power by the proletariat.

As controversial as Kautsky was, Antonio Gramsci and French and Spanish Eurocommunists took important cues from him in their own thinking. They came to think that working within the liberal parliamentary system might not be entirely antithetical to the aims of the revolutionary workers' movement. These thinkers emphasised the need for a more flexible strategy in attaining revolutionary change in the twentieth-century capitalist society, where people were successfully being co-opted into the system and where willingness to engage in radical revolutionary activity certainly seemed to be on the wane. Gramsci (1998 [1971]) famously argued for a long-term 'war of position', which would, through agitation in the parliament as well as civil society, eventually bring societal forces to the realisation that they were oppressed. Such a position ena-bled revolutionary activity in civil society but also, simultaneously, engagement with the bourgeoisie through the state and the parliament – in defence of, even-tually, socialist aims. Togliatti and other Eurocommunists followed this lead and argued for a pluralist approach to political action.

This meant building alliances with and listening to the views of non-workers and non-socialists *within* a bourgeois liberal democratic system. Spanish Euro-communist leader Carrillo summarised this well: 'We must bring into our pro-gramme as an integral part, not only the demands of the workers but also those of all sections of society which are under-privileged' (Carrillo, 1977: 185). This was a tactical decision: 'either one [engages in alliances], which will make it pos-sible to emerge in a new situation and turn socialist aims into something real – or else one preserves one's "revolutionary virginity" and does nothing' (Carrillo, 1977: 188). 'Revolutionaries can find within [state] apparatus, today, allies who are going to contribute towards changing it from within' (Carrillo, 1977: 189).

Kautsky's approach then has been followed and elaborated on by many social-ists throughout the twentieth century. These critics argue that Marx's delegative position on democracy fosters an unnecessary and misplaced refusal to partake in liberal democracy. While socialists, they accept, should always be sceptical of the dominance of business interests and the glorification of the ideology of rights within modern states, this does not mean that parliamentarianism, when engaged strategically, cannot be used to challenge the power of dominant classes. An extension of liberal democracy was envisaged here in:

- refusing to accept liberal democracy as the obvious gold standard of democracy;
- agitating for extensions of workers' control and democracy within the state, and
- emphasising the need for socially egalitarian economic and social policies to bring 'reality' of participation and control to parliamentary democracy.

This went further than reform liberal agitation for the sake of social stability or better functioning of the capitalist and democratic systems. Here, the end point was revolution and opening up of possibilities for radically reformed participatory kinds of democratic representation; yet, strategically, within the confines of the model which parliamentary democrats had built.

This Kautskyan approach, however, was always controversial and attacked fiercely by the so-called vanguard tradition in socialist circles. Its key front-man was Lenin, who in 'The Proletarian Revolution and the Renegade Kautsky', *Of Bourgeois and Proletarian Democracy* and the *State and the Revolution*, attacked the parliamentarians for his views. Against Kautskyites, Lenin emphasised the need not only to take control of the bourgeois state, but also to break it up (Lenin 1933: 30–2) as a key condition to any real union of peasants and workers for their emancipation. But what was to replace the shattered state machinery? A democ-racy, with the proletariat in a key role.

Lenin saw a return to 'primitive democracy', a move much derided by Kautsky, as necessary. A complete rethinking of the way in which democracy was to work would be necessary and starting out from this 'primitive' democracy, essentially a Greek idea of direct democracy, was a better starting point than that of the corrupt bourgeois liberal model. Lenin attacked strongly the system of parliamentarianism: it was a key institution of the capitalist state and hence antithetical to proletarian interests (Lenin, 1933: 37).

Yet, Lenin would not wish to destroy parliaments, but rather suggested that: 'The way out of parliamentarianism is to be found . . . not in the abolition of the representative institutions and the elective principle, but in the conversion of the representative institutions from mere 'talking shops' into working bodies'. This meant replacing liberal parliamentarianism with:

> institutions in which freedom of opinion and discussion does not degenerate into deception, for the parliamentarians must themselves work, must themselves execute their own laws, must themselves verify their results in actual life, must themselves be directly responsible to their electorate. Representative institutions remain, but parliamentarianism as a special system, as a division of labour between the legislative and the executive functions, as a privileged position for the deputies, *no longer exists*. Without representative institutions we cannot imagine democracy, not even proletarian democracy; but we can and *must* think of democracy without parliamentarianism, if criticism of bourgeois society is not mere empty words for us.
>
> (1933: 38, italics in the original)

Lenin (1933: 38) emphasised that Marx's study was not utopian but precisely focused on studying the real conditions of the '*birth* of the new society *from* the old'. Workers' control of affairs of work and state would in the end result in the withering away of state as we know it and a new order arising. It would make it impossible for the state to use its machinery to indoctrinate people to the false consciousness of their oppression and would allow the rise of the enlightened and emancipated working class.

This vanguard approach gives a central role to the proletarian movement in bringing about change. It was to be a proletarian democracy, with proletarian party of the people at its centre and as its enforcer. This was a democracy where not all interests were equal, for '[t]here can be no equality between the exploited and the exploiters' (Lenin, 1918: 7). For the Leninist vanguard approach, the Kautskyan 'opportunists' had then failed to think through and follow through with what revolutionary change and action would entail, thus vulgarizing Marx's democratic centralist views. For Lenin the Social Democratic acceptance of bourgeois political forms was a betrayal of Marx's views. The answer was not to ignore the state (as anarchists do) nor accept it, but to take up a revolutionary view of how it should change (in order to eventually wither away).

In sum

Much contestation has taken place over the idea of democracy within the Marxist and socialist lines of thought, as we have seen. There are those who see Marx's thought on democracy as compatible with a parliamentary strategy for revolutionary change – parliamentary democracy, for them, can be radicalised from within – and those who argue that the vanguard party approach is necessary. Many differences exist between these positions on issues such as: What constitutes the ideal democracy – proletarian or parliamentary democracy or something in between? Which representational methods should we use in democratic system – delegates, parliaments, vanguard, or combinations of all? By whom should the people be represented in a democracy – workers only, or all sections of society regardless of their class position? How is a correct marriage to be achieved between people pursuing their 'real interests' (of which they might be unaware) and respecting their *actual* views (parliamentary pluralism)? What is the end point of democracy – will it persist or ultimately wither away in equal communist society? Given all these differences, one might be tempted to think that there is no such thing as a Marxist politico-economic model of democracy. However, a significant amount is also shared among the Marxists and socialists regarding democracy, such as:

- Focus on exposing the problems of liberal democracy and argument for a deeper 'real' democracy that emphasises the need for economic as well as political systems to be restructured by democracy.
- Emphasis on greater worker control of social and economic processes; a workers' democracy, where workers have a say on communal life but also crucially on the economic processes of which they are part.
- Argument for radical equalisation of the status of citizens in democratic representation, and crucially adjusted kinds of representative systems within states. Even parliamentary variants of socialist thought, which rely on liberal representative government, place great emphasis on extending the involvement of individuals in governmental structures and decisions. Radicalisation of communitarian politics for social equality, even within the liberal system, remains the ideal.
- Emphasis on communal and societal values in democratic participation over simply personal interests. Delegates and representatives then are not seen, as in the liberal model, as market commodities to be 'supported' by those who benefit from what they have to offer, but as representatives (in the full sense of the word) of the views and concerns of the community, with also wider communal interests at heart.
- A view of the individual and society that emphasises the fact that individuals exist in structural circumstances, in social conditions that shape their thoughts and possibilities of action/inaction. Hence, Marxists and socialists all directly reject a conception of man as an egotistical individual separated from other individuals.

There is then enough to make up a 'politico-economic model of democracy' here. But what is the relevance of Marxist thought today and is there any meaningful democratic content to socialist thinking on democracy?

The Soviet experience has seriously discredited the cause of Marxism, many argue. The injustices and shambolic 'front' democracies hardly lived up to the kinds of idyllic ideals that Marx envisaged. Indeed, the victory of the vanguard approach of Lenin resulted in a socialist practice of governance in the former Soviet Union that was far from democratic. Although the Soviet system entailed all the trappings of workers' democracy, these were overshadowed by the all-knowing, omnipotent, 'Party', which became not only representative of particular interests but also dictatorial in its dealings with the Soviets and local delegative democracy. The Soviet experience has clearly shown us the potentials for Marxism to result in dangerous disavowals of its ideals.

However, while we must accept that there clearly are some real dangers in Marxist takes on democracy in paving the way to forms of authoritarian rule, this does not mean that the Marxist ideals *tout court* are necessarily discredited. As we have seen, Marxists can work with more liberal parliamentary routes to democracy too, and moreover make important points about the need to extend the reach of participatory modes beyond the mere parliamentary route. The Marxist critique of liberal democracy's failings too, while overstated in its extreme forms, is still rather pertinent. If we accept that there is relative autonomy in the state from capital, the role of capital in the processes, procedures and definition of 'legitimate' forms of interaction within the state is something that needs close attention. Indeed, there are many that would still maintain that there is a relevance to the Marxist critique of liberal democracy even today (Harrington, 1981; Callinicos, 2003; Williams, 2008).

Others yet, while they may not fully agree with Marxist takes, can still agree that the Marxist critiques and ideals, when built into alternative frameworks of thought, can be at least partially revived. Thus, many advocates of participatory democracy, feminism and green movements (see Chapter 4), do hark back in some ways to Marxist ideals of 'substantive' rather than merely 'formal' democracy.

There are also those who have built these ideals in a direction that has sought to reconcile socialist ideas with some core liberal beliefs, notably the belief in the liberal capitalist system as the most efficient producer of economic wealth. The social democratic line of thinking is one such tradition to have developed a distinct and successful alternative politico-economic model based on serious consideration of socialist criticisms of the liberal model. It is to examination of this model that we turn now.

Primacy of politics over the economy: the social democratic alternative

It is my conviction that much of present ideological debate in terms of socialism vs. capitalism is not only outdated but even outright dangerous as it blurs our deep understanding of the ideological problems of our society, and as it makes us less efficient in our fight for the socialist ideals.

(Adler-Karlsson, 1967: 7)

Much of the twentieth-century ideological debate has revolved around the opposition of capitalism and socialism as socio-economic systems. This debate has often been associated with two polarised positions, in one corner liberalism associated with Smith, Hayek and others and, in the other, socialism, understood essentially as a variant of Marxist thinking and inherently hostile to capitalism and liberal democracy.

There is another distinct alternative to these positions, however. Social democratic thought, as developed in Scandinavia especially, has sought to fundamentally challenge the assumption that capitalism and socialism are mutually exclusive. This highly original and innovative, and in the post-war Western context, surprisingly and surreptitiously influential ideology, has sought to combine: state intervention and capitalist economy; economic efficiency and social justice; respect for individual choice and rights and communitarian principles of solidarity; and electoral democracy with communal and economic democracy.

I will now examine this line of thought, which is often – quite unjustifiably – ignored in twentieth-century politico-economic thinking on democracy. This strand of thought I argue is far from a mere *ad hoc* collection of policies as sometimes suggested, and also far from an outdated framework of thought in thinking about the future of democracy in today's context.

One of the key contributions of the social democratic model has been to rethink the relationship between economics and democratic politics, that is, to shift the boundary between the two. As Sheri Berman (2006) argues the 'primacy of politics' is the core principle, along with communitarian values, at the heart of the social democratic model. While welfare liberals have, as we have seen in Chapter 2, introduced notions of equality of opportunity, the social democrats argue for primacy of, not liberal values, but democratic controls over injustices in society. The social democratic tradition then is quite distinctive. Indeed:

> If liberalism can be stretched to encompass an order that saw unchecked markets as dangerous, that has public interests trump private prerogatives, and that granted states the right to intervene in the economy to protect the common interests and nurture social solidarity, then the term is so elastic as to be nearly useless.

(Berman, 2006: 179)

Here, then, a dividing line is drawn between a liberal politico-economic model, even in its welfare liberal guises, and social democratic thinking. And with social democratic thought, I mean here the tradition that started from the socialist revisionism of the early twentieth century that became elaborated in various European social democratic movements, notably in Scandinavia. It is a tradition of thought that shares commitment to certain key principles, including the idea of 'integrative democracy', state as a defender of the individuals and national community, belief in complementarity of socio-economic equality and economic efficiency, and socially controlled market economy, and confidence in the public sector as extender of people's individual scope for choice (Tilton, 1990: 257–69).

Crisis of capitalism, liberalism and socialism

From the end of the nineteenth century, the problems of unfettered liberalism were becoming increasingly obvious. Socialists and Marxists were active in arguing that this should, and would, lead to the dissolution of capitalism as a guiding principle of economic and political life. During the 1920s many turned still to either liberal or Marxist alternatives, however, in thinking of ways forward. Yet, significant 'revisionist' thinking was starting to arise within both the socialist and the liberal camps. In the liberal tradition, as we have seen, some took their cue from J.S. Mill and started to argue for a more welfare-oriented vision of capitalism. Hobson and Hobhouse were at the forefront of such welfare liberal thinking. Among socialists too, revisionism was on the rise. The likes of Eduard Bernstein and Karl Kautsky, for example, pointed to the weaknesses of the Marxist view of revolutionary politics, and also to the positive economic consequences that the capitalist mode of production could have in generating growth. This revisionism created much infighting within the socialist parties but did not arise into full public consciousness until the 1930s and the onset of the Great Depression.

The 1929 Wall Street crash pushed the United States and many other states into a deep recession. It is this recession that many of the authors associated with social welfare thinking were responding to. All the authors examined here shared one basic conclusion: that the model of capitalist economic thinking dominant before and at the time of the crisis was inadequate and misinformed, either on value-based or pragmatic accounts, or both. Liberal capitalist economics and the model of state and democracy that went with it were considered quite inadequate as ways of responding to the crisis and as ways of thinking about organisation of social life. The liberal politico-economic model was seen in many ways to be at a breaking point.

Dealing with the recession and more widely the crisis of capitalism necessitated a rethinking of both economic and political systems, and *specifically of the relationship between the two*. Deep skepticism arose of the tendency of some of the classical economists to separate the economic from the political and to allow free rein to the forces of the invisible hand of the market. Instead of *laissez-faire* liberalism, these authors started to look beyond liberalism.

However, much of the social democratic thinking, while it arose from Marxist and socialist roots, went directly against the orthodoxy that Marxist parties had for a long time valued. Many came to argue that a better way to obtain change than calling for an abstract and increasingly unlikely revolution was for socialists to start developing concrete policies to deal with the hardship of workers in the societies in which they lived. This approach necessitated co-operation with the bourgeoisie and participation in the democratic instruments of bourgeois capitalism. Yet, it did not entail wholesale acceptance of the liberal economic or political system *as it was*, but could entail its transformation to a more just and democratically responsive system.

Keynesian thinking is perhaps the most famous line of thought that was critical of the neoclassical liberal economics. However, it should not be forgotten that already, before Keynes, some governments, perhaps most notably the Swedish government, had already started to apply very particular macro-economic policies and continued to develop a unique, and successful, model of social democracy in the post-war era. The Swedish model was not just a collection of Keynesian policies, but rather encapsulated and developed a very distinct ideology or political theory of social democracy. It emphasised the primacy of politics over the market (Berman, 2006) and highlighted the need for egalitarian principles to be wedded into the workings of an efficient and growth-prone liberal economy. It is a model of democracy, a social democratic 'ideal type' *par excellence*, which then deserves close attention, despite its seemingly 'peripheral' location in world politics.

Social democrats and the Swedish Model

If Keynes took steps towards a critique of liberal economics, such critique went much further and deeper with the emerging social democratic thinking. The Swedish social democratic thinkers were pragmatic in wanting to develop workable realistic policies for a very difficult time, but also highly principled in seeking to advance a unique combination of values in their societies: prosperity and equality, but also justice and communitarianism. Following these thinkers, social democratic ideas had a number of surges across the world, albeit at different times: in Sweden from the mid-1950s to mid-1970s, in Germany in the 1970s, in the United States under Roosevelt during the New Deal and in France and Great Britain just after the Second World War and again in France in early 1980s under Mitterrand (see Hahnel, 2005: 110).

Sweden was in many ways an unlikely site for the rise of the social democratic tradition. Yet, within this relatively marginal European state, specifically within its Social Democratic Party (SAP), unique lines of thought were developed on social democracy. The SAP, unlike many other social democratic parties, fully committed itself to support an electoral democratic approach to socialism and advocated active co-operation with the bourgeois parties. Instead of the divisive approach adopted by most class-warring socialists, the Swedes started developing the idea of a unified solidaritist nation, an idea encapsulated in the idea of 'folkhemmet', the state as the 'home of the people'. The core of the Swedish model consisted in re-interpretation of the role of politics in the economic sphere. The social democrats wanted to 'protect society from . . . the destabilising consequences [of markets] (Berman, 2006: 5). As Berman puts it: social democracy 'at least as originally conceived, represented a fully-fledged alternative to both Marxism and liberalism that had at its core a distinctive belief in the primacy of politics and communitarianism' (Berman, 2006: 8). Let's examine the key assumptions of the Swedish model.

The Swedish model involved in the first instance *limiting the independence of the markets* by exerting political control over them. Market forces were to be brought under state regulation and democratic control. This was done partly on value-grounds, to ensure a more just working of the market, but also on pragmatic grounds. As Wigforss argued, capitalism was perceived as wasteful in its use of resources (e.g. by not fully capitalising on employment resources), a problem that could be dealt with by promotion of more fully functioning economy. A combination of principled socialist value-led thinking and pragmatic reflection on weaknesses of capitalism led the social democrats towards a democratically controlled market economy. Instead of allowing the market forces and firms to follow market incentives alone, market forces were in the Swedish model built into, or integrated into, the political process and debate.

This meant that the Swedish model entailed a unique model of economics and also democracy, what Tilton has called *'integrative democracy'*. What this meant was that:

> from its origins Swedish Social Democracy has been committed to creating a society where first industrial workers and then employees in general participated on equal terms in the organization and governance of society. The democratic ideal ought to infuse not only political life but social and economic organisation as well.
>
> (Tilton, 1990: 257–8)

What is distinctive about this model is, first, that economic and political democracy are seen as infused together and it is believed that narrow 'political democracy' on its own is not sufficient.

Second, it is important to note that *participation, beyond the mere electoral sphere*, was a key aspect of this model. Notably, the views of labour should be considered and integrated into debates on developing economic policies. Capitalism and the liberal democratic model of democracy failed to do this: 'it foreclosed [to the worker/proletarian] not only the income from capital, but also participation in and responsibility for the organization of economic activity' (Tilton summarising Steffen, 1990: 258). The social democratic model was to remedy this through ensuring that workers would be in a position to exercise their power, both by integrating them into political and economic policy-making process and by in the first place schooling and socialising the workers to take up this role. The formalisation of the key role of trade unions in state-organised holistic wage-level negotiations was one key way of integrating labour. Another was the encouragement of the tradition of social movements (folkrorelse) within the state, which were tapped into and participated in by the 'representatives'.

The building in of labour's representation to the state and democracy, however, was to be consensual (Tilton, 1990: 259). Indeed, *emphasis on unity and solidarity* runs through the social democratic tradition. There was not to be class war but rather respectful debate among equals. Per Albin made the analogy between discussions in the state and those in the home: 'In the good home equality, consideration, co-operation and helpfulness prevail' (Albin quoted in Tilton: 1990: 259).

But if thought on democracy was unique in this model, so too was the politico-economic thinking that underpinned this system. As Tilton emphasises, social democrats were firm believers in the 'compatibility, even complementarity of socioeconomic equality and economic efficiency' (Tilton, 1990: 260). *Growth could be instigated and at the same time principles of social justice could be safeguarded.* The two aims were not contradictory but complementary. Social democrats then were not anti-capitalists, nor were they against encouragement of 'efficient' economic production and exchange. The social democrats still believed that inefficient firms should go under and that market forces should play a role in the economy. However, they wanted to ensure, within a capitalist system, first, equality of pay (same pay for same work) and security of the person (in event of unemployment).

Work creation was a crucial aspect of the social democratic ideas: instead of socialising ownership (socialist response), the key to a more just and efficient market system was the *encouragement of full or near-full employment.* There was nothing natural or efficient about persistent unemployment (an implication arising from liberal wage theories) for the social democrats. Full employment then was encouraged through the theory of wage policy developed by Gosta Rehn and Rudolf Meidner. These trade union economists argued that wage negotiations should be brought within the state to ensure that a just level of wages could be guaranteed across areas of work. So-called *solidarity wage* was to be negotiated in the mass trade union–employer union negotiations, which set the general wage level.

But how could such a policy be mixed with successful and non-inflationary growth in the economy as a whole? For surely fixing wage levels not only increased employers' costs, thus decreasing overall growth, but also would create rigidity in the economy that would restrict the free choice of firms to design their strategies. The Rehn–Meidner model maintained that 'squaring the circles' was possible through: (1) following tight fiscal policy to fight inflation and (2) promotion of an active labour market policy, through which individuals could retrain as and when needed and would be supported *out of* unemployment (Eklund, 2001: 55). The argument that Rehn and Meidner made was that as long as fiscal policy was regulated and support to workers sufficient, one could run an economy on the basis of higher basic wages and egalitarian principles and maintain growth. This is because with higher average wages the least efficient firms would be forced to improve their efficiency (without doing so at the expense of workers' wages), while the more efficient firms would gain profits (by paying lower wages than they could afford) (Tilton, 1990: 261). Crucially, because firms could not use wage levels to 'hide' their inefficiency in their sector of the economy, the solidarity wage was, in fact, not only just, but a very efficient way of encouraging efficient market behaviour.

It followed from the unique nature of the economic model that the role of the state in society and economy was to be very different in Sweden vis-à-vis the 'liberal democracies'. The key characteristics of the Swedish model according to Eklund (2001: 55) were:

- large public sector, providing free public services;
- generous transfer systems (pensions, parental leave, sick leave unemployment support);
- big unions;
- large firms in export sector, negotiating with big unions and government;
- full employment through the public sector; and
- social democratic political hegemony.

As Eklund has argued, the Swedish model can often jokingly be referred to as a model where 'Big business, Big government and Big unions' all play a role. This is a very apt description of the Swedish model, for it tries to combine those aspects which liberal and socialist models see as incompatible. Big firms working on the basis of capitalist principles can for the Swedish model be mixed in with labour power support and social welfare support. Instead of nationalisation the emphasis of the model is on politically and socially controlled economy.[1]

The Swedish model was attached to a belief in the *public sector as complementary to the realisation of the freedom of the individual.*Contrary to the liberals, the social democrats saw no contradiction between a large public sector that would provide individuals with security and essential services that they would need to individually invest in anyway, and freedom and liberty of the individual. This went together with the belief in communitarian and solidaristic values.

Social welfare democracy, today?

Sweden has been very keen to promote its unique model of democracy and this model has indeed been adopted to various extents in locales as different as Germany and New Zealand. However, not only is this model difficult to transport in any pure form, given that it relies on specific social and cultural conditions (Tilton, 1990: 9), but also its relevance today too has been questioned, as Sweden itself moved away from the classical social welfare model towards more liberal policies in the 1990s. Indeed, with globalisation of financial markets there has been an increasing push to deregulate the financial sector, something that the Swedish model with its belief in the primacy of political control had been very reluctant to do. Since the late 1980s it has been impossible for the Swedish system to resist these pressures. The resultant liberalisation has partially eroded the social welfare values, policies and consensus in Sweden (see Ryner, 2002). This is partly because of a psychological effect that the victory of liberalism over socialism seems to have engendered, but also quite simply because the rise of international finance gives 'international investors a powerful veto over any government policies they deem as unfriendly to their interests' (Hahnel, 2005: 118).

Does this mean that the Swedish model is no longer viable or of interest to us? Magnus Ryner's (2002) work is instructive in reflecting on this question. He has sought to understand the fortunes of the Swedish model in the last two decades in the phase of the 'third way' thinking (Giddens, 1998). The third way argued for a reformulation of social democracy based on liberalisation of market forces hand in hand with a revival of social citizenship, where social rights should be tied to recognition of 'responsibilities' of the individual. This model challenged social democracy for encouraging lazy, unproductive, un-market-friendly 'suboptimal' behaviour by the population. As Giddens (1998) argued, absenteeism and delays in search for work generated by high social support inevitably affect the profits and productivity of the system as a whole, resulting in a stagnating economy vis-à-vis purer market systems. To be able to generate adequate growth within the globalised market economy these negative consequences of social democracy need to be done away with and thereby social democracy 'renewed' (Giddens, 1998). His third way argued – persuasively – for very basic welfare measures only, which were seen to go hand in hand with support for business, privatisation of pensions and regulation of labour laws. A key aspect of Giddens's model is that individuals must take responsibility for their own work and income, they cannot be guaranteed by the state.

Ryner (2002) disagreed with Giddens's analysis. While he recognised that we must of course understand the changes that have taken place in the global economic system and in the demographic and productive structures of economy, these changes do not render the social democratic system incapable of dealing with such challenges. Ryner argued that the classical welfare model is much better placed institutionally and otherwise to deal with the challenges than the 'residual welfare model' where the market mechanisms is rendered 'the basic mechanism of social organisation' (Ryner, 2002: 26).

Ryner's argument is that we cannot understand the woes of the Swedish model as an externally conditioned inevitability, nor as a betrayal of ideals by social democratic leaders, but rather as a failure by social democratic leaders to adopt correct policies at the time of major international financial and economic restructuring. Ryner argues that the Swedish social democrats in the 1990s failed tactically both within the state, and internationally. Internally they failed to push through with crucial reforms that were needed within the stagnating economy. Options suggested by Meidner and others (notably the wage earner funds which would have deepened economic democracy) were not pushed through and fierce right-wing opposition to these proposals, and the very idea of the Swedish model so far accepted also by the right, was allowed to arise. Deregulation of financial markets in the mid-1980s compounded the moves away from the Swedish model, as the Ministry of Finance and Central Banks started agitating against the trade unions (see Ryner, 2002; Hahnel, 2005: 133). A right-wing neoliberal discursive system became dominant in these institutions: they took over the 'language' of freedom and rights and gave them a new spin. The failure of Swedish social democracy in the 1990s then was a *political and strategic failure not economically pre-determined*. It led to the downgrading of the welfare model and with it the distinct model of democracy embedded in it.

Ryner argued that alternative options were available and that what he calls a 'negotiated involvement variant of post-Fordism', a model that would have allowed macro-level negotiations on wages and staying true to social democratic goals, would have been a viable alternative. There is little evidence, he argued, that Sweden's classical wage determination policy and labour market laws would be *incompatible* with efficiency and productivity in a post-Fordist era (Ryner, 2002: 50).

There are then reasons to suggest that this model might be more attractive today than Giddensian critics imply. This is not only because of the wane of the neo-liberal ideology in the context of a new cycle of financial crises, but also because of the inherent attractiveness of the ideological values at the core of the Swedish model for many people around the world: values of equality, democracy, economic justice, solidarity, alongside economic growth. Indeed, in Sweden there has been a turn back to social democracy, albeit in a more moderate form because of the changes that the 1990s initiated. Further changes are to be expected.

Elsewhere too this model is considered an important alternative. Considering the effects of the neoliberal model for the global markets there has been a call from various sectors and nation-states for a return to Keynesian policies and protection of society from the harsh effects of global capitalism. In putting such principles to practice there is no better model around than the Swedish model.

This is a model which, while it cannot be straightforwardly transplanted to other localities, embodies a set of ideals that many new developing and democratising countries aspire to. Following such ideals may bring democratising states to similar, or possibly even quite different, institutional solutions. Pragmatic thinking and willingness to compromise are needed: this, if anything, is the core of the Swedish model, a key characteristic to bear in mind in thinking about its relevance in democracy promotion globally today.

Conclusion

This chapter has examined the alternatives to liberal democratic ideals. We have examined Marxist and socialist thought on democracy, or the variations in thinking as to how the inherent weaknesses of liberal democracy must be addressed. We have also examined social democracy as developed in the 'ideal type' form in the Nordic countries. It is important to bear these alternatives in mind, for they have not only been influential in twentieth-century politics but also, especially in the case of social democracy, have been rather successful in striking a balance between economics and politics, which has been difficult for the more liberal models. Indeed, we need to bear in mind that if we look past the hegemonic liberal rhetoric we can see that 'the ideology that triumphed in the 20th century was not liberalism, as the "end of history" story argues; it was social democracy' (Berman, 2006: 2). It follows that social democracy, and even some socialist ideas, may have unexpected strengths and appeal in the current era of repeated financial crisis and renewed democratic aspirations.

4 Reviving the direct democratic tradition

Participatory democracy and radical democracy

Whilst the masses are invited to the liberal democratic feast, and are the assumed beneficiaries of development, they must not spit, swear or speak too loudly, or they will spoil the meal.

(Luckham, 1998: 309)

The industrial system . . . is in great measure the key to the paradox of political democracy. Why are the many nominally supreme but actually powerless? Largely because the circumstances of their lives do not accustom or fit them for power or responsibility. A servile system in industry reflects itself in political servility.

(G.D.H. Cole quoted in Pateman, 1970: 38)

Power to the people! Community control! Let the people make the decisions that affect their lives!

(Cook and Morgan, 1971: 1)

In earlier chapters we have examined the liberal, Marxist and social democratic 'politico-economic' models of democracy. This chapter will examine other important, if often misunderstood, alternative traditions of thought on democracy, namely participatory democracy and radical democracy.

Participatory democracy has been one of the most vocal challengers to the liberal democratic ideal since the 1960s and 1970s. Participatory democrats in the United States and in Europe especially have been famously sceptical of the virtues of the liberal model, critiquing the conservatism and elitism characteristic of twentieth-century Western liberal democratic thought and practice.

While participatory democrats do not necessarily reject the liberal or representative model outright, they see it as insufficient on its own. This model is associated with the continuing disempowerment and de-radicalisation of society. They see modern Western democracies, not as paragons of democratic governance, but as decaying and compromised systems where the power of dominant elites through (electoral) liberal democratic systems, degrades the freedoms of individuals and communities, which in turn leads to the stagnation of human development and self-reflexivity, and breaks down the bonds of social solidarity. As Marcuse (1964) famously argued, the liberal democratic society is creating and sustaining a 'one-dimensional' uncritical man incapable not only of changing society for the better, but even of realising the oppressive nature of the very supposed 'freedoms' that they enjoy in the modern industrial society. Participatory democrats aim for a more truly democratic, critically reflective and participatory kind of society. They aim to reinvigorate the political system, and also beyond it the entire social system, including, importantly, the economic system, through a set of participatory reforms.

Radical democracy, on the other hand, is a term which refers to a conception of democracy developed by a set of thinkers from the mid-1980s onwards who explicitly sought to extend new-left thought through the insights of so-called poststructuralist or postmodern theoretical thought. Key figures in constituting and arguing for a radical plural democratic model, or a new 'ethos' of democracy, are Ernesto Laclau, Chantal Mouffe, William E. Connolly, Michael Hardt and Antonio Negri. The key thing to note about the 'radical theory' of democracy developed by them is that it explicitly seeks to expand the meaning of democracy beyond procedural liberal, delegative Marxist, participatory, as well as statist notions of democracy. It is an explicitly open, non-hierarchical and dynamic conception of democracy that uniquely does not envisage a particular form of ideal democratic society, but rather argues that many different actual forms of democratic politics are possible. Indeed, at the core of this 'model of democracy' (if it can be called that at all because of its resistance to the idea of universal 'models') is a resistance to 'fixing' right or wrong ways of being or acting 'democratic'.

This chapter will look first at the origins of participatory democracy and then radical democracy. I will examine the core values and assumptions that inform these conceptions of democracy, including their underlying politico-economic assumptions, as well as highlighting the kinds of concrete democratic reforms they envisage. Finally, I will also reflect on the relevance of these strands of democratic thought and practice today.

Origins of the participatory model

The origin of the idea of participatory democracy lies, as Carole Pateman (1970) points out, in the lost and often misunderstood tradition of 'classical democratic theory'. Joseph Schumpeter in his *Capitalism, Socialism and Democracy* made a fierce attack on the classical theory of democracy, which he perceived as utopian. Yet, it is not necessarily the case that the earlier thought on democracy was utopian or unrealistic, and as Pateman (1970) argues, Schumpeter (and many of his twentieth-century followers) failed to appreciate the contribution made by these thinkers. For Pateman, misunderstood thinkers included Jean-Jacques Rousseau and J.S. Mill, the two key forefathers of participatory democracy.

Rousseau's thought is important for participatory democracy because he was one of the key early critics of 'representative models of democracy'. For Rousseau, democracy was not just a way of protecting individual's interests against an overarching state (as it was for the liberal democrats at the time; see Chapter 2) but rather had value of a much more substantive kind. Rousseau held that the experience of democratic participation was of value in itself and crucially had consequences for the development of human personality. If a society could treat all men on an equal economic footing and if in this condition men would come to deliberate and assemble to construct laws, a 'general will' would emerge and all would become free (Pateman, 1970: 26). Crucially, in constructing the general will people would realise themselves more fully as human beings. Rousseau's emphasis on 'processual' and 'solidaristic' notion of democracy has become crucial for participatory democrats.

J.S. Mill built some openings towards participatory democracy too, but from the point of view of a liberal utilitarian perspective. As we have already seen in Chapter 2, while Mill ended up supporting a number of elitist rules, for Mill liberal democracy was not purely 'protective' but had another far more substantial and important function: that of allowing the development of each individual person. Crucially, for Mill, liberal democracy was educative and psychologically beneficial for participants. This is why people should play a role in it. The value of democracy was in its dynamic and interactive nature: in its ability to improve people's faculties and to bring them together with a sense of co-operative spirit.

Another key opening towards an 'extra-liberal' idea of democracy was to be found in the thought of G.D.H. Cole (1920), who in the 1920s advocated a guild system of self-governing participative associations. But participatory democracy in the fullest sense was the invention of the 1960s student revolutions. Why the rise of participatory democracy in the 1960s?

Many things came together in the middle of the twentieth century. While society was getting more affluent, materialism and consumerism also created a backlash against conformism. Feminists, the environmentalists and the New Left sought to counter the stifling de-radicalisation of politics. Critical Theorists of the Frankfurt School and later in the American context figures such as Herbert Marcuse made a point about the insidious ways in which conformism works in modern societies: people, while thinking that they are free, are insidiously being lured into ways of life that not only are bad for society, but also adverse for themselves as rational actors. A sharp critique of democratic governance was attached to this general critique. The liberal democratic system was conceived to be failing: while it provided a veneer of equality and representation, in fact, it was ridden with forms of power that twisted and manipulated the public in such ways as to 'make them want' what the elites wanted them to want. Critical thought and real democratic decision-making was seen to be drastically lacking.

This was reflected, Pateman (1970) argued, in the theories of democracy dominant at the time. The so-called 'contemporary theory of democracy', taking its cue from Schumpeter and Dahl, was conceived to be not only conservative in prioritising the present practice of democracy over possible alternatives, but also openly elitist: it had abandoned an interest in real inclusion of people in decision-making: as much as they mattered, they did so as silent apathetic automatons turning up at voting booths every four to six years. This 'empirical view' of democracy, with a very narrow conception of 'democratic participation', was prioritised as 'realistic'.

Participatory democracy, contrary to the liberal model, emphasised the need for a bottom-up grass roots approach to political interaction. The New Left advanced a sharp critique of 'top-down' visions of democracy and of modern expertise in administration of state affairs (Cook and Morgan, 1971). Simultaneously, there was of course a radical expansion of the area of the 'political': instead of connoting merely parliamentary public debate, the political was now also perceived in the social and economic 'private' sphere and also in the very ideas of the family or even the constitution of a person. For many the idea of participatory democracy was but a slogan and, as Cook and Morgan (1971: 23) have showed, remained poorly theorised. Yet, through the writings of a set of key participatory democrats – C.B. Macpherson (1977), Carole Pateman (1970), Benjamin Barber (2003) and Peter Bachrach and Arych Botwinick (1992) – a clearer sense of what this notion means has emerged.

Key assumptions, values and modes of participatory democracy

The cornerstone of participatory democracy is the strong belief in revitalisation and 're-democratisation' of systems previously reliant on the elitist and passive 'electoral liberal democracy'. This critique of liberal democracy as a system is based, however, on a much wider challenge to the very notions of the individual and society held by the liberal democrats. As Bachrach (1992: 18) argues: 'we consider liberal democratic conception of human nature as static and deficient, and liberal democratic conceptions of politics, equality and democracy as excessively narrow and elitist oriented'. The conception of man and society that the participatory democrats tend to work with draws on the Aristotelian and communitarian traditions. It emphasises the interdependence of individuals with others and political community in general. They also emphasise the fulfilment of individuals not in isolation, but rather in relation to others and wider societal goals and moral aims. Further, rather than assuming that power is always a visible coercive force, participatory democrats tend to emphasise the need for social analysis to appreciate how people's wills and wants can be insidiously structured and shaped. It is for this reason that merely assuming that people simply 'know what they want' when they elect leaders is insufficient for them. A theory of democracy must understand theories of power in society too and its key aim in many ways has to be to enable the overcoming of forms of insidious power, such as the influence of consumerism and possessive individualism (Macpherson, 1977; see also Lukes, 1974).

Electoral democracy is not enough for participatory democrats because political participation is not conceived instrumentally but as a value in itself. It follows that when participatory democrats emphasise that democracy does not just entail choosing of leaders but also, potentially, much wider and fuller senses of participation, they so argue for normative as well as pragmatic reasons. It is not just the case that fuller participation will create better policies in society, but that *in and of itself* there is value in the kind of self-developmental and co-operative processes that participation in society and politics can entail. The goal of democratic politics, then, is not mere representation of voices or views or interests of the people but rather, far more holistically, to 'provide political conditions to facilitate maximum self-development' (Bachrach, 1992: 20). Democracy, then, as Macpherson famously argued, is not just an institutional arrangement for electing leaders (one man, one vote) as it is for the liberals, but rather 'a kind of society' where people have not only the right to vote but the right to live as fully as they can. It is for this reason that participatory democrats are often taken to argue for a more 'substantive', rather than merely 'procedural' notion of democracy.

Ultimately, many participatory democrats seek to reinvigorate a sense of community and republican civic identity. It is principally the sense of alienation from each other that is the problem that participatory democrats see in modern society. Representative democracy – an oxymoron in itself for participatory democrats (Barber, 2003: xxxv) – is a way of alienating people from each other and also from their selves in assuming that they formulate their interests somehow in isolation from other individuals and community aims. Liberalism is to blame for this. As Barber (2003: xxxi) powerfully puts it: 'What little democracy we have had in the West has been repeatedly compromised by the liberal institutions with which it has been undergirded and the liberal philosophy from which its theory and practice have been derived.' Liberal democratic thought, while complex and contradictory in its impulses and traditions (Barber identifies anarchist, realist and minimalist dispositions within it), tends to reduce democracy to 'an artefact that is adapted and discarded as it suits or fails to suit liberal ends' (Barber, 2003: 20). Liberal 'thin' democracy guards people against each other and against the state, but remains sceptical of any substantive development of co-operative and mutualist feelings and dialogue. At the same time, liberals evoke various pre-theoretical assumptions about human nature (radical isolation of consciousness from others) to maintain the logical coherence of their argumentation (see chs 3 and 4 in Barber, 2003), which in turn leads to 'dispositional elitism' and misunderstandings of potentials for participatory democracy.

Participatory democrats take exception to many liberal democrats' belief in the universality and naturalness of apathy among 'the masses', and their insistence on the claim that overzealous participation will lead to instability in society. Participatory democrats argue that liberal democrats must be recognised as being more liberal than democratic (Barber, 2003) and that the democratic aspect of liberal democracy should receive more attention.

But how do participatory democrats claim to work towards a more democratic model of democracy? They do so by, first, emphasising the educative aspect of democracy. Democracy is not just about representation, it is about self-development.

> The underlying premise of participatory democracy – in contrast to liberal representative democracy – is that participatory democratic politics encompasses self-exploration and self-development of citizens. In sharp contrast, liberal doctrine conceives of democracy as merely facilitating passively the

expression of perceived interests, not in helping citizens discover what their real interests are.

(Bachrach, 1992: 10–11)

Key to participatory democracy, vis-à-vis liberal democracy, is the emphasis on decentralisation of authority structures. What this means in the context of participatory democracy is two things: (1) fragmentation and localisation of authority structures where possible, and (2) more direct involvement of people in everyday decentralised decision-making and administration. It is from grass roots participatory society that the call for and the impetus for participatory democracy on 'higher levels' comes from. Learning in other spheres of life directly influences the 'political efficacy' of the people in the formal public sphere: that is, it encourages more active participation, critical engagement and confidence in one's own views.

Beyond this, participatory learning fosters solidarity in society. Since participatory democratic theorists are sceptical of autonomistic individualistic conceptions of the individual, they call for more solidaristic and co-operative interaction: which is exactly what participatory democracy fosters, whether it be in the political system, in the school, or at the workplace.

These ideas, values and assumptions have played an important role in the practical development of participatory democracy. They have been highly influential in the practice of the New Left, the radical feminists and those of many green activists. These movements – feminist women's liberation movement, for example – put the emphasis on interaction at a social level, but in ways which encourage self-reflection on societal power relations and learning from oneself and others in deciding how to tackle, on various different levels, political disempowerment. Grass roots democracy and democratic learning and empowerment have been a key aspect of these movements. Instead of speaking of the 'masses' as the elitists do, these democrats speak of 'citizens'. Barber summarises this shift of emphasis and attitude to people well: 'masses make noise, citizens deliberate; masses behave, citizens act; masses collide and intersect, citizens engage, share and contribute (Barber, 2003: 155). But how is participatory democracy practically, on the level of institutional arrangements, to be put into practice?

Participatory 'institutions'

Concrete blue-print portrayals of what a participatory democracy looks like are few. Pateman's arguments, for example, focused largely on theoretical exploration of the possibility of participatory democracy, not on close examination of forms it could take. C.B. Macpherson's work went somewhat further and distinguished between two different variants of a participatory democratic 'model': (1) a pyramid delegative model and (2) a mixed pyramid model combined with a representational model. Yet, Macpherson's discussion of possible institutional arrangements for participatory democracy remained general in nature.

A somewhat clearer picture of possible participatory systems emerges from Cook and Morgan's (1971) reflections on different systems of participatory democracy. They distinguish, usefully, between co-determination structures and self-determination structures. Many seemingly 'democratic' workplace democracies work on the basis of co-determination structures, where experts co-operate with the people. These contrast with 'self-determination' mechanisms where non-experts are fully in charge of a given policy area or a given association, applying a direct democratic form of decision-making fully. Cook and Morgan (1971: 4–5) also distinguish different functional roles for participatory structures. Some have authority to make rules, others merely to implement them. Thus, one can have co- and self-determination structures that are applicable only to implementation of policies (e.g. in some workplaces where participatory democracy exists only on the level of factory floor) and those that are applicable on 'higher' levels of rule making. Participatory democracy can exist at different levels then and in different areas of social and political life, hence paying close attention to these different 'extents' of participatory democracy is important.

Participatory theorists are often interested in extending the level and reach of participatory governance. Already many managers in workplaces, for example, use participatory democracy at the level of shop/factory floor because it is efficient for productivity. However, for the participatory democrats the interest in application of participatory democracy is fuller and more extensive: it is not directed by end-value of effectiveness, but rather by the value of human self-development.

This is reflected also in the model of participatory democracy by Benjamin Barber. In his 1984 work *Strong Democracy*, Barber envisages a 'strong democracy' as:

> a distinctively modern form of participatory democracy. It rests on the idea of self-governing community of citizens who are united less by homogeneous interests than by civic education and who are made capable of common purpose and mutual action by virtue of their civic attitudes and participatory institutions rather than their altruism or their good nature.
>
> (Barber, 2003: 117)

Barber identifies seven conditions of participatory democracy: (1) conception of politics as active; (2) conception of politics as involving matters of 'public interest' (understood more expansively than as parliamentary matters); (3) necessity of making choices; (4) importance of choice; (5) reasonableness; (6) conflict; and (7) absence of independent ground. Strong democracy is described as a participation-oriented ideal of democracy (rather than authority-, arbitration-, bargaining- or consensus-oriented), and as a system that values above all else the activity of citizens (as opposed to order, rights, liberty or unity). Its institutional bias is populist, as opposed to executive, judicial, legislative or symbolic as for the other models, whereas its citizen posture is active (Barber, 2003: 141).

As for concrete models and institutions of strong democracy, Barber (summarised in 2003: 307) mentions the following areas of democratic innovation:

- A national programme of neighbourhood assemblies, from 1 to 5000 citizens, which would initially have only deliberative functions but later also legislative ones
- A national civil communications initiative to encourage debates to be televised (e.g. of town meetings)
- Civic education and information access, to ensure equal access to information for all
- Experiments in lay justice and decriminalisation
- Development of a national referendum process, permitting popular initiatives and referenda on congressional initiatives
- Increased electronic balloting, through means of interactive telecommunications where possible
- Selective local elections by lottery, to bring individuals closer to decision-making and participation
- Experiments with a voucher system for selected schooling and housing projects
- National (universal) citizenship service
- Development of local volunteer associations and programmes (e.g. retired people as neighbourhood watchers, etc.)
- Democracy in the workplace
- New architecture of civic and local space.

These would be united by the aim of bringing together people in camaraderie. They would not undo the liberal representative systems, but would re-invigorate them: indeed, the plan here is to be prudent in reform and to 'reorient liberal democracy toward civic engagement and political community, not to raze it' (Barber, 2003: 308).

The above view gives a fair picture of the kinds of participatory structures that could exist. Yet, it is also important to keep our minds open to ways of thinking about participatory democracy that extend beyond any 'whole system' views of participatory democracy. Indeed, there has been a move away from 'whole system alternatives' to democratising liberal democracy through incremental means (Luckham, 1998; 306). Thus, some analyse the ways in which specific measures such as participatory budgets could work in specific contexts (Nylen, 2003). This kind of 'participatory democracy practice approach' deserves to be taken into account, because there is something to be said for precisely conceiving of participatory democracy as an open process-oriented and dynamic ethos of democratisation. Participatory democracy encourages democratisation both in the form of, and through, self-governing principles, rather than a universalistic logic (see Barber, 2003).

Let's now turn to examine in more detail the politico-economic underpinnings of participatory democracy.

The politico-economic aspect of participatory democracy

The participatory model of democracy is not self-evidently 'politico-economic' in its appearance. Not all participatory democrats explicitly call for economic democracy. Barber, for example, explicitly focuses his strong democracy on the political sphere.

Yet, many do, and even Barber's understanding of politics is much wider than that of many classical liberals: it does involve, in important respects, economic issues. Crucially, poverty and inequality in society, for Barber, provide a key impetus for participatory democracy: he envisages, along with many other participatory democrats, that the cure to poverty and inequality is 'the empowerment of the poor citizens' (Barber, 2003: xxvii). Indeed, for all the participatory democrats, there is a strong concern about economic inequalities in society and participatory democracy, even for those that see it more narrowly as purely 'political', is seen as a way of addressing these inequalities. This is because economic inequality is seen as one of the core reasons for the malfunctioning of the political democratic system: some rich actors can use their power in 'mobilisation of bias' to direct democratic electoral politics in a direction that suits their interests, whereas poorer and more disorganised groups are unable to be adequately represented in the system, let alone being able to participate in it beyond the occasional elections.

Addressing questions of democracy then also entails addressing questions of economic equality for the participatory democrats. This means, if you like, bringing political and economic equality more into synchrony with one another. This does not mean that absolute equality of wages, for example, should be implemented, as for some of the Marxists, but rather call for attention to be paid to the gap between the rich and the poor. Participatory democrats warn that this gap should not grow into such proportions as to allow the system to be fundamentally compromised. Many participatory democrats then call for proportionality assessment of wages where, for example, the ratio of wage gap should never exceed 7:1 or 4:1 (Pateman, 1970). Establishing economic equality of some kind, or at least being aware of its dangers for the functioning of democratic politics, is a crucial aspect of participatory democracy.

Some go further. Workplace democracy is a strong theme in both Pateman's and Bachrach's work. This is because workplaces are where people spend most of their time and because it is at the level of the workplace that societal apathy and servility more generally are reproduced. If we are to challenge the structures of authority at the level of economic interactions within systems of production, this can have significant consequences for the overall structure of society and for reinvigoration of the participatory ideal of democracy.

But how is democracy to function in this area? Cole argued for a system of vertically and horizontally organised associations. The economic organisations would at their base entail electoral representation on a direct level of the factory. These basic economic units could be arranged vertically in relation to each other, to regional and national economic councils, delegates to which were to be elected by the lower level associations. Such systems were in place in the former

Yugoslavia, where worker's councils were to be directly participative and directly responsible to the factory floor.

Short of these arrangements, participatory democrats have envisaged ways of integrating participative structures and principles to basic everyday industrial decision-making. Many of these principles are already in evidence on the shop/ factory floor, in terms of employee units being given participatory decision-making power to implement general management instructions. Beyond these, some businesses have also dabbled in fully co- and self-determining structures at the higher levels of management. Pateman (1970) reviews some of these cases where decisions over redundancies, further investments and pay are taken by co- or self-governing councils of employees, rather than by expert management isolated from the workforce. Participatory democrats are at pains to point out that not only can such authority structures function well; they can also be conducive to economic productivity and employees' well-being. This is despite the occasionally low take-up of democratic roles by employees due to lack of confidence in managerial roles.

Another interesting development in recent years has been the growth of the idea of participatory democracy among economists. Michael Albert and Robin Hahnel represent a set of authors who are most directly associated with the idea of 'participatory economics'. The key starting point of the 'parecon' is to think about new ways of organising economic life, away from economics of greed towards more positive and democratic alternatives.

The core to participatory economy is a new way of conceiving economic planning in order to promote: (1) the value of economic justice or equity, defined as 'economic reward commensurate with effort, or sacrifice', (2) economic democracy, that is self-management 'defined as decision-making power in proportion to the degree one is affected by a decision', (3) solidarity, that is 'concern for others', and all this without sacrificing, (4) efficiency (Hahnel, 2005: 189). These aims are to be met through a selection of new institutional mechanisms: self-management of producers and consumers through workers' and consumers' councils, balanced job complexes, remuneration of labour on duration, intensity, onerousness and social value, and participatory planning (Albert, 2006: 2).

> [I]n participatory planning workers and consumers propose and revise their own activities in a process that reveals the social costs and benefits of their proposals for them and others to take into account . . . the planning procedure is designed to make it clear when proposals are inefficient or unfair. And other . . . councils can disapprove of proposals when they are unfair or inefficient, but revisions are entirely up to individual worker or consumer councils themselves.
>
> (Hahnel, 2005: 193)

'Parecon' is an innovative idea, which has developed some interesting answers to concrete challenges of shifting economic practices hand in hand with political ones. It provides one concrete vision of how to redirect social life in a positive way, to 'overcome cynicism that there is no alternative' (Albert, 2006: 7). But what really is the relevance of such participatory democratic ideals, today?

Participatory democracy, today

Participatory democracy is often misunderstood: it is conceived of as utopian and impracticable. Yet, the thinking that drives it is exactly the opposite of utopian: participatory democracy seeks to be grounded and realistic about how societal dynamics are driven and how they can be shifted towards more democratic directions. Participatory democrats remind us that society is not fixed but dynamic, history is not at an end but developing, we are not just calculating self-interested creatures but interactive and moral creatures. It provides a powerful normative as well as an explanatory vision of society.

It is no surprise then that many social movements continue to make reference to participatory democratic ideals in their work. So do, interestingly, a number of state actors today. Zittel and Fuchs (2007), for example, record the ways in which states have (rather paradoxically perhaps) started to utilise the idea of participatory democracy in order to engineer more participation, and hence legitimacy, for the laggard and failing Western democratic systems. The participatory democratic ideas are also evident and growing among a few socialist states and parties. Michelle Williams (2008), for example, traces the way in which the communist parties in both Kerala, India and South Africa have tapped into participatory democracy ideas as a way of re-invigorating their thought and political activity in the aftermath of the obvious problems of the Marxist and Socialist models of old.

Yet, a key question that we have not yet dealt with in any detail is, given the fact that participatory ideals are still advocated, even among some of the political elite, how are we to conceive of the role of participatory democracy in the age of liberal representative democracy? What is the relationship between liberal representative democracy and participatory democracy?

Many participatory democrats have been highly critical of the liberal tradition: its core assumptions, its philosophical underpinnings, and its capitalistic interest groups. Yet, arguably, participatory democracy, despite the rhetoric, is not necessarily anti-liberal democratic. It is also not anti/non-representational. In fact, it can be seen as an extension of the liberal democratic ideals. This is what Macpherson, for example, recognised. Macpherson (1977) pointed out that participatory democracy is in many senses the fulfilment of the ethic of liberal democracy, but crucially without the prioritisation of liberal market values but rather democratic participation. This is what Barber (2003) too argues – participatory democracy is not envisaged as hostile to liberal democracy but as complementary to it and in fact as a fulfilment of its ideals.

Yet, given that politico-economic models of democracy is our focus, it is important to note that all participatory democrats are deeply sceptical of the prioritisation of liberal values, especially liberal market values, as the premise of democracy

– as what democracy should 'protect'. The capitalist assumptions embedded in the idea and model of liberal democracy are challenged either head-on or in a reformist manner, but all participatory democrats are to some extent critics of capitalism and hence of the economist-driven strands of liberal democratic thought.

What this means in today's context is that if this model is to be applied it should be put into practice with economic models and alternatives in mind. Indeed, although many commentators and actors are eager to 'use' participatory strategies to re-legitimise political systems, or indeed in democracy promotion, one of the key things they often fail to note is that advancing the cause of participatory democracy would, if done properly, extend the scope of democratic governance to the economic and private spheres too, and would challenge the politics that protect economic inequality and liberty of the individual at the expense of citizen participation and communitarian learning and coming together.

Radical democracy in a postmodern world

A key motivating influence for post-Marxist thought, from within which radical democracy arose, was combining Marxist thought with poststructuralist theoretical currents. Instead of working from either universalistic liberal or Marxist conceptions of man and society, the so-called poststructuralist movement had advanced a radical critique of the idea of fixed identities, social objects and subjects. The implications of the poststructuralist critique for post-Marxist thought on democracy was developed by Ernesto Laclau and Chantal Mouffe. Their *Hegemony and Socialist Strategy* (2001) was initially published in 1985, at a critical juncture in left politics preceding the break-up of the Soviet Union but following the growth of social movement politics in the 1970s and 1980s. This work envisaged a new form of democratic left politics, underpinned by a specific theoretical critique of Marxist understandings of capitalism. It immediately became a popular reference point both in academia (trying to make sense of new spheres of politics in global settings) and among activist movements around the globe.

The cornerstone of Laclau and Mouffe's argument is that the old class politics of the left are at a cross-roads. They are not only losing out to new forms of politics, but crucially are premised on a problematic conceptual basis. Laclau and Mouffe, through a detailed analysis Luxembourg, Kautsky, Lenin, Bernstein, Sorel and Gramsci, trace the problems that Marxist writers have had in conceiving of class actors, their identity and the nature of the social struggle that they are engaged in. There is a tendency, they argue, towards singular, unified, and fixed understandings of the class positions that individuals hold. Class positions are also counter-posed to each other in stark 'class war' terms, which also presume that there are certain 'real interests' that drive class politics. Laclau and Mouffe – who perceived politics through a lens influenced by Gramscian but also Lacanian and Foucauldian thoughts – have criticised such Left politics as being premised on fixed identity positions. They argue that we need to radically reconfigure how we understand ideology, class politics and hegemonic struggles.

Laclau and Mouffe work with a number of key concepts which, once clarified and understood, give us a better sense of the core dynamics of their argument. Laclau and Mouffe's work is focused on tracing how the concept of 'hegemony' has developed in Marxist thought. They note its culmination in Gramscian thought, where hegemony meant no longer direct physical control of one class over another, but rather an ideological system embedded in the constitution of the identities and subjectivities of actors in society. Hegemonic struggle for Gramsci entailed not that proletariat should take over the state with physical force but that it 'can become the leading and the dominant class to the extent that it succeeds in creating a system of alliances which allows it to mobilise the majority of the working population against capitalism and the bourgeois State' (Gramsci, quoted in Laclau and Mouffe, 2001: 66). Hegemony extends beyond class interests, then.

Yet, Laclau and Mouffe (2001: 69) criticise Gramsci's inability to escape a view of political action rooted in a classical Marxist prioritisation of class as the core of hegemonic struggle, and hegemonic struggle as a zero-sum game among classes. They seek to build on the Gramscian view of hegemony as a more open and plural vision of social struggles.

Central to their vision of hegemony is the idea of 'antagonism'. Antagonism for Laclau and Mouffe (2001: xiv, 125) is 'not objective relations, but relations, which reveal the limits of objectivity'. Antagonism for them refers to antagonistic discursive movements or struggles by which politics, and democracy, proceeds: the ways in which positions and political discourses refer to each other in grounding their own claims. They distinguish their notion of antagonism, then, from those that refer to strictly physical oppositions (between classes) and urge us to focus on the analysis of discursive antagonisms.

> ' "Serf", "slave", and so on, do not designate in themselves antagonistic positions; it is only in the terms of a different discursive formation, such as the 'rights inherent to every human being' that the differential positivity of these categories can be subverted and subordination constructed as oppression. This means that there is no relation of oppression without the presence of discursive exterior from which the discourse of subordination can be interrupted.'
> (Laclau and Mouffe, 2001: 154)

This gives a crucial clue to their view of politics and political interaction: it is based on discursive constructions of struggles against objects or subjects. It is not premised *a priori* assumptions on power relations or prioritisation of specific forms of social struggle.

Another key notion for Laclau and Mouffe is the idea of 'chain of equivalence'. This refers to the multiplicity of legitimate voices or discourses of struggle in society. There is no prioritisation here of one struggle as prior to another (e.g. class over race or sex). Incidentally, this is why discourses such as democracy matter: 'it is only from the moment when the democratic discourse becomes available to articulate the different forms of resistance to subordination that the conditions will exist to make possible the struggle against different types of inequality' (Laclau and Mouffe, 2001: 154).

This brings in finally the idea of 'radical and plural democracy'. The demo-cratic revolution and collective struggle have become compromised by commodi-fication and bureaucratisation (Laclau and Mouffe, 2001: 162–3), which is why a 'deepening of democratic revolution' is called for (Laclau and Mouffe, 2001: 163). This idea of 'radical and plural democracy' for Laclau and Mouffe expresses the notion that there is no singular node or locality to democratic politics. Since there is no fundamental social struggle to prioritise, it is important to keep demo-cratic politics open. 'If we wish to construct the hegemonic articulations which allow us to set ourselves in the direction of [radical democracy], we must under-stand in all their radical heterogeneity the range of possibilities which are opened in the terrain of democracy itself' (Laclau and Mouffe, 2001: 168).

Laclau and Mouffe's framework chimes in some senses with that of participa-tory democrats in that they emphasise new sites, spheres and spaces of democratic politics. Yet their claims are theoretically quite distinct. Radical plural democracy does not have a conception of democracy that it prioritises as central, nor specific values that it attaches to democracy, or that it seeks to defend (such as participa-tion, learning or progress). Instead, radical and plural democracy as Laclau and Mouffe conceive of it is radically plural in the fullest sense of the term. It does not prioritise a particular form of democratic politics: it only entails that democrats keep their minds open to alternative spaces, spheres and views of democracy.

Crucially, Laclau and Mouffe's ideas have a very interesting relationship with liberalism. They recognise that there are some same leanings that they share with liberal forms of thought, notably the emphasis on pluralism. They also proclaim against anti-liberal democratic ideas (Laclau and Mouffe, 2001: xv):

> [L]iberal democracy is not the enemy to be destroyed in order to create . . .
> a completely new society . . . [T]he problem with 'actually existing' liberal
> democracies is not with their constitutive values crystallized in the principles
> of liberty and equality for all, but with the system of power which redefines
> and limits the operation of these values. Radical and plural democracy was
> conceived of as a new stage in the deepening of the 'democratic revolution',
> as the extension of the democratic struggles for equality and liberty to a wider
> range of social relations.

Indeed, they perceive their task to be a deepening of the liberal democratic ideal, not challenging or renouncing it (Laclau and Mouffe, 2001: 176).

Politico-economically, Laclau and Mouffe argue that a wholesale movement away from the structural and determinist tendencies within Marxism is neces-sary for adequate understanding of contingency, pluralism and openness of politi-cal action to emerge. Laclau and Mouffe then criticise all key aspects of Marxist theory of the economy.

First, they challenge the laws of motion of economy and the neutrality of pro-ductive forces. For them then 'it is not the case that the field of the economy is a self-regulated space subject to endogenous laws' (Laclau and Mouffe, 2001: 85). Second, they challenge the determinist view of the working classes: there is no singular subject position to these, but the working class is plural and segmented, also by other forces such as racism or sexism. Any notion of objective class or class interest is then difficult to maintain (Laclau and Mouffe, 2001: 83). There is no stable political and economic identity but rather 'a precarious unity of a tension' (Laclau and Mouffe, 2001: 121). '[T]he proliferation of . . . political spaces, and the complexity and difficulty of their articulation, are a central characteristic of the advanced capitalist social formations' (Laclau and Mouffe, 2001: 137).

The view of democracy then, is premised on a specific view of the economy, one which moves away from determinist Marxist, but also prediction- and interest-based arguments of the liberals.

Other 'radical democrats': Connolly, and Hardt and Negri

Laclau and Mouffe set the scene in many ways in thinking about radically different alternative democratic futures. Yet, others have contributed to this tradition. Notably, William E. Connolly has over the last three decades written a number of publications, which revolve around the idea of 'pluralisation', akin to Laclau and Mouffe's idea of 'radical plural democracy'. The foremost of these was perhaps the *Ethos of Pluralisation* (1995).

What is interesting about Connolly's thought is that he does not seek to support in any direct or unequivocal sense a liberal sense of pluralism. Liberal pluralism, Connolly points out, assumes a 'tree trunk' understanding of pluralism: while pluralism is emphasised, diversity is perceived as if it were 'branches' leading off a trunk as foundationalist assumptions about human nature ground pluralism. Connolly looks to move away from such a model, taking as his guide the idea of the rhizome, which grows and intersects in various ways, never settling on a single truth.

His approach then differs greatly from those of classical democratic theorists and those proceduralists for whom democracy consisted in the achievement of a specific social form. Connolly sees substantive or procedural democracy as impossible ultimate aims of democratic politics. Democratic politics ultimately should 'be pursued in ways that do not undermine either existing cultural pluralism or future possibilities of democratic pluralisation' (Connolly, 1995: 80). This does not mean that we need to turn against existing forms of politics, instead we need to look for and stay open to forms of politics that are open and pluralistic, rather than defining 'end states' of man or society. This allows us to remain open to multiple forms of democratic politics, and crucially a 'pluralising ethos' central to democratic vision. It also allows us to stay open to non-classical forms of territorial politics.

> What is needed politically, today and tomorrow, is a series of cross-national, nonstatist movements organized across state lines, mobilizing around specific issues of global significance, pressing states from inside and outside simultaneously to reconfigure stabilized convictions, priorities and policies.
>
> (Connolly, 1995: 23)

Even as he so argues, Connolly does not argue for a specific model and institutions of global democracy, but rather merely an ethos of democracy.

While often treated as a political theorist first and foremost, crucially for us, Connolly's thought does not remain silent on political economy. In thinking through the economic aspects and conditions of democracy, or pluralising ethos, Connolly takes his lead from a surprising source, namely C.B. Macpherson. Connolly argues, as does Macpherson, that economic equality is the key to robust democracy. Inequality is a threat to democratic ethos and must then be tackled. Yet, we must not try to achieve economic equality in ways that go against the principle of democratic pluralism. Connolly then seeks to temper, if you like, Macphersonite aims with something of a Foucauldian turn. He argues that pluralisation should be the aim, not equality in and of itself alone.

There are two key economic aims for Connolly (1995: 80–1). First, establishing a floor below which no one is allowed to fall and, second, setting out a glass ceiling which stops elites from trying to escape from general conditions of public economic life, making them less likely to (need to) want to make changes to these conditions. Connolly (1995: 82) argues that economic equalisation is a prerequisite of effective democratisation, but effective democracy is also prerequisite of equalisation. He argues that we must pay attention to it, then, and equalise conditions through taxes and so on – yet crucially, equalisation is not an ultimate end in itself, and should not infringe on the need to keep open pluralistic possibilities. Also, he rejects that equalisation is to result in a final harmonious society as Marxists and others had assumed: this is because he rejects the idea of a harmonious unitary self, seeing identities and subjectivities as plural (Connolly, 1995: 86). Equalisation does not result in search for our 'true identity', which has been alienated (Connolly, 1995: 92) or a true final form of harmonious human community (Connolly, 1995: 96). 'A democratic culture', he insists, 'that disrupts the dogmatic identities gear up possibilities for politics of pluralization' (Connolly, 1995: 98).

As for Hardt and Negri, they set out their line of though in *Empire* (2000) and *Multitude* (2005). In *Empire*, they argued for a new understanding of international politics as underpinned by a biopolitical 'logic of rule'. The Empire is not imperial: it is diffuse and non-territorial. 'Empire establishes no territorial center of power and does not rely on fixed boundaries or barriers. It is decentered and deterritorialising apparatus of rule' (Hardt and Negri, 2000: xii). A key aspect of empire is its moral and normative constructions. It hails universal ethical principles – of rights, of perpetual peace, of legitimate 'just' interventions – and it is these principles which become embedded to such an extent that it is difficult see beyond them. Universal values of justice open the door to legitimate interventions for construction of social life and behaviours and norms are 'internalised'. Thereby the power of empire is organized 'in the brain'. Empire is 'omniversal' and its rule communicated through communication technologies, non-governmental organisations, intergovernmental organisations, juridical systems, political actors, and indeed, in ways that we often fail to note, also, ourselves.

The rise of Empire is linked to the 'post-modernization of global economy' where the 'creation of wealth tends ever more toward what we will call biopolitical production, the production of social life itself, in which the economy, the political and the cultural increasingly overlap and invest on another' (Hardt and Negri: 2000: xii). Crucial to Hardt and Negri's analysis of Empire and, indeed, Multitude, is a different, non- or post-Marxist analysis of capitalism and its productive processes. They argue that to grasp power and Empire today, we need to grasp the changing forms of production within the capitalist world order. These forms of production are intimately connected with the rise of new forms of subjectivity, exploitation, domination, as well as resistance.

But what does this notion of Empire mean for the idea of democracy? Hardt and Negri's analysis leads to an analysis of democracy expounded in the *Multitude* (2005). Because Empire is never 'stable' or fixed, it is both more insidious in its workings and at the same time more directly challengeable. Empire offers not only new forms of domination and exploitation but also 'new possibilities and forces of liberation' (Hardt and Negri, 2000: xv).

The multitude refers to all those forces suffering of exploitation under Empire (Hardt and Negri, 2000: 53). They are not a unified actors, such as the 'working class' was for the Marxists, nor do they share interests or identities; they are a fundamentally diverse group of actors. Yet, they are capable of 'autonomously constructing a counter-Empire, an alternative political organization of global flows and exchanges' (Hardt and Negri, 2000: xv). They can do so through autonomous and seemingly unlinked rebellions. Hardt and Negri show that while the many rebellions, in Tienanmen Square, France, Chiapas or South Korea, seemingly share little, they all are underpinned by a critique of Empire and its logic of rule. The commonalities between these struggles are not at present easily 'communicable', yet they need to be noted for us to realise that all rebellions, however local, 'leap immediately to the global level and attack the imperial constitution' (Hardt and Negri, 2000: 56) for they are 'struggles over form of life' (Hardt and Negri, 2000: 56). Indeed, Hardt and Negri challenge the classical Left conception of resistance politics centred on localisation of struggles or the return to the state as the protector of interests. They envisage instead a radically open field of social struggles, where 'struggles slither silently across superficial imperial landscapes' (Hardt and Negri, 2000: 58). Because Empire is produced at multiple points in social and international life, it can also be challenged on all these multiple points and through very different strategies. There is great potential then for the 'multitude to sabotage the parasitical order of postmodern command' (Hardt and Negri, 2000: 66).

This means that because of the network power at work in the Empire, democratic forces too should work, and be understood as, network-like. Democratic hopes lie for Hardt and Negri with the multitude and its open-ended potential to challenge forms of power. Democracy, for them, is not reducible to party politics or representative institutions, or even participatory institutions – forms of democracy identified to be in crisis (Hardt and Negri, 2005: 234–5), but rather is an open-ended project attached to the multitude. Multitude does not aspire to classical 'patriarchal' representational democracy: multitude makes up an open network 'in which all differences can be expressed freely and equally' (2005: xiii).

A distributed network such as the Internet is a good initial image or model of the multitude because, first, the various nodes remain different but are all connected in the Web, and, second, the external boundaries of the network are open such that new nodes and new relationships can always be added.

(Hardt and Negri, 2005: xv)

The multitude is considered important for democracy because, first, it does not specify a particular identity or uniformity to political debate and struggle, while also calling for identification of 'common' ground. Second, its emphasis on bio-politics is crucial for our analysis of democracy: global democratisation suffers under, but also depends on, biopolitical power (2005: xvi). Multiple sites of 'life politics' is where struggles for alternative world orders are conducted. Third, Hardt and Negri's multitude is of importance because it emphasises not only social movements as essential to democracy, but also the need for social movements to be democratic; that is, open in themselves to a multiplicity of calls and modes of resistance and struggle.

Hardt and Negri's project, with its Foucauldian framework of analysis of power, in a sense seeks to create a new conceptual basis for democratic projects and global democratisation – one that is far removed from classical liberal or social democratic conceptions; one emphasising radical openness and plurality of struggles in the social sphere, and the immediacy of social and political struggle in challenging Empire.

Crucially, both conceptions of democracy have been attractive to a multiplic-ity of social movement actors in twenty-first century world politics. As power is changing and as politico-economic struggles are changing, political actors too are changing. Moving away from party politics towards new transnational spheres of social movement politics, many green, feminist and radical movements today look to 'the radical democratic' model, with its emphasis on rhizomes, agonisms, non-hierarchical social relations, networks and micro-politics of resistance (Eschle, 2001; Maiguascha and Eschle, 2005). While many liberal democratic democracy promoters may not have considered such democratic models, they must realise that for a multiplicity of social movement actors today – both in the West and in the developing world – a radical democratic model today serves as the closest ideal of democratic governance. The World Social Forum, for example, embod-ies the ideals of this model, not a liberal democratic one, in its attempt to build a global forum and a movement to struggle against neoliberal economic power.

Conclusion

The participatory and radical democrats provide challenging perspectives on democracy, which differ in significant respects from the liberal, Marxist and social democratic perspectives.

The participatory democrats provide a processual and dynamic view of democ-racy and democratisation. They also provide a people-centred and participa-tion-centred view of democracy, which sees civil society and citizen participation as central to democracy. The participatory view gives us a much wider view of democracy: it involves changing societal arrangements, in expanding what is perceived as democratic in society. Crucially for our interests, it provides a new interpretation of the relationship between the economic and the democratic: it sees participation of people in society, politics and the economy as a vital aspect of democratic politics.

As for radical democracy, central to this conception of politics has been the emphasis on pluralism, non-foundationalism, and conflict or opposition. For Mouffe, instead of seeking consensus, politics is tied in crucial ways to processing of conflict. This is what her notion of agonistic politics refers to, namely a processing through democracy of conflicts and antagonisms that are inevitable in politics. This view of democratic pluralism draws on Foucauldian sources in that it 'endorses a politics of diverse social, cultural and political movements organized around the values of cultural recognition, direct democracy, and performative resistance' (Gabardi, 2001: 552).

These visions of democracy are not dismissive of liberal democracy. Instead these traditions are conceived to work within, to extend and to re-invigorate liberal representative democracy. These traditions are critical of liberal democracy's inadequately pluralistic and overly consensual understanding society and politics. Crucial to these visions of democracy is the recognition of multiple power relations, economic positions, political claims and the need for improved contestation in democratic life. These visions, moreover, have been very pragmatic and relevant notions to many political activists. Participatory democracy is deeply influential and rooted in Western political life, and radical democracy is widely utilised by social movements, nationally and globally (see e.g. Eschle, 2001; Eschle and Maiguascha, 2005). It is for these reasons – not just theoretical reasons – then that we need to keep these democratic visions in mind when exploring democratic futures in world politics.

5   The poverty of state-based democracy

Cosmopolitan models of democracy

> [I]n an era in which the fates of peoples are deeply intertwined, democracy has to be recast and strengthened, both within pre-established borders and across them. The particular conditions which created the impetus to the establishment of the liberal democratic nation-state are being transformed and, accordingly, democracy must be profoundly altered if it is to retain its relevance in the decades ahead.
>
> (Held, 1995: xi)

Much of modern democratic theory, and also almost all of the debates in social and political sciences over democratisation and democracy promotion, have been premised on a 'statist' understanding of the conditions of contemporary democratic politics. While some radical democrats examined in the Chapter 4 have been highly sceptical of the territorial trapping of the idea of democracy, in classical democratic thought and practice the idea of democracy has been closely bound up with the idea of a sovereign territorial state. Liberal democracy, too, has been a model of democracy fundamentally bound up with the idea of the state, which developed in the context of, and as a response to, the rise of monarchical power within emerging nation-states in Europe. Thus liberal democracy continues in its representational as well as in its normative justifications to be inextricably tied to the idea of the state.

This 'entrapment' of the idea of democracy within the state is problematic, argue the authors discussed in this chapter. This is because, as David Held, one of the key advocates of cosmopolitan democracy, suggests:

> If democratic theory is concerned with 'what is going on' in the political world and, thereby, with the nature and prospects of democracy, then a theory of democratic politics today must take account of the place of the polity within geopolitical and market processes, that is, within the system of nation-states, international legal regulation and world political economy.
>
> (Held, 1995: ix)

In the current world political setting the nation-state based democracies struggle to deal with the challenges that trans-nationalisation and globalisation pose: the internationalisation of political decision-making; the extended role of international organisations and global civil society; the liberal movement of capital;

and the environmental problems that cross borders with ease. These issues are not easily tackled by single states, democratic or otherwise. The national states are also bound up within a global system of capitalism, which allocates resources and market roles beyond the jurisdiction of the individual state. Global capitalism has made political control of the market sphere increasingly difficult. This means that the legitimate scope of the 'democratic' within nation-states is in decline.

If power now lies at a global level of social relations, perhaps democratisation too should extend to these levels. Democracy, confined to the national, risks becoming irrelevant. Indeed as David Held so powerfully points out, it is curious that just at the time when democratic ideas are most dominant the dominant form of democracy – that is, liberal democracy based in states – is becoming redundant in many respects (Held, 1995: 21).

Various authors discussed here – whether 'cosmopolitan democrats' or advocates of 'global democracy' – have sought to formulate a set of ideal types of democratic order, as well as concrete institutional reform propositions, that could be used to provide the basis for a more global or cosmopolitan democratic future. The development of such ideas in recent years has been important, for cosmopolitan thought entails a deep challenge to traditional democratic theorising. Indeed, thinking about the possibility of cosmopolitan democracy has implications 'for the nature of a constituency, the meaning of representation, the proper form and scope of participation, and the relevance of the democratic nation-state' (Held, 1995: 18). Cosmopolitan ideas, moreover, have important challenges to pose to the ethical standards and justifications that exist for the idea of democracy, the notion of citizenship, and the idea of political community (Linklater, 2000).

Crucially for us, moreover, cosmopolitan and global visions of democracy are important because of the consequences that flow from them for thought about 'politico-economic' conditions and constituents of 'democracy'. Despite the many remaining differences of approach among the cosmopolitan and global democrats, many of them share a politico-economic outlook which recognises, and seeks to address, the global politico-economic power relations implicated in the thought and practice of democracy today.

This chapter will begin by a brief examination of the reasons for considering a more cosmopolitan or transnational form of democratisation. It continues with an examination of four key cosmopolitan, or global democratic, proposals, viz. those of David Held, Daniele Archibugi, Heikki Patomäki and Teivo Teivainen, and John Dryzek. The chapter concludes with my reflections with regard to the plausibility and urgency of global democratisation.

Global democracy and democratic theory

The interest in global democratisation or cosmopolitan democracy is a fairly recent one. So are the conditions within which it has become urgent or, indeed, possible to entertain such visions at all. The nation-state has been the dominant form of political actor since the mid-seventeenth century, and while it has had to respond to and negotiate a number of transnational forces – not least the increasing globalisation of the capitalist economic system – the state has remained paramount.

This is reflected in theory and practice of democracy. Liberal democracy has been the 'victorious' model of democracy in the modern era of the nation-state. The model has allowed large-scale political units to maintain legitimacy and has not entailed or facilitated radical challenges to the dominant forms of economic organisation, notably the capitalist market system.

Yet, today the nation-state is deeply enmeshed in global forms of social, cultural, political and economic relationships, which delimit the ability of individual nation-states to make decisions on behalf of their citizens.

Of course states have had structures in place through which they have represented their people in dealings with global problems. State representatives in the current international order are present in international organisations and regimes, although international organisations have been subject to the veto-powers of powerful states and hence do not represent all populations 'equally'. There is no global parliament to which representatives are elected, no global political parties or a global constitution. Decisions go through states, and also through the hierarchy of states. Thus, a clash of principles is evident in the current system. While the United Nations (UN) and various international legal conventions now enshrine the idea of human rights into global order, the absence of an adequate global institutional framework means that the possibility for individuals to be represented or to hold accountable states or international organisations does not actually exist.

An even deeper set of problems arises from the role of global capitalism. In a global capitalist system, less and less power is vested in the national elites and an increasing amount of power over economic affairs rests with international, non-democratic institutions and global private actors. In this context democracy is at peril: for even if states were to be purely democratic, the scope of democratic governance is minimal (Teivainen, 2002).

The lack of accountability in the international system and the narrowing of the scope of the democratic, and the widening of the scope of 'technical' governance (e.g. over global financial governance), is a concern for global and cosmopolitan democrats. This is because democratisation is clearly not just a matter of states, it is also a matter of the wider global power system, which, despite rhetorical moves in the democratic direction, has done very little to democratise the global setting.

Cosmopolitan and global models of democracy

But what would a cosmopolitan or global democracy look like and what do the concepts actually refer to? As we have seen, a key principle guiding much of modern international relations has been the adherence to the norms of sovereignty and non-intervention. All states, regardless of their size or make-up, are accorded sovereignty and scope for autonomy in decision-making. Such principles empower state actors and hence presumably communities to be self-determining, rather than subservient to the imperatives of the greatest powers in the international system. There is in principle nothing anti-democratic, then, about the international system, which as it stands could be seen at its core to have a democratic system of govern-ance, even if a flawed one (because of the hierarchical voting mechanisms within the international system).

Yet, equating democratic international governance with democratic representa-tion of states is not what the cosmopolitan and global democrats are after. Their interests extend far beyond the level of 'international or transnational democracy', where all states are represented. Instead they call for a system that is representative not only of states, but also of other actors, whether non-governmental organisations (NGOs), intergovernmental organisations (IGOs), or individual actors.

However, the problems in developing such democracy are many. Challenges arise from two directions: on the one hand, the power that some actors/forces have to shape the international system regardless of the limitations of sovereignty and non-intervention; and, on the other hand, the side-lining by some states of the rights of individuals within their states to democratic forms of representation and governance. How do the cosmopolitan and global democrats take on these challenges?

David Held

David Held's work on cosmopolitan democracy has been pioneering. Held has sought to provide both philosophical and theoretical principles for an extension of the idea of democracy, but also a set of reflections on the conditions of democ-racy and its putative institutional forms that might be entailed by the expansion of democracy to the global level. He outlined the core principles of his approach in *Democracy and the Global Order* (1995) and *Global Covenant* (2004). He sees his approach as an alternative to the neoliberal or neoconservative visions and the visions of the anti-globalisation activists (Held, 2004).

Held argues that the core substance of a democratic form of politics is its support for the idea of autonomy, that is the idea that 'persons should enjoy equal rights, and accordingly, equal obligations in the specification of the political framework which generates and limits the opportunities available to them; that is, they should be free and equal in the determination of the conditions of their lives, so long as they do not deploy this framework to negate the rights of others' (Held, 1995: 147). The principle of autonomy draws on the liberal democratic tradition. Indeed, he claims that autonomy is not adequately emphasised or valued in the participa-tory and radical democratic traditions (1995: 149). Yet, Held (1995: 156) insists that his model of democracy geared around protection and activation of autonomy is not individualistic but structural and not necessarily only liberal democratic. Indeed, Held emphasises that it would be false to think that a single liberal demo-cratic tradition exists, and that he remains critical of some of the narrowly elitist and more liberal versions of liberal democracy.

He proceeds to lay out the core conditions within which autonomy can be exer-cised, and hence the conditions of support that democratisation (on any level) should entail. These are extensive for the sites of power within which democracy is exercised are many. The seven sites of power he identifies are the body (health, basic needs), welfare (education, basic welfare), culture (diversity and toleration of difference), civic life (freedom to act in civil society), economy (rights in distribution and production processes), organisation of violence, and regulatory and legal institutions (Held, 1995: 176–85).

The key implications of Held's thought when it comes to international politics is the emphasis on cosmopolitan democratic law as a key complement to democratic public law within states (Held 1995: 227). This law 'transcends' the individual states and nations, but ends up entailing less than a federalist system of law (1995: 230). Crucially, Held (1995: 232) argues that such law needs to go hand in hand with a cosmopolitan political community, that is, 'a community of all democratic communities', a structure which comes to entail some new obligations for states and their representatives. This would comprise a system of multiple citizenships where people would be members of many different associations and communities which affect them, including states (Held, 1995: 233).

In *Global Covenant*, Held recognises that problems of coherence, inertia and accountability are of course very powerful within any attempt at global democratisation. This is why he advocates a reformed principle of subsidiarity: keeping decisions as close as possible to where they have these effects (Held, 2004: 100–1). This also involves recognising the limitations of the current system and tackling them: for example, promoting stake-holder decision-making, increasing the powers of negotiation by developing countries, allowing non-state actors to enter into negotiations, introducing panels investigating global problems.

But does this not sound rather vague and rather ambitious? How do we get there? We can start by reforming the present institutions, Held suggests, starting with the UN and the General Assembly. The General Assembly should be made a legitimate representational forum and the Security Council's hierarchy structure should be changed. Yet, this state-based international democratisation should also be complemented with a thicker mode of democratisation, one that would entail the recognition of non-state actors too and ideally some form of a new international assembly, a form of a global parliament. There should also be an increased recognition of multiple sites of politics, including recognition of the roles of regional authorities. The changes should also entail the opening up to public accountability of international functional organisations such as the International Monetary Fund (IMF) and World Bank and the creation of new bodies within the UN structure (such as, an empowered Social and Economic Security Council) to balance against the power of existing financial institutions. There should also be an empowerment of global judiciary, a more robust form of International Criminal Court (ICC) and International Court of Justice (ICJ), and a new framework for peacekeeping and humanitarian intervention. Various changes in relation to economic governance are also suggested (these are examined later).

Daniele Archibugi

Daniele Archibugi's *The Global Commonwealth of Citizens* (2008) is another recent contribution to debate on global democracy. It works, not with the principle

of autonomy, but rather with three much narrower, and arguably more conservative, democratic principles: nonviolence, popular control, and political equality
(Archibugi, 2008: 27–8).

These principles lead Archibugi towards an interesting criticism of the failures of Western states to take seriously the encouragement of democratic governance across the world. Archibugi argues that instead of sticking to the principles
of democracy, Western states have forcibly and in their own interests promoted
democratic governance. This is an approach doomed to failure in his view: a much
more consensual and dialogical approach is required, and one that starts with a
serious appreciation of the core principles and institutional forms that a cosmopolitan democratic order might require.

Yet, Archibugi's development of the idea of cosmopolitan democracy starts
from a belief that Western liberal democracy has been proved to be a success,
and that it is then a liberal form of democracy that should provide a guiding light
for cosmopolitan democratisation. However, cosmopolitan democracy must be
recognised to be a distinct form of democracy both in its core principles and the
institutional forms it takes. This also means getting away from the idea that 'West
knows best'. This means that we must recognise that there is no one single form
of governance that is democratic: this is why 'both researcher and the politician
championing the cause of democracy should . . . shun seeking the absolute "best
practice" in order to try out many "good practices" (Archibugi, 2008: 20). This
means remaining open to democracy problems also in the Western practices
and keeping an open mind to the 'endless' path to democratic development
(2008: 23). This means also recognising that the links between democracy and
peace or democracy and wealth are not straightforward or in easy causal relationships with each other.

But what should cosmopolitan democracy consist in? To avoid cosmopolitan
democracy being understood as simply a set of procedures, Archibugi (2008: 88–
9) sets out certain key objectives for cosmopolitan democracy, albeit minimalist
ones: control over use of force, acceptance of cultural diversity, strengthening
of self-determination of peoples, monitoring internal affairs (including levels of
democracy and human rights) and participatory management of global problems.
These principles should be aimed at various levels: local, state, interstate, regional,
and global. This would involve encouraging democratic principles, then, not just
on an abstracted global level but on multiple levels. 'Cosmopolitan democracy is
. . . a project that aims to develop democracy at different levels of governance on
the assumption that, although independent from each other, these levels may be
pursued simultaneously' (Archibugi, 2008: 110).

Archibugi argues that cosmopolitan democracy should use neither the confed-
eral nor federal models as simple guidelines: 'no historically significant experiences of cosmopolitan democracy exist' (2008: 109). He is sceptical of the kind
of centralisation of power that federal systems would involve on the global level,
but does not want to reduce cosmopolitan democracy merely to functional con-
federations either. 'Global democracy involves importantly world citizenship,
ability to transcend one's own local community' (Archibugi, 2008: 115). This is

not intended to replace national citizenship (as in a federalist system), but simply should pertain to 'several fundamental rights' (Archibugi, 2008: 116). The spheres that world citizenship should invoke include the universal declaration of human rights and institutional bodies should be prepared to monitor this. A world parliament is one possibility in terms of a body that could be turned to call up ICC and ICJ, on respect for such rights, financed by global taxes on currency transactions, for example.

In moving towards a cosmopolitan system, and indeed a world parliament, Archibugi highlighs the importance of reforming the UN system. His proposals follow many of the more widely discussed ones: reform of the Security Council and enforcement of actions and beliefs actually written into the UN system. Reform must also include reform of the judiciary: extension of role of the ICJ so that more states will join it, as well as an extension of its jurisdiction to include non-state members (Archibugi, 2008: 168). The UN also must start to consider a more representative world parliamentary assembly (WPA), although its jurisdiction should not of course be extended to those of states. This assembly would 'represent a forum where the main world problems such as economic and social development, the defence of human rights, the promotion of political participation and the safeguarding of environment, could be discussed' and would specifically focus on protection of fundamental rights, solving disputes in relation to definition of boundaries and jurisdiction of various political communities and identification of most appropriate levels of governance in case of cross-border problems involving many political communities (Archibugi, 2008: 173) . 'Even if it had no effective power, the WPA would be the visible and tangible demonstration of the institutionalization of a global commonwealth of citizens' (2008: 173). It would be elected, with authoritarian governments having to enforce democratic elections to qualify to attend. This institution should also work alongside a Council on Human Rights.

Heikki Patomäki and Teivo Teivainen

Patomäki and Teivainen's hopes for 'global democracy' focus less on expounding of 'cosmopolitan' philosophical principles and more on assessing proper applicability of a variety of reform proposals. Their focus is especially on evaluating UN reform proposals and reforms of international financial governance. They do so in a manner which seeks to recognise the potentials and limitations of current proposals, while also seeking to open up debate on radical new initiatives. Indeed, Patomäki and Teivainen argue for a dual track approach: reform of existing institutions (UN, IMF, World Bank, World Trade Organization) and the development of new alternative institutions (world social forum, global truth commission, world parliament, debt arbitration mechanisms, and global tax reform).

When discussing the reform of existing institutions Patomäki and Teivainen start from analysis of the UN. They argue for empowerment of the General Assembly, in terms of its decision-making power as well as its ability to empower NGO representatives. They also consider the General Assembly's extension through the idea of a People's Assembly (Patomäki and Teivainen, 2004: 30–1). It would not have legislative powers but would be a forum for debate. Its members would, however, be elected through universal suffrage. Crucially, Patomäki and Teivainen also suggest the re-empowerment of the EcoSoc, which was originally designed to be at the helm of the UN system, including the Bretton Woods system. If this committee were empowered and its decision-making mechanisms rejigged, it could provide the UN system with a more democratic and crucially a more social justice-focused approach to global governance.

As for the Bretton Woods system, Patomäki and Teivainen discuss many possible reforms here. These include, first and foremost, pushing through of the 'one country, one vote' principle and other possible limitations to the current power of key financial players, such as the United States, within these institutions. The other alternative they discuss is narrowing down the powers of the IMF; that is, lessening of its power in relation to other global bodies (Patomäki and Teivainen, 2004: 56–8). Also, transparency and accountability of these organisations are called for, for example, through formal independent auditing mechanisms of an ombudsman. Further, the role of NGOs should be elevated within these organisations.

Most interesting, however, are Patomäki and Teivainen's proposals for new global democratic mechanisms. They discuss, first of all, the World Social Forum (WSF) and its implications for global democratisation. Although this body has not overtly aimed to participate in global democratisation, they see it as important. While the WSF is not a self-evident 'actor', nor does it apply classical notions of democracy to its decision-making (see Chapter 4), it is trying to facilitate an alternative form of global politics though consensus-building and NGO/civil society politics (Eschle, 2001). Its 'radical democratic' imagining of democracy – both non-statist, and extra-liberal democratic – provides an interesting addition to thought about what might constitute global democratisation.

Yet, Patomäki and Teivainen do not mean to suggest that democratic explorations should stop here (see Patomäki and Teivainen, 2004: 125). Another idea suggested by Patomäki and Teivainen is the global truth commission, that is, the application of national truth commission ideas on a global level, for example, to investigation of systematic human rights atrocities. They also recommend consideration of the idea of world parliament, 'an assembly where representatives are selected on the basis of 'one person, one vote' (Patomäki and Teivainen, 2004: 139), which might entail that it is independent altogether from the UN.

Such proposals, may strike many traditional liberal democrats as dangerously ambitious. Patomäki and Teivainen (2004: 143–4) recognise this and warn against overly ambitious global democratisation. For example, they argue that it may be better not to have a single world parliament after all, but instead many parliamentary systems embedded in other functional organisations of the emerging global system. Also, world referenda, rather than parliaments, might be a better way to go (Patomäki and Teivainen, 2004: 146–7).

These authors thus call for a measured, balanced and pluralistic – not just ideologically fervent – global democratisation.

John Dryzek

John Dryzek is another figure who has developed a global model of democracy. Dryzek's focus is on outlining a distinctly informal *discursive* model of global democracy. Instead of focusing on reform of global institutions Dryzek focuses on recasting the discursive debates and contentions in international politics.

Dryzek, drawing on the trends for deliberative democracy in democratic theory, argues that discursive and deliberative processes should in fact be considered the central 'front' of democratisation in global politics. Instead of aiming to democratise specific institutional structures, then, he argues that the focus of democratisation globally should be on the democratisation of *public spheres and the dialogue within them* about crucial world political issues. At the moment there is a hierarchical system in place, which makes discursive democracy on global matters difficult to achieve:

> The reason is that deliberation closely tied to the constant application of formal authority in the international system is not easily rendered democratic, as it normally takes place among executives and nominees. Democratic legitimacy enters only tenuously, to the degree in which the executives are themselves elected . . .'
>
> (Dryzek, 2006: vii)

Despite the current problems of democratisation, both institutionally but also 'discursively', Dryzek (2006: vii) argues that democratic politics can, however, be fruitfully sought 'in the informal realm of global public spheres'. Indeed, he argues that discursive democratisation on such levels is the more feasible alternative for global democratisation than, say, Held's cosmopolitan model.

But what would this in fact consist in? It would consist in recognition of the space for discursive contestation in global public spheres to dominant discursive formations. Indeed, a set of challenges to predominant discourses have been emerging, and are increasingly powerful. 'Reflexive modernisation', increasing facilitation of competing discourses that bring up alternative ways of life and thinking holds the key to global democratisation (Dryzek, 2006: 21).

Democracy, then, in such a model of democratisation comes to have a very different meaning from that of liberal models, or indeed the institutional rewritings of Held or Patomäki and Teivainen.

> Democracy here cannot be interpreted in electoral terms . . . Transnational discursive democracy does not have to be integrated with any particular set of formal institutions (though it can target the influence over many such institutions, including states). Democracy is about communication as well as voting, about social learning as well as decision-making.
>
> (Dryzek, 2006: 25)

The influence of participatory democratic values on this deliberative communicative notion of democracy are clear here. Yet, this model is quite different from classical participatory democratic solutions in disembodying democracy from institutional forms altogether.

Political economy and cosmopolitan/global democracy

Not all theorists of cosmopolitan democracy are driven by a concern with global inequalities. Archibugi's account, for example, remains less interested in the economic: not only is he approving of liberal market forces as the producers of wealth, but also he reproduces the liberal tendency to separate discussions of global democracy from those pertaining to the market. This means that he also leaves the economic power of capitalism largely un-discussed in his theory of cosmopolitan democracy and indeed unchecked by democratic power in his model of cosmopolitan democracy. Yet, most cosmopolitan and global democrats are deeply concerned with global politico-economic relations. Held, Patomäki and Teivainen, and Dryzek all share in their critical reading of the role of the global market in constraining democratic practice today. For them, in order for democracy to work adequately the power of capital must be constrained through democratic forces.

Held's position is the clearest: he openly acknowledges his approach as 'social democratic' and sees it as an extension of the logic of social democracy in the global sphere. The core of such a project is subjecting 'market instincts, private property and the pursuit of profit within a regulatory framework' (Held, 2004: 13). Held, as do the social democrats examined in Chapter 4, accepts markets as central to well-being, and liberal democratic institutions as a vehicle towards a socially solidaristic and just state (Held, 2004: 15). This politico-economic vision, which emphasises both economic efficiency and social justice, he argues, must now be extended to the global level to tackle global financial power and environmental degradation. This is because of the growing inequities and instabilities that have emerged globally through globalisation (Held, 2004: 35). The approach of the economic liberals such as Nozick or Hayek fail to understand the power relations involved with market democracy: 'Not only does Hayek's conception of the rule of law drastically restrict consideration of the proper form and scope of democracy, but it also removes (by design) consideration of the impact key sites and sources of power on the possibility of democracy' (Held, 1995: 244). Economy cannot be left to function 'spontaneously', for the ideal of equality, which that perfectly free market would entail, is not the reality of capitalism (Held, 1995: 245). 'Democracy is embedded in a socio-economic system that grants a "privileged position" to certain interests' (Held, 1995: 247).

There are tensions between capitalism and democracy, then. Held, it follows, deems capital liberalisation and the one-size-fits-all approach to economic reform in global financial organisations as especially problematic and hence, while accepting the dominance and productiveness of a capitalist system (when regulated), keeps open the possibility that alternatives to capitalism might still arise (Held, 1995: 249) as well as advocating a new politico-economic 'policy mix' within the present capitalist order (Held, 2004: ch. 3). Indeed, he points out that 'capitalism is not a single, homogenous system world over' and that variations in its workings are possible (Held, 1995: 249).

This is based on according the state, and also global institutions, a key role. Governance actors must be active to maintain the proper functioning of the system. The aim of intervention is not to control the system, but 'to ensure the conditions for the pursuit of individual or collective projects' (Held, 1995: 251). Held attacks the present focus on mere free trade, market liberalisation, foreign investment, transfer of assets from public to private and cutting of government expenditure, balanced budgets, tax reform and TRIPS (trade related aspects of intellectual property rights) (Held, 2004: 55). He argues instead for balanced markets, strong government, social protection and distributive justice at the global level (Held, 2004: 56). To such a process of developing global 'targeted egalitarianism', the values of autonomy, human rights and cosmopolitanism are crucial. We must be ethically concerned for the poor and for the developmental capacity of 'distant others'.

This also means 'entrenchment of democracy in economic life': 'key groups in the economic will have to be rearticulated with political institutions so that they become part of the democratic process' (Held, 1995: 251). People should then be free to pursue their own interests in the economy but within the confines of democratic procedures and principles. This means not only regulation of markets nationally and globally, but also respect by corporations to requirements of autonomy of workers in specific contexts. Indeed, in his early work, Held argues for a form of industrial democracy: if not collective ownership, commitment to 'access avenues to decision-making apparatuses of productive and financial property' (Held, 1995: 253).

Local workplace democracy aside, how is the transformation brought about on a global level and indeed a concrete policy-level? Through a number of policy reforms, Held argues in the *Global Covenant* (Held, 2004):

(1) We must create a rule system for regulation of markets and of market access.
(2) We must increase levels of aid and make it more attuned to local conditions (e.g. local supply chains). We must also look into debt relief.
(3) There should also be new streams of money for the tackling of illiteracy and extreme poverty at the global level. These could draw on, for example, new systems of global taxation (on energy extraction or currency flows).
(4) There should be a change to global financial governance with more equal voting arrangements and with phasing of integration of emerging markets into the global market, so as to protect them. There could be a consideration for new Bretton Woods institutions more attuned to tackle the current global economic order.
(5) There should be increased regulation, first voluntarily, on multinational corporations.

There should be, in short, a move towards a social justice oriented economic system on a global level, where markets would be controlled by democratic processes.

Patomäki and Teivainen too place heavy an emphasis on control of the global economic system in order for global democracy to function adequately. Their ideal for global democratisation is underpinned by a realisation of the need to transform not just the UN system, but first and foremost, the global economic system of decision-making.

Within this system, particular kinds of expertise and knowledge-making dominate and alternatives are not given adequate attention. Voting systems in international financial governance are hierarchical and dispossess developing states from the system of global economic decision-making. Not only should these organisations be reformed, as is discussed earlier, Patomäki and Teivainen also suggest the creation of two new economic institutions: a debt arbitration mechanism and a global tax system. The debt mechanism is precipitated by the fact that 'foreign debt continues to be one of the main obstacles to democratic will-formation in most parts of the world (Patomäki and Teivainen, 2004: 150). Because of the power held by Bretton Woods institutions and credit agencies over many states, these states, democratic or not, have the scope for limited autonomous democratic governance in their economic affairs. This means that the separation of debt-provision mechanisms from political and democratic decision-making must be challenged. This is what the new debt organisation seeks to do: to insert political and moral considerations into debt arbitration. There is a need for fair processes of dealing with debt: double standards continue to exist (Patomäki and Teivainen, 2004: 153). Fair legal rules are needed for global financial matters. With support from global civil society, movement in this direction may be possible.

But what about a global tax system? It is argued that global forms of taxation would be not only fair but also productive in generating income which could be used to tackle important global problems independently from individual 'shareholders'. Taxes have been proposed for currency transaction, pollution, arms sales, travel, telecommunications, mining and extraction of raw materials. Of these the currency transfer tax (CTT) is the most advanced idea, associated with the ATTAC (*Association pour la Taxation des Transactions financière et l'Aide aux Citoyens* or Association for the Taxation of financial Transactions and Aid to Citizens) as well as James Tobin (see also Patomäki, 2001). Environmental taxes have also emerged. While taxation in and of itself would not be democratising, it would have important global democratising effects, when combined with democratic global policy-making. It would provide revenue and political control over the global markets and for this reason is, as Patomäki and Teiveinen argue, 'an obvious' proposal to consider: 'If there is a global integrated economy, there should also be taxes' (Patomäki and Teivainen, 2004: 163).

Dryzek's analysis is also interesting for it, too, rests on a politico-economic argument. He developed this in superficial form in *Deliberative Global Politics* (2006) but in more detail in his earlier work *Democracy in Capitalist Times* (1996). In this work he argued that while the global demise of socialism seems to have left as us with a single 'capitalist' model of democracy, this model was 'not easy, happy or perhaps even sustainable' (Dryzek, 1996: vii).

This provides the background to his discursive model of democracy: global inequalities and the problems of capitalist 'discourse' underpin the need to revise and re-contest the sphere of the economic and the kind of future politico-economic policies that should be evaluated. At the moment there is a dominance of liberal market ideas. These are creating the very consequences that they predict, but through the application of the ideas by policy-makers, not because they are necessarily true. Drawing on Colin Hay's work, Dryzek shows how the belief in urgency of deregulation of markets is precisely what brings on the kinds of dynamics that the discourse of market liberalisation predicts: the liberal prophecy that markets will punish those who do not conform become 'self-fulfilling' (Dryzek, 2006: 7). Yet, there is nothing inevitable about this and policy-makers could challenge the discourse that seemingly implies that 'there is no alternative' (Dryzek, 1996: 6, 101).

Indeed, the neoliberal discourse is after all just that, a discourse: it is not objectively true or the only way to interpret global economic affairs. It is for this reason that we need discursive challengers that scrutinise this discourse and set it up in comparison to other ways of thinking, from human rights thinking to environmental thought. Global democratic politics in the economic sphere for Dryzek, then, means challenging the neoliberal hegemonic discourse and challenging the power of those institutional actors who seek to solidify it. Global democratic politics can challenge neoliberalism in the following ways: by showing the cracks in the TINA-discourse (There Is No Alternative [to neoliberalism]), by challenging centralising discussion and decision-making on economic matters, by introducing ideas of democracy to global governance devoid of them, by encouraging the global resistance movement, by encouraging communication across borders, and hence by being able to fill some aspects of the institutional void that exists globally (Dryzek, 2006: 107). Dryzek (2006: vii) envisages his global discursive democratisation as an 'alternative to the dominance of market liberalism'. It shows the cracks and tensions in the liberal capitalist order.

All these cosmopolitan and global democrats then are critical of the unequal distribution of power as well as the power of certain economic processes and actors over others. They are interested in equalising such relations of power and having some form of democratic control over the global economy. In fact, they see such control as a key condition of any attempt at successful global democratisation.

Conclusion

The advocates of cosmopolitan and global democracy agree on a number of things. First, they agree on the fact that the state is an inadequate locus for solving global problems and ethically not self-evident as a site of political community or democratic decision-making. Second, they agree on the need to think about political, normative and theoretical justifications for global and cosmopolitan democracy and the need to think seriously about institutional forms that such a global or cosmopolitan democracy might take. They also are broadly on the same lines when it comes to the kind of cosmopolitan democracy they envisage. For all, reform of the

UN system is key, with the institution of world parliament and global legal principles and judicial bodies as key auxiliary steps towards global democratisation.

They all, however, shirk away from global federation or a state-like structure
and emphasise the multiplicity of the avenues and levels of democracy that should
exist in a global democracy. They all also agree on the need to keep an open-
minded approach to democracy: democratisation is not settled or complete even
in the West and, crucially, multiple different kinds of democracy can be instigated
at different levels of governance and in different parts of the world. Indeed, all
cosmopolitan democrats, while holding a liberal democratic ideal in mind, keep
their minds open to multiple models of democracy. They are all also adverse to
the forcible promotion of democracy in world politics, preferring, if not limiting
themselves to, an autonomous form of democratic development as the ideal of
democratisation.

Another aspect that these authors agree on is the crucial role of economic forces.
These authors consider it essential that a politico-economic order is taken into
account in global democratisation. This means going beyond the classical nation-
state based democratic theory and practice and development of global (social)
democratic principles and ideals. These are embedded in the proposals for debt
arbitration mechanisms, global forms of taxation and prioritisation of economic
and social committees in the work of the global institutions.

The advocates of cosmopolitan and global democracy allow us to conceive
of the idea of democracy in ways liberal democratic theorists would not dare
allow us to imagine. Here democracy is seen as a global challenge, a politico-
economically rooted challenge and a challenge which calls for pragmatic, open-
minded and conceptually diversity-accommodating approach to envisioning the
meaning of the idea of democracy.

6 Orientations towards the empirical study of conceptual orders in democracy promotion

As discussed in the Introduction to this book, the aim of Part II which follows is to analyse the politico-economic models of democracy currently at work in democracy promotion practice and in the work of the key actors who advocate the institution of democracy in other countries. We are not interested in models of democracy as just theoretical possibilities, but as political visions which are played out and shaped in practice. It is simply not the case that social democracy, participatory democracy or cosmopolitan democracy are utopian visions but are they part of democracy promotion or support today?

How do we identify politico-economic models examined in the previous chapters in the practices of democracy supporters? The models presented in Chapters 2–5 are, after all, but 'ideal types' set out by democratic theorists.

I suggest here that we can do so by analysing carefully the conceptual leanings with regard to democracy's meaning in the democracy support discourses. Democracy promotion practitioners or policy-makers, of course, are *not* democratic theorists and may not have developed, or be expected to have developed, systematic philosophical frameworks for how to understand democracy and its politico-economic context. Indeed, detailed and systematic engagement with democratic theory is, as we shall see, conspicuously absent in today's democracy support. This does not mean, however, that models of democracy – conceptual leanings which conform to or support certain models of democracy – are not present. Through careful interpretation of the conceptual basis of democracy promotion discourses we can gain a sense of the conceptual, and hence also 'ideological', leanings of democracy support activity, even when such leanings are accepted or worked with in rather unconscious or unsystematic ways.

Before we proceed to such analysis, a word or two is needed on the philosophy of science and 'methodological' leanings of this analysis. The analysis here is based on conceptual analysis. Such a form of analysis has certain key strengths. Yet, it also harbours specific weaknesses which we have to explicitly acknowledge at the start. This brief chapter seeks to set out where the orientations of the study arise from, how it is conducted and what caveats need to be born in mind. I will discuss here, first, the importance of post-positivist philosophy of science as the context for this study and the meaning of hermeneutic approach to social analysis. I will then make some comments on the nature of the 'conceptual analysis' conducted here, and the strengths and the weaknesses of such a form of analysis. Finally, I set out a series of tables which summarise the core ideas of different models of democracy. These serve as ideal types which we can keep in mind in the concrete analyses that follow. Chapters 7–10 seek to find values set out here either expressed or omitted in the engagements with the idea of democracy.

Postpositivism and interpretative engagement with conceptions of democracy

There has been a crucial shift in the social sciences in recent years, against classical 'positivist' approaches to the study of social reality. Postpositivist or postempiricist scholars, while of various different persuasions, share common ground in critiquing the mode of scientific analysis that is applied to social reality by the positivists, which assumes the existence of laws or regularities, their usefulness for studying causal relations, regularity-deterministic causal relations (given we have discovered a law, we have grounds to state 'when A, then B'), separation of values and facts, and objectivity of social science. The critics contend that not only is this form of analysis not the dominant one in the natural sciences any longer, but also in the analysis of social reality it misses the crucial aspects of what makes social life ontologically distinct from the natural science objects. Objects of study in social sciences are people, their social relations and social structures, including their ideas and understandings of reality. In grappling with such objects of study we are compelled to apply interpretation to the meanings people hold, as well as deal with the fact that our relations to social reality are neither objective nor removed from it, but rather intricately tied to its fabric. Objectivity and norm–fact distinctions then are problematic notions for postpositivists and, crucially, for them, social science has to be able to analyse not just patterns of behaviour but also patterns of meaning.

The postpositivist or postempiricist turn in social sciences has given rise to various different approaches to the study of social reality: constructivism, post-Marxism, discourse analysis, and so on. All of these approaches draw on a previous turn to 'hermeneutic' social inquiry. But what is hermeneutics?

Hermeneutics is a school of philosophy of science which emphasises the need to engage seriously with the meanings that people hold. Hermeneuticians, originally interpreters of religious texts, emphasised that the way in which we capture truths in social sciences is necessarily through interpretation of meanings of ideas that people hold; not through the observation or measurement of their actions. Thus, just as the observable action of 'blinking' does not in and of itself relay to us the meaning of a 'wink' (a socially meaning-laden action), in the same sense social science which merely focuses on capturing observable patterns, variables and measurements, fails to capture what it is that social action consists of, how its driven, and for what purpose, and how social life acquires meaning and structure.

One of the key contentions of second-wave hermeneuticians in twentieth-century philosophy of science has been the emphasis on not only interpretation of meaning but also the need for the analyst to remain aware of the way in which their own interpretations are tied up with the meaning structures which make up social objects. Thus, unlike studying rocks, studying social structures or ideologies entails that the student of the 'object' is necessarily in close relationship with, or possibly clouded by, their own embeddedness in its ideational premises. Analysing the state, globalization, or democracy involves interpretational relationships with the objects of study, persons' understandings of these objects, and our own world views, which may influence our readings of the meaning of such objects of study for others. Analysing these concepts or their uses, then, is not the same as analysing the molecular structure of granite or physical constitution of atoms, for example: the objects of study are inherently interpretational in nature.

This creates specific problems for social analysis. Obtaining objective data from the object of study is almost impossible. This means that a student of social affairs has to make sure that they are constantly aware of and reflective of their own embeddedness in the structures of meaning and their reproduction, and that they stay attuned to the contexts and meaning structures within which others interpret concepts. Even so, social scientists may and often do unwittingly not only mis-interpret meanings, but also reproduce their social causality. What makes social sciences peculiar and peculiarly difficult is the inter-meshing of its objects and subjects and the resultant subjectivity of findings.

I draw here on the hermeneutic trends by placing them in the context of a phi-losophy of science which mitigates their worst excesses of subjectivism and rela-tivism. I adopt here a critical realist philosophy of science as the backdrop for a hermeneutic interpretation of actors' conceptions of democracy (see also Kurki, 2008). What this means is that I accept that while we cannot but have inter-sub-jective understandings or interpretations of the meanings of social concepts or of actors' understandings of such concepts, such interpretations reflect better or worse a 'reality' of social life.

Thus, unlike some philosophers or theorists informed by radical hermeneutics I refuse to accept that the reality of the social world is reducible to our interpre-tations of it, and that we cannot speak meaningfully of the correctness of our analysis of meanings and beliefs in social life. I argue that through engagement with evidence and reasoned theoretical argumentation we can make the case that some interpretations of reality of meanings or beliefs are more correct than others (Kurki, 2008). Thus, while my analysis here is certainly interpretive and subjective, it is also criticisable and falsifiable in the sense that another analyst can review the data and the interpretations and come to different conclusions as to whether they accurately reflect the reality of democracy promotion discourse. Indeed, the readers are invited to critically engage with the interpretational judgements made here.

Maintaining this 'realist' context to hermeneutic analysis advanced is consid-ered an important commitment for 'critical social science' (Sayer, 2000). It is only in the context of statements made about objective realities – conceptual or other-wise – that we can come to debate and evaluate claims about the social world. It is, then, the critical realist approach to emancipatory social science that I seek to build on here, rather than the Wittgensteinian tradition of hermeneutics informative of poststructuralist approaches.

This means that I explicitly analyse conceptions of democracy in discourses through the hermeneutic methods of interpretation and self-reflection, but also accept that interpretation always takes place in the context of real social structural constraints, the nature of which we aim to get at through hermeneutic engagement with subjects. What this means is that, crucially, we cannot and should not reduce our interpretations to relativistic or 'subject-glorifying' narratives only, but also be prepared to critically examine whether subjects themselves may, in fact, be mistaken or misled in their understandings or conceptual framings of objects.

Conceptual analysis of models of democracy

A few key assumptions direct the conceptual analysis here. The first is that discourses, with specific conceptual frameworks, construct as well as reflect social realities around us. Discourse, not just behavior or action, matters for social life. We are social beings, who come to define our reality, live our reality and structure our reality through 'discursive' or 'conceptual' engagement with objects, others, and indeed ourselves. This means that 'discourse' and 'concepts' have real and potent power in shaping social reality (Sayer, 1992; Fairclough, 1995) and the study of their contours – empirically and theoretically – is central to understanding how social life is ordered.

The object of analysis of such an approach is the structures of meaning within which social actors exist, the structures of meaning which provide consistency to our understandings and world views. Discourse is a central notion in analysis of structures of meaning. Discourse, for our purposes, can be defined as *'specific ensembles of ideas, concepts, and categorisations that are produced, reproduced and transformed to give meaning to physical and social relations'* (Hajer, quoted in Fischer, 2003: 73). Discourses structure how people understand objects and subjects and what counts as accepted views of reality. Our interest is in understanding how discursive constructions – and specific understandings of concepts within such constructions – underlie political dynamics, even though they do so often in quite unconscious ways.

The focus of discourse analysis need not, however, be specific sentences or words as such. Rather, discourse analysts are interested in 'patterns of reasoning' that texts or practices exhibit (Fischer, 2003: 75). Indeed, discourse analysis is interested in how specific understandings are regularised or repeated in discourse, and thus naturalised, as well as in how discourses can be underpinned by discursive disagreements or contradictions.

These dynamics are important to pay attention to, partly because discourses, far from being mere rhetorical structures, also have built within them relations of power (Fairclough, 1995). Understandings of social life, and specific conceptual meanings, can reflect and reproduce specific social positions, interests and hence social power relations. All discourses, and conceptual settings within them, favour some ways of looking at the world over others, and thus specific groups of people and their interests over others. This is why we need to be wary of 'consensus' or lack of disagreement on conceptual foundations of specific ideas: if agreement or consensus exists, it may be that one discourse or conceptual meaning structure has assumed 'hegemonic' status in societal and cultural power relations.

There are various ways in which such hegemony can be achieved. As Gramscian and Foucauldian approaches to discourse analysis emphasise, construction of hegemonic or consensual understandings is the aim of most social interaction, that is, one system of meaning always struggles for power over another. Often hegemony is achieved through co-opting or integrating structures of meaning within each other.

Yet, not all discourse analysts are interested in structuring of hegemonies or power alone. Some are interested in understanding – somewhat less ambitiously – the patterns of decontestation between concepts, how relations between concepts appear in discourses, how in discourses concepts become linked in specific ways so as to fix meanings, and in so doing come to designate some concepts as central and others as peripheral. Michael Freeden's (1996) morphological approach to ideology analysis is one such approach referred to here in the empirical analysis.

Freeden's approach has been concerned with analysis of patterns of 'decontestation' between concepts in our discourses or conceptual framings of the world and how these structure our 'ideologies'. Specifically, he has been interested in the study of the morphology of concepts in liberal philosophy: how liberals have framed in different ways the relationships between core liberal values in their thought.

Patterns in hierarchy of values and concepts are what Freeden's approach focuses on. In drawing on his approach, I too seek to study the patterns of values and concepts – their hierarchies in specific discourses of democracy. I do so in order to trace specific patterns of meanings, or absences of meanings, attached to the idea 'democracy' in democracy promotion discourses.

As the earlier chapters have shown, different politico-economic models exhibit different understandings of democracy by the way they structure differently the value commitments surrounding democracy's meaning. While 'Hayekian' liberal democrats emphasise economic freedom of the individual as a core starting point value, for socialists the meaning of democracy is inextricably tied to the idea of social and economic equality of citizens. The role of civil society, of community, of solidarity and of property rights too are understood differently as they are positioned in different ways in relation to other values. From these differences of value orientation – from different conceptual commitments attached to democracy and different hierarchical positioning of values – arise different politico-economic models of democracy with different understandings of how democracy should function, for whom, and how. Thus, institutional as well as policy orientations of different types of democrats differ. This is even as some room is left for representational democracy by most streams of democratic thought.

What I am interested in studying here, then, are the hierarchies and relations between concepts surrounding the idea of democracy and how they may reveal orientations towards one or the other politico-economic model of democracy. Like Freeden (1996), I too am interested in the patterns of decontestation that come to highlight some values or concepts – liberty, economic freedom and rights for example as opposed to equality, participation and justice – as core aspects of the meaning of democracy. Other ideas appear as adjacent to the core notions, others as relatively insignificant or peripheral. Hierarchies and relations of concepts construct 'ideological frames' on democracy's possible meaning.

Yet, the adoption of 'Freedenite' orientations, does not mean that I seek to here implement the entire morphological system of Freeden's method. Freeden's way of 'sorting out' discourses, conceptual systems and ideologies through hierarchies of conceptual relations is valuable as a general orientation, yet I do not seek to rigidly apply all his concepts in the analysis of discourses here, partly because his method too has its limitations. Notably, the method is more suited to analysis of ideological frameworks that have been well thought-through, and it is less suited to the study of 'messy' empirical realities of actors who are not necessarily systematic in their conceptual framings or decision-making. For this reason, I seek here to construct but a very broad set of concept-hierarchies, which we can use as the basis for identifying 'politico-economic orientations' in the democracy support discourses. These are set out below, and provide rough guides to the interpretive analyses provided in the chapters which follow.

Ideal types of 'politico-economic models'

Table 6.1 Classical liberal democracy

Core concepts	Liberty – individualism – (minimal) sociability – rational governance – constitutional representation of interests and defence of freedoms
Adjacent concepts	– Political equality – Economic liberty – Democratic representation of 'interests' of the people through elected representatives – Electoral competition – Active democratic culture and civil society (to act as check on state) – Rule of law (in defence of freedoms) – Property rights (primarily those of individuals)
Peripheral concepts	– Education – Minimal, or moderate, state regulations of economy
Combine to provide a core meaning of democracy as:	Democratic institutions of liberal representative democracy: elections tempered by respect for liberal rights and constitutional principles. Facilitation of economic freedom and separation of politics and economics. Minimal interest in socio-economic considerations and active regulation of economic sphere.

Table 6.2 Reform liberal view of democracy

Core concepts	Liberty – individual freedom in the context of (strong) sociability – community – rationality – common good and constraints on freedoms
Adjacent concepts	– Socio-economic equality – Property rights (individual, potentially communal) – Democratic controls over the economy (to prevent untoward use of power by some individuals over others) – Education
Peripheral concepts	– Civil society
Combine to provide a core meaning of democracy as:	Democratic institutions of liberal representative democracy: elections tempered by respect for liberal rights and constitutionalism, together with active respect for limits to individual liberties if they endanger common good and socio-economic 'equality of opportunity' to act in democratic decision-making.

Table 6.3 Neoliberal democracy

Core concepts	Liberty – individual freedoms – constitutional, procedural defence of freedoms – limited state – right to property – spontaneous order as basis of economic and, it follows, political system of governance
Adjacent concepts	– Economic liberty – Minimal, and 'pro-market', regulation of economy/society – Rule of law – Electoral competition – Free trade and economy
Peripheral concepts	– Learning/education – Pro-market civil society
Combine to provide a core meaning of democracy as:	A system of governance consistent with defence of individual economic liberties (primary value) which support political liberty. Democratic procedures include electoral choice of governors in the context of rights to property and efficient 'rule of law'.

Table 6.4 Embedded neoliberal idea of democracy

Core concepts	Liberty – individual freedoms – constitutional, procedural defence of freedoms – right to property – stability of social order

Adjacent concepts	– Economic liberty
	– Active interference in defence of market freedoms in state and
	   civil society
	– Strong regulative pro-market state
	– Flanking measures against instability in society (including
	   basic welfare and education)
	– Rule of law
	– Free trade
	– Active pro-market civil society

Peripheral concepts	– Democratic innovations
Combine to provide a core meaning of democracy as:	A system of governance consistent with defence of individual economic liberties (primary value). Democratic procedures include electoral choice of governors in the context of defence of civil society, rights to property and rule of law. State can act as an active interfering actor in defence of market and competition-oriented state and civil society activity.

Table 6.5 Socialist delegative democracy

Core concepts	Community – welfare – equality – democracy as embedded in socio-economic system
Adjacent concepts	– Critique of liberal representative democracy: towards more direct forms of democracy – Immediate revocation of delegates – Expansion of sites of democracy: worker's democracy – Equal pay for delegates and workers – Education: 'learning' for communal good (and to realise 'real interest')
Peripheral concepts	– Constitutional separation of powers – Individual liberty
Combine to provide a core meaning of democracy as:	Direct forms of delegative democratic governance or modified forms of (contestation-premised) representative democracy. Emphasis on ensuring communal bonds and equality, and control over the economy.

Table 6.6 Social democratic model of democracy

Core concepts	Liberty – community – solidarity – equality (political and economic) – stability of social order
Adjacent concepts	– Welfare – State regulation of economy and representation of wage earners – Property (individual and communal) – Learning/education – Big state – Full employment – Grassroots civil society ('solidaristic' community organisations)
Peripheral concepts	– Rights claims – Free trade
Combine to provide a core meaning of democracy as:	Liberal democratic system with strong controls over the economy. A dual track system of democracy. Strong emphasis on value of solidarity and communal grounding of democracy in social interaction and controls over excessive political or economic power. Education as basis of social unity.

Table 6.7 Participatory democracy

Core concepts	Community – development – learning – participation – active individuals in defence of rights and community – expansion of sites of democracy
Adjacent concepts	– Liberty and rights; but pushed beyond 'liberal' foci – New spheres of democracy beyond formal politics: workers' democracy, everyday decentralised democracy – Democratic innovations for participatory democracy – Self-reflection and realization through community and dialogue – Non–interest-driven communal representation – Civil society (as active sphere of democracy) – Property (communal and individual)
Peripheral concepts	– Constitutional representative democracy
Combine to provide a core meaning of democracy as:	Direct forms of local democracy combined with circles of democratic control over all areas of social life, including the economy. Active notion of citizens as learners and developers of their faculties.

Table 6.8 Radical democracy

Core concepts	Civil society – agonism – non-hierarchy – pluralism of values
Adjacent concepts	– (Global) civil society – Network democracy – Contestation – Non-hierarchy of claims – Against fixing democracy's meaning or institutions
Peripheral concepts	– Representative democracy – Class politicss
Combine to provide a core meaning of democracy as:	Radical non-state based democracy based on debate and agonistic politics. Non-hierarchical non-institutionalised idea of democracy.

Table 6.9 Global democracy

Core concepts	Autonomy – global power structures – politico-economic justice
Adjacent concepts	– Global representative institutions – Global controls on economy – Global civil society – Learning and dialogue
Peripheral concepts	– State-based democratization
Combine to provide a core meaning of democracy as:	Non-state based democracy as basis for national democratisation of a meaningful kind. Need for global economic and democratic controls.

What is crucial to note about these 'ideal type' models and their value orientations is that the constitutive concepts of democracy are understood in different ways: some place equality in the socio-economic sphere as a core notion of democracy, others decontest democracy as an essentially liberty-defending mechanism. Some traditions advocate and place emphasis on liberty and defence of rights, while others emphasis learning and community. Some emphasise controls over the economy, while others separate democratic concerns from those over the economy.

This conceptual matrix, while an ideal type categorisation, provides us arguably with some useful pointers in approaching analysis of the complex discourses on democracy promotion. What I try to do in the chapters which follow is to identify the concept hierarchies and decontestations over democracy's meaning in democracy support discourses. Such analysis cannot be categorical but is necessarily 'interpretive'. Given that the same values can characterise, or be valued in different ways, in various models, interpretation has to pay attention to what is emphasised, in what context, and what is also omitted from value delineations. The ideal types set out above make it possible to try and decipher conceptual orders. Thus, if classical liberal priorities over individual liberties would emerge as central, a classical liberal model would seem to be promoted; if concern with equality and solidarity were set out as central, socialist or social democratic models would seem to inform the texts analysed. If both sets of ideals were to emerge, social democratic, embedded liberal or reform liberal models may be most appropriate interpretive categories to consider. Orientations towards 'models' in turn tell us about the ideological centours of democracy support, even as no overtly 'ideological' frames are seemingly present.

But how exactly do I go about analysing the democracy promotion discourses? What sources do I look at in determining conceptual orientations in the discourses? Does it not matter where we look, for what we find?

Data and cases

The analysis here is based on two key reference points. First, I base it on a close reading of the textual discourses identified in key policy documents, guidance manuals, strategy papers and reference works. I have identified in each case a set of sources which I analyse, or others have analysed, with conceptual bases of democracy-building in mind. While the study is not comprehensive in that not every policy document is subjected to detailed analysis, I seek to cover most of the key policy documentation and practical guidance manuals which structure democracy promotion policy-making and practices.

Second, I analyse the 'practical' discourses of a selection of democracy support practitioners. While it would be impossible to interview all the thousands of people involved in democracy support, I have interviewed a small cross-section of experts working in fields or facets of democracy support that the empirical chapters have chosen to focus on. Fifteen interviews were conducted: with European Commission officials, US democracy promotion officials, representatives of political foundations, and private contractors. In the case of international financial institutions, detailed analyses of interviews conducted by other researchers were drawn on.

This data is drawn on to construct a two-stage analysis of democracy promotion, consisting in a documentary analysis of general discursive and historical context of the actors' democracy promotion and a more detailed 'case study' analysis of a selection of areas in which the actor engages in democracy promotion.

The primary focus of the analysis has been specifically on gaining a sense of – or interpreting – the conceptual orders which democracy promotion documents and practices reveal. The analysis then turns to identification of value preferences or foci, which may be revelatory of the kinds of ideological or conceptual 'model inclinations' characteristic of the different actors. As we shall see, the reality of democracy promotion today reveals an interesting and rich, if still predominantly and unsystematically liberal, conceptual matrix; one which tells us interesting things about democracy support as a practice of world ordering.

Part II

Politico-economic models of democracy in democracy promotion practice

7 Liberal democracy

Its multiple meanings in United States democracy promotion

Jeff Bridoux and Milja Kurki

The world must be made safe for democracy. Its peace must be planted upon the tested foundations of political liberty. We have no selfish ends to serve. We desire no conquest, no dominion. We seek no indemnities for ourselves, no material compensation for sacrifices we shall freely make. We are but one of the champions of the rights of mankind. We shall be satisfied when those rights have been made as secure as the faith and the freedom of nations can make them.

> (Woodrow Wilson, war message, 2 April, 1917)

Our action, our leadership, is essential to the cause of human dignity. And so we must act, and lead, with confidence in our ideals.

> (Barack Obama, speech at Westminster, 25 May, 2011)

The United States has for a significant length of time seen itself as the beacon of democratic rights and freedoms. Its cultural and political identity has, from its very beginnings, tied together the norms of democracy and liberty. Importantly, the United States has also taken on an active role in the promotion of democratic rights and ideals globally. Alongside the promotion of democracy, it has also advanced the cause of open markets and trade: indeed, discourses of democracy have historically been closely tied to understandings of how the economy should be organised. The United States has been, and still is, firmly committed to the promotion of a liberal democratic model with a market-capitalist twist.

Yet, the conceptual foundations of US democracy promotion are more complex than often appreciated. It is true that the commitment to political and economic liberalism and their promotion globally are grounded in American history, and more specifically, in the way in which the US Republic came into being (Appleby, 1992: 424; Perkins, 1993: 8, 51) and liberal democracy and capitalism have played a unique role in the institution of this particular type of 'revolutionary' state. Through careful conceptual analysis, we can identify, however, shifts over time in US democracy support and its conceptual foundations. There exists, often unnoted, significant debate within the United States about the precise meaning of liberal democracy; over the precise variant of liberal democracy that the country is premised on, and should promote. Thus, while debate on democracy's meaning in the US scene remains firmly within liberal democratic tradition, this does not mean that singular, fixed or non-negotiable ideas on liberal democracy emanate from this key democracy promotion actor.

To highlight the trajectories of development in the conceptual foundations of US democracy support, we will start by identifying five 'paradigmatic moments' in US democracy promotion. These moments reflect both shifts in definitions of the role of democracy promotion in US foreign policy and, crucially, shifts in understandings of democracy in US democracy support. We will then focus on analysing in detail contemporary practices and specifically the conceptual contours defining President Obama's current democracy support. Our analysis shows that not just historically but also today, US democracy promotion is conceptually more diverse than many commentators have appreciated. Indeed, US democracy promotion has combined and oscillated between classical liberal, neoliberal and reform liberal models of democracy. Against Robinson (1996) then, we contend that a far from singular or clear procedural understanding of democracy emerges from conceptual premises of US democracy support, even as efforts to engage with alternative ideas – reform liberalism most recently, for example – remain disappointingly unsystematic.

Finally, we examine some concrete facets of US democracy support in order to tease out how complex liberal democratic conceptual parameters in the United States play out in shaping practices of US democracy support. We build a picture of an ideologically liberal democratic democracy support actor – but one which, even today, continues to look for the exact 'politico-economic' meaning that promotion of 'liberal democracy' should take.

Paradigmatic shifts in historical context

The first paradigmatic moment in US democracy promotion was, without doubt, the Wilsonian push after the First World War for democratic republics in international politics (Smith, 1994; Latham, 1997: 34; Williams, 1998: 32–41; Ikenberry, 2001: 119, 124, 127, 155–60). For Wilson, military power and imperialism, both caused by autocracy, were to be replaced by a rule of law in which a world public opinion rather than alliances and armaments would structure the international order. It would be America's international order, based on its principles and meeting its interests; an international order based on peace, economic well-being, political stability and social cohesiveness, values shared by liberal democratic regimes (Iriye, 1993: 104, Ikenberry, 2001: 19, 20, 122–8; Williams, 2006: 47–50). Ikenberry summarises the importance of President Wilson's ideas embodied in his Fourteen Points speech as the bedrock of American democracy promotion: 'the war was to inaugurate a democratic revolution not only in the Old World but worldwide. [. . .] Wilson's view was that the rest of the world was coming to embrace American principles, and this would overcome all the great postwar problems' (2001: 127–8).

American liberal democratic principles were to be at the heart of the democracy support effort – constitutional rights and liberties, electoral democracy, and free market economies would make the world a safer place. Classical liberal rights, procedures and defences, with a distinct concern for economic freedom, stood at the heart of this agenda, if in a far from 'rigidly defined' manner (Smith, 1994, 2011).

The outcome of promulgation of these values proved rather different from what Wilson envisioned. The Great Depression, the rise of fascisms and Nazism, and the most destructive conflict ever experienced in human history put an end to Wilson's world order. Yet, it is precisely on the ashes of Wilson's world that a new opportunity to promote democracy arose.

Indeed, the 1940s and 1950s constituted the second paradigmatic period of US democracy promotion: it brought forth the 'New Dealers' democracy promotion'. In the post-Great Depression era, American identity, and its foreign policy, allowed for distinctly 'reform liberal' agendas to arise. New Deal led to a need to balance the demands of liberty and equality also in the sphere of foreign affairs. Awareness of socio-economic concerns 'made American foreign policy much more conscious of the social dimensions of domestic and international politics' (Nau, 2002: 74). As Franklin Roosevelt's Annual Address to Congress in January 1941 clearly explicated, the United States at the brink of war and in order to counter the threat of autocracy, should focus – domestically and internationally – on the protection not only of democratic rights and liberties, but crucially of 'a social economy' for we should always bear in mind 'the social and economic problems which are the root cause of the social revolution' (Roosevelt, 1941).

The US post-war democracy promotion efforts reflected these concerns, which led to support of the Marshall Plan and the Bretton Woods system, and the advocacy, at home and abroad, of a much more 'reform liberal' version of democracy and capitalism, which some have even labelled 'social democratic' despite the absence of the full range of 'dual track' democratic controls (see also Bernstein 1972; Lacey, 1989; Merrill, 2006; Berman, 2011; Smith, 2011).

This 'reform liberal' approach to democracy support took seriously the need not only to 'liberalise' the political systems of the states, which still remained an aim, but also to reflect as well as mitigate the power balances apparent in the societies in question. It was openly recognised that economic stability was crucial for social and political peace. For this reason, the stabilisation of economies of target states, not through open market systems but controlled and regulated social market economies, was important. This entailed recognising the role of active employment policies, welfare safeguards as well as limited trade union representation within economic policy. Even though full dual track democracy of a Swedish kind was not advocated, reform liberal concerns for a more social market and an active welfare providing state were clearly at the heart of the activities at this time. Thus, the version of democracy promoted in Japan and Germany at the end of the Second World War, for example, was not 'liberal' in the sense meant by Hayek (see later section) but rather much closer to the sense meant by Hobson or Hobhouse, or even Keynes. Democratic liberalism was balanced by concern with economic equality, stability and well-being and hence democratic regulation of the economy of the state (Dower, 1999: 220–1; Wolfe, 1984; Cohen, 1987; Schonberger, 1989).

However, the realities of the Cold War soon triggered a reverse course in countries undergoing democratisation (Dower, 1999: 271–3, 525–6, 546, 551–2; Bridoux, 2011a: 151–60). From the beginning of the Cold War, the United States systematically privileged a national interest defined by security and economic concerns over democracy promotion. The overall objective remained to provoke the downfall of the Soviet Union and international communism through numerous proxy wars, and by supporting authoritarian regimes if need be, as long as they were anti-communist. Interestingly, it is in this rather unfavorable context that US democracy promotion experienced a rebirth.

In the 1980s, President Reagan pushed for a new way of engaging the proxy states: they were to be democratised (Carothers, 1999; Guilhot 2005). This strategic move was, as Guilhot (2005) and others (see e.g. Robinson, 1996; Carothers, 1999; Burnell, 2000) have documented, a part of the Reagan administration's strategic rethinking of its relations with difficult proxy states. Counter-insurgency warfare and support to friendly forces was of decreasing utility and was causing embarrassment to the administration. A 'softer' approach was to be developed. Reagan's Westminster speech in 1982 set the course for the renewal of democracy promotion.

Crucially, Reagan moved away from reform liberal commitments in the conceptual model promoted in the 1950s in favour of a model which saw individual freedoms as a cornerstone of democracy. This is because, echoing Hayek, '[h]istory teaches the dangers of government that overreaches – political control taking precedence over free economic growth, secret policy, mindless bureaucracy, all combining to stifle individual excellence and personal freedom' (Reagan, 1982). This leaning to liberty was, he argued, a generally accepted principle now:

> Whether it is the growth of the new schools of economics in America or England or the appearance of the so-called new philosophers in France, there is one unifying thread running through the intellectual work of these groups – rejection of the arbitrary power of the state, the refusal to subordinate rights of the individual to the superstate, the realization that collectivism stifles all the best human impulses.
>
> (Reagan, 1982)

A newly reinvigorated policy area of democracy promotion was launched, guided by highly liberal Hayekian political and economic philosophy. Individual liberty, economic freedom, and anti-communitarianism stood at the heart of this agenda, which put procedural democratisation at the centre ground of activity.

As the plans unfolded a cadre of progressive forces for democratisation was recruited to the cause. Often these forces adopted a 'classical liberal', rather than overtly and aggressively 'neoliberal', stance on democracy; arguably because such a conception was conceived as more palatable to many recipients of democracy aid. Thus, the National Endowment for Democracy (NED), a bipartisan non-governmental organisation funded by the US Congress, for example, adopted as its mission the promotion of a classically liberal set of ideals founded on promotion of liberal political freedoms: individualism, constitutionalism, electoral democracy, and civil society activism in the context of a continuing belief in the democracy-facilitating qualities of a liberal economic open-market system alongside advocacy of 'political liberty' (NED, undated).

In the run up to and in the aftermath of the fall of the Soviet Union, US democracy promotion geared up, by this time, with a rather unquestioned combination of both classical liberal and Hayekian neoliberal approaches to democracy promotion. These liberal ideals were transmitted to Central and Eastern Europe, as these countries were democratised while their economies were systematically liberalised. Classical and neoliberal agendas in a sense merged and a consensus on a liberal democratic set of ideals was firmed up. So much so, that even Democratic President Clinton, when reflecting on the role of democracy, without consideration of alternative models, made a firm commitment to promotion of democracy but also to 'market democracies' around the world.

The 1990s policy of liberal democratisation fitted in with, and arose from, the triumphalist ideas promulgated by Francis Fukuyama (1992), for example. Fukuyama famously argued that the liberal democratic model was the final blueprint for organisation of governance and liberal capitalism was the only real alternative for economic development. With this in mind the history had 'come to an end' in so far as it had previously involved the juxtaposition of alternative ideological systems of thought. Also, in 1993 Marc F. Plattner felt brave enough to declare that the US model was the way to go for all societies around the world, and that hence the United States should not shy away from promotion of its own model elsewhere. The United States took on self-consciously the role of democratising the world – as part of its 'distinctively American liberal grand strategy' (Ikenberry, 2000). In this grand strategy, classical liberal and neoliberal ideals mingled together rather comfortably.

Yet, as triumphant as democracy promotion was in the early 1990s, through diplomatic dialogue and increasingly through democracy aid, not all were happy with the developments that ensued. Not only did critics challenge the United States' triumphant role in promotion of what was perceived as a 'low-intensity' form of democracy (Gills et al., 1993), the United States was also accused of promoting a limited type of 'polyarchic' model, which ensured the continuing dominance of class power of transnational capitalist elites in target countries, while undermining participatory and radical aspirations of developing state publics (Robinson, 1996). Criticisms also started to emerge from within the so-called liberal democratic 'mainstream'. Thus, Fareed Zakaria's (1997) critique of the overdone focus on electoral democracy made a big splash in the US scene in the late 1990s. Thomas Carothers's critiques too – of the transition paradigm (2002) and Western electoral, civil society and rule of law programmes (see Carothers and Ottaway, 2000; Carothers, 2005, 2006a) – pointed to various problems in the US administration's democracy aid.

Yet, despite the mounting criticisms, in the wake of the 9/11 attacks, President George W. Bush went on the offensive with democracy promotion. The Bush administration made strong rhetorical commitments to democracy promotion as a security response to 9/11 and defined a major role for democracy promotion in US foreign policy through the 'Freedom Agenda'. Encouragement of liberties was now seen as a security concern. Bush's aggressive democracy promotion did not constitute a paradigmatic shift in itself but a more intense continuation of Reagan's and Clinton's commitments to promote a combination of classical liberal and neoliberal ideals of democracy globally. Nevertheless, the identification of the Freedom Agenda with the invasion and occupation of Afghanistan and Iraq prefigured an over-stretch of US democracy promotion, which in turn, led to a final paradigmatic shift, which has been undertaken by the Obama administration.

The US actions in Iraq and Afghanistan caused a 'backlash' against the US democracy promotion project – both within and outside of the United States (Carothers, 2006b, 2008, 2009a; NED, 2006; Rupnik 2007; Diamond 2008b, 2008c 2008d;). The failures to stabilise Afghanistan and Iraq generated not only criticisms of the model of democracy promoted by the United States, but also the very notion that democracy is exportable (see e.g. Fukuyama and McFaul, 2007; Coyne and Cofman, 2008; Goldsmith, 2008; Barany and Moser, 2009). Carothers (2007: v) concluded that 'the future of democracy promotion as part of US foreign policy is uncertain'. It is in the midst of this backlash that the current Obama administration conducts its business today.

Models of liberal democracy in US democracy promotion today

How is democracy conceptualised today in US democracy support? Through a detailed reading of the value hierarchies embedded in US foreign policy discourses, we offer an account of how liberal democracy is understood today. Crucially, we point out that liberal democracy's meaning is partially being reconfigured as shifts between different 'variants' of liberal democratic ideals play out in US discourses and practices. We argue that, far from being a conceptual black box, US democracy promotion is conceptually diverse. We focus our initial documentary analysis on the discourses of the Office of the President, the Department of State and the United States Agency for International Development (USAID) as these are most important policy actors that contribute to definition of democracy's meaning today. In the section that follows we examine in more detail specific programmes and activities of the implementors of democracy aid, such as NED and the Millennium Challenge Corporation (MCC).

Let us start by examining the context for the current democracy promotion agenda. The Obama administration inherited the US democracy promotion system at a time of crisis. On the one hand, the backlash against democracy promotion instigated by Bush's Freedom Agenda was in full swing with an increasing number of countries resisting and domestic critics complaining. At the same time, the Obama administration was faced with a momentous financial crisis, a development which undermined the target countries' belief in not only the commitments of Western states in terms of aid, but also in the very model of capitalist democratic development that they espoused.

In this context, President Obama's commitments to democracy support seem to have been reactive at best. Indeed, on the campaign trail Obama did not build his foreign policy rhetoric on sweeping statements about democracy, freedom and human rights. At the onset of his presidential mandate, Obama shied away from democracy promotion, which took a supporting role to economic development in the strategic planning. Hillary Clinton, at her Senate confirmation hearing, defined the three pillars of US foreign policy as defence, diplomacy, and development; prompting some observers to ask where democracy had disappeared to. However, gradually, Obama has sharpened the role of democracy promotion in his foreign policy. His National Security Strategy 2010 (NSS) mentions the word democracy 24 times, and related concepts more than 160 times (Wollack, 2010: 20). Obama reaffirmed the commitment of the United States to democracy and its promotion abroad as a component of US foreign policy.

However, in contrast to the previous administrations' value-laden rhetoric of expanding democracy globally, Obama's democracy promotion is placed alongside economic and security interests and is subordinated to those as required. This led some observers to label the Obama administration as 'realist' (Thayer, 2010: 4).

Yet, US democracy promotion is far from being on its deathbed. As Bouchet argues, 'There has been a stark and deliberate rhetorical break from the Bush era, but the president and many of his foreign policy appointees are basically liberal internationalists with a conventional view of democracy promotion' (2011: 584). US democracy promotion is evolving and is a reflection of the challenges faced by the United States today. It is also undergoing a 'paradigmatic shift' it would seem.

Obama's new conception of democracy: an incipient paradigm shift

Obama's democracy promotion has now dealt with its withdrawal symptoms and is experiencing a partial revitalisation. Yet, still, in contrast to the previous decades, contemporary US democracy promotion is not woven into a grand narrative of US foreign policy. Today, in an increasingly multipolar world, the United States does not seem to have the confidence, or the political willingness, to adopt a highly normative foreign policy that echoes past attempts to remake the world in the United States' image. What does this mean for the kind of democracy which is then promoted?

We argue that present policy is characterised by a discursive incertitude regarding the role, content and purpose of democracy promotion. This in turn translates into a lack of precision and discrepancies in the *meaning of democracy* in US democracy promotion. Today, US democracy promotion is characterised by a surprisingly broad discursive constellation of meanings of democracy. This incertitude in many ways emanates from Obama's presidential discourse.

What is interesting about the Obama administration is that, at home, Obama has adopted a committed 'reform liberal' orientation in his thinking on the future of the country. In December 2011, Obama delivered a speech on the economy in a small Kansas town called Osawatomie. At the very same location, in 1910, former President Theodore Roosevelt delivered a very provocative speech, which was labelled 'communistic', 'socialistic' and 'anarchistic' by the American establishment. Quoting Abraham Lincoln, Roosevelt argued that 'Labor is the superior of capital, and deserves much the higher consideration' (quoted in Roosevelt, 1910). While recognising, again quoting Lincoln, that 'Capital has its rights, which are as worthy as protection as any other rights (quoted in Roosevelt, 1910), Roosevelt made clear which side he was on:

> New nationalism[1] regards the executive power as the steward of the public welfare. It demands of the judiciary that it shall be interested primarily in human welfare rather than in property, just as it demands that the representative body shall represent all the people rather than any one class or section of the people. I believe in shaping the ends of government to protect property as well as human welfare. Normally, and in the long run, the ends are the same; but whenever the alternative must be faced, I am for men and not for property.
>
> (Roosevelt, 1910)

Obama said much the same when he spoke in Osawatomie. His speech on the economy was a clear statement of reform liberal intentions regarding the relationship between state and economy. Obama does not question that free market remains the most formidable force for economic progress but he questions the classical or Hayekian economic theory's assumptions that the market will naturally regulate the economy and that more deregulation and less taxes are synonymous with economic growth. On the contrary, Obama argues that to give a free hand to the market results in growing economic inequalities in the market. Hence, the government must act and legislate to redistribute resources and protect the weakest members of society:

> 'The market will take care of everything,' they tell us . . . there will be winners and losers. But if the winners do really well, then our jobs and prosperity will eventually trickle down to everybody else. And, they argue, if prosperity does not trickle down, well, that's the price of liberty. Now, it's a simple theory. And we have to admit, it's one that speaks to our rugged individualism and our healthy skepticism of too much government . . . that theory fits well on a bumper sticker. But there is a problem: It doesn't work. It has never worked.
>
> (Obama, 2011a)

This position is reiterated in Obama's latest State of the Union speech, in which he also outlines concrete institutional steps to implement a reform liberal democratic policy: new rules to hold Wall Street accountable, a financial services watchdog (the Consumer Financial Protection Bureau), and a review of the tax code for a better redistribution of revenues across society (Obama, 2011a, 2012a, 2012b).

Capital and the market are to be not only regulated but subject to democratic controls for the benefit of the populace. Markets are not to rule the country but must be made to work for the citizens.

This is all very well, but how does Obama conceptualise democracy when it is to be promoted abroad? Do his reform liberal value orientations translate to foreign policy? Some shifts in democracy support rhetoric are indicative of such a reorientation of democracy promotion.

First, Obama has shown reluctance (despite having co-sponsored the Advance Democracy [2007] Act) to engage in Bush-like coercive democratisation. This is because mechanistic electoral views on democracy do not capture, for Obama, what democracy is about. 'This yearning [to freedom] is not satisfied by simply deposing a dictator and setting up a ballot box. The true desire of all mankind is not only to live free lives, but lives marked by dignity and opportunity; by security and simple justice' (Obama, 2007). Schumpeterian proceduralism then clearly is insufficient. So it would seem is mere advocacy of individual freedoms, for equality of opportunity, a key reform liberal ideal, is attached to democratic aspirations.

Given this belief in a somewhat more holistic view of democracy, it is not a surprise that 'sustainability' became the buzzword of Obama's administration regarding development aid as well as democracy. Obama's approach to development is based on an intertwining of economic and political development. By going beyond a 'classical' liberal model of democracy, which separates the economic and the political, Obama's discourse brings economy and politics together to a more holistic view of democracy and its context of sustainability.

> Delivering on these universal aspirations requires basic sustenance like food and clean water; medicine and shelter. It also requires a society that is supported by the pillars of a sustainable democracy – a strong legislature, an independent judiciary, the rule of law, a vibrant civil society, a free press, and an honest police force. It requires building the capacity of the world's weakest states and providing them what they need to reduce poverty, build healthy and educated communities, develop markets, and generate wealth. Finally, while America can help others build more secure societies, we must never forget that only the citizens of these nations can sustain them. . . . [I]n these places where fear and want still thrive, we must couple our aid with an insistent call for reform. We must do so not in the spirit of a patron, but the spirit of a partner – a partner that is mindful of its own imperfections. Extending an outstretched hand to these states must ultimately be more than just a matter of expedience or even charity. It must be about recognizing the inherent equality and worth of all people. And it's about showing the world that America stands for something – that we can still lead.
>
> (Obama, 2007)

Declarations such as this confirmed Obama's approach to democracy promotion as part of a wider policy in which democracy, human rights, and development were conceived as mutually reinforcing. A widening of the remit of democracy work then has ensued; it has been increasingly integrated into a wider range of policy agendas (Interview with Senior State Department Official, 2012). As a result, the Obama administration has also identified a wide range of partners – citizens, communities, political and civil society leaders. There has been a shift away from US-based market-dominant contractors towards trying to make sure aid gets to the recipients on the ground in target countries (Interview with Senior State Department Official, 2012; Interview with representative of a private consulting firm, 2012).

This new conceptual approach was developed in the Presidential Policy Directive on development (PPD 6), the first of its kind. The new global development policy gives priority to economic growth, identified as 'the only sustainable way to *accelerate* development and eradicate poverty'; with democratic governance, understood as the best means to *consolidate* economic development, in a supportive role. However, this supportive role does not mean a passive role. Obama argues that the values of liberty, equality, and social justice are intrinsic to democracy and should be present when democracy and human rights are promoted abroad (Obama, 2011b). The simultaneous concern for social and economic equality through greater state interventionism in economic affairs and political democratisation is arguably a goal identifiable with the reform liberal ideas.

Reform liberal rhetoric then is now solidly anchored in Obama's discourse on democracy in general and in some regards also in his discourse on democracy promotion. But what does this mean for how other actors in the US governmental sphere approach democracy? We observe that, interestingly, despite shifts in Obama administration's discourses on democracy, so far there is little evidence of any concrete transitions to systematically reform liberal practices in the discourses of the US State Department and USAID.

US Department of State

This is seen clearly in the discourse of the State Department. In 2010, the US Department of State published its first Quadrennial Diplomacy and Development Review (QDDR), which identifies the core missions of the Department of State and of USAID. Hillary Clinton's speeches also specified how the administration concretely thinks of democracy support and such a position is not entirely in line with President Obama's turn to reform liberalism.

Similarly to Obama's understanding of the purpose of democracy promotion, Clinton links economic development and democracy: 'The US is committed to advancing democracy, human rights, gender equality, and sound governance to protect individual freedoms and foster sustainable economic growth'. The end point of US economic and political assistance to developing countries is to make assistance unnecessary in the long term. Consequently, Clinton argues that recipients of US aid must 'seek to build their own capacity, maximize the impact of the assistance they receive, and provide for their people' (US Department of State 2010b: 94). In line with Obama's discourse, sustainability through ownership of development policies by recipient countries is thus also supported by the Department of State.

Yet, such an emphasis on sustainability and ownership also means that only countries that are able and responsible economically and politically qualify for US support. Hence, US development strategy prioritises investments 'where partner nations have demonstrated high standards of transparency, good governance, and accountability—and where they make their own financial contributions to development' (US Department of State 2010b: 95). This means that US partners share responsibility and are accountable to their people and to the United States regarding their progress in the direction of good international citizenship.

Good international citizenship is, according to Hillary Clinton, characterised by three mutually supportive essential elements: 'representative government, a well-functioning market, and civil society [which together] work like three legs of a stool' (Clinton, 2010). Interestingly, in so arguing, it would seem that Clinton's definition of democracy is fairly classically liberal, with a priority given to values as individual liberty, negative rights (civil and political rights like freedom of speech, private property, freedom of religion, right to a fair trial . . .) and institutions of representative democracy (constitutional protection of rights, rule of law, free enterprise and trade, and civil society as counter-balance to state power), while the market is separated as a supporting leg of the stool. In contrast to Obama's reform liberal rhetoric, here in Clinton's thinking, democracy is essentially a political regime, which facilitates an economic regime of liberal markets, and vice versa.

Also, in contrast to Obama's discourse, the Department of State does not call for any concrete shifts towards greater regulation of economic forces in society but seems to work on the basis of continued belief in the efficiency of a free market economy. For example, a look at the Department of State's operational arm of democracy promotion reveals the importance of democratic regimes for a global open economy. The Bureau of Democracy, Human Rights and Labor (DRL), which oversees the Human Rights and Democracy Fund (HRDF), and the funding of which has grown from $7.82 million in FY 1998 to over $207 million in FY 2010, (DRL, 2011), has not substantively redirected its programmes.

For the DRL, in line with Obama's discourse, democratic governance helps governments to address socio-economic challenges. Democratisation programmes thus include political and fiscal reforms to deal with internal grievances, improved access to health care services and education, and measures to reduce poverty and to strengthen natural resource management. Social stability is also an objective of US democracy promotion, through support of worker rights and well-regulated labor markets (DRL, 2010a).

Yet, it is interesting to note that the country programmes do not include the institutional commitments necessary for the exercise of reform liberalism. Despite advocacy of labour rights, there are little signs of shifts to advocacy of democratic controls over economic power centres in society and to bring about an actively regulated market economy in target states. On the contrary, there is still a studious separation of the political and economic spheres in most country programmes. Indeed, social and economic welfare support to developing societies strives to achieve social peace and stability, both necessary for smooth operations of a free market economy, rather than a genuine empowerment of the government and the people in their relations with a capitalist economy. A slippage towards more instrumental and stability-driven 'embedded neoliberalism' seems to take place here (for more detail see Chapter 10).

Moreover, for all the discussion of the political aspects of democracy promotion – freedom, human rights, elections, civil society – it is probably the DRL's process of application for grants that best underscores the continued role of a market-driven liberal economic conceptualisation of democracy. Despite Obama's scepticism of market logics in the context of democracy, and his emphasis on a greater role for the state over private actors, in democratic societies, the delivery methods of democracy aid seem, paradoxically, to contradict such beliefs. This is because it is defined that democracy programmes should be contracted and implemented on the basis of liberal economic market-competition logic. This means not only objectifying the idea of democracy – programmes must define objectives that are 'ambitious, yet measurable and achievable' – but subjecting delivery of 'democracy' (a supposedly political value) to a market logic. Democracy promotion is paradoxically to be conducted on the basis of a 'private actor-based' business model, rather than with politicised democratic values in mind (Clary, 2009; DRL, 2010b, 2010c). As we will see in a later section, this creates tensions in the delivery of more politicised or reform liberal democracy support activity.

USAID

But what of the work of USAID, the key implementer of democracy projects within the administration? USAID activities being carried out in field-based operating units in country missions account for 85 per cent of the US$2.25 billion democracy assistance total budget as of fiscal year 2008 (GAO, 2009: 4). What is interesting to note is that in USAID discourse there has been a distinct shift away from the promotion of free-market based economy alongside limited state regulation.

Much has changed since 1998, when in that year's programming document USAID set out a classical/neo-liberal view of democracy (USAID, 1998). In this view, first, respect for the rule of law and a well-developed justice system is crucial because of its role in facilitating not only 'a democratic society', but also 'a modern economy' (USAID, 1998: 7). Rule of law, as for Smith and Hayek, enhances predictability and equitable treatment as well as respect for basic human rights and in so doing helps to curb the arbitrary exercise of power by elites and other branches of government. A key output of the rule of law is the promotion of market-based economy 'based on the principles of private property ownership, the free purchase and sale of goods and services at prices established through supply and demand, with the minimum regulation necessary to protect the public interest, and minimum state intervention' (USAID, 1998: 20). Second, on classical liberal democratic lines, elections and political processes, it was argued, should be free and fair: the essential objective was to achieve impartial electoral frameworks, credible electoral administration, effective oversight of electoral processes, informed and active citizenries, representative and competitive multiparty systems, inclusion of women and other disadvantaged groups, and effective transfer of political power (USAID, 1998: 11–13). Third, a civil society, in line with classical liberal view, was seen as constituted by organisations that allow for the 'freedom of individuals to associate with like-minded individuals, express their views publicly, openly debate public policy, and petition their government' (USAID, 1998: 15). A vital labour sector was also important to support political and economic liberalisation: 'in the absence of income growth in the labor sector, consumer-market demand stagnates, depriving both in-country commercial producers and US exports of potential markets and thus undermining broad-based economic growth' (USAID, 1998: 16). Finally, good governance principles such as transparency, pluralism, citizen involvement in decision-making, representation, and accountability were seen as essential. Five elements are identified as contributing to good governance: democratic decentralisation, legislative strengthening, governmental integrity, policy implementation, and civil-military relations.

What is interesting is that the 1998 programming handbook seemed to laud the classical liberal political system together with a free-market economy, deregulation and minimum state intervention as organising principles of the economy in developing countries. In contrast, in its 2010 programming handbook, USAID's objectives are different. Specifically, free-market economy is conspicuously absent as a definitional component of democracy. While the political dimension of democratisation is similar to that contained in the 1998 document, it is interesting to note a focus on tackling business practices 'that are exploitative of labor and the environment'. The aim now is to promote broad-based, equitable economic growth, improvement of health through workplace health education and prevention, and gender equality (USAID DCHA/DG, 2010: 53, 57). Such a shift can also be observed in the cooperative agreement *Global Trade Union and NGO Strengthening*, which was awarded by USAID to The Solidarity Center to support anti-sweatshop activities. In addition, the 2010 handbook argues that more transparent and accountable governance must be encouraged, with the government responsible for social peace, law and order, the creation of conditions for economic growth, *and* minimum level of social security (USAID DCHA/DG, 2010: 22).

This shift of emphasis from unabated open economy and limited state to a seemingly more controlled economic development with a clear role for the state as a provider of economic welfare and stability, could pass for a more reform liberal understanding of the relationship between the state and the economy. Superficially, at least, it is in line with Obama's shifts to more reform liberal position.

Yet, again, systematisation of these new ideals leaves something to be desired. First, we must note that the measures we describe all contribute, in USAID discourse, to social stability and effective functioning of open-market societal institutions. They can then be compatible with (neo)liberal policies, and be reflective of a more 'embedded' stability-oriented neoliberal model. Indeed, it is interesting to note that there is no questioning in the documents of USAID of free enterprise and open trade as general organising principles of economic life, despite the concern with stability and sustainability. Also, projects do not seem to translate to very firm concrete policy commitments in systematically 'reform liberal' directions: little attention is now given to new agendas such as development of economic democracy, tighter financial regulation, or greater redistribution of wealth as a condition of 'sustainable democratisation'.

This conclusion is confirmed in the most recent USAID strategy document. Similarly to Obama's and the Department of State's positions, USAID *Policy Framework 2011–2015* locates democracy promotion in the general development strategy of the administration (USAID, 2011a: 24). In the political dimension, USAID concentrates on classical components of liberal democracy: support to civil society in its balancing role to the power of the state, citizen participation, democratic accountability, and civil society support (USAID, 2011a: 26). But the USAID also argues that, when not present, a new social contract between government, civil society and the private sector is necessary. Is this an opening in a reform liberal direction? It does not seem so. While clearly a better dialogue between state and private actors is the end point, the aim of this interaction is not, it seems, increasing the state's role in the private sphere *per se*. While concern with stability of the state and dialogue within the state are central in this initiative, the end goal has not shifted. The core of democracy support of USAID is still considered to be 'traditionally'-focused institutional and civil society work (Interview with Senior State Department Official, 2012).

Again, in implementation methods of USAID, any skepticism of liberal capitalist modes of operation is quickly forgotten. We observe that USAID, much like DRL, is fixated on efficiency and 'return on investment' for aid funding. Two organising principles are central: competition and quantification. These two factors originate in the need to measure the impact of democracy assistance projects and to rationalise aid projects to achieve 'efficiency'. This efficiency entails a procurement process that helps to select the most apt USAID partners, which are defined as viable economic actors, accountable, transparent and having the skills and knowledge necessary to deliver results. While USAID officials show some skepticism of relying purely on for-profit private actors – a tendency which intensified in the Bush years – the procurement policy is clearly in line with a business model understanding of the use of public funds. In light of such a policy, it is unlikely that USAID procurement methods will produce room for new diverse and politico-economically 'alternative' actors, projects or agendas. This is because the procurement process depoliticises the democracy agenda, does not facilitate 'debate' on democracy's meaning in delivery of projects, and continues to privilege technically superior but politically unconnected, poorly committed or inadequately reflective private contractors.

Moreover, USAID's constant reference to the need to buttress the private sector in developing countries, and belief in 'out-sourcing' and private-sector based delivery of public goods at home, leads to a protection of free-market economy as the key principle in democracy support. USAID's Administrator, Rajiv Shah, confirms that the actual rationale for US assistance is above-all instrumental to US growth through markets: 'To win the future, we must continue to reach developing world consumers through innovative business models and targeted assistance, accelerating the peaceful rise of the markets they represent' (Shah, 2011: 6, 10). A politicised critique of open markets, in practice of USAID's democracy support, is thus directly undermined through glorification of the market as a delivery instrument.

US Democracy promotion today: conceptual diversity

The analysis of the US discourses on democracy promotion shows that US democracy promotion is in transition and, partially and unsystematically, undergoing a paradigmatic shift. This shift involves the rejection of regime change in favour of democracy support that is more receptive to political, social and economic realities of developing countries. The shift also translates into the co-existence, or confusing oscillation between, several politico-economic models of democracy in the US discourses on democracy promotion. President Obama lauds a reform liberal model. Yet, the Department of State's discourse sees capitalism and democracy as mutually reinforcing concepts and advocates at best an embedded neoliberal rather than reform liberal orientation. In the case of USAID, the contested nature of concepts like democracy and capitalism is more readily apparent. USAID has broadened its concept of civil society action and good governance by integrating social and economic justice issues, conceiving of a form of social pact between government and people to address socio-economic inequalities. Yet, USAID's latest policy framework and review of procurement and assessment methods still work on the basis of curiously liberal economic rationale, which seems to leave little room for 'critical' redirection of state–democracy–market relationships in US democracy support.

Interestingly, despite the incipient conceptual shifts in understandings of democracy's meaning, the Unites States seems to be unable to move away from a democracy promotion paradigm that puts liberal democracy and free markets at its centre. The existing discourses reveal an incipient return to debate on the exact meaning of liberal democracy and what it means for the state–economy relationship. This explains why classical liberal democracy, neoliberal, reform liberal, and embedded neoliberal ideals, all seem to feature in US discourses on democracy promotion today. Yet, the more the analysis moves from the rhetoric to the practices of democracy assistance, the less this diversity is evident. A closer look at how, what could be termed a 'cosmetic diversity of liberal variants of democracy', plays out in concrete activities of US democracy promotion is the subject of the next section.

Facets of US democracy promotion

We now examine a plurality of facets of US democracy assistance. This is essential to gain greater clarity as to how specific conceptual and ideological inclinations regarding politico-economic models of democracy within the US administration express themselves and influence outcomes. After all, so far we have only examined the general level discourses of US governmental actors involved in democracy support. We now examine examples of US democracy promotion: first, as part of their post-conflict reconstruction efforts, notably the differences in conceptual models which came through in US actions in Japan and Iraq; civil society funding work of the USAID and NED; and, finally, the models of democracy which come through in the work of the United States' Millennium Challenge Corporation (MCC). Examination of these diverse facets of US democracy support gives us, while not a complete view of all US democracy support, a broad sense of how 'models of democracy' thinking in policy frameworks translates to practices of implementation. We can see that while clearly far from conceptually singular practices have taken place, there is a tendency in US democracy support not only to work within the confines of liberal democratic ideals, but also to veer towards a neoliberal interpretation of democracy's meaning.

Reconstruction in Japan and Iraq

In its history, uniquely among 'democracy promoters', the United States has intervened militarily on numerous occasions. In the aftermath of such engagements, in most cases, the United States has then engaged in some sort of politico-economic reconstruction of the target countries (Meernik, 1996; Peceny, 1999; Enterline and Greig, 2008). To gain a sense of how 'models of democracy' emerge from concrete actions in post-conflict reconstruction as practiced by the United States, this section analyses the reconstruction of Japan and Iraq.

In Japan, the democratisation of the political and civil society, and of the economy, was in the 1950s genuine and extensive. The Occupation revised the economic, financial and trade structures, aiming at greater democratisation; the political institutions and the bureaucracy were reformed along democratic lines; a new democratic constitution was written from scratch; Japanese civil society was infused with democratic values and norms; reform of trade unions, education system, religious activities and youth organisations was undertaken. But what model informed this extensive effort?

The democratisation of Japan in the 1950 went – in line with US democracy promotion ideology at the time – further than pushing for a 'minimal' classically liberal procedural model. This was not 'electoralism'. Nor, interestingly, was the democratisation driven by 'neoliberal' ideals of the kind we have learned to expect since the mid-1980s. Led by a generation of F.D. Roosevelt's New Dealers, the democratisation of Japan was first of all a political project, a genuine and vast exercise in democracy engineering that attempted to reach deep in the hearts and minds of the Japanese people. This meant prioritising the political over the economic and subjecting economic liberalisation to concerns of genuine democratisation. Crucially, genuine debate on controls over the economy was facilitated, communist and left-activists were not curtailed and trade unions' role was seen as crucial. Japan's reconstruction in the early years reflected reform liberal ideals, rather than hard and fast 'liberal' economic and political ideals.

Eventually, US policy was to shift away from this position. Indeed, democratisation was put on hold and 'controlled democratisation', with a focus on economic recovery and partial remilitarisation, was instituted. At this point, the Occupation authorities started to orient Japan towards American values and interests too, which in turn included a turn to emphasis on liberal values: liberty of individual and protection of market freedoms. By the end of the Occupation, Japan's institutional landscape was thoroughly liberal.

Despite this 'reverse course', it is interesting to note that the American administration in Japan displayed remarkable flexibility and pragmatism regarding the politico-economic model of democracy that was promoted. The first phase of the Occupation reflected a political project that aimed at the eradication of authoritarianism and 'in-depth' instillation of democratic values and norms in Japanese political and civil society, and in the economy. This translated to the adoption of surprisingly reform liberal or even social democratic ideas of democratisation, including facilitation of strong trade unions and deep-going economic dialogue. The second phase saw the advancement of a more liberal model – in order to re-configure the power of former Japanese political and economic elites, who were more in tune with the US foreign policy objectives of repelling Communist advances in East Asia.

Interestingly, the post-war reconstruction of Iraq was also a two-stage affair: but in the opposite order. Between March 2003 and June 2004 the US-led Coalition Provisional Authority (CPA) led a reconstruction programme that built the structures of a liberal democracy with free markets. But due to lack of progress with ideologically-driven Hayekian liberalisation, the American government shifted its efforts in 2007 to a more pragmatic and conceptually open stance, focused on achieving national reconciliation through economic development and political grass-roots engagement.

From the beginning of the occupation, the democratisation of Iraq has faced two antagonistic trends. Internationally, the US objective to promote democracy in the Middle East through regime change in Iraq sat uneasily with other security-based justifications for intervention: to eliminate Saddam Hussein's weapons of mass destruction (WMDs) and to reduce the threat of international terrorism.[2] To deal with these challenges, in the immediate aftermath of the invasion, the CPA developed a strategic plan comprising four dimensions: security and stability, infrastructure development (to resume the provision of essential services), economic development through liberalisation, and democratisation of the Iraqi state and political society (CPA, 2003: 5).

The democratisation of the country did not benefit from optimal conditions. However, the challenges were arguably aggravated by the two first decisions made by the CPA: the purge of Iraqi political and civil society of Ba'athists and the disbandment of the Iraqi army. These two decisions were highly ideological in the sense that they aimed to eradicate challenges to the political and economic liberalism that the United States intended to impose on Iraq.

Indeed, a hyper-liberal version of democracy was promoted in the first phase of the occupation of Iraq. This was mainly due to two reasons. First, this liberal model, which put emphasis on individual freedoms, representational democratic structures, and minimal state intervention to preserve the private sphere from public encroachment, was perceived as the obvious model, which had worked in Central and Eastern Europe. Second, to promote a minimal model of democracy made sense because it would show that democratisation of the country progressed rapidly. Because of the need to show quick results, liberal democracy seemed to fit the bill: if successful in instituting a constitution, elections and rule of law – the procedural trappings of liberal democracy – the United States could show it had endowed the Iraqi state with democracy before transferring sovereignty to an Iraqi government.

However, the political liberalisation of the country proved far from straightforward. Democratisation in the relative safety of Baghdad progressed more quickly than in the provinces where dire security conditions impeded democracy promotion projects. As a result, centralisation took over decentralisation of power. This meant that, paradoxically, in the provinces traditional power structures were preserved and came to hinder power sharing and genuine representation of all segments of society (Bridoux and Russell, forthcoming). The individualisation of democratic exercise did not happen in Iraq; individuals remained entangled in tribal and sectarian power structures. The local traditional elites acted as a filter of democratic norms and values, which distorted liberalisation on the ground.

As a result, a model of liberal representative democracy and its structures was established in Baghdad but showed its limitations through its inability to adapt to non-Western conditions, made worse by dire security conditions. This lack of flexibility created a hollow shell of democracy (Howard, 2002) in which processes and structures – constitutional process, electoral procedures, rule of law, defence of individual freedoms – allowed liberal democracy to work but were ineffective at forcing the adoption of core democratic norms and values at the grass-roots level.

When the US administration reviewed its reconstruction strategy in Iraq, it was obvious that the original policy, which favoured the military to improve security and stability, was at a dead-end. A new plan, called *The New Way Forward*, was put together in late 2006 to early 2007. On the governance side, a fundamental change took place: G.W. Bush and his advisers reached the conclusion that national reconciliation would not be the product of a nationwide agreement of what Iraq should look like but would come from a long and piecemeal process involving all actors. Thus, a more comprehensive approach to Iraqi problems translated into more grass-roots-based work in the Provinces while the institutionalisation of democracy continued in Baghdad. Alongside the January 2007 *Surge* of military personnel that added 27,000 soldiers in Iraq, *The New Way Forward* focused on the role of Provincial Reconstruction Teams (PRTs) and their role in gaining loyalties of the local population. The objective was to facilitate the support to moderate elements seeking peaceful ways of resolving political differences (SIGIR, 2007: 75; 2008: 81). PRTs worked on four areas: local governance, community action, economic growth, and community stabilisation (USAID, 2007: 1). They implemented local governance programmes that targeted local empowerment to facilitate political decentralisation. In addition to fostering good governance with local officials, the PRTs worked with Iraqi civil society organisations to empower women, deal with youth issues, and advocate work for a democratic and tolerant Iraq (USAID, 2007, 7).

In the second phase, interestingly, the liberal model of democracy co-habited with a more socially attuned and even participatory approach to democratic politics. The need to address the dire economic conditions and political sectarianism that plagued continuously the post-war reconstruction of the country, called for a decentralisation of decision-making. These projects could only achieve success if the local communities were in a position to define their needs, rather than Washington or Baghdad deciding on what specific projects to finance. Here, then, the US democracy support on the ground displayed interesting flexibility in its approach to democratisation and reconstruction. Pragmatic concerns led towards 'reform liberal' engagements with the publics, and even participatory democratic engagements of subjects – partly because neoliberal and classical liberal ideals did not seem to work (Bridoux and Russell, forthcoming).

Yet, this 'instrumental' use of 'alternative' ideas on democracy in the context of the failure of one's own model could not, within the broader (neo)liberal democracy project go very far. The heart of US action in Iraq was still to institute a liberal capitalist state with a liberal representative political system. Any dabbling with alternative models was to be pragmatic only and never to challenge the full vision of liberal democratisation, which the United States continued to push for on the general policy level. The impracticability of the liberal model was realised – yet, arguably, the full lessons remained to be learned. No systematic shift to participatory or social democratic alternative models of democratisation, for example, has resulted from US thinking on post-conflict reconstruction it would seem, despite the strong hints the experience of Iraq gave to policy-makers as to the inadequacy of implementing liberal ideals in places where they do not resonate with local contexts.

USAID and NED support to civil society organisations

In the last 10 years, since the realisation that electoral democracy support only runs risks, US democracy assistance has strongly focused on encouragement of a bottom-up approach, with civil society organisations (CSOs) deemed the most efficient partners in democratisation. As Clinton affirms: 'civil society undergirds both democratic governance and broad-based prosperity' (Clinton, 2010).

Crucially, US democracy promotion sees both a political role and an economic role for civil society. The political role is to create space for citizens to communicate their interests and values to each other and their government. Civil society represents the plurality of views which liberal societies hold, and simultaneously ensures that the government is held accountable and in check. The economic role of civil society, interestingly, consists in contributing to a social climate that is conducive to stability and the creation of conditions friendly to the operations of a free-market economy. Professional organisations, labour unions and business associations all contribute to channelling potential social tensions created within the capitalist economy. This is not all, for in recent years, under the Obama administration, civil society can also play a role in protecting the weakest members of the society: 'without consumer advocates, unions, and social organizations that look out for the needs of societies' weakest members, markets can run wild and fail to generate broad-based prosperity' (Clinton, 2010).

But what kind of models of democracy emerge from US CSO funding? We will start by analysing the USAID, one key actor in civil society assistance. What is crucial to note is that the USAID holds a number of expectations as to the CSOs it works with.

First, civil society must adopt fundamental freedoms as a given and as the basis on which to push for democratic reforms. Hence, CSOs are considered as autonomous and change-inducing actors (USAID, 2011a: 27). Second, civil society is supposed to be autonomous and free from the state's influence, because civil society acts as main counter-balancing force to the power of the state (USAID 2010: 3; Clinton 2011). Third, USAID considers civil society as partner on the same footing as the target state government and is identified by US diplomacy as an 'efficient path to advance foreign policy objectives' (US Department of State 2010a: 59). Civil society thus becomes a partner of choice and is given an ideological role to play: to counter authoritarian governments and help spread liberal democratic values. Fourth, CSOs are expected to be entrepreneurial, economically viable, and competitive actors, thriving to sell their expertise on an open market of funding opportunities.

Indeed, interestingly, USAID profiles itself as a corporate actor, a risk-taking and flexible development entrepreneur that does not consider development and democracy promotion programmes as aid but as an investment in a better future for the United States and the world (USAID, 2011b: 1). Consequently, USAID seeks to boost its partners' capacity, and increase competition between recipients of funding assistance. This focus on competition translates into an obligation for CSOs to have specific skills and knowledge to partner with USAID. Above all, a reliable partner involves economic viability, with CSOs asked to provide 'proof of financial resources to perform the project, or the ability to obtain them', 'projected budget, cash flow, organizational chart, and past performance', and 'applicable policies and procedures' like accounting, personnel, property management, and so on (USAID, 2011b). A CSO must be 'a reliable organization that is respected by its beneficiaries and partners, that delivers on its work, and that handles money appropriately' (USAID, 2011b).

Finally, civil society actors are expected to conform to specific rules and procedures to access funding. USAID's definition of 'partner' from the perspective of compliance is very straightforward:

> A USAID partner is any entity or individual who enters into an agreement with USAID to support the achievement of our foreign assistance goals via our overseas development programs. We expect our development partners to act in the spirit of partnership while delivering effective and sustainable development solutions to the beneficiaries we work with in more than 100 countries worldwide. We expect the USAID partner to take all steps neces-

sary to ensure integrity within their organization, systems and personnel, and to meet the compliance standards of the U.S. government.

(USAID, 2011c)

To this end, USAID recently set up an Oversight and Compliance Division for Partner Performance that is specifically responsible for tracking partners' performances, compliance with US federal regulations and takes appropriate corrective measures if needed. CSOs are thus seen as well-trained, responsible, conscious agents of development that further US development goals on the ground.

USAID's objectives not only reveal specific assumptions about civil society actors and their role in democratisation, but also, arguably, a specific understanding of the democratic state these actors should promote. One trend sees CSOs as an instrument of shifting priorities in the administration's democracy support. Supporting the weak and capacity of the state to deliver for them is now the role of civil society. At the same time, USAID literally contracts CSOs to fulfill this role, rather than empowering the state. Thus, paradoxically, the role of the state is minimised, which is more in line with classical or even neoliberal ideas on the role of the liberal democratic state.

As a result of the procurement system in place in USAID work, far from benefiting from freedom of action, CSOs are captured in a web of administrative and competitive rules that seeks the maximisation of aid investments and the insertion of free-market economy ideas, as essential to multiplying the impact of aid in target countries. It is interesting to note that for all the discourses on democracy – ownership of development and sustainability, a free-market economy and its principles of rationalisation – efficiency, profit-making and risk-taking remain central in democracy support not only as an end in itself, but also as organising principles of how development aid is dispensed (Bridoux, 2011b).

A competitive selection process impacts CSOs, which must bow to efficiency principles that secure the best return on investment for aid donors. CSOs sell their expertise on democracy promotion on a market that is regulated by competition and comparative advantage. Procurement rules based on a business model philosophy condition the way private actors of democracy promotion offer their services, even if the competitive process itself is not rigorous, it would seem, given that key US-based actors tend to win most of the contracts. Indeed, some companies work exclusively for USAID (Interview with representative of a private consulting firm, 2012).

But what about the NED? Do same dynamics play out here? Has this organisation not got more flexibility in its delivery of aid and what does this mean for CSO support it disburses? The National Endowment for Democracy (NED), a bipartisan non-governmental organisation (NGO) funded by the US Congress, was founded in 1983. NED provides funds for civil society organisations, primarily to its four 'mission'-specified institutes: the International Republican Institute (IRI), the National Democratic Institute (NDI), the American Center for International Labor Solidarity (ACILS), and the Center for International Private Enterprise (CIPE). NED's purpose is 'to encourage free and democratic institutions throughout the world through private sector initiative', essentially through non-governmental American participation 'in democratic training programs and democratic institution-building abroad' (American Political Foundation, 1983: 9). NED offers grants to US-based and foreign NGOs to strengthen democratic electoral processes and to reinforce the spread of values, institutions and organisations promoting democratic pluralism.

What is notable about the NED is that its conception of democracy is classically liberal in its formulation. NED counts defining elements as: freedom of choice; freedom of expression, belief and association; pluralism; free and competitive elections; respect for the inalienable rights of individuals and minorities; free communications media; respect for the rule of law; the existence of autonomous economic, political, social and cultural institutions; and a separation between the political and economic dimensions of democracy.[3] While the NED recognises that 'a democratic system may take a variety of forms suited to local needs and traditions, and therefore need not follow the US or any other particular model' (NED, undated), its operating principles clearly prioritise a classical liberal ideal, which moreover separates the economic and the political. Thus, promotion of socio-economic rights, for example, is not what the NED focuses on: it is 'not our thing' (Interview with Barbara Haig, 2012).

But what of the dispensing methods of the NED? Its stated approach to promoting democracy is 'a bottom-up approach to grant-making that empowers the most effective grassroots activists and is responsive to local needs' and adopts 'a global perspective that enables it to show solidarity with *all* those defending democratic values and freedom' (NED, 2012: 2, 7, italics in original). NED is also ready 'to take risks on new groups and innovative projects' (NED, 2012: 7). It specifically hopes to help NGOs that are starting out and may not have structures for project implementation. If the actors seem 'right', the NED will provide help in the process of developing board-passable projects.

But what does NED mean by supporting '*all* those defending democratic values and freedom' and the 'most effective grassroots activists'? Does this mean that NED considers funding organisations that could have an alternative conception of what democracy means? Is NED really ready to risk funding radical democratic actors? Certainly, NED activities indicate that some work on socio-economic rights and democracy, for example, is tolerated (Interview with Barbara Haig). Yet, this only goes so far. Thus, the work of CIPE and Solidarity Centre, for example, should be such that they are not in contradiction with each other. Work on shadow economy by both, for example, is in line with the idea of bringing economic processes into the field of open-market economics (Interview with Barbara Haig, 2012). Little contestation over politico-economic ideology or end points is encouraged, or seems to exist, within the work of NED or its core grantee organisations, including the CIPE and the Solidarity Centre.

Also, a survey of NED's recipients of aid funds shows that NED's partners in 90 countries develop and implement programmes in fields that traditionally pertain to a liberal understanding of democracy. The NGOs financed by NED provide training and technical assistance in the following fields: human rights;

electoral assistance; political parties training; inclusion of youth; strengthening of independent trade unions; development of strong and free media; the rule of law and good governance; fighting corruption; civic education; accountability of local authorities and elected officials to citizens' needs; empowerment of women; enhancement of the representation of women in public life and reinforcement of the representation of ethnic, religious and cultural minorities; and development of citizen's input in policy-making (NED 2010).

Why are NED's partners so inclined in promoting liberal democratic values and processes? Is there not room at all in the selection process for alternative democratic values and institutions? Certainly NED's procurement process, which is less market-based than that of USAID, should allow this. Indeed, while competition for funds exists in NED framework, it is 'assisted' or 'regulated' competition where NED works actively with specific organisations, rather than unleashing the powers of market competition on NGOs. A more politicised and strategic edge exists in NED work. Thus, small NGOs without a solid administrative structure should be able to apply for funding as long as they respect principles of transparency and accountability in their operations, and are happy to work with NED principles and priorities (Interview with Barbara Haig, 2012). Only the CIPE's application process is more specific and clearly identifies business-supporting programme objectives to adhere to (CIPE, undated). NED's more strategic, politicised and directed form of democracy aid holds the hope for a more open kind of democracy support.

Yet, unfortunately, in terms of its guiding conceptualisation of democracy, no such room is actively created, it would seem. In contrast to USAID, no shift in guiding ideology has taken place in the NED conceptualisation of democracy. A classically liberal commitment remains at NED's core, which explains its continued classical liberal orientation.

The dynamic in a sense is the exact opposite of that in the work of USAID then: while USAID works with a conceptually much-shifted mission discourse but on the basis of liberal economic delivery methods which undermine this, the NED works on the basis of an enviably flexible and strategic delivery methods but a narrower mission ideology. In both cases the result is the same: promotion of an unchanged classical/neoliberal democratic ideal.

The Millennium Challenge Corporation

The MCC is an independent foreign aid agency created by the US Congress in 2004 with the aim to fight global poverty. The agency delivers bilateral aid to the world's poorest countries, but only to those committed to good governance, economic freedom, and investment in their citizens. The MCC's criteria of eligibility have democracy at their centre: 'strong democratic institutions are some of the very institutions which enable sustainable, locally owned, positive economic outcomes' (MCC, 2007: ii). Thus, the MCC's aid compacts are conditioned by the acceptance by the recipients of aid to political and economic liberalisation in their societies.

An analysis of the MCC's discourse on the relationship between the economic and political dimensions reveals that democratic institutions are considered as facilitators of the operations of a free-market economy. Indeed, just and democratic governance means: to promote political pluralism, equality and the rule of law; respect to human and civil rights; protection of private property rights; encouragement of transparency and accountability of governments; and combating corruption.

These values and institutions are representative of a neoliberal democratic conception of democracy with a neoliberal edge. Indeed, the MCC encourages its partner countries to develop policies that encourage firms and citizens to embrace and support global trade and international capital markets, to promote private sector growth, to strengthen market forces in the economy, and to respect workers' rights including the right to form labor unions for the sake of social stability, conducive to smooth operations of a market economy (MCC, 2011: 5–6).

The finality of the politico-economic model of democracy promoted by the MCC, then, is 'neoliberal'. This is despite the fact that there are some rhetorical openings suggestive of alternative politico-economic models of democracy at work in the MCC's discourse too. For example, the recommended involvement of stakeholders (government, private sector and citizens) in the definition and the oversight of the implementation of aid contracts, and civic participation in government, are reminiscent of participatory ideals. Yet, these are only light touches within a more generic neoliberal orientation. Indeed, it is important to note that the link between the political and the economic spheres in the MCC's conceptualisation of democracy does *not* involve a degree of control by the state over market forces. On the contrary, the democratisation of the MCC partners translates into the facilitation of the operations of free markets in recipient countries. This is achieved through the erection of a legal framework that preserves social stability: legal framework provides stability and predictability, both indispensable to a smooth working, open economy. Neoliberal concerns dominate the MCC. This surely stands in sharp contrast to Obama administration's priorities in democratisation: the vestiges of Hayekian neoliberal ideas on democracy also continue to play a role in the Obama administration's democracy support.

Conclusion

The United States is a unique democracy promotion actor. Not only is it the first to enter the scene, and hence a trend-setter in important respects in this policy area, it is also unique in that it has been one of the only openly ideologically committed democracy promotion actors worldwide.

For historical reasons, the United States' commitments tend to be liberal democratic in nature. However, some shifts, historically and contemporarily, have taken place in US democracy support activities. It is not a uniform, one-size-fits-all democracy promoter, because the exact meaning of liberal democracy even today (and especially today) remains under some debate or question. As Foley (2007) has highlighted, debate on the relationship between capitalism and democracy continues in US domestic politics, and this is arguably, if very unsystematically, also reflected in shifting discourses in its external democracy support. A more holistic discourse on democracy which ties it to questions of economic justice and inequality is played out today in US policy discourses – especially in the Office of the President and USAID's work. Yet, these developments are contradicted by continued, and often 'technically' or 'implicitly'-justified, promotion of classical and neoliberal ideas in discourses of the US Department of State and USAID itself and in the actual delivery of US democracy support (e.g. through, MCC, USAID and NED). Crucially, the business-driven procurement method which is tied to US democracy support disenables the possibility of politicising US democracy support and conceptualising very far-reaching re-directions of US work away from core liberal democratic and economic ideals.

There is little likelihood then that US democracy support can soon shift towards reform liberal, let alone radical, participatory or socialist models of democracy support: too deeply is a generically liberal democratic discourse embedded within its history and its political, economic, and bureaucratic discourses and structures. Debates are confined: primarily between the liberal versions of liberal democracy.

Nevertheless, it should be noted that a Robinsonian (1996) analysis of US democracy promotion misses essential aspects of its inner workings, crucially, the role of conceptual diversity and oscillation within generically liberal democratic commitments. This new reading advanced here reveals not only the consistencies, but also the contradictions, and potentials for debate, contestation and redirection, in US democracy support.

8   The European Union

A fuzzy liberal democracy promoter

> The USA tends to use more procedural and liberal definitions of democracy in
> its policy-making, while Europe, because of its history and its development of a
> welfare state, develops policy that is more in line with the definition of substantive
> democracy.
>
> (Landman, 2009: 7)

The European Union (EU) is an important new foreign policy actor. Its role in trade
and global multilateral financial order has in recent years been complemented by
a concerted effort to act as a foreign policy voice of a coherent kind. Not only has
the EU sought to render consistent its external policy in the aftermath of the various crises in the Balkans and Iraq, but also it has sought to elevate its role in global
affairs across policy sectors – from military and defence policy and peacekeeping,
to development, human rights and democracy promotion. The effort to create the
so-called European External Action Service (EEAS), a structural reform called for
in the Lisbon Treaty, has galvanised the hopes of many EU politicians and policy-
makers for a more visible, coherent, and active transmission of European power
and principles on the international scene.

But what kind of democracy promotion does the EU engage in, and more specifically, what kind of model of democracy does the EU advance? This is a rather
more complex question than one might expect.

While much academic debate has taken place in recent years over how to
understand the EU's role in external democracy promotion (see e.g. Youngs,
2001, 2003, 2008a, 2008b, 2009; Santiso, 2003; Kelley, 2006; Manners, 2006,
2008; Sjursen, 2006; Aggestam, 2008; Barbe and Johansen, 2008; Bicchi, 2006;
Crawford, 2008; Hyde-Price, 2008; Pace, 2010; Wetzel and Orbie, 2011) and
many studies have been written on the effectiveness of EU democracy promotion (Schimmelfennig and Scholtz, 2008; Lavenex and Schimmelfennig, 2010;
Youngs, 2010), the conceptual framings of the EU approach are still unclear.
Many commentators have pointed to the contradictory and paradoxical characteristics of EU democracy promotion (Santiso, 2003; Raik, 2004; Pace, 2009;
Youngs, 2010) and a few have specifically commented on the curious conceptions of democracy in EU discourses (Pridham, 2005; Kochenov, 2007; Manners,

2008; Pace, 2009, 2010; Wetzel and Orbie 2011; Reynarts, 2011). Pridham (2005) and Kochenov (2007), for example, have highlighted the distinct vagueness and unspecificity of the EU's conception of democracy. Manners (2008), Youngs (2011a), and Pace (2009) on the other hand, have emphasised the fact that there are indications that, at least potentially, the EU goes beyond the promotion of 'liberal democracy' in its democracy support. As Landman (2009) too highlights, the EU seems to have the willingness to be a more 'substantive' democracy supporter than the United States. Some authors remain optimistic, then, that the EU can represent a more attuned, socially just, and diversity-accommodating actor in world politics (Jacoby and Meunier, 2009).

Such hopes are certainly supported by the pluralistic and socially attuned rhetoric of the EU. Yet, what this amounts to exactly is unclear. Thus, Wetzel and Orbie (2011), for example, identify the EU as essentially a liberal democratic actor in democracy promotion as do other commentators on EU foreign policy (Tsoukalis, 2003; Smith, 2008; McCann, 2010). Reynaerts (2011) and Hurt, Knio and Ryner (2010), on the other hand, point to essentially neoliberal policies at the heart of EU democracy support, as has some of my own work (Kurki, 2011b).

In the light of these different perspectives, what are we to make of EU democracy support? Has it moved beyond the US focus on liberal democracy to some sort of post-liberal democracy support, or is there a unique European social model on offer here? Or does the EU really promote '27 models of democracy' as practitioners believe?

I argue here that in some regards the EU goes further than the United States in extending debate on democracy's meaning through a somewhat more pluralistic, or at least fuzzy, discourse on democracy. Yet, it also fails to deliver on this incipient pluralism. I argue that the EU, then, is not just a liberal-democratic democracy promoter, or a social democratic actor, but a very specific kind of liberal democracy promoter – a 'fuzzy' liberal democracy promoter. Rather than setting out a clear set of principles in terms of what kind of democracy it promotes – pluralistic or otherwise – the EU, I argue, *fudges* the question of what kind of democracy it promotes. This leads to curious tendencies in EU democracy support. On the one hand, democracy can be recognised to be a contested concept (see e.g. European Commission, 2006a) and various slight differences of focus are allowed in EU democracy support – from Trade DG's promotion of neoliberalism to DG Development's exploration of reform liberal, social democratic and participatory values. On the other hand, EU discourse, despite its seeming pluralism, also reduces any substantive political or ideological debate over democracy and introduces technocratic tendencies to EU democracy support: while seeming pluralism exists, a technocratic 'implicit' liberalism delimits pluralism characteristic of the EU's fuzzy discourses.

These tendencies structure how alternative models are engaged with. Despite seeming to lean towards reform liberalism, social democracy or even participatory democracy at times, the actual practice of EU discourses de-radicalises such alternatives and promotes them, if it does at all, as secondary to an essentially 'liberal' and often technocratically neoliberal set of commitments.

Study of the concrete facets of EU democracy support confirms this. When we examine case studies of EU democracy support, we find that both fuzzy 'diversity-accommodation' and far more rigid technocratic logics play out in them.

I do not here suggest that the EU's democracy promotion is singular or has a single set of interests or drivers at its heart. Indeed, I argue that it is very important to note the structurally determined nature of EU's fuzzy liberalism: it emerges from the context of politico-economic demands, bureaucratic complexity and political pluralism of the actor. Yet, the limitations of fuzzy liberal democracy promotion have to be taken seriously, despite the fact that there is some potential here for alternative, more consistent and persuasive, conceptual redirections too in such a conceptual system.

This chapter begins with a run-through of the core documents of EU democracy promotion. This is where the contours of fuzzy liberalism are set out. I then analyse the different ways in which fuzzy liberalism plays out in different sectors of the EU's democracy support: (1) its electoral and parliamentary support, (2) its civil society support, (3) its neighbourhood policies and (4) its democracy promotion through trade policy. I conclude with a substantive analytical section which reflects on the structure, functions and power political consequences of the EU's 'fuzzy liberalism' in democracy promotion.

Conceptions of democracy in EU democracy promotion discourse

History of EU democracy support

Democracy promotion is a relatively new project for the EU. It was only really taken up in formal terms in the mid-1990s as part of the EU's attempt to build a role for itself as a significant international actor. In its search for increased legitimacy in the eyes of both the general public in EU countries and external actors, the EU started to develop a variety of policy instruments to facilitate democracy in third countries.[1]

The idea of democracy has of course been at the heart of the EU's discourses since the 1950s. This is partly because membership of the EU has been conditional upon democratic principles being practiced. The Copenhagen Criteria attached to enlargement codified this, and through the enlargement policy the EU has, even before democracy promotion's adoption as a policy instrument, been an important democracy promoter in its local neighbourhood (Pridham, 2005). This is despite the fact that, paradoxically, even the requirements of the *acquis* have not always been very democratically pushed through in applicant states (Raik, 2004).

I am not concerned here with enlargement policy, however, but the role of democracy support beyond this, in EU 'foreign policy'. What is the role of democracy support there? While the EU was slow to get involved in this agenda, by mid-2000s it has amassed an impressive array of declarations and instruments on democracy (see e.g. European Commission, 1995, 1998; 2001; 2003; 2004a, 2004b; 2005b; 2006a, 2006b, 2006c, 2006d, 2007a, 2008, 2009, 2010a, 2010b, 2010c, 2011a, 2011b; European Community, 2006; Council of the European

Union, 2009). It has developed a rather distinctive approach in that it has focused on setting out a 'positive' approach which involves active but positive external assistance to democracy. This approach, further, has gone hand in hand with a rather unusual 'mainstreaming' of the idea of democracy across policy sectors. Unlike in the United States, where the democracy sector is predominantly in the hands of the Bureau of Democracy, Human Rights and Labor (DRL) and United States Agency for International Development (USAID), in the EU structures, Trade, Development, Enlargement Directorate Generals as well as the newly formed foreign affairs services (nowadays EEAS) deal with democracy-enhancing instruments.

But what model of democracy does the EU promote? This is a very complex question; far more so than in the (already surprisingly complex) case of the United States. To gain a general orientation, let us first examine in detail the conceptual leanings evident in the EU's core declarations and strategy papers on democracy promotion.

Conceptions of democracy in EU documentation

The European Commission's 1995 declaration, which first instituted the democracy and human rights agenda into the EU scene, provides the first explicit statements of the EU's intentions in the sphere of democracy promotion. It sets out the 'positive approach' that the EU is to take to the promotion of these values and sets out its move towards inclusion of essential elements clauses to the EU's co-operation and development agreements, including the penalties and positive incentives that can be provided in support of democracy. It calls for greater 'consistency, transparency and visibility of community approach' and greater 'sensitivity' to the perspectives of third countries (European Commission, 1995: 3). But how is democracy conceived?

Interestingly, in defining democracy the document is remarkably vague or undefined in nature. Indeed, despite seeking to provide a contractual basis for better democracy and human rights policy, curiously no definition of democracy is offered in this document. The declaration is simply concerned with the addition of 'democratic principles and human rights' into co-operation agreements.

The final page of the document provides a 'key' to how various policy communities or treaties have conceived of democracy – various references on human rights and democracy policy are listed from Helsinki final act, to Charter of Paris – and links democracy to 'pluralism and free and democratic elections'. Yet, beyond this no normative position is specified on democracy. This 'key' provides a poorly determined and somewhat confusing set of reference points for a reader seeking to decipher the meaning of democracy in EU discourse. Crucially, while it links democracy to (neo) liberal preference for economic freedoms, it does so in an unsystematic and *ad hoc* manner, and provides a meagre set of reference points for identification of any distinct conceptual model elements – whether liberal, social democratic or participatory. What can be deciphered is that democracy is attached in a loose manner to concepts such as freedom, equality, justice and, in one instance, to the development of rights and democracy in the context of 'economic freedom'. No specific value hierarchies are specified and no clear model of democracy emerges from this document – liberal or otherwise.

Yet, the following agreements on democracy promotion provide more 'conceptual meat' to the concept of democracy.

The 2001 communication from the European Commission on the EU's role in promoting human rights and democratisation provided some crucial conceptual clarifications. The aim of this document was to bring to light problems of EU democracy promotion, to refocus EU human rights and democracy strategies, and 'ensure that these issues permeate all Community policies, programmes and projects' (European Commission, 2001: 3). It placed great emphasis on improving the coherence of EU action and elevating the priority ranking of human rights and democracy promotion in EU policy hierarchies, as well as calling forth the new civil society-focused democracy assistance instrument, namely the European Initiative (now Instrument) for Democracy and Human Rights (EIDHR) (European Commission, 2001: 5). But how is democracy defined in this new era of democracy mainstreaming?

Again, no direct effort is made to define in a focused way what democracy means. Instead the meaning of the concept is implied through references to other principles, institutions and documents. Yet, a clearer sense of principles to which democracy is attached can be gained here. It could be argued that a core reference point to the meaning of democracy is given by the reference to the Union's *Charter of Fundamental Freedoms* (European Community, 2000). EU democracy promotion is to work with a belief in these principles and these principles are seen as tied to the idea of democracy, as a core value of the Union. If this is what the EU promotes, it is worth examining these principles in more detail.

The EU's charter of rights (European Community, 2000) defines the Union's core principles as the following 'indivisible, universal values of human dignity': dignity, freedom, equality, solidarity, citizen's rights and justice. These principles are, at their core, classically liberal in nature. Thus, the emphasis is on inviolability of the freedoms of the individual. As the document declares: the EU's fundamental rights place the individual at the heart of its activities (European Community, 2000). It is defence of individual freedoms of consciousness, association and information that are central, as are procedural notions of equality between citizens and before law, as well as gender equality. Democracy as a notion is attached primarily to electoral and judicial equality and, thus, the model of democracy that emerges is by and large in line with the classical liberal notion.

Yet, it is interesting to note that the Charter, exceeding many other such charters, also explicitly recognises solidarity as a key aim and also explicitly discusses the rights of labour and demonstration (European Community, 2000). There is, besides rights of individuals, also a clear recognition of communal interests and rights. This is in line with a reform liberal ethos. Although the document stops short of advocating full 'dual-track' social democracy, the concerns of reform liberals with regard to communal context of individual's rights are recognised here.

The 2001 document is not only significant in providing the charter of fundamental rights as a key reference point of how to define democracy in EU democracy promotion. It is also important in fleshing out some strategic focal points of EU democracy promotion. These are indicative of some interesting conceptual leanings too, and hence worth a mention.

First, it is important to note that the document emphasises important strategic concerns which the EU's democracy promotion is now adopting. The EU's strategic interest centrally is in promoting liberal democratic governance: *democratic elections and human rights and freedoms*. This indicates a classically liberal orientation, in line with Schumpeterian foci.

However, that is not all. References to trade policy emphasise the need for *trade unions'* role to be recognised in democratisation (European Commission, 2001: 8). Their rights are clearly seen as important in the context of democracy and human rights promotion, and all these things are now considered as a key in terms of 'poverty reduction'. The exact relationships between these things and the notion of democracy are not defined, but the interest in poverty, labour standards and need to recognise trade as an aspect of democratisation, indicate an awareness of economic context and conditions for democratisation.

Nevertheless, it would seem that the priorities are still of a 'reform liberal' kind at best: while liberal democratic in their core, they go beyond classical liberalism in tentative ways only, and fail to extend to a full conceptual shift indicative of social democracy, let alone socialist, radical democratic or participatory models. The core activity envisioned for the new EIDHR, for example, revolves around the defence of classical liberal ideals of equality of participation, development of pluralist political process, free media, justice system, rights of association and assembly, and electoral processes (European Commission 2001: 16).

The 2006 declaration on financing of EU democracy promotion procedures also places clear emphasis on what seems to be a classically liberal democratic model. This paper (European Commission, 2006c) repeats that the Union is based on principles of liberty, democracy, human rights, fundamental freedoms and rule of law. These are classically liberal sets of priorities, and are *not* discussed in conjunction with prioritisation of equality, solidarity or justice. Indeed, a classical democratic model emerges from this document, one in which, even though questions of justice are referred to, these are seen as secondary concepts to the notion of liberty and representative democracy. In a classically liberal style, democracy, human rights and liberties, democratic controls and separation of powers, alongside rule of law, are seen as essential to each other. They are linked in meaning and sustain the core meaning of democracy (European Commission, 2006c: 2). Civil society is accorded a role too, but is conceived in line with liberal democratic principles, as a check to the state (2006c: 2).

In Article 2 (2: 1.a.vi.) reference is made to equal participation of women and men, and also to promotion of core labour standards and corporate responsibility, (2:1.b.vii), yet these references are clearly not central, or one might even argue of peripheral character, to the core principle of liberty and are placed alongside other minor concerns, such as right to education. Indeed, in democracy promotion efforts focus is on maintenance of core human rights and electoral observations, alongside international co-operation efforts in these spheres. Questions of social justice, poverty reduction, equality of the socio-economic kind, or principles of solidarity are not core concepts here, but at best adjacent ones. And acceptance of core labour standards and corporate responsibility is as far as recognition of alternative agendas goes.

This tendency is arguably repeated in the EU's Neighbourhood Policy (ENP) documents (e.g. European Commission, 2004a). Here emphasis tends to be on highlighting core liberal democratic and liberal economic principles as the Union's core values, and as such the values that are to serve as the basis for 'shared values' in the neighbourhood. Trade union rights and core labour standards are recognised as linked issues; social dialogue and working conditions are a concern, but no systematic effort to drive reform liberalism or social democracy is apparent. In fact, the discourse seems to even suggest a neoliberal set of concerns with the economy as central: the ENP process is concerned with 'investment climate, excessive regulation, property rights and improved market access to public procurement' (European Commission, 2004a: 16; see later section on ENP and Ukraine for more detail).

However, interesting developments were to take place in EU discourse on democracy with the 2003 government and development communication (European Commission, 2003), and following it, the European Consensus on Development (European Community, 2006). These documents both placed poverty reduction and locally generated development at the centre of EU's development policies, and, crucially, linked democracy and human rights policies to this agenda. As a result, an interesting move away from the classical liberal model took place. There was now an increased recognition of *socio-economic* agendas as a key context for and a site of interaction of democratisation and human rights agendas. The social dimension of globalisation and the decent work agenda are tied to the democracy and development agenda (European Community, 2006), while this agenda is simultaneously tied to the agenda of international organisations, including the Poverty Reduction Programmes of the World Bank (European Community, 2006: 14). While being far from ambitious in tone, there is a clear shift in this document from prioritisation of classical or neoliberal concerns to the recognition of the importance of socio-economic development, justice and poverty reduction as a condition of good democratisation. This is suggestive, if not of a systematic shift towards social democracy, of the kinds of concerns that have exercised social democrats and reform liberals.

But this confuses the picture: what on earth does the EU stand for in its democracy support? Multiple models seem to be at play here, though none is clearly defined or delineated.

Interestingly, the latest EIDHR policy documentation (European Commission, 2010d) clarifies the linkages between different value hierarchies and thus models of democracy in EU democracy support in productive ways. The EIDHR, as the EU's main focused democracy instrument, has an important role in investing funds in grass-roots civil society activities and also has been an important point for reflection on the meaning of democracy. Thus, noticeably, the 2006 EIDHR strategy document (European Commission, 2006a) was responsible for the recognition of, by democracy promoters' standards rather astounding admission, that democracy is a multifaceted and contested idea. This was an important admission, even though it was quickly undermined by the very same document going on to define what democracy 'actually' consisted of – on classically liberal lines. The latest EIDHR strategy paper is even more interesting. It shows important shifts in EU's democracy promotion policy away from a classical liberal point of view towards a more socio-economically geared, if somewhat confused, conceptual principles on democracy.

The latest strategy document (European Commission, 2010d) reflects on the findings that have been made on the basis of the EIDHR's first few years of activity as well as the general challenges of democracy and human rights promotion and what this means for its activities. In so doing, it seeks to build on the trends and objectives of the EU's new development policy as well as ensuring complementarity of action with other instruments, neighbourhood policy and stabilisation instruments. Three key developments emerge in the latest strategy document. Two of these – shift towards recognition of post-conflict environments and shift towards building global and transnational alliances – are marginal to our concerns here. But another key shift is important for us, namely the shift towards recognition of social, cultural and economic rights.

What is interesting is that, despite the document assuring that the recent global economic crisis has not affected the EIDHR's activities in any substantial way, the EIDHR has made a concerted effort to integrate social, cultural and economic rights into the objectives. Objectives 1 and 2, especially, which used to be more classically liberal in nature, now clearly emphasise the need to focus on trade union rights, core labour rights, defence of socio-economic opportunities and engagement with vulnerable groups.

There is also recognition of the consequences of financial crisis and the need for a 'socio-economic approach' (European Commission, 2010d: 2). Recognition of Western states' internal weaknesses is also present (European Commission, 2010d: 7). This document opens up room for the EU to act as a far more 'socially', critically minded and politico-economically attuned actor in democracy promotion.

Yet, even so, we must also note that calls for better dialogue on democracy promotion still tend to revolve around instigating better management cycles, monitoring of projects and more flexible funding instruments. Despite the powerful rhetorical argument for socio-economic human rights and democracy promotion, much of the document (European Commission, 2010d) is concerned with improvement of technical detail of democracy aid delivery. Importantly, no politicised or systematic shift to fully blown social democracy, or even reform liberal concerns, is instigated; despite the fact that the language used indicates clear openness to such perspectives.

Similar concerns with 'socio-economic' matters are also reflected in the very latest adjustments to EU democracy support in the aftermath of the Arab Spring. The revised ENP policy has explicitly moved in its promotion of democracy to promotion not of 'democracy' only, but rather 'deep democracy' (EEAS/

European Commission, 2011). This means facilitation of liberal political systems and civil conditions and military–civilian relationships which facilitate sustainable democracy. The EU's concern with deep democracy also clearly goes with concern for economic reforms and labour conditions in the Middle East. Support to deep democracy is not just about institutions and elections but about holistic reform of societies' economic, civic, cultural and political structures.

In this context, however, we get a distinct, and again different, view of the socio-economic possibilities. In ENP documentation there is clear interest in two additional aspects besides concern with social and economic rights: concern for the stability of the countries concerned, and liberalisation of economic prospects of the target countries. Here then a more socio-economically attuned approach mingles with arguably embedded neoliberal tendencies. In terms of ideas on democracy, a rather classical liberal democratic core remains too, viz. the idea of 'deep democracy'. The EU does not make socio-economic equality the heart of efforts to structure a state's democracy (say, dual track democracy). Rather, the EU seeks to make democracy promotion more attuned to challenges which economic inequalities can raise to achievement of liberties in communities. The success of democratisation, and the success of economic reform, depends on this. Crucially, there is very meagre *value-based* commitment to reform liberal or social democratic concerns. An embedded neoliberal model would seem to be the closest ideal type relevant here.

Fuzzy liberalism

As we have seen, the EU's democracy support discourse is confused and wide-ranging. The EU discourse of democracy is so under-determined that it can provide grounding for various ideals of democracy – classical, neoliberal, reform liberal or even incipiently social democratic ideas. At the same time, pluralistic principles about the contested nature of democracy are also explicitly accepted, albeit rather superficially.

Where does this leave EU democracy support? Rather confused and, for want of a better word, 'fuzzy'. Not only are practitioners advancing, simultaneously, various somewhat differently oriented democratic conceptions, but also the pluralistic beliefs in the EU being a unique promoter of '27 different models of democracy' is accepted by many officials (Interviews with EEAS and European Commission Officials). Yet, this pluralistic picture seems to also give way to prioritisation of EU as a primarily liberal actor, if a different type of actor vis-à-vis the United States.

In the context of the confused conceptual underpinnings of EU democracy support it is not surprising that practices are confused or unclear. Indeed, while moving away from clearly or rigidly liberal democratic ideals, at present the EU is not explicitly developing any clear 'alternative' models to classical and neoliberal democratic ideals.

Moreover, as the latest Council statement confirms, there is also a distinct lack of interest in the EU towards developing conceptual coherence for EU democracy support: it is argued that there is no need for the EU to 'renegotiate existing norms, values and central principles as to what constitutes the building blocks of democracy, nor set out new policies' (Council of the European Union, 2009: 2). The focus is squarely on improving the implementation of existing policies.

This is an interesting conclusion for it recognises neither the shifts in EU policy on meaning of democracy, nor the potential conflicts of definition between liberal, reform liberal and incipient social democratic ideals. While policy coherence is the aim, conceptual or ideological coherence, it would seem, is not deemed necessary to achieve this. This is a striking – if not surprising – conclusion for the Council to draw, and reinforces the tendency within the EU democracy promotion system to elude conceptual concerns but also questions of ideology and political commitment. As a result engagement with hidden ideological and power-political conceptual leanings that might be present within its own approach is sidestepped. The OPPD's recent (2009) report arguably demonstrated exactly this disinterest in exploring definitions of democracy of a unique kind and their ideological leanings and consequences.

But how, then, is this fuzziness played out in practice? To gain a clearer picture of the ways in which conceptual fuzziness is played out in concrete democracy promotion activities of the EU, I examine in the next section a plurality of different facets of EU democracy support. While different facets of EU democracy promotion demonstrate that a variety of slightly different forms of democratic ideals can be at work in the EU's actions, deep-running 'implicit liberalism' also underpins the EU's democracy promotion activities, as we shall see. The EU's ideological basis, while fuzzy and incoherent (or pluralistic), is in some regards and at the same time, surprisingly coherent and (implicitly) 'confined'.

Facets of EU democracy support

In the previous chapter we observed the multiplicity of actors and instruments at work in US democracy support, and the somewhat different discursive and conceptual orientations of their work. The fuzziness of EU discourse is likely to exacerbate the diversity of activities. Indeed, it is important to note that in the EU there is no one actor that promotes democracy but a plurality of actors that are connected with each other in more and less 'loose ways'. Here I will examine briefly four facets of EU democracy support: (1) its more traditional work on electoral and parliamentary systems; (2) its support to civil society organisations (CSOs) through EIDHR; (3) its actions through the ENP, in the case of Ukraine; and (4) its democracy promotion through trade policy.

An interesting picture emerges from such a study. I will argue that, paradoxically (vis-à-vis much critical literature), it is in the EU's traditional procedural and institutional work that it promotes, most effectively, 'neutral' or potentially pluralistic models of (liberal) democracy. Indeed, especially its electoral assistance projects are commendable for their attentiveness – within limits – to fostering a plurality of ways of engaging with the idea of democracy. However, as will be seen, in its more 'substantive' work, from CSO support to neighbourhood and trade policy, far less pluralistic and in fact strongly neoliberal ideological leanings on democracy, I argue, start seeping through the EU's fuzzy liberalism. It is also notable that these cases demonstrate the strong leanings towards neoliberal and embedded neoliberal tendencies rather than social democracy support in EU democracy promotion.

Electoral and parliamentary support

Proceduralism is, following Schumpeter, often associated with obsession with elections. Yet, procedural interests of democracy promoters today are rather broad: they involve interest in constitutions, and structure of the legal system, the party system and even civil society in so far as it contributes to institutional stability and efficient functioning of executive, legislative and electoral processes. This section will examine the EU's activities in relation to 'procedural' democracy promotion: notably its electoral assistance work and its parliamentary support. These are examined because the EU has historically paid close attention to this sphere of work (see e.g. Kopstein, 2006). Electoral assistance was arguably the earliest step in the EU developing its 'democracy promotion' activities. Providing concrete support for planning, resourcing and monitoring elections was considered a concrete, but also fairly technical and neutral, way of supporting democratic governance at EU borders and beyond. Significant resources then have been placed, within various instruments, to facilitation of electoral assistance and monitoring by the ENP, the Development Co-operation Instrument, and perhaps most notably, the EIDHR (European Commission, 2006a). Parliamentary support is an emerging area but equally important as a site of facilitation of democratisation.

Electoral support

Although electoral assistance programmes have been criticised by some academics and commentators (see e.g. Carothers and Ottaway, 2005), the EU has, arguably, developed a sophisticated, reflexive and contextually responsive approach to electoral assistance and monitoring. Indeed, the EC's latest 'Methodological Guide on Electoral Assistance' (European Commission, 2006d) provides not only a comprehensive but also a reflectively engendered, dynamic framework for electoral assistance. The EU has moved away from narrow 'event-only' approach to electoral assistance and now aims to provide assistance throughout the electoral cycle; also, at the point of post-election legal reform, it has developed a variety of different funding modalities through which to provide support: from traditional project funding, to pooled funding and budget support (European Commission, 2006d).

But what does the EU do in electoral assistance and what politico-economic models are facilitated in such support? It is notable that the EU places great emphasis on neutrality of action in its electoral support and explicitly avoids any form of intervention which may be interpreted as partisan or biased. Objectivity, neutrality and impartiality form the core of the EU's actions in this area.

This focus on neutrality might be interpreted to mean that the EU ignores the politics of electioneering, that it does not recognise that being involved in structuring the electoral systems and procedures of third countries is a deeply political activity. Yet, interestingly, the EU's latest guidance shows a relatively sophisticated understanding of the political contestation involved in this area. The politics of polling systems, border drawing and electoral systems are openly recognised, for example: this is why the EU tries to ensure that local decision-makers make decisions on such issues, and that the EU's involvement in any such decisions is minimal (European Commission, 2006d: 25). The Commission also recognises the need to include a variety of different kinds of political actors in the political system; and not simply the obvious 'friends' of the EU or the West (2006d: 75). In so doing, the EU tries hard not to negate the politics of election assistance but tries to explicitly minimise its involvement in advocacy of specific systems which may benefit some groups over others. Also, although electoral support is known and recognised to be a 'highly technical area' this 'should not cloud the fact that an election is above all a political event' (European Commission, 2006d: 31).

As regards accusations that non-governmental organisations (NGOs) are sidelined in electoral support, this is a wrong-headed accusation, too, vis-à-vis today's EU electoral assistance practices. NGOs, in fact, play a crucial role in electoral assistance. Numerous projects are funded seeking closer co-operation, monitoring and facilitation roles for NGOs in the electoral cycle (European Commission, 2006d). While NGOs in this context are perceived of as relatively 'functional'; that is, in the context of what they can do to ensure efficient functioning of elections, they are included extensively in plans for electoral assistance.

But are there specific politico-economic preferences in the electoral assistance system? This is an interesting question for arguably the EC's electoral assistance support, far from being un-reflexively biased towards *a narrow* liberal democratic view which would prioritise a capitalist elite structure (Robinson, 1996), is perhaps among the most explicitly self-reflective and 'politics aware' of all of the EU's assistance activities. This is because the EU seeks through its electoral support to ensure support for all parties and constituencies – radical, left as well as liberal – and explicitly does not seek to advocate a specific politico-economic model, or an electoral system which would benefit liberal economic elites, in its electoral assistance. This is, paradoxically, while the work in electoral support clearly does take place within an area of activity at the centre of a 'procedural' framework of thinking about democracy. Curiously, then, proceduralism is *not* necessarily a key threat to plurality of politico-economic models of democracy in EU democracy support. While the EU *promotes* liberal democracy (and not other models), such support is in and of itself *not anti-thetical* to the promotion of other models (see also Chapters 3–5). Neither, so it seems, is parliamentary support by the EU, while also focused on promotion of a fairly limited supposedly liberal democratic institutional model.

Parliamentary support

Parliamentary support is of course a much more controversial area of intervention than election planning; for it involves support to parties and hence partisan leanings of a kind that may be easily judged as a form of bias. Yet, here too the EU's actions are far more pluralistic and supportive of alternative possibilities than is often recognised by critical literature. Far from supporting merely liberal elites or parties, the point of EU's recent parliamentary support is to provide support to all parties, including those in opposition or those too small to be able to effectively challenge well-funded hegemonic parties. Political leanings are not used as criteria for support; and if nothing else, there is a general preference in the support provided for somewhat more marginal parties, these often including left or radical parties. Indeed, evidence shows that the EU's parliamentary support is actually rather sophisticated in nature and is about improving the efficiency of parliamentary systems.

Yet, in parliamentary support two minor ideological biases creep in, which we must note. First, there is an association made in the documentation between open democracies and open liberal market economies (European Commission, 2010b). It is stated that liberal market economy provides a key condition for open parliamentary activity: for it opens systems based on state control of resources to better scrutiny. This association is curious and rather surprising given the otherwise non-committal tone of the EU's work in the parliamentary support area. Yet, the fact that this assumption 'slips' into the discussion is far from surprising: self-evidence of such notions, as we will come to see, is a widespread tendency in EU democracy support in other areas.

A second bias which emerges from the documentation concerns the way in which participatory democracy is discussed within it. The EU's document on parliamentary assistance makes a point about highlighting the need for participatory as well as representative aspects of parliamentary work (European Commission, 2010b). Yet, on closer analysis, it is clear that the conception of participation here is very narrow in nature, having been reduced to consultation of people's views through referenda and civil society's role in effectively monitoring and pressuring parliaments. The original radical agenda of participatory democrats is *not* present here: there is no push for extended and politico-economically grounded forms of participatory politics. Rather, the participatory democracy notion is taken on as a rhetorical move, which both gives an added justification to parliaments' roles vis-à-vis the traditional 'liberal' representative functions, but also, arguably, simultaneously dismisses any more radical views of this notion.

Despite these biases, we must acknowledge that the EU's parliamentary support, as with its electoral support, is rather reflective of the need to defend and keep open multiple views on democracy, on politico-economic alternatives, and electoral and parliamentary systems.

The EU, it follows, tries to the best of its ability not to guide the electoral or parliamentary reforms but asks local 'buyers-in' to do so. At the same time, it recognises the contextuality of any action, including the fact that on many occasions it may be better for the EU not to take action than to do so. While talk of local ownership is cheap in development policy today, as many critics have shown (Cooke and Kothari, 2001), strangely, in its electoral and parliamentary work – because of the potential political explosiveness of work in this area and the visibility of the

EU's expertise nationally and internationally – the EU has made an especial effort to remain attuned to the plurality of political and economic perspectives.

It is true that the contestability of democracy's meaning is not openly recognised, and hence the self-evidence of the core liberal institutional modes is not critically reflected on. It is also true that despite some fairly knowledgeable reflections on democracy's various forms and structures, a 'checklist' approach (albeit a non-quantitative, 'reflexive' one) is adopted. Yet, despite the generally 'liberal democratic' structure of electoral work and the minor slippages towards a somewhat more 'ideological' association of democracy with elections and parliaments and liberal economies, this democracy support leaves, potentially at least, room for critical non-liberal actors too – important to consider when we remember that advocacy of liberal democracy is not an anathema for extra-liberal democratic actors *per se* despite their more extensive visions.

Yet, this is not the end of the story: the pluralist qualities of EU democracy support may be, and indeed are, undermined in other non-procedural policy areas.

Civil society support: the EIDHR

The aim of the EIDHR is to fund civil society organisations in the area of democratisation and human rights. The EIDHR, much like USAID and National Endowment for Democracy (NED) in the United States, aims to 'defend the defenders' of democracy and human rights. The idea is that local actors own and direct their activity, while the EU (co-)funds their projects. The aim is then not to dictate to actors, but rather to open room for grass-roots engagement in local contexts by CSO actors.

The budget of the EIDHR is not substantial but significant. It receives around 1.104 billion Euros per financial period (2007–2013) to be distributed between NGO projects. The funding is administered through the EuropeAid Co-operation office, although decisions on project funding rest in most instances with Country Delegations, which also are in charge of (in reference to generic EuropeAid guidance and documentation) of setting out the calls for proposals for EIDHR funding.

But how well does the EIDHR live up to the promise of open-ended, pluralistic democracy support through civil society funding? And what kinds of democracy-enhancing activities does the EIDHR envisage itself funding? Are there conceptual biases in the kinds of democracy-enhancing CSOs that are funded?

Formally, documents (European Commission, 2006a, 2010d) and also staff working on EIDHR administration (Interviews with European Commission Official, 2011) assure us that there is no political, economic or partisan bias in the kind of funding the EIDHR grants. The funding, first, is conducted on a calls-for-proposal basis, not on the basis of partisan, interest-based or ideological alliances. This enforces competitive applications from civil society actors, on the basis of which country delegations or EuropeAid staff make decisions on how well CSOs meet the criteria of the EIDHR objectives and how well the projects are conceived and measures of success elaborated. It would seem that all CSOs can and should turn to EIDHR funding, and can moreover receive help from the EIDHR, delegation staff or appropriate other bodies in making the applications. No overt political or partisan bias is acknowledged and the plurality of NGO activity and foci is accepted (Interview with European Commission Official, 2011).

However, we must dig a little deeper to gain a full appreciation of the EIDHR's conceptual leanings. In so doing, we come to appreciate the rather deep-running but crucial sets of *implicit* conceptual and ideological assumptions in its workings.

I have documented elsewhere how the EIDHR's discourse about the role of CSO actors, its calls-for-proposals, and management structures, create specific leanings or biases in funding (Kurki, 2011b). Let us revisit these arguments here.

One of the significant characteristics in this regard is the sets of assumptions that are made about the CSOs that should apply for money. Not only is it assumed that actors which are democratising should not be anti-European, but also they are perceived in a very particular role, that is, as the defenders of individual rights against the state. They are to be civil society actors as liberal democratic tradition perceives them, as self-standing, autonomous, but at the same time entrepreneurial actors in defence of a limited individual-protecting state. While this does not mean that only 'liberal' actors are funded – for trade unions or Left-leaning organisations *can* also be funded – it does mean that to obtain money it is assumed that the CSOs will adjust themselves to the core expectations and aims of the liberal democratic rhetoric indicated in the EIDHR documentation.

Other interesting, seemingly innocuous, conceptual characteristics include emphasis on CSOs providing, when necessary, 'services' to society. This seems to imply that social democratic ideas are promoted. Yet, service provision support may in fact undermine directly a social democratic idea of the state. It is *in place* of the state that CSOs are to supply services, thus undermining the state's role in service provision.

Another crucial assumption relates to the expectation that CSOs are self-managing. They are to be professionally structured and governed organisations that are willing to 'perform' managerially for the EU, for they are to be 'responsible' project managers *for* the EU. They should then respect the managerial guidance that the EU provides, including careful empirical measuring of effects or results of projects and financial management in line with EU guidance (Kurki, 2011b).

Now these assumptions are not surprising as such. Of course, it is important for the EU to insist on responsible and liberal-rights-respecting commitments from organisations ultimately funded by the European public. However, it is noteworthy to keep in mind that because of such assumptions not *all* kinds of organisations fall within the remit of EIDHR's funding streams, as they do not in the US context either. Non-professional, anti-European, non-structured, volunteer-based, non-'activity' based organisations do not fit in well. Just like in the United States, there are limits to who is willing to and able to successfully engage with the funding structure requirements of democracy aid through the EIDHR.

Even more interesting characteristics are embedded in the calls-for-proposals system utilised by the EIDHR. As NGO representations have confirmed, this structure of funding is considered with great scepticism among the CSO community, for not only does it raise the bar high for CSOs to apply, but it also drives

CSOs into competition with each other (Interview with CSO representative, 2011). Thus, far from creating civil society solidarity (one of the key constituents of social democratic and participatory understandings of democracy), the calls-for-proposals actually call forth entrepreneurial competitive, self-interested and 'driven' CSOs. The competitive 'market-model' approach to funding arguably seeks to (if inadvertently) embed CSO actors into a market logic of thinking, with important consequences for their ability to work with others and, importantly, to conceive of themselves, if relevant, as non-market-oriented actors. The calls for proposals, although they have raised standards of applications (Interview with European Commission Official, 2011), bring with them hidden logics averse to particular types of non-market, non-liberal thinking.

Such tendencies are further re-enforced in the management structures of the EIDHR projects, which demand that log frame analysis be conducted as a pre-condition of funding. This of course specifies what type of activity 'counts' for the EU, thus constraining the kinds of activities actors would like to engage with. Thus, trainings and seminars work well as they can be measured; whereas strategic volunteer-based structural reform attempts or dialogues are less easily expertly measured (see Chapter 9 for effects on NGO actors).

Problems with the rigidity of EU funding structures have long been recognised and, as a result, adjustments have been made (European Commission, 2010d). Yet, still the basic structures remain the same, and crucially the pressures on CSOs are essentially the same. Thus it is reluctantly accepted by Commission staff that some hidden biases may creep into whom the EIDHR funds. There are certain organisations that are easier to work with than others (Interview with European Commission Official, 2011).

A crucial thing to note then is that the EU's EIDHR funding, while seemingly neutral, is not necessarily so in practice. Moreover, it is far less openly reflexive and politically attuned to the problems and ideological consequences of management practices than, say, openly political electoral work. So, *creeping conceptual and ideological* leanings are embedded into the EU's civil society support. Through the assumptions embedded in management processes of the EIDHR, not only the EU action, but NGO actions and activities in the field are modified, moulded and structured according to a particular, seemingly neutral, but implicitly ideological conceptual mould.

I have argued elsewhere that the ideological logic that underpins many aspects of EIDHR is best characterised as 'neoliberal' in a Foucauldian sense (Kurki, 2011b). What this means is that actors in civil society are expected to adopt for themselves a liberal democratic and liberal market attitude on the basis of which they come to be voluntarily incorporated into funding structures. Whatever their political leaning – and some leanings fit in better than others – their thinking, management structures and activities in civil society are shaped and moulded – crucially, even if funders are 'played' for money. Whatever the promise of pluralism on the level of over-arching rhetoric, in the civil society funding sector, management pressures bring within them implicit, and seemingly, neoliberal tendencies.

Thus, not only are CSO actors to be pro-European and willing to subject themselves to the EU's managerial gaze, but also social democratic actors, for example, are to accept the view of themselves as 'private actors' in defence of a liberal state. Thus, even if 'service providing' – a category of NGOs that the EU is today very interested in funding through its civil society work because of its 'poverty reduction' strategy – NGOs are to act as a supplementary private actor which provides a service, *in lieu* of the state itself. Such a logic, while seemingly social democratic, renders impossible the very idea of a solidaristic, extended service-providing social democratic state, because of hidden neoliberal assumptions.

Paying attention to implicit as well as explicit conceptual assumptions about the idea of democracy and related concepts of civil society and participation is important to gain a sense of the ways in which fuzzy liberalism plays out in concrete EU democracy support.

ENP: the case of Ukraine

The EU's Neighbourhood Policy provides an equally interesting site for analysing hidden conceptual dimensions in EU democracy promotion. The ENP is clearly a continuation of the accession policies. It draws heavily on the accession strategies, to the point of occasionally plagiarising accession documentation (Kelley, 2004). However, it seeks to develop partnerships with countries which are unlikely to be offered a membership prospect, but which are deemed of significance in development of trade and security relations. Democracy and human rights, association agreements attest, are also central 'shared values' between the neighbourhood states and the EU, and the EU's Action Plans for reform seek to duly develop the neighbourhood states' democratic credentials.

As an example case, I examine here Ukraine's engagement with the ENP. This is a particularly interesting case for it is one of the most advanced and most closely engaged neighbourhood states, but also one where democratic developments have halted after initial progress, while simultaneously, the EU's co-operation is gaining increasing momentum, with a Free Trade Area now in negotiation.

What is interesting is that, despite its pluralistic democracy promotion rhetoric and 'fuzzy liberal' commitments, the EU in Ukraine has actually a surprisingly clear idea of what kinds of democracy and economic system it would like to see in place. In promoting democracy, the EU's actions and statements are, contrary to usual democracy promotion rhetoric, quite ambitious and, indeed, rather forceful: contrary to local ownership rhetoric, ENP reform plans actively seek to bring about specific ideals in target countries. The high-rhetoric fuzziness of EU discourses in this ENP case translates into low-politics concreteness.

The initial ENP strategy (European Commission, 2004a) envisaged a partnership based on common shared values, such as democracy, human rights, solidarity and peaceful interaction. These values were to guide the Ukrainian partnership with the EU too and were indeed embedded into the Ukraine Action Plan: it called for 'an increasingly close relationship, going beyond co-operation . . . to promote stability, security and well-being . . . founded on shared values, joint ownership and differentiation' (European Commission, 2005a: 1). At the core of these documents lay an emphasis on liberalising economic reform 'including a stake in the EU's internal market' and as such 'convergence of economic legislation, the opening of economies to each other and continued reduction of trade barriers' (European Commission, 2005a: 2). However, given emphasis on the economic sphere it was also interesting to observe that the first priority for the action was 'further strengthening the stability and effectiveness of institutions guaranteeing democracy and the rule of law' (European Commission, 2005a: 3), alongside the more traditional priorities of political dialogue, security, migration, and nuclear policy.

Commitments at this stage were fairly general in nature: although the Action Plan specified priorities for democracy and human rights reform. The Action Plan argued for electoral reform and strengthening of local government; it also called for judicial reform, especially speeding up of court processes, maintenance of judicial independency, and anti-corruption efforts (see Chapter 10). It also mentioned in this context, albeit in a more minor way, human rights protection and fostering of civil society and media freedoms. The plan went on to detail a set of human rights abuses that the EU stands against and mentioned the rights of labour as specified by International Labour Organization conventions (European Commission, 2005a: 5–6).

Yet, the EU also calls for rather more specific reforms too: these relate to the economy of the country, or the 'functioning market economy' in the country (European Commission, 2005a: 2.2). Here the focus of the reforms is more specific: reforms seek to creating a price-stable economy where state aid is controlled and 'legal environment ensures fair competition between economic operators' (European Commission, 2005a: 2.2.16). This remains to be done, and sure enough, the EU proceeds to specify what is needed: improvements to the 'business climate' through 'ensuring transparency, predictability and simplification of regulation' (European Commission, 2005a: 2.2.18), and a set of measures for speeding up the economic courts. Independence of the central bank, too, needs to be improved, it argues (European Commission, 2005a: 2.2.19) as well as fiscal sustainability and tax and pensions reforms. Further, structural reforms are needed in the economy, including privatisation of state-owned assets and reduction of the state's role in price-setting and trade distortion. In trade, emphasis is on regulatory reform and harmonisation of standards on products, removal of 'all export and import restrictions' (European Commission, 2005a: 25) to enable access to the World Trade Organization (WTO).

A whole set of details are laid out on company law reforms, freedom of capital and services provision. Taxation reform on the lines recommended by the WTO is also set out (European Commission, 2005a: 2.3.5), but a key focus is competition policy, which seeks to push through controls on state aid 'which distort trade between Ukraine and the EU' (2.3.6.39). Property rights also need to be protected, entailing reforms to legal structures and enforcement. Public procurement is also crucial: it needs to be done on principles of transparency, non-discrimination, competition and access to legal recourse (2.3.7.42).

All the reform priorities, we have to note, are strikingly neoliberal in nature. A market-friendly liberal economic state is what the EU has in mind for 'democratising' Ukraine. Interestingly, interest in democracy seems secondary to safe-guarding of liberal preferences. Crucially, however, the EU's views on the economy of Ukraine specify very clearly the kind of politico-economic vision it perceives as central: liberal economy, with adequate legal protections for liberal trade and competition, and a culture of support for such policies in government and civil society.

The progress on these principles by the Ukraine has been meticulously and perseveringly measured by various reports prepared by the EU (European Commission, 2006e). The progress reports urge Ukraine onwards, for example, in drafting of a new competition policy law, controls on state aid levels and forms of taxation in Ukraine, the public procurement process and budgetary sustainability of the current levels of welfare support (2006e: 8–11). Defence of property rights is also seen as central (2006e: 12) as is tackling of stumbling blocks to Ukraine's market economy, such as 'cumbersome decision-making, excessive bureaucracy . . .' and 'uncertainty over investor's rights, red tape and heavy tax pressures' (2006e: 8).

More specific Country Strategy Papers and National Indicative Plans have followed, which aim at promoting 'Ukraine's transition to a fully fledged democracy and market economy' (European Commission, 2007b: 3), even while democracy as an aim is sometimes conspicuously absent from the discussions, as economic agendas are in the driving seat. The emphasis is on an almost instrumental democratisation of the state: the aim is for a competitive economy, and slim and efficient public and social administration; democratisation and human rights are, in a sense, characteristics which are instrumental towards that end.

What is interesting, when one closely observes the lists of reforms specified for Ukraine, is just how little emphasis is actually placed on democratic reforms, even on the 'procedural' level of the polity; the focus is rather on economic and social reforms. While the non-procedural focus might imply for some a 'broader' socio-economic understanding of democracy as operative in the EU thinking, this would entail a misunderstanding of the conceptual orientation. It is clear that substantive social democratic or reform liberal ideals are not at play here: the priorities are primarily neoliberal in nature and driven by economic concerns.

The EU's reports also make some reference to values outside of these specific 'neoliberal' reforms. Perhaps most significantly, the progress report evaluates progress in terms of labour rights: the EU shows interest in core labour standards and trade union rights in the Ukraine (European Commission, 2006e: 5). This interest, however, is driven by concern about competition generated by Ukraine's possible 'race to the bottom' on labour rights, not by altruistic or principled commitments with regard to labour in the country (Interview with EEAS Official, 2011). Thus, at best, an embedded neoliberal interest comes through in the consideration given to issues of basic welfare support and labour rights. These are needed for the sake of stability in the context of the wider aim of economic liberalisation.

Little appears to have shifted in this regard now that the EU is advancing towards a new Deep Trade Agreement with Ukraine. Indeed, progress has been made in this process *despite* the *democratic* backsliding in Ukraine.

The notion of 'partnership' in this kind of context is a curious one (Korosteleva, 2011). The ENP process is about evaluating Ukrainian progress in social and economic reforms on the basis of EU-set standards. While actions plans are agreed between the EU and Ukraine, clearly little discussion of what 'shared values', notably the idea of democracy, might mean is undertaken. The EU cannot really make full use of conditionality in relation to the neighbourhood, but nevertheless in setting up the conceptual parameters of its action, it can direct ENP countries in certain directions. Indeed, despite the lack of explicitly ideological language in the documents, specific kinds of ideological leanings are revealed. These tie in most comfortably with neoliberal notions: in terms of separation of the economic and the political, but also in their simultaneous bringing together in defence of economic liberalisation; in terms of emphasis on liberal state and law which regulates the economy in order to defend private property, competition and business climate; in terms of support for civil society that is expected to act as a defence for individual rights; and in terms of interest shown in separation of powers and independence of judiciary and central bank.

Minor interest is shown in the discourse to questions of labour rights, freedom of assembly, or gender equality. Also, an abiding concern is access to and reform of the social and welfare services. Yet, these interests are clearly secondary to the creation of a liberal market economy, and crucially, are underpinned by a liberal interpretation: thus, welfare reform is encouraged because it facilitates fiscal tightening up of state expenditure. The central underpinnings of a viable state consist of a competitive market, facilitated by correct pro-business and pro-stability rule of law; regulation that facilitates smooth market transactions; and efficient and cost-effective welfare systems that enable people to engage effectively in a flexible labour market that liberalisation of the economy will bring about.

It is not facilitation of 'democratic controls over the economy', or even meaningful procedural democratisation that are the key concerns here. Democracy is about creation of transparent and effective dialogue within the state for the sake of economic liberty. While interest is shown in some corporatist actions (social and economic conventions), red tape and big bureaucracies are seen as the problem.

As a result the EU, curiously, despite the partnership language, ends up dictating to Ukraine and creates a dynamic in 'democracy support' which is clearly not in line with pluralism or debate – or even 'fuzziness'. In Ukraine, the EU's fuzzy liberal discourse has turned surprisingly specific.

Democracy promotion through trade

One of the most ambitious and unique aspects of the EU's democracy promotion policy has been its 'mainstreaming' into the area of trade policy. Uniquely among trade actors, the EU has sought to use its considerable trade power in the world to push forward the aims of democratisation. This has been ambitious not only because trade policy usually is an interest-driven policy area, but also because the EU's competences in this area are, while extensive, divided in complex ways between various Directorate Generals, and thereby affected by various different sectoral interests and values.

Thus, promoting democracy through trade is not likely to be easy, which indeed is what experience has shown. The EU's enforcement of conditionality clauses through trade power has been poorly and inconsistently applied (see Smith, 2008).

Yet, to leave the analysis here would be to mistake the power the EU has in trade beyond mere traditional conditionality structures. I will argue here that through its actual trade agreements, with or without democracy clauses, the EU is arguably inadvertently pushing particular kinds of governance reforms alongside hard-driven liberalising economic reforms. The EU then is, inadvertently, more of a democracy promoter through trade than would initially be apparent – and, crucially, is a rather 'pushy' and deeply interventionist liberal politico-economic actor.

The key instrument of democracy enforcement through trade is *supposed* to be the so-called democratic conditionality principle, now included in most (although not all) EU trade agreements. Since the Cotonou Agreement (2000) the EU has placed especial emphasis on including the so-called essential elements clauses into trade agreements. These refer to respect for democracy and human rights as essential elements of these agreements, infringement of which may result in suspension of the agreement. Such clauses are now included widely. Most extensively, such clauses have been incorporated into the EU's generalised system of preferences (GSPs) and GSP+ frameworks, where preferential trade status is directly tied to human rights and democracy clauses, but to a lesser extent they also play a role in the EU's other agreements.

However, their enforcement has been poor: that is, the EU has not sought to either actively monitor or actively sanction states on the grounds that they fail to live up to these commitments. The EU has only exercised this conditionality twice in the context of a GSP, namely, in relation to Burma and Belarus. Many other cases have gone repeatedly unexamined and unpunished: the Commission is not actively interested in investigating, let alone willing to act on investigations of infringement (Interview with EU official, 2011). On this basis, then, it seems that 'democratic' conditionality of the EU's trade policy-making has proved rather a weak instrument. Indeed, some have claimed success (e.g. in Szymanski and Smith, 2005) others have demonstrated that the EU's democracy promotion through trade lacks teeth because of the poor enforcement of clauses (Kelagama, 2010).

Yet, other means besides 'explicit conditionality' also exist for the EU to enforce its preferences on democracy promotion through trade. Crucially, it should not be forgotten that trade agreements *themselves* constitute deep-running efforts at restructuring governance of target states on lines which are, at least eventually, envisaged to be 'liberal democratic' in nature. Thus, lest we come to mistake the EU's trade policy as 'weak' in structuring target states, we should not forget that the EU's trade agreements – which it concludes on a regular basis with various target states – now entail deep-running reforms to the legal structures of states, their procurement policies, their ministries, their structures and preferences in service provision, and so on. These reforms are considered necessary for the kind of 'beyond the border trade' that the EU considers central to safeguarding its core business. Thus, facilitation of opening up of service sectors and public procurement in third countries to EU providers is a key aim of EU trade policy and such market access can only be provided through such reforms.

Through the backdoor, then – by means of economic reform policies necessitated by trade interest – the EU does seek liberalisation of target states and thereby also liberal democratisation of these states. As European Commission officials accept, the EU's trade policy is not first and foremost a democracy promotion instrument. Yet, its end goal is precisely that – the liberal democratisation of target states (Interview with EU Trade official, 2011). An implicit modernisation theory seems to underlie the activities of trade actors.

But what are we to make of the claim that the EU's trade policy is in fact 'reform liberal' in nature, given the emphasis that is placed within it today on labour rights and solidarity as core principles of trade engagement?

Core labour rights through trade

The EU's role in core labour rights (CLRs) promotion through its trade policy is interesting, yet dubious in its 'social democratic' credentials. The EU has, for sure, had an important role in pushing these values in trade agreements; yet, they have often been pushed for bureaucratic interests, or quite simply from self-interest: the EU is keen not to let trading partners gain an advantage on account of their poor labour rights (Interview with EEAS Official, 2011).

At the same time, it seems that labour rights become easily interpreted in rather minimal ways as Orbie (2008) and Novitz (2008) have argued. Their meaning in the EU discourse is taken and moulded to fit an essentially neoliberal 'defensive' and minimal interpretation, rather than acquiring full substantial positive value, as in the social democratic tradition, for example. In this context it is crucial to note that the European trade unions have for some time been warning that the EU's *Global Europe* strategy involves a turn away from prioritisation of decent work and a shift towards a more neoliberal policy. The EU is accused of not properly standing for the CLR agenda, but letting it be hijacked by market-led rationales. Orbie and Tortell (2009), who are key experts on CLS, agree that there has been a tendency to sideline real labour concerns. The promotion of CLR as part of the 'democracy' agenda through trade entails, it would seem, enforcing of liberal trends rather than social democratic trends in target countries.

Despite the seeming weaknesses of the EU's democracy promotion through trade, it is important to keep in mind that EU trade dialogue is far from impotent in bringing about structural and governance changes in partner societies. Indeed, despite the ideologically 'neutral' and technical tone of EU actions in the trade area, it seems that, in reality, EU democracy promotion through trade entails a rather forceful attempt at (neo)liberalisation of target states. Democratic pluralism, taking account of the existence of many possible politico-economic ideals in reforming target country governance (economic and political) is clearly not a priority here. A rather rigid ideological neoliberalism comes through in the EU's trade policy, despite the concern with 'flanking measures' such as labour rights.

Fuzzy liberalism: implications for EU democracy promotion

In this section I will develop some conclusions from the above analysis of different facets of democracy promotion. I focus here on two issues. First, I want to reflect on the role and character of EU's fuzzy liberalism and why it matters that we understand in some detail how this particular conceptual position works. Second, I wish to reflect on the power politics and the causes of EU's fuzzy liberalism and to deal with the difficult question of 'intentionality' in evaluating fuzzy liberalism.

Fuzzy liberalism is a conceptual framing that places liberal democratic values at its core, while at the same time making unsystematic or peripheral references to other values, such as solidarity, labour rights, participation, and social welfare. This brand of liberalism is not explicitly 'liberal' as such: it does not celebrate or clearly demarcate liberal ideological values or logics. Rather, it is based on a conceptual fudging of democracy's meaning in the high-level policy discourse and technocratic and technical specification of the content in particular sectors of activity. There is no clear 'politico-economic model of democracy' in EU action guided by conceptual fuzziness. This does not, however, mean that fuzziness does not have concrete consequences. Indeed, as we have seen, it results in very interesting, and often surprisingly neoliberal, democracy promotion practice.

Reading the EU as a fuzzy liberal democracy promotion actor makes more sense, I argue, than concluding that it is either a principled liberal actor (Tsoukalis, 2003), a 'fallen' liberal actor (Youngs, 2010), a 'social democratic' actor (Manners, 2006) or a genuinely 'pluralist' actor (Zielonka and Mair, 2002). It is only through understanding the EU as fuzzy liberal that we can understand why it does what it does: why much of its activity is liberal in its core but why it remains 'shy' about its liberalism, while peppering its discourses with seemingly, but unsystematically, social democratic and even participatory language.

So what functions exactly does fuzzy liberalism serve in the EU's external actions? Arguably, it serves a fundamentally important function by taking the 'edge' off the potentially fiery debate on the meaning and ideological orientation of democracy promotion. In a sense, this is what allows the EU to engage in democracy support in the first place.

The EU as a 'democracy promoter' is in a difficult position. Its own experiences with democracy are multiple and contested. Liberal democracy, reform liberalism, participatory democracy and social democracy all have played important roles in European experiences of democratisation. It cannot then easily commit itself to a singular – say universalistic liberal – position as the United States can. Nor can it declare itself fully to be any particular kind of democracy promoter, say social democratic actor, for within its borders are (increasingly today) also liberal and neoliberal states and a wide array of parties which would not agree on a social democratic orientation for the EU. In this way, and confusingly insisting that it must act in support of democracy, fudging of the meaning of democracy is in many ways essential for the EU, more so than for other actors, which are more ideologically unitary.

Yet, fuzzy liberalism has more uses. It also provides the EU with a surprisingly flexible, malleable and rhetorically powerful set of commitments, which enable its external activities. The EU, with its fuzzy liberalism in tow, can be a more flexible actor than others: it can, through its fuzzy rhetoric, justify a whole range of positions. So while social service delivery organisations are funded on one hand, giving a seemingly (although poorly) social democratic edge to the EU's activity, at the same time, with its fuzzy liberalism at hand, the EU can also argue for a highly liberal orientation in its trade policy . With fuzzy rhetoric at hand, the EU can recognise social rights and labour rights, while at the same time can push for liberalisation of the legal and governmental structures of states.

This fuzzy liberal discourse is, moreover, more palatable for many recipients than a more hard-edged 'ideologically clear' discourse. This is why the Office for Promotion of Parliamentary Democracy (OPDD, 2009), for example, argues that the EU should adopt an open, United Nations based, flexible understanding of democracy. Such fuzzy, open discourse provides the least controversial and most acceptance-generating definitional backdrop to EU action. The EU then, the OPDD argues, should resist the temptation to define democracy in any specific 'EU-way'.

However, what this overt advocacy of a 'fuzzy' position on democracy's meaning misses is *the hidden politics of the 'no-model'* approach. As we have seen, models do also emerge from the practice of a no-model approach. This position also ignores the contested nature of democracy's meaning and, crucially, the already-existing contradictions in EU practice. It also ignores an important aspect highlighted by another report by the International IDEA (2009a). This report records the confusion of recipients with regard to the EU. Recipients are confused as to whether the EU is a liberal actor or something else and remain disappointed by the lack of engagement with social democracy as a core pillar of EU democratisation. It is the social democratic model that recipients are interested in but do not consistently perceive in EU's own activities.

This is arguably because no consistent social model exists in EU democracy promotion! Despite the fuzzy rhetoric the actual practice of EU democracy promotion falls short of advocacy of systematic dual track democracy, or even reform liberal democracy. As we have seen in the case of the EIDHR and the ENP, for example, it is in fact (embedded) neoliberal models which seem to emerge, even from the promotion of supposedly social democratic or reform liberal principles.

Nevertheless, despite the lack of systematic promotion of non-liberal models, fuzzy liberalism should not be entirely faulted. It also creates considerable room for at least potential diversity in the EU's external action. Already some seemingly contradictory policies seem to exist within the EU democracy support structure (e.g. compare EU's development and trade policy rhetorics). Through systematic engagement of alternative conceptual positions, such incipient pluralistic promotion of potential differing models could be cashed into something more truly pluralist, as I suggest in Chapter 12.

However, crucially, any potential debate on democracy in the EU will only be able to work within specific conceptual confines. This is because hidden in fuzzy language are also limitations to debate and contestation on democracy's meaning.

Hidden coherence of fuzzy liberalism

Is there any ideological coherence to fuzzy liberalism? This is an important question. I suggest here that there may, indeed, be some level of ideological coherence to fuzzy liberalism after all. This clearly delimits any potential radicalisation of pluralistic debate within the EU.

As the analysis of some of the facets of EU democracy promotion under fuzzy liberalism has already suggested, there do seem to emerge, within the fuzzy and open language used by the EU, specific kinds of tendencies in EU thinking and practice of democracy support. Thus, the economic and legal technical reforms in Ukraine as well as the managerial requirements for CSO's funding all point in a surprisingly uniform direction: that of the neoliberal politico-economic model of democracy. It seems to me then that the kinds of actions that fuzziness, by empowering bureaucratic and technical logics, legitimises are in the end often primarily 'neoliberal' in nature. By this, I mean sets of tendencies where market logics are made primary and depoliticised. Arguably, fuzzy liberalism is particularly apt tool in accommodating neoliberal demands because it removes from discussion any specific openly ideological debate and, under the semblance of vague rhetoric, facilitates a set of rational technical (market-led) solutions to problems.

The kind of liberalism that Youngs (2010) has called for, and hoped for, in the EU is arguably a *principled ideological* kind of liberalism, the centre ground of which is the belief in the rights of individuals, democracy and freedom. The neoliberal logic, which actually seems to *implicitly underpin* EU's fuzzy liberal democracy promotion, is a very different kind of liberalism. This is a form of implicit and hidden liberalism, where it is no longer necessary for liberalism itself to be justified ideologically or ethically. Liberal principles become embedded into 'natural' assumption about how individuals, states or civil societies should conduct their life. Implicit liberal assumptions 'conduct the conduct' of individuals and societies on the level of everyday practice and techniques, rather than principles. It is EU's underlying slippage to this sort of liberalism that we need to be wary of. It is implicit liberalism which explains the EU's tendencies to depoliticise its democracy promotion discourse, its contradictory activities in democracy promotion, and its hidden entrepreneurial management logics.

Noting this is crucial for how we read the EU: the structure of its actions, the effect of its actions and the potentials of its actions. Recently, another set of authors has also pointed to the role of neoliberal governmentality in EU democracy promotion (Hout, 2010; Reynaerts, 2011; see also Apeldoorn, Drahokoupil and Horn, 2009; Hurt, Knio and Ryner, 2010). Will Hout's conclusions are of significance here. They point out that:

> The dominant understanding of (good) governance in policy circles fails to recognise the essentially political character of governance issues. . . . EU development policies are essentially neoliberal in character and [. . .] their governance-related strategies in effect display a technocratic orientation and are instrumental in deepening market-based reform in aid-receiving countries.
>
> (Hout, 2010: 3)

This study is in agreement with this conclusion; but I have highlighted here the origins and complexities of the neoliberal tendencies in the EU. Fuzzy liberalism is the conceptual underpinning of the EU's increasingly fuzzy neoliberalism.

But is this fuzzy liberalism an intentional practice or strategy on the EU's part? In my view, and as will be specified in Chapter 11, the form of implicit neoliberalism that emerges is not intentional as such, nor strategic. Crucially, interviews with practitioners in the European Commission have confirmed that individual officials in the EU do not perceive themselves as committed to anything like a neoliberal effort: instead a variety of 'conscious' political leanings characterise their work. Neoliberalism is less about principles and more about practice, about everyday 'common sense'. Neoliberal management principles or beliefs in economic technical reforms are not so much intentionally argued for as unintentionally fostered by a particular kind of a discursive environment. So self-evident are they that they need not even be discussed. There is no 'ideology' in a fuzzy liberal EU democracy promotion practice: a curious turn of events indeed for a policy agenda which is supposed to be at its core, about the ideological advocacy of specific normative principles!

Conclusions: EU and world order practices

The EU is an actor in the work of which liberalism, it seems, has gone 'underground'. Arguably, the depoliticising and fuzzy liberal tendencies in the EU's democracy promotion discourse are indicative of a new and potentially very useful and effective form of power in world politics. The United States' ideological commitments have gotten it tangled in unsavoury and unpopular interventions. The EU wants to avoid such entanglements and cannot hold openly ideological positions for various internal reasons. Yet, this does not mean the EU's politics of democracy promotion are non-existent or necessarily even more pluralistic or benign. Indeed, it is my contention here that the EU's fuzzy liberalism, while advocating no clear model, does come with its own conceptual politics. Indeed, the EU of today rather successfully liberalises and democratises countries at its borders, it seems.

Yet, this is not a fully pluralist practice of democracy support. Despite the centrality of partnership and dialogue principles in EU foreign policy, meaning-ful deep-going dialogue on democracy is not evident in EU democracy support. Indeed, it is made near-nigh impossible by the strong slippage towards prioritisa-tion of EU rules, principles and values in concrete EU actions or funding instru-ments. Crucially, debate on democracy's meaning, so much valued rhetorically, only takes place within specific bureaucratic and technical confines. As a result, despite Landman's claims that the EU promotes more substantive models, par-ticipatory and social democratic alternatives do not emerge from EU actions. The language of substantive models must shift and mould into new forms that fit the EU's fuzzy liberal and often neoliberal management practices. Pressures exerted by fuzzy liberalism are such that, while it seemingly opens up some room for debate and exploration of extra-liberal ideals in EU democracy promotion, all such ideals are swiftly returned to the magnetic field of (embedded neo)liberal core assumptions, with crucial consequences for EU's ability to set out a clear 'alternative' or 'pluralistic' stall in democracy support. While less committedly liberal in its democracy support than the United States, a fuzzy depoliticised lib-eral core emanates from its practices, with important effects for maintenance of an essentially neoliberal world order, as we will discuss in Chapter 11.

9 Democracy promotion by non-state actors

Alternative models in action?

In Chapters 7 and 8 we examined the role of two key actors in democracy promotion: the United States, and an international organisation, the European Union (EU). We have seen that in both cases interesting things are going on with regard to the 'conceptual orders' adopted. US democracy support discourse has worked within the confines of a liberal democratic orientation, although debates within liberal democratic thinking, or at least oscillation between different variants of it, seem to have taken place. The EU, on the other hand, has been characterised by this author as a 'fuzzy' liberal actor. Despite the rhetoric promise of more 'pluralistic' practice and the refusal to provide clear definitional contours to the values of democracy, the EU's democracy support is characterised by surprising delimitation of debate on models of democracy and tendencies towards implicitly neoliberal conceptualisations of democracy.

State actors and international organisations, such as the United States and the EU, while arguably important in structuring the field of democracy support, do not exhaust the possibilities of democracy promotion activity today. This is because multiple 'non-state' actors are also involved in democracy promotion. While they are often dependent on funding of the donor states or international organisations, equally the main donors too are dependent on the projects designed by these organisations and their local knowledge and expertise in country contexts. These organisations are part and parcel of the democracy support industry today. It would be quite wrong then to draw conclusions about the contours of democracy promotion's conceptual orders without paying attention to these organisations.

However, these actors span a wide range. There are various specialised state-funded, but independent/semi-independent, non-profit organisations involved in democracy promotion. The most famous is perhaps the National Endowment for Democracy (NED), examined in Chapter 7. Organisations modelled on the NED in Europe include the Netherlands Institute for Multiparty Democracy (NIMD) and the Westminster Foundation. These organisations rely directly on public funds for support of their activities but act (at least in principle) independently from government agencies. There are also increasing numbers of parliamentary democracy support agencies, which bring together parliamentary resources for democracy promotion but under semi-independent non-governmental organisation

(NGO)-type set-ups (e.g. DEMOS, OPPD). In addition, we have the inter-governmentally funded but non-governmentally run, transnational, non-profit organisations like the International IDEA. Furthermore, numerous network NGO-actors exist, such as InterAction in the United States, and ENoP and EPD in Europe.

Then there are the political foundations. In the United States context 'political foundations' (NDI, IRI, CIPE and Solidarity Center) are all wrapped up in the NED structure and are, while linked to parties, relatively non-partisan in their approach to democracy support. In Europe, however, foundations exist independently of a single funding foundation. These organisations are primarily state-funded, yet they are to be independent of the state, and crucially have historically adopted openly ideologically partisan approaches to advocacy of democratic principles. Alongside them there exists a number of advocacy NGOs ranging from transnational ones, such as Amnesty International, to local grass-roots organisations advocating for democracy and human rights issues in target countries.

And this is not even to mention the role of private 'for-profit' corporations in democracy support. Especially in the US scene, where delivery of democracy aid is now almost fully privatised, the role of such 'for-profit' organisations is also important to note. Thus, Chemonics and DAC are examples of influential and well-networked private firms acting in democracy support delivery (for more detailed analysis, see Bridoux, 2011b).

It is clearly impossible to examine all the different types of non-state democracy promotion organisations here. For the sake of space, I will focus here on examination of three types of 'intermediary' non-state organisations, which all do some democracy support but also position themselves in democracy promotion debates internationally. They are all not only substantial organisations well-known for their role in democracy support, but also not tied in their agendas to specific issues or country contexts. As such, they are analysed here as 'prisms' for accessing some of the recent developments in the NGO sphere in democracy support (hence the non-diachronic structure of this chapter vis-à-vis chs 7, 8 and 10).

I examine first the International IDEA, a Sweden-based intergovernmental organisation engaged in a variety of democracy support activities (while formally an IGO, it functions akin to NGOs and is classified as a non-state civil society actor by United Nations Development Programme). It is famous for its distinctive 'consensual' and 'technical' approach to democracy promotion and acts as an active consultant and deliverer of democracy support knowledge and 'best practice' in democratising context around the world, often at the behest of other organisations or donors, whether United Nations (UN) or EU. Second, I examine the work of a selection of the political foundations, the 'Stiftungen'. These are perhaps the most interesting set of democracy promotion organisations for us to pay attention to, because they have historically been openly ideologically or politically driven. They are in many ways the best hope in terms of identifying practices in support of 'alternative' non- or extra-liberal politico-economic models. Third, I examine briefly the work of the EPD (European Partnership for Democracy), the ENoP (European Network of Political Foundations), and NIGD (Network Institute for Global Democratization), three distinct kinds of 'network' actors involved in democracy promotion.

The organisations I study here are relatively rarely discussed in the academic literature on democracy promotion, but provide a fascinating picture of the dynamics of democracy support through non-state actors. Their discourses demonstrate the dynamics towards more depoliticised democracy support today, and the concomitant 'mainstreaming' trends in the 'conceptual foundations' of democracy support. These are *not-for-profit* outfits – the role of for-profits also today deserves close study,[1] especially in the US context where they are most widely found – but, interestingly, these organisations too increasingly 'make their living' out of 'selling' specific products in the democracy promotion industry to funders or from facilitation of such selling process by subsidiaries. In so doing, they often have to – and willingly do – play down the 'politics' of their democracy support in favour of more marketable, and results-led management aesthetic of the donors. Those organisations – the NIGD, for example – that do not, suffer severely in not being able to raise funds for activities.

Interest in the organisations chosen as the 'cases' here is driven primarily by recognition of their considerable, yet often unappreciated, role in democracy promotion. Yet, there are also wider theoretical interests that must be kept in mind with regard to these actors. Certainly, any analysis of these actors has to appreciate the changing nature of NGOs in today's global governance. Since the 1990s, NGOs have not only gained power in the international political scene, but they have also thus become part of the professionalised elite of advocacy, aid and assistance. It is argued that they are now the hand-maidens of governments and international organisations in structuring global policy agendas (Sending and Neumann, 2006, 2010)

It follows that interesting questions arise as to the power dynamics at play within and through these organisations: what is precisely their role in wider structures of world ordering, and what are the exact relationships between states and these organisations? Indeed, this chapter seeks to pay attention to the questions informed by critical literature on NGOs (e.g. Hulme and Edwards, 1997; Cooke and Kothari, 2001; Sending and Neumann, 2010). How overtly political/ideological are NGO actors? How technocratic are they? How pluralist are they? How interest- or market-driven are they? How participatory/locally-driven are they? Crucially, I ask: What overt and covert ideological or conceptual predilections drive them in their democracy support? As will be seen, and analysed in more detail in Chapter 11, the role of NGOs in the global democracy support industry tells us some interesting things about shifts in the liberal world order as well as in democracy support.

International IDEA

The International Institute for Democracy and Electoral Assistance (International IDEA) is a Stockholm-based organisation, instituted, supported and funded by a group of 25 countries. It is responsible to the board consisting of representatives of states but acts essentially like a non-state actor. Its programmes seek to: '[p]rovide knowledge to democracy builders; provide policy development and analysis; and support democratic reform' (International IDEA, 2012).

Its work starts from the principle that democracy is a value that is much appreciated throughout the world and the 25 member states can, through the International IDEA's framework, provide measured and appropriate assistance to making democracy work in the many contexts where support for democracy is needed. The International IDEA (hereafter often referred to as IDEA) is perceived to be particularly influential in providing expertise in devising constitutions, electoral systems and party systems, and in evaluating the 'state of democracies' and in dealing with questions of gender-and-democracy and democracy-and-development.

The IDEA works on the basis of five core principles, which give us some indication of its distinctive starting assumptions, vis-à-vis key donors, in democracy promotion (International IDEA, 2008: 7):

* Democratisation is a process that requires time and patience.
* Democracy is not achieved through elections alone.
* Democratic practices can be compared but not prescribed.
* Democracy is built from within societies.
* Democracy cannot be imported or exported but can be supported.

The International IDEA takes change and dynamic evolution of governance systems as a key principle underlying its approach (International IDEA, 2009b) and accepts that the work on democracy for them is never 'done'. They take a distinctively long-term and continuous approach to democracy building. Also, it is significant that they explicitly go beyond a narrowly electoral approach to democracy support. While most democracy promotion actors, including the United States and the EU, now accept such principles and dabble in extensive civil society support and 'locally grown' processes, the IDEA seems to attach special emphasis on reaching beyond electoral, and prescriptive institutional, support. In this context it is significant that the IDEA recognises the universality of the value of democracy, but also the 'inherently local political processes that must be supported through context-sensitive approaches' (V. Helgesen, in International IDEA, 2008).

Crucial for the IDEA is also the slogan that emphasises that 'democracy cannot be imported or exported, but it can be supported' (International IDEA, 2009b). With this in mind the IDEA takes a non-aggressive support based approach to democracy assistance: 'Quintessentially, we bring experience and options to the table but do not prescribe solutions – true to the principle that the decision-makers in a democracy are the citizens and their chosen representatives' (International IDEA, 2009b).

The IDEA, then, acts as an advocate, an expert and a knowledge-centre for democracy promotion undertaken by other organisations, but does not seek to impose specific prescriptions on them or target states. It co-operates closely with the OSCE (Organization for Security Co-operation in Europe), the UN, the EU and other donor agencies, but does not consider itself an actor 'in cahoots' with any of them. The IDEA's democracy support is not interest-driven, nor driven by specific national values: it is a neutral and non-interfering democracy assistance organisation. But how does the IDEA approach the notion of democracy in democracy support?

Conception of democracy

One might presume that the IDEA's non-coercive, neutral approach based on prioritisation of local perspectives would be reflected in its approach to the idea of democracy. And so it is. The IDEA does not adopt a strict definition of democracy in its work, but rather chooses to leave its meaning rather open. Just two key principles guide its take on the meaning of democracy in its democracy support:

- that democracy refers to popular control over policies; and
- that in that popular control citizens should be equally treated.

Based on these two principles, IDEA maintains, democracy can take many forms (Helgesen, 2010).

While in many ways reminiscent of the EU's rather 'vague' and 'broad' approach to democracy support, what is striking, in comparison to the EU's discourse, is that the IDEA has *not* shied away from conceptual debate on democracy's meaning. Interestingly, during the last decade or so, the IDEA has commissioned a number of studies specifically tackling the complexities of the concept of democracy and its implications for democracy support (see e.g. International IDEA, 2008; Landman, 2009; Pace, 2009). Crucially, it has sought to deal with the debate over the meaning of democracy and, specifically, the counter-positioning of 'procedural democracy', 'liberal democracy' and 'substantive democracy' in debates on democracy support (Landman, 2009).

In recognising the importance of debate over democracy's meaning, the IDEA claims to keep its mind open to *all* conceptual approaches to democracy. Indeed, most documentation now explicitly makes reference to all these three ideals and refuses to take a specific stance in relation to which conceptual approach is being preferred. The IDEA supports a procedural view, given that one of its key foci is electoral support. Yet, IDEA explicitly argues that democracy goes beyond elections and emphasises 'liberal' cultural aspects, with human rights at its centre. At times, IDEA emphasises the pulls of substantive democratic traditions, the role of social and economic rights, for example, in democratisation. Indeed, Landman (2009: 8) goes as far as to say that 'the IDEA has in many ways followed the European approach to democracy building', which he (somewhat mistakenly, as seen in Chapter 8) associates with the 'substantive' democratic ideal.

What is also distinctive is that the IDEA's view of democracy is dynamic and self-reflexive and encourages all actors, including Western states, to measure and reflect on the weaknesses and strengths of their democratic systems. Indeed, the IDEA's democracy promotion documentation produced by researchers associated with IDEA's 'State of Democracy' assessment give a good indication of this. The core principles of *popular control* and *political equality* of voice and respect can and should be measured in *all* democracies, not just developing ones (International IDEA, 2008). Questions related to the quality of (1) citizenship, law and rights; (2) representative and accountable government; (3) civil society and popular participation; and (4) democracy beyond the state, are relevant to all states – including democracy promoting states themselves.

It seems that the IDEA's framework allows for some extra-liberal, as well as procedural and liberal conceptions, to be considered. Yet, it is noteworthy that on the basis of the understandings of democracy discussed in this book, arguably, the IDEA's core principles and mediating values stop short of encompassing full range of alternative models or discussion of contestation between models.

Notably, socialist, radical, participatory and even the fully extended social democratic principles of dual track democracy, it would seem, are in fact rather silently incorporated, if at all. While social and economic rights are indeed included in the considerations, democratic forms which seek to control the economic in any substantive ways do not arise from this framework. Socio-economic rights can be accommodated, but are not set out as core principles; these remain liberal democratic in nature. The model of democracy here seems to be liberal in its core, with values relating to 'substantive democracy' considered as additional extras.

The core of the understanding of democracy, it could be argued, is more in line with liberal values and notions, and less so with participatory, socialist or even social democratic notions where direct or indirect controls over economic processes, workplace and international and global institutions would be considered central. Global democracy does, interestingly, make an important entry point here (International IDEA, 2008), but the framework does not capture the core values or principles of 'cosmopolitan' projects on global democracy, but focuses on analysis of states' interactions with international organisations. Thus, it could be argued that the model of democracy that arises out of the IDEA's documentation is at best what might be termed a 'liberal democracy +' model. Its central focus is still on the state institutions and primarily liberal democratic political processes.

Interestingly, while recognising the crucial nature of conceptual issues, the IDEA also seeks to intentionally avoid some of the most *contested* aspects of the debates on democracy. In the end, it focuses on technical and institutional issues of democracy promotion: elections and constitution support. Crucially, it does not claim to advocate a specific approach to democracy or its politico-economic foundations, but stays clear of such debates. Thus, its 'development and democracy' work, for example, is not focused around exploration of contested models of democracy and development, but rather, somewhat more neutrally, on recognising that these two ideas interact.

The International IDEA dares not take a firm stance on what kind of democracy (or model of economic development) it seeks to facilitate because it is to be strictly neutral in its approach. Non-partisan support for democracy is then what the IDEA provides in the bulk of its constitutional and electoral support, even as this neutrality-seeking position may hide not only specific 'liberal' focal points in IDEA's work, but also potentially some subtle differences in the work of different communities within the IDEA. This is also despite the fact that, paradoxically, such neutrality seems an elusive notion in an area of policy-work which is focused on the advocacy of a contested and ideological concept.

While Landman claims there are substantive notions at work in IDEA's work, this may be an exaggeration. In my assessment, it is fairer to say that there is a 'liberal +' approach at work in IDEA's discourse: it is open to socio-political alternatives but stops short of advocating such solutions (presumably because this would be political or ideological, unlike, curiously, technical work in promotion of liberal democracy!). The core concerns in constitution-writing, election work and reform of party political systems and media are maintenance of basic liberal rights and freedoms. In our terms, the broader socio-economic aspects are second-ary to the 'core' aspects of democratisation which still revolve around liberal rep-resentative institutions and constitutions. Simultaneously, debate on democracy's meaning is explicitly depoliticised in fear of accusations of 'political bias'.

But how about political foundations? Are more politically open, partisan and pluralistic alternatives to be found there?

Political foundations

In the United States, as we have seen, the 'political foundations' (International Republican Institute [IRI]; National Democratic Institute [NDI]; Centre for Inter-national Private Enterprise [CIPE]; and Solidarity Center) exist within the NED structure. In that context they also remain, while informed by party-lines, non-partisan in their approach to conceptions of democracy. Within the NED structure their work on democracy and understandings of democracy are united by a classi-cal liberal democratic discourse, with which all are in agreement (Interview with Barbara Haig, 2012). Thus, the Solidarity Center, while concerned with labour's role, does not seek to attack or undermine core classical liberal representational principles; nor will IRI and NDI openly advocate party politics in their respec-tive traditions. In the US scene a common liberal democratic discourse unites the actors, and within this the idea of democracy can be 'depoliticised'. No debate on democracy's meaning is necessary, despite the differential orientations in terms of division of labour of the different institutes.

However, in the European context the role of political foundations is very dif-ferent and deserves close attention. This is because the European foundations are, arguably, the most openly and self-avowedly radical *political* and *ideological* among democracy promoters today.

The Stiftungen are not only the oldest but are historically very important democracy promotion organisations. They are civic education foundations, ini-tially established in Germany and then replicated in the context of other European countries, which are associated with or 'close' to (Mair, 2000: 129), yet at the same time 'independent' of, specific political parties in these countries. As such they have been explicitly political and value-driven in nature: they have been tied to and have sought to advance specific sets of political or ideological ideals that emanate from their party-political history. Thus, the social democrats have focused on social democratic agitation, involving support to social democratic actors such as trade unions, women's or farmers associations and (to a lesser extent) parties. Liberal foundations, in contrast to both of the above, advocate property rights and free markets (see e.g. Mair, 2000).

Various political ideologies, then, have classically characterised the work of the political foundations. This makes them of particular interest, given our interest in analysis of the role of 'ideological' leanings and alternative conceptual understandings of democracy in democracy support. If technical and depoliticising tendencies have been on the rise, here is a set of actors that have developed, over a long time, a very specific niche in democracy promotion, which is focused on openly ideological, political and hence 'subjective' rather than 'technocratic' or 'universalistic' conceptualisation of democracy in democracy support.

Or so it would seem. I argue here that, while this remains the case to some extent, important shifts are taking place in the work of the political foundations. While they seemingly represent a counter-weight to the technicalising and depoliticising tendencies in democracy promotion, evidence suggests that trends towards depoliticisation, consensus ideology and marketisation also exist among these actors, partly as a result of the discursive and managerial tendencies which are imposed upon them as they join the global fight against poverty and autocracy, through governmental development agencies or external donors.

Nature of the foundations

Today in the European context, at least 63 political foundations exist. Their roles vary somewhat but most are involved in 'political education' in domestic contexts of their home countries and simultaneously in their interactions with outside actors, including developing and democratising states. The German foundations are the model for political foundation activity in many countries in Europe now. The oldest of the German Foundations is the Friedrich Ebert Stiftung. It was set up in 1925 to provide the basis for social democratic civil society engagement and expanded its activities to the international sphere in 1957. Since then in the German context five other Stiftungen have been established, namely the Konrad Adenauer Stiftung, the Friedrich Naumann Stiftung, the Heinrich Siedel Foundation, the Heinrich Böll foundation and Rosa Luxemburg Foundation. These foundations represent the political traditions of all major parties from right to left and beyond (Greens, Christian Democrats). Many more foundations, similarly representative of the national political range in home societies, now exist Europe-wide.

The emergence of these foundations in the post-Second World War setting was initially tied to the fear of anti-democratic trends arising in European countries in the absence of active political education of citizens in the values of democracy. Because the organisations originated from state concerns with the stability of European democracy, they are traditionally government-funded and work in conjunction with political parties in the home states. Their funding generally reflects the distribution of votes to the associated parties in the political system and is distributed through the Ministries of Finance and Development for projects proposed by the foundations.

As Mair (2000: 128) has shown, because of their close nexus to the state and the protection of their budget line within the state, the political foundations have tended to be rather secretive and low-key in their activities. Some have even suggested they act in defence of respective home country interests (rather than 'democracy') in the target countries where they are based. Yet, they are more than 'tools of foreign policy' of the home states. This is particularly because of their interesting conceptual foundations.

While in the United States a liberal democratic consensus discourse exists on democracy, what is notable in examining the conceptual foundations of the political foundations in European context is that this is not the case. Instead the full gamut of political leanings has been explored and celebrated in the foundations. This is partly because they have been funded in such a stable way by the state, which has believed in their diverse ideological projects' contribution to democracy at home. Such funding has also insulated them from market pressures of having to compete for funds on the global funding scene. This in turn has facilitated continuance of their more politicised and ideological discourses of democracy and democracy promotion.

Thus, it is interesting to note that the foundations have resisted their instrumentalisation and have remained committed for the most part to their specific ideological predilections. This is re-enforced by the fact that the foundations work on the basis of substantial freedom of action: the desk officers for individual organisations hold great power in responding to situations on the ground. While monitored from the headquarters, the political foundation desk officers have developed close and long-term relations with partners. As a result, there exists a considerable level of trust between the foundations and their partner organisations (Mair, 2000).

It is notable that these foundations are explicitly founded on values, that is, respective political values of the party-political tradition *but also* on value pluralism.

> The principle of pluralism . . . is the democratic way to curb state omnipotence. Just as different political parties struggle for votes and power in a democratic system, democratic political education must always reflect the diversity of opinions, of political options and models.
>
> (Friedrich Naumann Stiftung, 2002)

One of the key aspects of the work of foundations, then, is the recognition of the need for openly political and ideological debate as an underpinning of democratisation – at home or abroad. While liberal democracy can be supported, so should social democracy and radical democracy of the Left. Democracy support should consist of recognition of the full gamut of political traditions in home countries and thereby also in target countries and crucially open dialogue and struggle between political foundations is considered a positive and natural state of affairs (Mair, 2000). Far from 'depoliticising' democracy support, explicitly political and pluralist principles are at work here.

This is reflected in the conceptions of democracy that can be found within the foundations' work. While the liberal foundations – Friedrich Naumann in Germany and Jarl Hjalmarson in Sweden, for example – tend to promote the Hayekian 'liberal economic rights first' idea of liberal democracy (see e.g. Ashford, 2003), the social democratic foundations – the Friedrich Ebert Stiftung in Germany and the Olof Palme Centre in Sweden, for example – work with a philosophy of democratisation which prioritises 'managing fragmentation tendencies and neutralising socioeconomic conflicts of interest' through being attuned to the role of under-privileged actors (FES, 2012). The Christian democratic foundations, on the other hand, work with religious and political groups towards the advancement of a social market economy, while the Green and far left foundations such as the Heinrich Böll foundation and the Rosa Luxembourg foundations agitate for global justice agendas. The political traditions and ideological debates between them is reflected in their work. The approaches to democracy could not be more different. While some call for liberal market economies as a crucial *a priori* condition of democratisation, others explicitly argue that democracies premised on market principles are in danger of collapsing in the face of democratic illegitimacy. Here then, alive and kicking, is a truly pluralistic and ideological contestation of different models of democracy in democracy support. Or so it would seem.

Towards depoliticisation, consensus ideology and market-led approach?

While interviews with practitioners and documentation of the foundations emphasise their distinct ideological and hence 'democratic' orientations, we need to dig deeper, and study some of the worrying dynamics affecting the work of these organisations in recent years. Here, I want to reflect briefly on the ways in which depoliticisation and hegemonic 'liberal' consensus-building is affecting the ideological premises of the foundations' work.

In one of the few academic studies on the foundations, Mair (2000) records some important shifts in the work of these foundations in the last two decades. Mair notes that there have been increasing shifts towards micro-projects as opposed to fostering long-term strategic alliances with key actors in the target countries. Also, the foundations, Mair points out, suffer from increasingly insecure funding bases, which forces them increasingly to look for external funding in the competitive global development field and the 'democracy promotion industry'. There has also been a shift towards employing a new generation of 'young technocrats' in desk offices, who are familiar with new and increasingly demanding development aid requirements: these young professional technocrats are replacing the locally based politically connected actors (Mair, 2000: 136–7).

What interests me is that this process may be undoing what has always been distinctive about the foundation actors: that is, their ideological orientations in democracy support. Subject to the pressures of increasingly technocratic and professionalised aid delivery mechanisms, the political nature, the flexibility and distinctiveness of the activities of these actors is being undermined. While in the past, volunteers from local party branches would visit target states to engage in strategic debates (e.g.

with union activists), nowadays foundations too increasingly 'organise workshops' and 'train' civil society actors. These types of activities fit within the requirements of output-oriented development aid: 'recording an impressive number of seminars that have been funded makes the expenditure easier to understand and defend, compared to justifying the core funding of a partner on the grounds that it might play a more useful role in democracy in the future' (Mair, 2000: 139).

While a state has always had some control over these actors, that state at least was committed to ideologically pluralist but also ideologically principled democracy support. When development aid bureaus have shifted to output-oriented management models and as other international organisations have increased their role in the foundations funding, the foundations, along with many other non-state actors, seem to have increasingly shifted towards more 'co-operative' but also, as a result, more ideologically consensual results-led approaches to democracy support.

Interviews and discussions with foundation actors confirm these trends. The foundations are increasingly both subject to shifting trends towards standardisation in development aid delivery structures and are looking for external funding from the EU and other development funds for their work. And they are feeling the effects of the funding requirements and the management criteria. Many foundation practitioners complain of the heavy paperwork their work involves now and recognise shifts in their work as a result. In some contexts, these contextual changes are compromising the democracy promotion of these organisations. No longer will volunteer-based dialogue and strategising take place as technical multi-party projects win out. There is a danger that the shifts '[do] not increase ownership but promotes opportunism instead' (Mair, 2000: 140).

Note in this context the increasing shift towards micro-projects over long-term commitment to specific ideological actors. This approach has the advantages of avoiding dependency on organisations, which may also turn out to be corrupt and inefficient (a problem in the past), yet it also means that target organisations on the ground are increasingly being subjected to not only the process of open competition for funding (same process foundations themselves are increasingly subject to from their funders), but also partial and piece-meal funding that is likely to be un-conducive to long-term democratisation (Mair, 2000).

The managerial requirements of international development aid are increasingly complex for the foundations to manage. They necessitate that the foundations possess formal 'development expertise' and that they have undergone training in international development management practices, requirements which are difficult to fulfil by some of the more traditional volunteer-based political foundations, for example. Such requirements also limit the foundations' ability to engage in the traditional 'political' activities and agitation in democracy support. The social democratic foundation actors, for example, have noted the difficulties that arise in developing direct trade union contact between donor and target country populations. The explicitly political/ideological underpinnings of such activities are not easily accommodated within the depoliticised management practices of the development agencies. This is not to even mention the complications caused by the inability of volunteer actors to complete complex management documentation now required by development institutions (Interview with representative of a political foundation, 2010).

In this context, interestingly, the political foundations are also increasingly becoming a form of democracy aid facilitation, rather than a political democracy promoter themselves. While they used to 'deliver' projects, now they rely often on 'subcontractors' on the ground. They provide assistance in application for money, project management and subcontract activities to local NGOs, rather than acting as a direct political democratising agitator. They are intermediaries to which donors turn to deliver their goods on the 'ground'.

While depoliticising and 'marketisation' are distinctive dynamics in the operating practices of the foundations, this is not to say that there are no ideological leanings or distinct conceptual understandings of democracy remaining in their work. Their respective philosophies do still come through in how activities are structured. Yet, there is also a notable rise of a 'common perspective'. What is interesting about the rhetoric of foundation activists, including social democratic activists, is their unwavering commitment to liberal democratic 'core' principles on which democracy support is to be founded. As one foundation representative stated: we 'follow more or less Dahl's paradigm' (Interview with representative of political foundation, 2011).

Interest in contestation over democracy between multiple perspectives, of course, was not the strong suite of a Dahlian perspective, which sought to pin down the 'realistic' meaning of democracy to core liberal notions.

What does this say about the 'politics' of democracy support through political foundations? It says that while such historically ideological actors as these have and do play important roles in democracy support, their roles and activities are increasingly being shifted in directions which may undermine their historical roles. Thus, while the foundations have actively sought a new role for themselves in democracy support and have started to rebrand themselves in order to keep their competitive edge in the democracy promotion market, some foundation activists, especially on the Left, also increasingly note the dangers and the weaknesses of the new dynamics. Not only do the new managerial practices shift the nature of the activities of actors, but also they change their self-perceptions. No longer are they political, ideological and principled; rather they are increasingly efficiency-seeking, product-selling, opportunistically co-operative and results-led. This shift has allowed these organisations to increasingly obtain funding from other key funders, such as the EU, but also in so doing, runs the risk of stunting their political edge in democracy support (see also Mair, 2000: 140–2).

Network actors

If the political foundations have been a rather poorly understood set of actors, there is another distinct kind of actor in democracy promotion today, which hardly receives a mention. There are nowadays an increasing number of so-called 'network' actors. In the US context, organisations such as InterAction play an important role in bringing together US-based NGOs working in development. In

Europe, ENoP and EPD are key actors in networking political foundations and NGOs to European funding structures and to each other. These are interesting actors to examine for they give us an insight into the workings of democracy promotion scene in today's global context. These organisations seek to influence the policy processes and thus, if you like, represent or 'lobby' for changes in democracy promotion structures which may be of benefit to their 'stakeholders'. Not all network organisations are of this nature, as we will see, but such networking and, if you like, interest-representation, now plays an important role in the democracy support industry.

The European Network of Political Foundations (ENoP) is a conglomeration, or network organisation, that brings together political foundations in Europe. It was established just a few years ago to feed the foundations' views to the European decision-making scene, where their work, curiously, was being ignored. They wanted to bring their perspective specifically to the Commission and the Council in order to institute changes to the structure of the EU's civil support organisation (CSO) funding in democracy support. Having been successful in so doing, the ENoP is itself part-funded under the EU's NSA-LA programme.[2] They have also, through training arranged for members, been successful in helping member foundations to receive grants through the EU's funding streams.

But what conceptions of democracy, if any, does the ENoP work with? On the face of it, the organisation's president was clear about what is meant by democracy: the ENoP works with the EU's Copenhagen criteria in defining the meaning of democracy. Democracy for ENoP purposes means democratic institutions, rule of law, human rights, minority rights and free press as defined by the EU in its accession criteria. These constituents make up 'European democratic values' (Interview with Arjen Berkvens, 2011).

It is arguably not just a principled commitment to these 'European values' that motivates the 'consensual approach' to the meaning of democracy of the ENoP: the discourse on democracy is informed by very pragmatic considerations. Given the EU's preference for depoliticised or apolitical action in democracy promotion, arguably the foundations' 'partisan' edge has been intentionally played down by the ENoP in its lobby efforts (Interview, Berkvens). This has arguably made the ENoP's approach to political society as a central aspect of democratisation more palatable to the Commission which abhors partisan language.

This has, however, meant some movement away from the overtly political language previously central to the political foundations. The foundations, whatever their ideological orientation, have in their ENoP co-operation agreed to work with a consensual, in some regards 'lowest common denominator', discourse on the meaning of democracy in order to avoid disruptive political debate between them. As a foundation representative explained in a different context, the core liberal rights agenda – electoral representation rights, minority rights and human rights – are less contestable in nature than the idea of democracy and hence provide a better grounding for action (Interview with representative of a political foundation, 2011). Openly dealing with contestation then might endanger the ENoP's stance vis-à-vis the Commission by potentially exposing partisan leanings. Although a liberal consensus discourse does not of course exclude that individual political foundations push for views on democracy which go beyond the liberal democratic Copenhagen Criteria in their own activities, it is simply the ENoP's preference that, in the EU context, it is best to avoid engaging foundations in ideological or political debate. As Arjen Berkvens states, 'the EU will never finance national social democratic foundations, so we go for a multi-party and depoliticised approach' (Interview, Berkvens). As a result, the ENoP tries to keep out of contested politics of democracy and 'stick to lobby work' (Interview, Berkvens).

This stance, while entirely understandable, is far from straightforward as the basis for ENoP's actions in 'representing' the political foundations. This is because arguably some interesting tensions characterise the ENoP's take on the conceptual premises of democracy support.

What is distinctive, first, is the tension between the ENoP's conceptual approach, which places emphasis on 'political society', and its simultaneous reluctance to discuss the 'political ideologies' that make up a 'political society'. The ENoP rejects the more technical institutional approach to democracy promotion advocated in many EU programmes. Reflecting the political foundations' general orientation, the ENoP places especial emphasis on political society and encouragement of democratic reforms and attitudes within it as a key condition of successful democratisation. Indeed, this is perceived as the 'niche' of ENoP members' democracy promotion. Yet, fascinatingly, the politics or ideologies of political society, embedded in the individual foundations' charters and positions in their local political systems, is not something the ENoP wants to discuss in explicit terms. Instead it pushes for the opposite: for more consensual, mainstream, co-operative actions, such as projects on elections or multi-party systems. In such projects, which can bring together multiple 'partisan traditions', the individual partisan foci of foundation work can be sidestepped and foundations made more palatable for funders. While focusing on political society, the politics of political society are curiously undiscussed.

It is also notable that while opting for a common consensus on the meaning of democracy and avoiding ideological debate, the political foundations of course do accept that there are many models, including participatory models, at stake in debates on democracy promotion. Berkvens too recognises that on occasion debates between conservatives and radicals, for example, can raise their heads (Interview, Berkvens). Yet, despite these disagreements the ENoP political foundations also share a common goal: shaping the structure of EU's democracy support in their shared interest. Ultimately this pragmatic shared goal trumps any ideological contestation over democracy's meaning. This is further reinforced by the view, expressed by another political foundation actor, that even if you break democracy down to different models, you would still get from all of them the same core elements (Interview with representative of a political foundation, 2011). Despite conceptual differences between the foundations, the ENoP – paradoxically – works with the assumption that at their roots all models of democracy are liberal democratic in nature. While accepting pluralism, the ENoP narrows down the meaning of democracy to a single 'core' meaning, on which additional elements can be built.

Another interesting conceptual assumption is sidestepping of the politico-economic aspects in political foundation or ENoP work. Not only do different ideological traditions have different views on democracy, they also have very different views on the politico-economic contexts of democracy as we have seen. The ENoP, however, wishes to sidestep debate on this – despite its members' interests in the nexus of development and democracy. The ENoP recognises that there are indeed very different approaches adopted to economic development among its members. However, the implications of this for democracy promotion are not explored in detail; rather the issue of developmental ideologies is sidestepped as an issue of no direct concern for ENoP (Interview, Berkvens). The ENoP is not aiming to be 'political' in this sense, but rather is opposed to political infighting on politico-economic ideologies (Interview, Berkvens). It seeks to create political consensus on democracy as a key concept, which in turn means sidestepping questions of politico-economic contestation around democracy's meaning.

This is demonstrated also in another characteristic of ENoP's work: its focus on national democracy as the location of perceived democracy – enhancing activities of its members. Again, because 'global democracy' is not a focus shared by all, it is best to narrow down common interests to conceptual foci which all can agree on. This of course silences within ENoP's stances the specific interests in global democratisation of some of the more radical actors.

In sum, the ENoP's treatment of democracy is curious in many ways. Crucially, it is underpinned by a slippage towards a classical liberal paradigm. While on the one hand it is agreed that democracy does not come in a single model, the ENoP for various pragmatic reasons tends to work with liberal democratic principles. This core conception on liberal democratic lines excludes discussions of the economic as part of the political.

The ENoP demonstrates the extent to which even the explicitly political and ideological actors in democracy support today have adjusted to the existing policy scene by accepting the importance of lobbying, interest-representation and consensus-building for their work. In a global industry where organisations increasingly compete for funds under competitive processes, means to represent sectional interests are important to foster. While such lobbying and pragmatic coming-together serves common interests – arguably, the political foundations' representation has been far more successful since the generation of ENoP as an umbrella organisation – at the same time it also demonstrates and embodies shifts in 'conceptual' thinking on democracy. The rise of a consensus agenda of liberal democracy promotion and the depoliticisation of democracy's meaning are key trends reflected here.

They are similarly reflected in the work of other network actors, such as the European Partnership for Democracy (EPD), which is a civil society initiative, with three foci of action: (1) to influence policy debate and advocacy (EPD's emergence is tied to development of EU Council Conclusions); (2) to engage in knowledge-sharing between CSOs in Europe ('transition belt'); (3) to channel funding towards third countries; and (4) to facilitate CSO access to funding (Interview with CSO representative, 2011). The EPD is conceived essentially as a 'platform for donors and CSOs to meet and come to a common agenda' (Interview with CSO representative, 2011).

What kind of conceptual debates are played out here then? The EPD was designed to bring the uniqueness of the EU context to democracy promotion activity in Europe. The EPD was to reflect the uniquely open and diverse approach to democracy within Europe – all its 27 member states' visions of democracy – and thereby also the unique flexibility and dynamism of European approaches to democracy support. The philosophy underlying EPD was recognition of diversity and the pluralism of EU's experience with democracy and the aim was to highlight the problems of homogeneous narratives on democracy, characteristic of US democracy promotion, for example.

The aim was also to highlight the importance of listening carefully prior to assistance. Thus, the EPD has primarily funded platform discussions where donors and CSOs in specific countries have been able to come together to discuss their specific needs, aims and demands, so as to bring forth more genuinely dialogical and interactive democracy promotion funding. The EPD's agenda has been about 'pulling the break and rethinking' democracy promotion done in a 'hard driven way' (Interview with CSO representative, 2011). The best the EU can do, it is believed, is stay at arms length and tell its own stories about different experiences with democracy, and to address the rigidity and incoherencies in its own actions. This is what the EPD seeks to achieve.

According to a CSO representative, the motivation for EPD is driven by perceived scepticism by CSOs of the EU's actions. Especially the 'calls for proposals' structure of EU democracy funding is perceived as a failure: it sets CSOs up against each other and reduces room for flexibility and strategic action both by CSOs and funders themselves. Trust funds and more flexible instruments should be looked to. The EPD also calls for a more openly political approach to democracy promotion. The EPD, then, in part shares the ENoP's agenda; they are for more open and political funding in democracy promotion. Yet, the EPD also in some regards competes with the ENoP; this is partly due to the structure of EU funding and policy-making; it drives CSOs and political foundations to compete for the same funding and hence to treat each other with scepticism (Interview with CSO representative).

But what conceptions of democracy does the EPD work with? Again, curious conceptual choices emerge from a close study of the organisation's discourse. When asked how the EPD conceives of democracy, a CSO representative stated that 'key elements' of democracy need to be understood in line with the core liberal consensus view. Basic consensus on liberal democratic foundations is needed on which to build democracy action (Interview with CSO representative, 2011).

Yet again tensions abound. First, the commonly agreed liberal view seems in some ways to clash with the EPD's push for a distinctive European agenda. Indeed, it is rather curious that despite a concern for a distinctive European approach, the EPD does not seek to push a specific conception – for example, a social democratic conception – of democracy. The starting point is that the EPD will not take sides either on meaning or context of democracy but rather seeks to keep its view open. Much like the ENoP, the EPD does not wish to get into political debates on democracy (Interview with CSO representative, 2011). A strange kind of pluralism then stands at the heart of the EPD's activities: it highlights diversity as a basic principle of the European approach and does not wish to support the more narrow institutional democracy promotion only; yet, there is no clear ideological basis on which narrow views or diversity is highlighted and it is not clear what this means in practice for distinctiveness of the EU's democracy promotion. For example, what seems for external actors to be most interesting about the EU's democratic experiences – social democracy – is not openly highlighted as a unique ideological or political approach to democratisation in Europe or through the EPD (International IDEA, 2009a). This is because of a wish not to alienate potential target organisations or the EU, but yet again the curiously depoliticised approach to democracy, and the adoption of a common consensus on liberal model, is characteristic of the EPD's discourse.

NIDG: another type of a network

The Network Institute for Global Democratisation (NIDG) is another network institute in the area of democracy promotion, but one that differs in crucial and consequential respects from the other two examined above. The NIDG is, vis-à-vis the mainstream democracy promotion scene, a much less 'mainstream' actor, although it is far from insignificant in that the UN Secretary General Kofi Annan, for example, has given this organisation his endorsement, stating that it is a 'pioneering form of electronic network that has furthered the democratisation process' (NIGD, 2012). But what does this network do and where does it stand on the meaning of the idea of democracy?

What is noteworthy about the NIGD is that it is a network structure. However, it differs from ENoP and EPD in two crucial respects: (1) it does not seek to explicitly represent specific constituencies of CSO or NGO actors, and (2) it is based on the loosest possible network structure: 'the concept of "network institute" stands for our principle of maximal light-weight infrastructure' (NIGD, 2012). Its aim is somewhat less specifically defined than those of ENoP and EPD, and that is to defend the interest of specific kinds of actors or to advance specific democracy promoters' aims but to 'strengthen global civil society by producing and developing emancipatory knowledge for democratic movements, organisations, and states' (NIGD, 2012). Indeed, a member of the NIGD interviewed reinforces that it was conceived as an organisation that would act as a 'collective organic intellectual', 'organically connected to different worldwide transnational social movements, some of them struggling also for democracy in their local context' but also with a significant focus on global democratisation (Interview with Heikki Patomäki, 2011). In its role, then it does not 'represent anything', rather it is 'about taking the initiative, struggle for hegemony, as it were, developing new ideas, giving new directions . . . always in dialogue' (Interview, Patomäki).

The NIGD does so through disseminating knowledge and generating dialogue through seminars, workshops and conferences. Its members also engage in specific non-NIGD funded projects, which are fed through to NIGD work. One of its core aims is facilitation of debate and knowledge-dissemination on the World Social Forum; of which it is a founding member. This 'radical democratic' experiment that has now been running for numerous years seeks to explicitly bring together anti-capitalist and other reform movements 'to make another world possible'.

As for its structure and membership, the NIGD is 'composed of a transnational network of nearly 100 researchers and practitioners who strive to promote democratisation' and is run by a structure of partially overlapping activist-based hubs responsible, respectively, for newsletters, website, administration and funding. The NIGD is run from Helsinki, Finland and Lima, Peru, and works on the basis of a board and annual meeting conducted online (Interview, Patomäki). Working on the basis of the participatory democratic principle of self-organisation, many of its projects are run by individual project leaders responsible to the board. The core principle of management is that many people take responsibility and leadership shifts often, with no single individual remaining in control of the organisation for any great length of time.

The organisation suffers from severe constraints in funding. Having received core funding from Nottingham Trent University, the Finnish Foreign Ministry and the Ford Foundation, the organisation in recent years has struggled to raise NIGD-specific funding. This is partly because it has, while applying to a whole set of international foundations, refused to 'compromise' on its principles and radical reform agenda (Interview, Patomäki). Given that the funds are small-scale most of the activity is volunteer-based. This organisation, while structured and professional, is not the same type of professional NGO found on the Brussels scene. It does not pitch itself to the European CSO funding market: in fact, its members have been rather skeptical of the bureaucratic requirements of EU funding and also do not think the EU would be very forthcoming in terms of provision of funding for such an organisation. This is also partly because the NIGD has engaged in agendas which run counter to the views of Commission, for example on the idea of Tobin Tax. Indeed, Patomäki reveals that while he has engaged with the European Parliament, he has on occasion argued for by-passing the central EU institutions because they have been opposed to the kinds of reforms that NIGD has proposed. Instead of seeking to get into bed with any major funder, the NIGD looks towards activist organisations and the academic establishment to provide funding, drive, and audience for its activities, although strategic interactions have also been had with state officials, Members of the European Parliament and the UN. Crucially, however, the NIGD is centrally *not* a lobby organisation but interested in instigating critical thinking on alternatives to current democratic trends.

In terms of conceptions of democracy, its work is noteworthy in three key aspects with regard to conceptual debate, and it is here that crucial differences from ENoP and EPD arise. First, the NIGD adopts a global democratic perspective and openly moves beyond a statist framework of democratisation. When examining the foci of projects, it becomes immediately apparent that a global perspective is adopted as the framework for democratisation, and crucially national level democratisation is discussed in relation to democratisation of global political and economic institutions. This means that civil society too is encouraged on the basis of conceiving of it as global activism rather than as 'functional' in facilitating national liberal democratisation (cf. EU and US political foundations).

Second, it is to be noted that the NIGD adopts an openly politico-economic approach to democratisation. Indeed, much of its focal concerns revolve around restructuring of global economic and financial governance structures, not simply national political systems. In many respects the global democratisation of economic structures is precisely seen as a precondition of any meaningful national democratisation. Conceptions of democratisation are then clearly seen as bound up with economic systems, structures and processes and economic reform as essential to democratisation. As Patomäki puts it: 'Many of our proposals have to do with how global political economy is governed: new regulations . . . taxation . . . ways of controlling in a democratic way global financial systems. These are keys to understanding global neoliberalism. By tackling these first we open up space for other democratic reforms. So the focus is very often on political economy' (Interview, Patomäki).

Third, there is radical democratic and also a dialogical philosophy underpinning the NIGD's work. First, its origins lie in a radical democratic initiative undertaken in the Finnish context and it seeks to extend radical and participatory democratic ideals of increased participation of people on multiple levels, sites and spaces of democracy (Interview, Patomäki). Second, it works on the basis of dialogical and non-imposing principles: 'All of NIGD's work is based on the conviction that globalization, defined as the coming-together-of-humanity, must be based on cross-cultural dialogue concerning both philosophical fundamentals, and concrete reform proposals' (NIGD, 2012).

This means that the kind of sidestepping of debate on the meaning of democracy characteristic of other networks is made, by principle, difficult, and debates on the meaning of democracy become tied up with the very idea of reform. These philosophical and political (rather than pragmatic instumental) set of commitments are important to appreciate, for they render this organisation less closely bound to specific interests and hence to specific visions of democracy. Indeed, there is open recognition of the need to contest the notion of democracy and remain open to dialogical debate on its meaning. Notably the liberal consensus view of democracy is not attached to the activities here – unlike in the frameworks of the EPD and ENoP. This organisation is then a very different kind of a network organisation from those of ENoP and EPD; it is more idealistic and radical, although not less concrete, in its proposals and its activities. A key call it makes for democracy promoters is that they should remain far more open in their engagement with the idea of democracy. This sets a bold challenge for them; and their liberal-democracy-preferring mainstream discourses. As Patomäki powerfully argues:

> In the spirit of critical responsiveness . . . you should provide funding for
> actors that are promoting different contested notions of democracy, including

also democratising democracy promotion itself and all these other related relations of power. It is very short-sighted to promote only those conceptions of democracy that you yourself, or political party behind you . . . are willing to advocate in your own location or place . . . you should be much more open minded . . . It is possible to organise it that way: there are many institutions that provide an example . . . universities in neoliberal era, we are based on the very idea that states are willing to fund autonomous organisations within which you can do whatever in terms of learning . . . It's a good idea . . . it benefits the society as a whole.

This is a bold challenge and brings into focus not only the failures of major funding agencies in engaging with radical agendas but also of the other NGOs which, according to Patomäki, follow the mainstream agenda of the Organisation for Economic Co-operation and Development (OECD) and the EU far too closely. The NIGD explicitly does not do so: 'We haven't bothered to look very closely at these documents, except when we do critical research on them' (Interview, Patomäki).

But how successful can the NIGD be then, existing outside of mainstream agendas and looking for radical global solutions through activist networks and the World Social Forum? Patomäki admits that successes are few, in fact in concrete terms non-existent: no concrete proposal has been implemented. Yet, the NIGD has successfully informed policy agendas of the UN, of the Belgian state, of activists on the ground in places such as Middle East. Also, some of its proposals, for example, with regard to global financial tax, are now becoming more mainstream.

While lack of concrete achievements may be disappointment, NIGD remains proud that they 'have not only kept the spirit of critical civil movements alive but have provided concrete utopias to the discussion and these have played a role in shaping the agenda' (Interview, Patomäki). The grounds for measurements of success are rather different here than for the more output-oriented, efficiency-driven democracy promotion actors: they are not just about influencing policy, or successful delivery of measurable democratisation training or projects, but about keeping correct ethical principles of participatory democracy and traditions of alternative thinking on global problems alive. *Ad-hoc* engagements have been had and some relative successes too achieved, despite the difficult working context of 'neoliberal globalisation'. The aim is simple in that 'you bring in ideas of democracy that are not so conventional and might encourage people to participate' (Interview, Patomäki) and in this regard limited successes have been achieved.

Yet, this organisation is far less connected to the hubs of democracy support or its funding. It is, some might say, a marginal democracy enhancement organisation. This is because its open opposition to neoliberal politico-economic solutions, and its refusal to examine democracy merely as a representative institution devoid of economic and global context which needs to be democratised. This means it suffers from very specific limitations. As Patomäki summarises: 'I think that is the difficult story of the neoliberal era. Unless you want to be very accommodating to the neoliberal discourse and ideas . . . it is very difficult to get funding, and we have seized all the opportunities that there have been' (Patomäki, Interview).

But are such organisations today inevitably marginal in democracy support frameworks? Do politics of democracy support demand to be toned down? And what does this all tell us about NGO and CSO actors in the field of democracy support?

Conclusion: ideologies in non-state democracy promotion

This chapter is based necessarily on a limited analysis of NGO actors. For the sake of focus and space, we have examined some of the most important NGO-type actors funded within international democracy programmes today: International IDEA, foundations and network actors. As limited as such an analysis is – we have not specifically tackled organisations 'delivering' aid on the ground or specific projects of democracy aid delivery – some key trends are identifiable in the work of NGOs today.

We have seen that funding is a key concern for NGOs involved in democracy support, but also that funding concerns interestingly direct their conceptual decisions. In today's context the NGOs must actively seek funding from external as well as public sources, and in so doing need to create niches and market opportunities for their activities. They need to 'sell themselves' and in so doing create trust and show conformity to development aid and expertise standards of funders. This means professionalisation of their work and increasingly widespread adoption of development industry's management tools in NGO work: from log frames to results-based measures and financial audit systems.

These funding structures and changes clearly create pressures towards de-politicisation and consensus-ideology. This is most evident with the political foundations, some of which openly recognise the need to tone down their ideological specificities in democracy support towards more 'mainstream' and more clearly results-based management systems and activities. The need to demonstrate concrete results creates an aesthetic of measurement and reporting to which funders and receivers of aid should conform to. This progressively removes, or moulds, the conceptual and thus ideological commitments of NGO democracy support. Social democratic actors, for example, record increasing problems in voluntary and principle-based democracy support because of increasing management and funding pressures on them. While the state still funds democracy support of most foundations, the move to privatisation and subcontracting (and hence 'NGO-isation') of democracy support drives as well as reflects the increasingly depoliticised tendencies in democracy support. As Sending and Neumann (2006) warn: NGOs are becoming the tools of the state and the global governance organisations and are embracing this role for themselves.

These tendencies give rise to many paradoxes. As we have seen here, many foundations in democracy support claim to support pluralism, yet it is consensual 'liberal' pluralism that increasingly drives the activities, while engagement with *contestation* over models of democracy is sidestepped. Pluralism and full debate on democracy's meaning might entail levels of debate which would undermine the democracy support agenda. Too much democratic debate in the democracy support industry is not good for business.

Even when full-marketisation of democracy aid has not taken place (as in the EU) partial pushes in that direction are already evident in funding frameworks. Public money still plays a role but is decreasing and is also becoming more stringently managed on the basis of efficiency and result-delivery principles. The strategic and the political is giving way to results-led work and de-politicisation – a curious set of aims for democracy promotion, a historically uniquely ideological and normative policy aim. While actors such as the NIGD still retain hope of alternative avenues in democracy support, this chapter has shown that there are curious trends in democracy support through foundations and NGOs. It has shown that these actors are by no means more liberated, more politically open or independent actors in democracy support. We should not turn to them, then, in an idealistic hope that they would provide an alternative 'critical' edge to democracy support: in an 'implicitly liberal' world order, these organisations seem to increasingly form part and parcel of the governmentality structures of liberal world ordering (see Chapter 11).

10 International financial institutions and democracy promotion

We have examined in earlier chapters organisations that self-consciously perceive themselves as engaged in democracy support. However, to understand the democracy support of the main 'democracy donors', we need to also have some understanding of the role of global financial and economic organisations – or international financial institutions (IFIs) – in 'governance support'.

To suggest that the IFIs would have a role in democracy support seems counterintuitive for some. Why? Because these organisations see themselves as purely 'economic' in nature, and many commentators in economic and political sciences perceive them as such (Swedberg, 1986; Teivainen, 2002; Kurki, 2012b). These organisations, so the conventional story goes, do not explicitly concern themselves with 'political' matters and could not do so because of the restricted mandates that constrain their activities. Yet, curiously and importantly, these organisations have also come to realise that not engaging with the interaction of the economic and the political will jeopardise their wider aims with regard to economic growth, development and poverty reduction. Thus, a considerable part of the agenda of the IFIs has been 'governance-oriented'. Also, these activities have structured in deep-running ways the activities of other democracy promotion actors, not just non-governmental organisations (NGOs) but also bigger organisations, such as the European Union (EU). Hence, it is crucial to appreciate the extent and nature of the IFIs' democracy promotion – not least because of the role of specific 'politico-economic models' within their activities.

In this chapter, I will first examine briefly the role of IFIs and the evolving role of 'governance' engagement within them. I then examine a set of 'cases' which suggest in more detail how these institutions, notably the World Bank, engage in democracy support 'by proxy'. I will examine the Bank's good governance agenda, the IFIs' anti-corruption work and the participatory Poverty Reduction Strategy Papers. The general discourse and each case study suggest interesting dynamics in terms of the 'model' of democracy which emerges from the IFIs' work. While we can observe language of social equity and participation in their discourses, these terms acquire their meaning within a market- and competition-driven discourse. There is then, I argue, remarkably little meaningful debate beyond embedded neoliberal and neoliberal approaches within the frameworks of these organisations. This is not helped by the depoliticisation of governance work within the IFIs. Finally, I will reflect on the 'structuring' role of the IFIs for global democracy support. Their role, I suggest, is more important than is often perceived by students of democracy promotion and needs to be analysed more carefully through conceptual as well as politico-economic lenses.

IFIs and democracy support: an historical trajectory

In the aftermath of the Second World War a series of international financial and economic organisations, often referred to as Bretton Woods organisations, was set up. Their role was to facilitate the macro-economic management of international capitalist systems in such a way that would guard against structural instability. The International Monetary Fund (IMF) was set up to facilitate the financing of countries in liquidity or debt difficulties. The General Agreements on Tariffs and Trade – which later became the World Trade Organization (WTO) – was set up to encourage the liberalisation of world trade. The World Bank, on the other hand, was set up to facilitate lending to countries in need of development assistance.

Each of these organisations was accorded a very specific set of mandates. Crucially, these mandates were 'limited' or 'restricted' in nature: they only covered strictly economic questions of how to facilitate increasing efficiency, liquidity, solvency and stability in global trade and financial transactions. At the same time, though, they set up a rather ambitious and globally expansive system of economic facilitation, covering both macro-financial stability pacts and micro-projects facilitating economic growth 'from below'.

But what do these organisations then have to do with democracy promotion? Much more than one might think. While these organisations have worked with restricted mandates – mostly focusing on macro-financial stability, monetary cooperation, facilitation of trade, and reduction of poverty – and while for most of their existence they were blind to democracy's role in development, preferring to instil stability and economic development as priorities, they have also come to play crucial roles in facilitation of democratic governance practices globally (Abrahamsen, 2000: 26–7).

Arguably, they have always had an implicit role in 'political' 'governance' matters. The IMF, for example, has sought not only to monitor exchange rates, but also to lend emergency funds and thereby set reform conditions on its borrowers. It has also provided detailed policy guidance as to how to deal with monetary problems, guidance which extends to matters that are 'governance-related'. The WTO, on the other hand, facilitates the trade liberalisation of countries, a process which in turn necessitates deep-running legal and social reforms in target states. Especially since the focus is on 'beyond the borders' trade, much of the WTO's activities are today geared around facilitation of liberal economic structures, and concomitant cultural values and political attitudes in its member countries. The World Bank provides loans to countries, but also acts as a knowledge producer on development as well as a development actor which seeks to facilitate poverty reduction and economic growth in its borrower countries. This has taken the form of not only policy advice on how to structure the economy and the state in such ways as to improve efficiency, but also encouragement, through conditionality or otherwise, of deep-running reforms with regard to good governance and anti-corruption.

The activities and advice of IFIs have come under much scrutiny in years past because of their apparently 'neoliberal' and 'economistic' nature: they advance, critics argue, very specific, extreme versions of liberalisation, with little consideration to the 'political' or 'social' effects of economic decisions (Teivainen, 2002). Yet, from the point of view of this study, what is essential to note is that they are *not just economic* in nature but also confine and prescribe the extent and role of democratic controls in target countries.

When we examine them from the point of view of 'politico-economic models of democracy', we can see that, in important respects, these organizations are democracy promoting organisations: their actions target the 'political' as well as the economic structures, which have substantial consequences for the structuring of the target societies, their polities and economic systems (Williams, 1999, 2011; Abrahamsen, 2000). It is not just the case, then, that once 'economics enters, politics exists' (Teivainen, 2002); what is of interest to us here is that the two discourses, the economic and the political, despite their seeming separation, are closely intertwined in the work of the IFIs. Also, it should not be ignored that these organisations have since the early 1990s – rather paradoxically – started to openly embrace their role in governance work. Thus, under the auspices of improving accountability and efficiency of loan management and development, the IMF and the World Bank have both come to take on rather explicit roles in facilitation of good governance, state effectiveness and civil society (see e.g. Spanger and Wolff, 2003; Crawford, 2006; Limbach and Michaelowa, 2010; Williams, 2011).

Indeed, in many ways the whole rise of democracy support is tied to the actions and priorities of IFIs. What is often neglected or left aside in accounts of the history of democracy support, is that its rise as a policy area in the 1990s was in fact closely tied to a set of changes in the workings and shifting economic reasonings of the IFIs. Far from emanating merely from the US or German foundations (as many historical accounts suggest), arguably, a key facilitator of democracy support was the changing paradigm of economic development in the early 1990s. As Peter Burnell (2000: 40–1) documents, the sway of modernisation theory, which required economic development as a condition of democratisation, was diminishing in power in the early 1990s, while a new line of argumentation was on the rise, which placed democratisation alongside, or even as a condition of, economic development:

> An increasing number of development economists specializing in development policy came to the view that primary responsibility lay in the political sphere. Shortcomings in respect of political representation and governmental accountability produced economic policy regimes and styles of public sector (mis)management that were oriented to maintaining the power and enriching the prerequisites of the privileged few, not advancing public well-being.
>
> (Burnell, 2000: 41)

Significantly, then, it could be argued that it was changes in economic develop-ment paradigms and the views of economists in key global development organisa-tions that dictated the moves towards democracy promotion as a legitimate and crucial policy aim of states, NGOs, and crucially also of the IFIs. 'Once govern-ment is perceived to be a significant part of the problem, so attention to political matters must form an important part of the solution' (Burnell, 2000: 41).

But how are we to think of IFIs in democracy support? And crucially what kinds of politico-economic models emerge from their discourses and practices?

The work of a number of interesting scholars has already analysed the polit-ico-economic discourses of the IFIs. If democracy support has lacked politico-economic analysts, the IFIs' work has been subject to much rigorous politico-economic engagement, including analyses of the conceptual foundations of its activities. Yet, the conceptions of democracy in IFI work have arguably not been examined in detail. Drawing on the existing literature, research conducted within the project 'Political Economies of Democratisation', and original readings of various IFI documents, I argue here that certain important dynamics are played out in the IFI discourse on governance (and hence implicitly in discourses of democracy). Crucially, a shift towards a post-Washington consensus has taken place and with it a move towards an embedded neoliberal model. The language of participation and social equity plays an important role now in facilitation of 'stability' of social orders, yet the key notions that drive the IFI logics are neo-liberal in nature.

Outlines of conceptual orientations: the post-Washington consensus

As mentioned, a key shift took place in the work of the IFIs in the late 1990s. The most triumphant years of the post-Cold War era were subsiding and the strong neoliberal '*laissez-faire*' policies associated with Structural Adjustment were clearly failing in target countries. In this context, the World Bank turned to renewed thinking on the role of the state. The 1997 report *State in a Changing World* and the report of 2002 *Building Institutions for Markets* had a key role in pushing a paradigm-shift in thinking on states and markets. It is important, before we examine specific facets of IFI work, to appreciate the general discursive context within which democracy's role is conceived in the new post-Washington consensus paradigm. This has important consequences for the kinds of politico-economic models envisaged by the IFIs.

In 1997, no longer was development work to be guided by an ideological com-mitment to the idea of a limited state: instead an *effective state* was now required (World Bank, 1997: 1). Purely technical or technocratic solutions to economic growth were likely to fail, it was recognised, and thus the state had to be acknowl-edged as central in the process of generating sustainable development. Accounta-bility and transparency of the state and its ability to work in conjunction with civil society and markets were seen as paramount. An efficient state, able to provide for citizens in an effective manner, would arise if the state's roles were actively and systematically restructured.

A key in such restructuring was subjecting 'state institutions to greater competition' (World Bank, 1997: 3), for example, through better public–private partnerships. Indeed, state and private actors were now seen as 'complementary' (World Bank, 1997: 4) and the state's role was seen as pivotal in fostering a successful and attractive market system (World Bank, 1997, 2002).

The restructuring, however, also required a more 'stable' state. Thus, increased provision of basic welfare functions was seen as necessary to quell any 'fertile ground for violence or instability' (World Bank, 1997: 4). As a result efficient basic welfare services which could deal with disaffected populations, for example, were seen as having potential in stabilising governance systems. The secret of success in reform to public services then was to find the right balance of measures to 'incentivise' individuals to engage in the correct kinds of non-corrupt–pro-growth activities.

Broad coalitions – state, private sector, civil society and labour unions – should come together to 'achieve greater security at lower cost' (World Bank, 1997: 5). 'Lock[ing] in mechanisms that are costly to reverse' (World Bank, 1997: 6) was seen as a way forward as was partnership between private firms and citizens. The pressure such alliances could provide on the state was seen as crucial – the checks and balances that would emanate from private actors and partnerships would 'check arbitrary state action' (World Bank, 1997: 7). Private and NGO actors could also thus be called on to deliver state services and decentralisation and modernisation of bureaucracies in general was seen as an important aim (World Bank, 1997: 7).

Some of the reforms envisaged were seen as difficult to deliver. Yet, the 1997 report also had in mind new ways of delivering projects. Since changes on the level of perceptions and feelings of target state actors were seen as the key to efficient delivery of change (World Bank, 1997: 8), focus of implementation became localised and 'participatory'. State leaders could only do so much; 'effective leaders' in society would explain and sell reforms to their publics (World Bank, 1997: 14).

A few key conceptual trends indicative of specific politico-economic ideas on democracy are evident here. First, as David Williams (2011) has powerfully insisted, since 1997 a narrow neoliberal 'economistic' mode of development does *not* govern at the World Bank. Williams argues that there is instead 'a liberal transformationalist' project at work in the World Bank: this project perceives governance of civil society, as well as social and political life in general, as central to its aims. Given that irrationality of bureaucratic and political decision-making in target countries was seen as a major problem in obtaining economic reforms, it is these forces that should now be directly tackled. They are now seen as the 'major cause of economic decline', which in turn serve to justify a more 'intrusive development strategy' (Williams, 2011: 58). Following the precepts of New Institutional Economics, the states' capacity to collect information and manage economic processes has become seen as central: to have a strong market there is a perceived need to have a strong state with strong legal and regulatory systems (Williams, 2011: 85).

These moves in the World Bank have been replicated in crucial respects in the IMF. Ben Thirkell-White (2005) records the shifts towards 'political' over mere 'technical' requirements in the IMF's work too. It was especially the response to the Asian crisis that seems to have turned the tide in the IMF: it brought IMF to the centre of the project of facilitating 'market confidence' and the concomitant project of legal and institutional reforms. The role of the IMF is now perceived to be the restructuring of states, not just 'reducing them' (Thirkell-White, 2005: 2). Governance reform – good governance – and political conditionality to lending is now being tied to global efforts of democratisation, even if for IMF, because of the restricted mandate, good governance is interpreted in a rather technical way, as promotion of good governance for the sake of market and investor confidence.

As Thirkell-White (2005: 3) then argues, the IMF from 1997 onwards should be analysed as an institution of political, not just economic, management. Its policies have deep political and social impacts beyond 'questions of economic efficiency': they have impact on 'inter-ethnic redistribution, industrial policy, state-business relationships, welfare system, the debate on economic risks in society and the very basis of political power (Thirkell-White, 2005: 15).

This shift to facilitation of strong pro-market governance has brought with it some interesting dynamics. A crucial one is the 'governmentalisation' of the IFIs' work in governance. Rita Abrahamsen (2000, 2004) and Jonathan Joseph (2012) have pointed to important dynamics in this respect. They have pointed to the ways in which the IFIs have shifted the onus of responsibility for reforms, but also for control and compliance mechanisms, to the target countries. The states working with the IFIs are to now 'watch themselves' in moving towards better reform. Not only participatory modes internally within the state but also the so-called Review Mechanisms outside the state are all geared around 'locking in', through voluntary consultative processes, the kinds of incentive-based reforms the IFIs would like to see implemented (Abrahamsen, 2004). It is creating the correct mechanisms of pressure, checks and balances, both internally and internationally, which is behind the success of good adequate modernising reform. What this has meant, though, is the transference of duties, if you like, for reform programmes to national elites and local consultation groups, and increased subjection of states to various forms of voluntary as well as compulsory review mechanisms.

Whether this has worked or not is under some dispute. Jonathan Joseph (2012) notably argues that, unlike in Europe where self-regulatory governmental techniques succeed in gaining results in societies by shifting subjectivities as well as states towards the neoliberal governmental mode of thought, in the action of international organisations towards developing states, this has not succeeded. This is because, Joseph (2012) argues, there are not the adequate structures and social dynamics in place to facilitate these shifts.

Whatever the case, it is clear from the discourses of the World Bank and the IMF that today in the minds of development actors such as these are particular kinds of states: pro-market states, effective states and stable states. At the heart of their agendas are 'embedded neoliberal' ideas about the state.

The presence of neoliberal aims is evidenced by the fact that competition and market logic are at the heart of the IFIs' thinking. Whether it be merit-based human resources policy or business-climate building, at the heart of thinking on good governance lies the idea of a pro-market state. This is the most accountable and modern kind of state. Indeed, fears for arbitrary government, over-spending government, corrupt government and red-tape government are rife. It is smallish but efficient and measured pro-market government that is envisaged. As the 1997 report so well summarises:

> Taxes, investment rules, and economic policies must be ever more responsive to the parameters of a globalized world economy. Technological change has opened new opportunities for unbundling services and allowed a larger role for markets. These changes have meant new and different roles for government – no longer seen as sole provider but as facilitator and regulator.
>
> (World Bank, 1997: 2)

As much as democracy serves as an end for development, it does so through a specific vision of the macro-economic environment of democratic polities, it seems. Democracy nor development can viably exist in the context of high 'reckless' fiscal spending, non-transparent 'corrupt' public procurement, non-open 'protectionist' trade, non-meritocratic 'corrupt' bureaucracy, big 'laggard' non-accountable public sector, and non-professional 'non-incentivised' civil society. Clearly, some ideals about democracy come through here. Specifically, the kinds of values that motivate alternative models of democracy – primacy of politics, communal learning, big employment-providing state – are *not present* in the World Bank's discourse on the state.

At the same time, interest in development of *embedded neoliberalism* comes through in the World Bank's discourse on the state and markets. Reforms are not just about open markets, but also stability of social systems. Stability is now the name of the game: not just limited states are called for but stable, basic welfare-providing, pro-market states. States which regulate and oversee, manage and encourage, market solutions, are needed today: not big states, nor small states, but active pro-market states. But how do the discursive parameters play out in concrete actions of the IFIs?

Cases of 'democracy support' by proxy

Much deeper and broader analyses of the IFIs' activities in 'democracy field' should be undertaken by democracy support scholars, and indeed by the Bank itself (which continues to deny its own role in 'democracy'-support by focusing on 'governance'). To contribute to such a research agenda, three facets of the IFIs' work in the democracy field 'by proxy' are examined briefly here.

Good governance and the World Bank

The World Bank has taken a central role in governance work and is the global driver of governance thinking today. It aims to come up with the right strategies and modalities for introducing more transparent and accountable governance. Its work is central in setting out the key focal points of governance work and also measurement and indexing of states' 'performance' in governance. This work is needed not only because the quality of governance is seen as 'linked' to development performance (Levy, 2007: xix), but also because recipients have a commitment to ensure that aid is used effectively in the target states (Levy, 2007: xix).

The work done by the governance sector is focused on assessing and facilitating reforms to public sector governance, public administration and service provision. Since, as Brian Levy powerfully shows, these aspects are seen as closely related; it is important to develop measures – objective measures – of governance performance, quality of bureaucracy and performance of institutions (Levy, 2007). Despite the difficulties in measuring governance, various indicators have been developed, which are used as the basis for improvement of performance. Based on such assessments, advice on public sector finance, accountability structures, administrative processes, national checks and balances and service provision is given, including detailed advice on human resources policy, procurement, financial regulation and transparency mechanisms. The Bank is concerned about processes and incentives but also wise, efficient use and 'high-return investment' of money (Levy, 2007: xxix). Public sector governance reform is a key focal point as are sets of tax administration and legal structure reforms. Indeed, the World Bank, Williams (2011: 97) argues, is 'concerned intimately with the actual practices of government and capacities needed to pursue them'.

At the same time sequencing problems are noted. The secret is to find the correct balance of forces which enforce the right pressures for change. Levy, for example, argues for 'orchestrated imbalance', which 'builds momentum by embracing entry points for reform that have development impact in the short term, and also rachet up tension in the governance system' (Levy, 2007: xxxv). Clearly, the aim is to change governance structures of societies through a gradual and measured process of incentive-based reforms. Both top-down and bottom-up avenues are explored: reforms of institutions from on high, and citizen capacity-building in information gathering and dissemination (Levy, 2007: xxxii).

Yet, reforms envisaged are seen as essentially 'technical'. Despite critique of 'technocratic' approaches, in line with the Bank's mandate, the focus of work is on specific detailed governance mechanisms and how to improve them, not on politicisation of how governance should be organised, nor facilitation of debate on how it should be conducted.

But what models of democracy are envisaged here? None overtly; but implicitly a curiously modified neoliberal image emerges. Governance of the state should be pro-market, capable, and also participatory.

As we have seen, since the late 2000s the World Bank has taken decisive turns away from purely economistic approaches and the Washington Consensus ideals of liberalisation without concern for state capability. Capable, effective state and participation now stand at heart of its agenda (Levy, 2007: 1; see also Williams, 2011). This is clearly seen in the good governance programmes. What is of concern here is not liberalising, or undermining, state structures to such an extent that they would become subject to adverse pressures or compromised by poor resources. An embedded neoliberal concern for the stability and effectiveness of the state is central for development and aid accountability. It is why, after all, strong financial regulations, procurement systems, human resource systems and accountability should exist and must be measured and regulated. This is also why cutting services is not necessarily the aim of service sector work, but rather more effective delivery of it, through private sector co-operation and reform of public–private partnerships.

Interestingly, this orientation towards stable states, goes hand in hand with a varied set of 'participatory' agendas today. These agendas seek to leverage bottom-up forces for change, given that it is recognised that technocratic agendas alone do not work (Levi, 2007: xxxii). As a result, 'participatory' open governance is now a key focal point of the Bank's activities. Multiple programmes aim now to foster 'Open and Collaborative Governance', for example. This kind of governance 'facilitates an active dialogue between government and its citizens regarding, for example budget allocation and utilization and provision of social services. Citizens have improved access to their leaders and mechanisms in place to demand better services, and government has the capacity to respond' (World Bank Institute, 2012a). These ideas for open governance include: 'ensuring Open Budgets through Public Financial Management, strengthened Public Accounts Committees . . . ensuring Open Public Procurement . . . engaging with parliaments to enhance their capacity and ensure all branches of government are accessible to citizens; promoting collective-action against corruption . . . and, strengthening the capacity of journalists to hold the government accountable' (World Bank Institute, 2012b).

There is also a search for increasing private input into policy design as well as projects seeking to improve accountability and transparency, as well as efficiency, in policy design and administration.

These reform programmes are, moreover, tied to detailed projects of civil society reform. Indeed, in today's governmentalised context, mere projects are not enough. Real change and real leadership entails: 'a process that enables change agents to influence attitudes, mindsets and values of stakeholders' (World Bank Institute, 2012b). In regard to the activities in the civil society sphere, again the Bank is involved in 'an extraordinarily detailed attempt to change large areas of social, political and economic life' (Williams, 2011: 93). Thus, educational projects as well as civil society projects are funded to foster entrepreneurial spirits and utility-maximising individuals (Levy, 2007; Williams, 2011: 109).

Is the World Bank now a 'participatory democratic' actor? This does not seem to be the case, because the community development projects and training in participatory procedures seem to have a very specific set of foci: they are 'designed to promote community groups and instil in individuals an understanding . . . of a market economy and the skills, attitudes and patterns of thought and conduct which the Bank thinks necessary if the market economy is to flourish' (Williams, 2011: 113). This means that civil society groups or communal action is 'not to be composed of groups bound by affective ties, but rather recognisably modern associations, bound by their common interest in engaging with the market economy and thus brought within the purview of the state' (Williams, 2011: 114). A neoliberal 'conduct of conduct' seems to be the aim of participatory governance.

What is notable about the World Bank's activities in good governance then is that, despite more 'social', 'strong-state' and participatory tones, it is still closely geared around the promotion of specific economic and political visions. 'Despite the formally apolitical stance of the Bank . . . there is little doubt that underlying the . . . vision of good governance is a Western model, ringing with Weberian echoes, with its emphasis on free markets, individualism, and a neutral but effective public administration' (Leftwich, 1996: 16).

This is why the World Bank projects which involve participatory processes do not amount to what democratic theorists understand by participatory democracy. True participatory democracy would involve collective democratic ownership of workplaces, as well as educational structures, and not simply decentralisation of power to local governments or tribal councils or polling of citizens for the sake of efficient delivery of services. It should involve deliberation and co-decision, communal interaction and exchange, not merely 'customer evaluation'. Indeed, arguably, the very essence of participatory democracy clashes with the World Bank's insistence on an essentially liberal conception of civil society as a sphere of autonomous, interest-driven individuals looking to challenge and check the state.

It follows that in terms of the 'model of democracy' promoted, little has changed in the World Bank despite the new foci or work and participatory language. As Crawford, too, concludes:

> Theoretical or conceptual modifications [to World Bank's conception of the state or economy] remain firmly embedded within a neoliberal paradigm. Thus, democratic controls of the market or wage levels or property are not pushed for: rather, emphasis is, despite rhetorical openings, on private actors as key models of efficiency. Market requires a market model of society where private actors represent and vocalise their interests and preferences. The state is to act 'in the service of the free market economy'.
>
> (Crawford, 2006: 117)

The promotion of an essentially neoliberal ideal, even if with embedded stability-safe-guarding qualities, goes together with a depoliticisation of the idea of governance in the Bank's work. While critical of technocratic tendencies itself, there is a clear trend towards objectification of the idea of governance and lack of debate on democracy's many possible meanings. Levy's work (2007: xxi) on the indicators of governance demonstrates this well: a belief in objectivity of measures of 'successful' service delivery is unshaken and guides work on public sector reform and accountability building. A technical apolitical idea of governance, participation and hence democracy is dominant in the Bank's work and is underpinned by embedded neoliberal ideals.

Anti-corruption consensus

Anti-corruption work of the IFIs is another important area of democracy support 'by proxy'. The so-called international anti-corruption effort has become central in the activities of most IFIs and also those of various democracy promoters. It has been especially attractive as it has constituted a more technical and difficult-to-resist policy area through which politico-economic ideals can be 'promoted' in target states without the contestation that some of the more overtly political agendas, such as good governance or democracy support, can experience. But what is anti-corruption about and how exactly does it contribute to / reveal the democracy promotion aims of IFIs?

The idea of corruption is a powerful and evocative negative concept. Yet, it also has a positive side. Indeed, as Mark Philp (1997) has argued, implicit in the negative idea of what counts as corruption lies also a sense of what the ideal is that is being corrupted. Anti-corruption work always works on the basis of politico-economic ideals, which it seeks to instill in society, economics and politics of target states.

It is this characteristic of anti-corruption efforts that makes them important to examine in the context of democracy promotion. If democracy promotion is overtly about the advancement of a particular set of democratic (and economic) ideals, the corruption fight is covertly about very similar aims. Thus the fact that democracy promoters, and perhaps most notably the more economistically and technically oriented IFIs, engage in the global anti-corruption campaigns reveals an important role which they hold in the broader democracy promotion paradigm.

But what do IFIs do in relation to corruption? A great deal: they implement numerous measures, goals and projects which seek to structure the actions of states and publics within them. These manifold projects on how best to fight corruption have been far from successful, albeit at the same time increasingly central to their work (see e.g. Gebel, 2012a).

How do these projects work and what kinds of politico-economic ideals are they driven by? Anja Gebel's (2012b, unpublished) doctoral work has traced the principles underlying anti-corruption discourses in great detail. Her work gives us direct indications of the politico-economic models of democracy, which emerge, if implicitly, from the work of the Bank and other actors in anti-corruption work.

Gebel studies how IFIs fight corruption through structuring the incentives through which the work of public sector and the state more generally are supposed to function. They assume that a self-interested, rationally calculating individual will only stop corrupt practices if correct institutional incentives are in place. Crucially, however, in defining what these correct incentives are and where they should lead, the World Bank, and other, related organisations such as Transparency International and the United Nations Development Programme (UNDP), come to define in unique ways distinctive ideas of the good society that they envisage as the counter-point to a corrupt society.

Gebel has powerfully documented the role that international anti-corruption efforts play in structuring particular sets of politico-economic visions of governance, economy and civil society. She argues that at the heart of the anti-corruption effort lies a prioritisation of a market-driven competitive liberal economy. This economic vision, moreover, is tied to the structuring of the political life in target states: both within the state, its public sector work and in civil society. Incentives, these organisations assume, can be directed so as to ensure that competitive rational interest-driven individuals will not abuse their power to the detriment of society but 'automatically' contribute to the ideal vision of society.

Competition, transparency, accountability, control mechanisms and calls for integrity provide key reference points in such a discourse. These concepts all gain their meaning from and come to re-enforce a neoliberal understanding of the role of the state, and its link to the economy. In so doing, they also come to constrain the politico-economic visions of democracy associated with an 'integer' state. A socialist or a social democratic state, with a heavy role provided for public sector workers and state expenditure, alongside 'life-long' and well-protected welfare provisions for civil sector workers, provide the wrong kinds of 'incentives' for 'efficient' state functions. They do not encourage merit-based competition between public servants or the levels of accountability and transparency that a good civil service should observe in order to 'safeguard' efficient use of public money. Moreover, any state intervention in the economy that goes beyond the safeguarding of competition in the private sector can only be seen as detrimental to the efficient working of private sector actors, providing opportunities for corruption rather than minimising them.

Gebel argues that while neoliberal ideals dominate in international anti-corruption discourses, there are discursive chains which attach to the idea of anticorruption made up of a wide range of notions or signifiers that point in the direction, hardly expected, of potentially non-neoliberal ideals. Thus, development, equality, integrity/ethics, context-sensitivity and participation, for example, play a key role in the discourses of World Bank, Transparency International and UNDP.

Might these openings point in new directions for anti-corruption? Doubtful, concludes Gebel. This is because, Gebel argues, while these new terms appear in the discourse, their meaning becomes quickly interpreted along the lines of the existing neoliberal orthodoxy. The meaning of participation or integrity becomes circumscribed within the discursive context in which it is placed within pre-existing discursive structures, which are neoliberal in nature (Gebel, 2012a, 2012b). At best, then, discourses shift towards adjusted forms of neoliberalism, that is, embedded neoliberalism. Few signs of openings towards meaningful participatory democratic or social democratic thinking on the state emerge (Gebel, unpublished). The technical agenda can only shift so far and within specific well-defined discursive or conceptual parameters. Moreover, in the context of being unable to 'politicise' debates about alternative routes to development, good governance, or integer states, limited room for exploration of the meanings of the incipient openings in the discourse exists.

It seems that the anti-corruption work of the IFIs is far from inconsequential for democracy support. Gebel's work hints strongly that anti-corruption work, while technical in tone, in fact deeply structures – or at least attempts to do so – the economic and the political possibilities within target states. As a result, some ideals are 'in', while others are 'out'. Competitive market economies are 'in'; big uncompetitive solidarity or ideology-driven redistributive markets are 'out'. Competitive, state-checking civil society is 'in'; anti-liberal non-rational, non-interest-realising civil society is 'out'. Transparent and accountable, small, efficient, states are 'in'; big, unaccountable, reckless public-spending states are 'out'. It matters then, despite the depoliticised discourse of these organisations, which kinds of implicit politico-economic models emerge from the activities of these actors.

This matters, further, because the technical criteria, indexes and working practices of the IFIs are copied and reproduced by most actors which also act in 'democracy support' more overtly. Thus, the United States and the EU, for example, are increasingly active in the anti-corruption field as part of their development policy. Given that this is the case, and if anti-corruption 'best practice' of these donors is often drawn from the IFIs, as it seems to be, the activities in this sector of the IFIs have an even wider reach. They inadvertently set the standards in anti-corruption policies globally. We need to be aware of the possibility that as the practices in anti-corruption due to the World Bank and Transparency International become the 'gold standard' in the development field, so may their normative visions of the 'good life' gain hegemony.

It is for this reason that any aspiring supporters of 'social democracy' or 'reform liberal democracy' must critically evaluate not only 'democracy' programmes, but also associated socio-economic and socio-political programmes such as anti-corruption efforts. These policies can incorporate the neoliberal economic prescriptions of market liberalisation and mainstream competition as a way of tackling public corruption. The political ideals of a limited state and active state-challenging civil society emerge here too. Embedded in anti-corruption programmes, then, are specific ideals, which the advocates of anti-corruption pass on and disseminate knowingly and unknowingly in their projects, programmes and knowledge construction. Far from a merely negative technical project, anti-corruption emerges as a deep-running positive and normative political project.

Poverty Reduction Strategy Papers

The PRSP programme marks a significant shift in the World Banks's and IMF's engagements with developing countries. The failure of the Structural Adjustment Programmes and conditionality in many developing countries prompted serious soul-searching in the IFIs and the response that emerged surprised most, even critical, commentators. The IMF and the World Bank would now make funding for debt facilitation for the heavily indebted countries conditional on the completion of a 'nationally owned' and 'participatory' Poverty Reduction Strategy Paper. Crucially, the PRSPs were explicitly seeking to not only get indebted countries and their publics to directly engage with the reform programmes of the IFIs, but also to contribute to the 'democratisation' of these countries. The PRSP programme is one of the flagship initiatives of the IFIs which have directly tied poverty reduction to democratisation and vice versa.

But what has been the effect of PRSP for democratisation? The role of PRSP and its participatory qualities have been judged from many angles and the literature is divided. Many studies record that not only does IFI support on the whole tend to have negative consequences for democratisation (Abrahamsen, 2000; Barro and

Lee, 2003), but also the PRSP is doing little to help in this regard as it provides but a rhetorical patch on a process in which no real substantive debate can be had on the content of reforms (Joseph, 2012). Other commentators are more positive. Nelson and Wallace (2005), for example, concluded that IMF programmes can in general contribute to democratisation. Limbach and Michaelowa (2010) found specific long-term evidence of successes, specifically of the PRSPs bringing about democratic improvements in target countries.

The question of effects then remains contested. But what is of interest here is not just the results – successful or not – of PRSPs, but rather the models of democracy that they come to support or disenable – the politico-economic visions embedded in this process of 'participation'. On the face of it, the PRSPs could be seen as prime examples of 'participatory democracy' in action. After all, the two core aspects of these papers are precisely 'ownership' and 'participation'. Ownership refers to the need to involve the target country in the process of poverty reduction; participation to inclusion of various domestic stakeholders in the debates on the nature of PRSP commitments.

But how participatory is the process, and does it really imply participatory or substantive democratisation? Joseph (2012) argues that the PRSP process is but a governmental technique for monitoring and enforcement of implementation of neoliberal economic reforms in developing countries. It is about getting states to commit to self-regulated reform, which is externally set and conditioned while seemingly voluntarily conceived. Reaching out to stakeholders entails better 'performance', it is argued, while also legitimising the process which is ultimately controlled by the World Bank and IMF boards (Joseph, 2012). The focus of PRSPs is not in 'democratisation' at all, Joseph's argument would suggest, and its participatory qualities seem limited.

It does seem that indications of deep-going participatory democratic commitments are questionable in the PRSP process. Evidence suggests that in practice the results are variable. In some cases there has been more extensive consultation than others, and in some cases core aspects of IFIs' programmes have been modified somewhat. Yet, as Spanger and Wolff (2003) indicated, in many cases, even if innovative breakthroughs towards inclusion of various actors have been made, the participatory qualities of the PRSP process are limited in crucial respects. First, it should not be forgotten that the IMF and World Bank accept or reject the PRSPs of the target countries and hence little room is left for real debate on macro-economic alternatives. Indeed, as Spanger and Wolff perceptively noted, in the poverty reduction process through PRSPs, structural reforms, poverty reduction, and democratisation make up a 'harmonious triad' (2003: 26). This means that not only are poverty reduction and structural reforms seen as part of democratisation, but also democratisation itself is a process tied to these reforms. While the course of democratisation is fixed, simultaneously so is the course of economic governance. Thus, through the PRSP, democratic and economic debate on alternative models are in fact undermined rather than encouraged. Also, as a result, many of the more economic aspects of PRSP have been left least discussed: it is merely their social and political results that civil society actors are consulted on.

Second, it is noted that the PRSP processes are often government-led and in many cases so much so that little real power is left for stakeholders in the process. They are 'directed' in nature and poorly 'participatory'. Crucially, not all NGO or CSO actors have been equally represented in the consultation processes – women, the poor, and trade unions, for example have been less enthusiastically incorporated than more moderate business and political forces.

Third, worryingly, the consultations conducted do not often include representative consultation through parliaments but rather focus on civil society consultation only. Indeed, it would seem that even its purely procedural and liberal democratic credentials are rather poorly formed, as critics have contended that PRSP process reaching out to stakeholders tends to undermine the role of national parliaments.

There are many problems, then, attendant to the PRSP process. A key problem, one could argue, is that it seems to run on the basis of an understanding that the course of participation, reform and economic progress is determined and known; there is little expectation that alternative courses of action or visions of democracy or economics exist in target countries. From the IFIs' perspective, the '[a]ssessment is that neoliberalism is in the interest of poverty reduction and therefore development of democracy can only lead to their confirmation' (Spanger and Wolff, 2003: 26).

There is then an underlying ideological model on politico-economic organisation that underpins the PRSP process, and it is not participatory but rather neoliberal in nature. Participatory democracy would involve direct discussion and debate on the substance of the economic policies and real ownership of the debate by the people. As for social democracy, this model too is disabled by PRSPs on two grounds: first, by lack of emphasis on state sovereignty in 'ownership' of macroeconomic decisions, and second, in disfranchisement of social and economic policies of the Left through the focus on IFIs' preferred sets of reforms. As for global democracy, this is not viewed as a concern here either: if anything, IFIs' goal is the localisation of the democratic process, and thus the reverse of global democratisation. Interestingly, even liberal democracy of a national kind can be sidestepped in this process.

The democratic credentials of PRSP processes, then, are shaky. This is important to note for, as Spanger and Wolff powerfully argue, a limited form of 'consultation'-only participation, which does not allow people to express their real worries about economic forces, can undermine both the stability of the countries and their democratic credentials. The lack of real democratic reach not only creates the potential for these processes to provoke social and economic unrest in countries, but also the sidestepping of democratic procedures can entail a regression in democratic control of a country over its economic social and political life. Spanger and Wolff put it succinctly: 'a phoney participatory process can undermine democratic processes as well as autocratic processes do' (2003: 53).

Despite the innovative nature of the PRSP processes and the potential for more participatory engagement they provide, we have to then remain skeptical of the democratic qualities of the PRSP process. It may not only entail the promotion of specific liberal politico-economic ideals for reform, but can also, curiously as a result of its 'participatory' qualities, end up damaging rather than advancing democratic progress – of even liberal kind – in developing countries.

IFIs as structural causes in democratisation

The case studies above have examined the active 'agential' role of IFIs in democracy support: how they try through their actions to contribute towards democratisation. We have seen that they do so through advancing an essentially neoliberal model with an emphasis on economic freedoms and property rights together with a liberal vision for civil society and the state, which are co-opted into the 'transformationalist project'.

However, as Doorenspleet (2004) and Gasirowski and Power (1998) contend, it is clearly not enough to examine the mere agent-centric aspects of democracy promotion activities: this is because they may be effective in only the right kind of socio-economic or geographical contexts. Abrahamsen too (2000) contends that more structural analyses of democracy promotion of IFIs are needed to understand the wider structuring effects they have on democratisation, outside of the purely observable actions undertaken in target countries in the name of good governance.

This point is worth remembering here not least because the IFIs play crucial roles not just in 'democracy support' – implicit or explicit – but also in structuring of the field within which democratisation in third countries takes place. As Abrahamsen (2000) has persuasively pointed out, external actors' role is much greater in structuring the possibilities and limitations of democratisation in Africa, for example, than is often acknowledged. Considering that socio-economic factors have been seen as crucial conditioning factors in democratisation, it is crucial to remember that, besides being engaged in democracy support, the IFIs, more than many other international organisations, structure the contextual and structural environment of democratisation in such ways as to enable and disenable considerations of specific politico-economic models of democracy.

The role of the IFIs is to encourage first and foremost liberalisation of world trade, macro-economic stability of states and free movement of capital and economic growth and development, and thereby poverty reduction, in world economy. In so doing, the plurality of actions that are taken have deep roles in shaping the contexts within which states exist and their developmental trajectories. If states are to have open economies, with independent central banks, commitments to external rule systems on global capital and open trade flows, the extent and nature of democratisation within these states is inevitably limited to specific kinds of democratic developments. National sovereignty and solidarity-based models of democracy are by definition excluded and international organisations become, as Pevehouse (2002: 525–6) has suggested, external defenders of the rights of capital and the business interests. Radical democratisation against capital and business forces becomes, by definition, circumscribed by the developing states' association with the IFIs and their rule commitments. So does social democratic control of procurement processes (preferencing of national procurement, for example).

Thus, alternative politico-economic models become structurally impossible to insist on, even when commitments to such models on the ground are strong.

Consideration of the wider structural role of IFIs in the global scene is important then. Those who focus on study of governance reforms and democracy promotion need to pay attention to economic structures and institutions which act as constraints on the possible forms of social, political and economic organisation in the world today. The orientations, economic models, anti-corruption measures as well as governance work of IFIs structure the fields of action and strategic possibilities of democratising actors on the ground as well as within the global democracy support industry itself.

If indeed the structural confines within which democracy and the economy can be envisioned today are set by the IFIs and are set in rather rigid conceptual terms, what room is there for the EU, the United States or the NGOs to develop alternative politico-economic alternatives in their democracy support, even if they wanted to support alternative visions of democracy? We will return to this difficult but essential question in Chapters 11 and 12.

Conclusion

I have argued here that we need to understand better the role of IFIs in democracy support – implicitly and explicitly and structurally. Not only do the activities of these organisations span a wide range, with important consequences for the development of democracies in developing countries, but their 'technical' and non-partisan discourses strengthen the impact of their politico-economic structuring of developing – and, arguably today also of developed – countries.

It is in analysis of IFIs that the politico-economic approach to analysis of democracy promotion is of most use: we cannot understand IFIs' role in democracy support unless we understand democracy support as an agenda embedded in both economic and political spheres, and affecting both sets of considerations. Analysis of IFIs' activities shows that not only are these institutions deeply concerned about and involved in the structuring of social and political fields and possibilities in countries, they also seek to impart through their activities very specific understandings of the politico-economic alternatives open to countries.

These alternatives are predominantly neoliberal in nature: they involve privatisation of economies and public companies, undermining of classical service-delivery model of a state (if not service-delivery itself), construction of a business-friendly set of legal and political rules and the construction of a state-challenging entrepreneurial (and service-delivering) civil society which supports rather than challenges the IFIs' macro-economic and developmental blueprints. Democratisation and participation are of interest to IFIs but only, it seems, in so far as they support the economic aims of the organisations. It is the economic, then, that is firmly in the driving seat, while the political and the social are increasingly considered legitimate spheres through which to structure the economic.

This is the case even as the criticisms of Washington consensus model has been taken into account. The role of the state is no longer conceived as minimal or restricted, but rather is conceived as an important lynch-pin in capacity-enablement of a good, strong liberal-market state. Strong (pro-market) regulations, good basic social services, and efficient legal and civil society support for entrepreneurial society are needed. These aspects are central in the making up of a fortuitous context for the correct type of stable liberal democratisation.

The politico-economic model advanced, then, is embedded neoliberal in nature. Not only are social democratic and radical democratic alternatives undermined, while seemingly being incorporated in the language of development and basic social services, but also, paradoxically, while national democratisation (rather than global democratisation) is advanced, at the same time national sovereignty of democratic publics is undermined. While there is a broader reach of democracy, the meaning of democracy, in the context of global pressures, it could be argued, is getting shallower (Teivainen, 2002).

Where does this leave us in terms of thinking about prospects of democracy support in the global scene and the prospects, specifically, of alternative politico-economic models in democracy support? The final part of this book seeks explicitly to draw analytical conclusions from the empirical studies conducted here.

Part III

Conclusions and policy provocations

11 Democracy promotion, implicit liberalism and the liberal world order

The previous chapters have documented the nature of democracy promoters' understandings of democracy. We have identified a number of conceptual characteristics individual to each case: the United States' debate structure within liberal democratic tradition, the European Union's (EU's) fuzzy liberalism, the World Bank's technocratic neoliberalism, and the non-governmental organisations' (NGOs') more diverse yet increasingly pressured attempts to deal with various models of democracy. There are also indications of some overlapping characteristics between the cases, however. In most cases we have seen that liberal democratic understandings of democracy seem still to dominate, albeit (and significantly) in somewhat different forms: practice is informed not just by classical liberal or neoliberal orientations but also by indications of liberal reform leanings and embedded neoliberalism. It seems that multiple understandings of democracy and its politico-economic context do have a relevance to democracy support, even if they have been given rather marginal roles, as a tendency towards consensus on liberal democracy is more pressing than interest in exploring the contestations over (liberal) democracy's meaning.

This chapter aims to review the findings presented here and analyses them in the context of some core trends in world politics. Notably, I ask: What are the core characteristics this conceptual analysis has identified in democracy support and how can we understand trends in conceptual foundations of democracy support in the context of developments in the liberal world order today?

What makes such an analysis interesting in the context of democracy promotion studies is that it goes against the grain of the dominant case- or donor-focused analyses in the field. The role of democracy support as a global endeavour and one undertaken in wider politico-economic or world political structures is relatively rarely considered in the 'problem-solving' mainstream of democracy support analysis. In relation to International Relations and interprofessional literature; on the other hand, it is also interesting to re-visit the question of democracy support's role in liberal world order. If democracy support has shed its liberal trappings, how does this fit within understandings of trends within the liberal internationalist world order more widely? Strangely, while many interesting analyses of shifts in liberal world order have emerged in recent years (these are reviewed in section three below), analyses of the role of democracy support have not featured heavily in these analyses. William Robinson's (1996) critique of US democracy support still remains one of the only systematic studies of democracy promotion in the context of the global world order dynamics. Yet, some revisions to this analysis are necessary in today's context.

Contrary to Robinson, I will argue here that the role of democracy promotion as a practice of 'liberal world ordering' is rather unconscious, unreflective and remains in large part 'hidden'. While democracy promoters deny they are the harbingers of a single-minded liberalism – as some call it 'large-L' liberalism (see e.g. Dunne and Koivisto, 2010: 622) – a 'small-l' 'implicit liberalism' plays an increasingly important role in structuring democracy promotion discourses and practices today. Such implicit liberalism comes together with three further characteristics of democracy support today: diversity-accommodating consensus discourse; liberal interpretation of the meaning of social and participatory democracy; NGO- and civil society-oriented democracy support delivery; and support to 'strong' stable liberal states.

In accounting for these key trends it helps if we turn to two theoretical orientations: Gramscian and Foucauldian logics. These in combination, I argue, account persuasively for the key dynamics of democracy support pointed to here, and moreover allow us to speculate on how these dynamics fit within wider shifts in the global order.

The chapter will proceed in three parts. First, I summarise the findings of the previous chapters. Second, I set up a theoretical framework within which to account for the findings. Third, I place the findings in the context of some of the wider debates on liberal world order today.

Conceptual contours of democracy support

In the classical liberal internationalist vision, democracy support constitutes a crucial underpinning of the activities of liberal world ordering. States and institutions encourage domestic democracies because this encourages more stable and peaceful interactions between states. Liberal ideals, then, as many argue, are the guiding tenets of democracy support and democracy support is a core underpinning of liberal world order.

Yet, the obviousness of liberalism as an underpinning of democracy support or of democracy support as a supporting pillar for liberal world order have been in some doubt in the last few years. Their obviousness has been attacked from various sides. On the one hand, practitioners and specialists of democracy support have come to argue that democracy support is not an ideological agenda but rather an unbiased un-ideological agenda (cf. Chandler, 2006a, 2009). At the same time critics have argued that democracy support has become less and less about consistent defence of liberal principles. Richard Youngs' (2011b) recent attack on EU actions is noteworthy here: he argues that the EU does not anymore stand for liberal principles in its foreign policy. Instead, it is reneging on its commitments and lapsing into inconsistent and poorly justified pragmatism which falls radically short of 'defence' of liberal principles in democracy support.

Yet, the evidence in Chapters 7–10 suggests that both positions are mistaken. It seems wrong to suggest that liberalism no longer plays a role, or to suggest that it provides a conscious framework of thought which democracy promoters refer to in justifying their actions. Liberalism, it seems, is increasingly *implicitly embedded* in democracy promotion practice. Liberalism in democracy support has changed its stripes, is (at least potentially) multifarious, and is often hidden. As such, liberalism is also less and less contested. It seems that there is little need to debate or justify core liberal values today – even as various somewhat different forms of liberal orientation can underpin democracy support practices. Liberalism in democracy promotion then can be not only diverse in its forms, but also unstated, unreflective and in fact quite un-strategic. More often than not liberal leanings are accepted as 'common sense', they are 'in the air' that practitioners breathe, even when practitioners seemingly work with diversity-accommodating or pluralist conceptual logics. This has important consequences for our study, for 'implicit liberalism' deeply impacts on which politico-economic models are advanced, and how.

Summary of empirical findings

The empirical chapters in this book have recorded six distinct sets of findings which we need to make sense of, and which the 'implicit liberalism' thesis, and adjoined explanatory tools proposed here, seek to account for.

First, we have noted that the conceptual assumptions of democracy support are less openly ideological and universalist than one might expect, given the central role of liberal ideas in democracy promotion historically. No longer is democracy promotion justified as a straightforward liberal ideological project, advanced for the sake of liberal ideological end points. Neither is democratisation seen as an unproblematic linear process which can be encouraged with ease by outside actors. Also, no longer are justifications for democracy support simply 'normative'; rather, more instrumental and pragmatic justifications have emerged as, it is argued, democracy is good for development, security and economic prosperity. Crucially, a distinctly less triumphalist tone characterises democracy support today vis-à-vis the 1990s heyday. 'Liberalism with a big L' has been seen as increasingly unproductive as the backdrop for democracy support in the context of various failings in transitions, backlash against democracy support and the financial crisis. Instead, a far less openly and self-avowedly liberal discourse surrounds democracy promotion today.

Crucially, we have found in the analysis of conceptions of democracy in democracy support that diversity of possible meanings of the idea of democracy are recognised by many actors, even if this recognition remains rather superficial in nature. This recognition goes with an emphasis on context-sensitivity of democracy support, local ownership and civil society participation in democracy support. No longer do democracy promoters aim to coercively push an unproblematic one-size-fits-all approach to democracy support.

Second, we have found that when analysed in detail, despite the less overtly liberal framings of democracy support, the discursive frameworks still primarily make reference to liberal democratic ideals as the cornerstone of democracy support. While there has clearly been a movement away from narrow electoral and procedural notions of liberal democracy, and much wider civil society based ideas of democracy are dominant, at the same time the background model is still deeply liberal in nature. Thus, it is liberal political constitutions, liberal party systems, liberal parliamentary systems, liberal rule of law structures, and liberal civil society that are encouraged – even if their liberal nature is not overtly emphasised but rather emerges from the way democracy is 'assumed' to function.

However, despite this dominance of liberalism, this type of liberalism, we have noted is somewhat more complex in structure than often assumed by critics. There are various traditions and value hierarchies suggestive of different liberal democratic framings at work. Thus, we have seen that the US scene today demonstrates shifts towards reform liberal framings, alongside classical and neoliberal understandings of democracy. In the EU too, classical liberal, reform liberal, neoliberal and embedded neoliberal traditions wax and wane in a complex manner. Thus, the exact meaning of liberal democracy is not as firm and fixed as many might expect – even as liberal democratic tradition dominates!

Further, paradoxically, other extra-liberal values of democracy have also been accommodated within the broadly liberal democratic discourse. Notably, in the work of the international financial institutions (IFIs) and of the EU, it would seem that some social democratic notions of social equality and participation, for example, make their appearance. Indeed, it is evident that consideration is given to social justice or socio-economic rights today, even if such concepts are incorporated in rather unsystematic and un-thought-through ways. Indeed, what is striking is that characteristics of such alternative models appear, but are not systematically reflected upon, but rather simply 'accommodated' with core liberal framings.

Third, we have seen that there is a surprising amount of consensus between different democracy promotion actors on democracy support, its legitimacy, how to do it, who to interact with and what conceptions of democracy to work with. This is despite the seeming competition between actors for prestige in the field. Underlying superficial differences are a lot of commonalities and a broad, and somewhat vague, liberal consensus on the order of governance that democracy promotion should advance. A global democracy promotion system, then, does seem to exist, which is surprisingly uniform, both discursively and practically.

Crucially, any challenges to this consensus are seen by practitioners – across actors – as 'dangerous' or 'foolish': to question the consensus is to delimit the chances of democratic success in target countries and to downgrade or dismiss the authentic aspirations for (liberal) democracy of actors in these countries. Hostility and surprise characterise responses to any suggestions that there may be untoward political bias or power involved in the consensus that dominates. This consensus is, after all, reflective of the contentions over democracy's meaning and can make reference to social democratic and participatory ideals!

Fourth, the role of civil support organisations (CSOs) and private actors has arisen in democracy support, as we have recorded. In the everyday practice of democracy support through development agencies, no longer do states and their development agency staff *do* the democracy support. Rather, the tendencies are towards privatisation of democracy assistance and, as a result, resort to CSOs and private actors as delivery organisations. This has been taken farthest in the United States where democracy support delivery is almost fully privatised, but is also characteristic of different EU 'calls for proposal' practices.

As a result the role of managerial demands has become more and more technical and demanding. No longer are strategic interactions with specific organisations favoured, because the market model is seen as the solution to 'effective delivery of aid'. 'Democratic market competition' (as envisaged by theorists of 'market democracy'; see Chapter 2) for funds is the name of the game. This ensures the realistic nature of projects, and crucially, efficiency and accountability of delivery; the key criteria on which 'democracy-enhancing' action is now measured. As a result, the democracy promotion 'industry' has become professionalised.

This has had the effect of unifying democracy promotion discourses of NGOs with those of the main agents: discourses of the United States and the EU on democracy support now deeply influence those of grass-roots actors on the ground and are further strengthened through the 'management speak' and aesthetics imposed on engagement with deliverers. This arrival of ideological 'consensus' on democracy support has been important in empowering new kinds of actors, such as the network actors. However, as we have seen in Chapter 9, it has also effectively dampened any political disagreements or debate on the meaning of democracy among these actors. Debate on radical alternatives in democracy support is now considered *passé*, as all actors, including NGOs and social democratic foundations, increasingly work within the broad (if at its core liberal) democracy promotion consensus, with its emphasis on facilitation elections, effective party systems, efficient rule of law, non-corrupt administration and active entrepreneurial civil society. As a result democracy support is increasingly depoliticised.

Fifth, despite the generally liberal orientations of the democracy support framework, surprisingly, the role of the state is today considered central in it. It is not a *laissez-faire* liberal 'Washington Consensus' model that is advocated in democracy support today. Indeed, a 'modest-sized state' is considered necessary, which is strongly supportive of market liberties and open trade, but in so doing also regulates and manages conflicts and instabilities. This has entailed not only budget support for states, but also increased use of public–private partnerships. Also, civil society work today has the aim of impacting on the state and its administrative and legal structures in ways which seek to render the state more accountable as well as 'efficient' in the delivery of good service. Liberal state, then, does not mean weak state; rather democracy support is all about encouraging a specific idea of a 'strong' liberal state that defends not only liberal ideals but also a stable mixture of liberalising reforms. This suggests a preference for an embedded neoliberal state, although in some discourses genuinely 'reform liberal' tendencies have also been present.

Sixth, we have also noted that democracy support is, for most actors, not an idealistic normative aim as such, but is also crucially about stability. Liberals and social democrats, donors and NGOs, the United States and the EU want the social order that they promote to be stable. In this sense, at the heart of democracy support there lies a commitment to stability or order first. Crucially, this is why some democracy promoters place such a strong emphasis on social justice measures in democracy support today: these measures stabilise target countries, hence affecting the chances of success of democratisation. Yet, even so, crucially, it is not the idea of democracy itself that dictates the emphasis on social justice or social democratic modifications of liberal democracy; it is the interest in order which dictates the shift to more stable models.

How can these developments be theoretically accounted for?

These findings arise from the empirical chapters above. But how should we make sense of these findings? What theoretical tools help us to make sense of them? International Relations (IR) Theories, surely, should be able to help us.

Yet, it would seem that classical IR theoretical tools struggle to cope with the trends identified here. This is because they tend to approach social explanation in specific, and for us, problematic ways. IR theorists tend to be interested in explaining why states promote democracy and where and when it serves their interests or meet their identity requirements to do so. It is in answering these types of questions that they come to their differential assessments of the role and nature of democracy support in the world system. Realists highlight state interests as the guiding explanation of the hypocrisy that is evident in democracy support; liberals and constructivists note the increasing tendencies towards agreement, consensus and institutionalisation of democracy support; Marxists dismiss democracy support as a tool of transnational capitalist classes to mould states into submission.

For sure, such assessments can be helpful and meaningful in making sense of democracy support today. Thus, realists, for example, are on strong ground in being able to, in part at least, explain why big-L liberal democracy support does not work: it is an illusion which hubristic liberal actors adopt. Liberal democracy support will, for the realists, at one point or another, reveal its political power underbelly. Recognising the hard power politics inevitably tied to democracy support, realists argue, helps us to understand the implicit nature of liberalism today. In a context where liberal ideas do not work anymore, it is best to downplay their role. Yet, realist theorists arguably struggle in helping us deal with the consensus on such implicit liberalism throughout different kinds of actors – from NGOs to IFIs. They also struggle to understand the deeply embedded and often rather unconscious nature of 'implicit liberalism' in democracy support.

Liberals and constructivists, on the other hand, would no doubt point to the durability and power of liberal ideals in structuring world order. Construction of ideational hegemony of certain values and concepts has durability and can explain also why liberal ideals today may be less overtly celebrated, yet still there. Liberal ideals have been socialised and institutionalised within the world system and this is what explains the shared consensus on them. Indeed, they may even point out that so engrained are these values now in the everyday practices of liberal world order that we do not even need to notice their role – hence the increasingly implicit nature of liberalism. Liberals can also account for the diversity of views and pluralism of thought that seems to characterise democracy support today: liberalism can accommodate various frameworks of thought and is quite adaptable.

Even so, the liberals will arguably find it difficult to explain the deep implicit nature of liberal commitments. Why the depoliticisation? Why the small-l liberalism? Why the accommodation of alternative ideals, if liberal values in the end are superior? Arguably, the liberals and the constructivists have some problems in accounting for the changing nature of the liberal world order. Also, they find it difficult to deal with the power dynamics of such ideals. Institutionalisation or socialisation of liberal ideals may indeed be happening, but why these ideals? How are they tied to power structures, economic power relations and potentially shifts in such power relations?

Marxists and neo-Gramscians have some answers: the depoliticisation of liberalism and its accommodation within wider strands of thought is a tool of liberal ideological hegemony. The liberal order is premised on a powerful ideological consent-building strategy, which explains the tendencies noted here. While the explanation may be plausible, not only is the consensus today less self-evident, given all the tendencies in pluralistic directions alongside depoliticisation, but also this process of depoliticisation and relative pluralisation seems rather unintentional and unstrategic. It does not seem to be driven by transnationalist capitalist classes but quite independent or autonomous democracy support of NGOs themselves.

A theoretical set of tools are needed that allow us to deal with the unconscious and unstrategic nature of implicit liberalism today. I argue here that a combination of Gramscian and Foucauldian ideas seems to take us furthest in explaining these trends – even if they may not holistically account for all trends in democracy support (i.e. realism, liberalism or neo-Gramscianism can quite conceivably still account better for certain *other* trends in democracy support – see Conclusion).

Gramsci and Foucault on implicit liberalism and associated trends

Four key arguments are made here, which seek to narrate and give a theoretical account for the six key trends identified in the empirical analysis. These arguments emanate from a combination of Gramscian and Foucauldian theoretical concepts and ideas. Curiously, I do not seek to systematically separate Gramscian and Foucauldian insights, but to utilise both theoretical frameworks together, side by side.

I do this because I find that Gramsci's and Foucault's ideas, rather than opposing or clashing with each other, blend together well to form a coherent picture of the conceptual dynamics in democracy support. I concur with others who have come to the conclusion that in empirical analysis these theoretical frameworks are not, despite different ontological assumptions and foci, oppositional systems but rather speak to each others' concerns in an interesting way (see e.g. Murray Li, 2007; Joseph, 2012). Before I move on to the concrete arguments, let's first examine Gramscian and Foucauldian systems of thought in some detail.

Comparing the thought of Gramsci and Foucault

Antonio Gramsci was a Marxist thinker, who in his fragmentary *Prison Notebooks* (1998) developed an important new line of inquiry for Marx-influenced critical social science. He was interested in understanding how and why capitalist societal forces have durability in excess of what one might expect, given that they seem to contradict the 'real interests' of most people in society. Why do people agree to societal power structures which weaken their own power and in fact can actively oppress their ability to live fulfilling lives? He was also interested in explaining how progressive change could be achieved given the increasing co-optation of radical social forces, even the workers, within the bourgeois state. This was an important and practically important puzzle for him as an active communist agitator in Italy of the 1930s.

His key theoretical insight related to the idea of *hegemony*. Instead of relying on pure domination and control of subordinate classes, power of the bourgeoisie, he argued, was exercised through generation of consent among the ruled. Civil society was a key site for generation of such consent. A *hegemonic bloc* would be an assemblage of social forces which generated consent of the governed through adoption and co-option of various different social and civil society forces in a manner which disenabled critical challenges to the existing social order. Thus, for Gramsci, it was because of the co-optation of churches, guilds, and even trade unions to a hegemonic consensus revolving around a consensus belief in the benign and progressive nature of capitalism and liberal democracy that communist parties and activists in the 1930s had such difficulty in bringing about revolutionary change.

Gramsci also developed the idea of *common sense* as a way of understanding how hegemonic ideas worked in concrete social settings. Whereas 'high philosophies' explicitly defined particular ideological notions and logics for social life, 'common sense' was the sphere where 'high philosophies' and their ideological precepts (about the nature of man, society or social order) transformed into commonly acceptable 'everyday' ideological logics and practices. 'Common sense' is 'the diffuse, uncoordinated features of a generic form of thought common to a particular period and a particular popular environment' (Gramsci 1998: 330).

Crucially, in 'common sense' understandings of how society worked, how power relations were constructed and what the role of people was in society, purity or singularity of thought was not required. Thus, it was not abstract and pure systems of 'philosophical individualism' that were passed on. Rather, in a cultural hegemony ideological principles of the ruling classes, such as belief in individualism, mixed and mingled with many locally developed everyday notions and visions of social life. Yet, Gramsci argued, in common sense developed within an ideological hegemonic bloc, particular ideological understandings tended to win out. Thus, abstract individualism could mould itself into everyday belief in people's ability to improve their lot in society.

Crucially, what makes common sense so powerful is its apolitical and 'self-evident' nature: there are certain beliefs which within the common sense are uncontested and uncontestable. Important also is its ability to embrace different interests, values and ideas, and yet make them work for specific overall ideological aims. Even though common sense tends to present itself as a rather spontaneous offspring of the dominant higher philosophy, or ideology, it is actually a calculated 'generic form of thought common to a particular period and environment' (Gramsci 1998: 330).

What is critical here is the link between ideology and practical life. This link is established by common sense. Consequently, if one wishes to challenge an existing ideology, the field of battle is located in the realm of ideas.

Indeed, in terms of revolutionary strategy, Gramsci argued that a *war of position*, a gradual long-term battle over ideas – a strategic struggle for hearts and minds and for 'common sense' in the context of the cultural hegemony of capitalism – was what was needed. Revolutionary action which did not base itself on gradual ideological war of position could be easily snubbed out and be delegitimised in the context of the hegemony of capitalism and liberal democracy. A passive revolution, so well conducted by capitalist forces at his time, was what needed to be considered by revolutionary activists.

Michel Foucault's ideas, on the other hand, were developed in the very different context of France in the 1960s. He saw himself as a critic of Marxist thought and developed in his historical studies of social institutions very distinct directions vis-à-vis the mainstream structuralist Marxist ideas. Genealogical historiography is what Foucault is best known for: his studies of genealogy of sexuality, prisons, medical practices and academic knowledge, provide key reference points for much of post-Marxist and poststructuralist thought today. Here he developed key moves on *disciplinary power* and *micro-power*: forms of power which emanated from everyday practices and inter-relations and which involved the active self-control of the individual as a key site of activation of power. What is of interest here, especially, are the arguments on *governmentality* which he developed in the late 1960s.

Governmentality is a concept which Foucault (2008) defined through the idea of 'conduct of conduct'. Governmentality was an attempt through various practices, techniques or modes of regulation to shape the nature of the activities and thinking of actors in society. Instead of exerting power coercively on individuals, governmentality logics and techniques in modern societies in the West shaped individuals' understandings and notions of self in such ways that they came to adopt 'freely' particular pro-market understandings of self, others, and social relations. The exercise of this form of governmentality power, then, relied on the adoption of 'responsibilities' by individuals themselves for the passing on of particular ideals or understandings of life.

The form of governmentality Foucault identified in advanced liberal states was neoliberal in nature. What this meant to him was that it was not classical liberalism that was passed on by the Ordo-liberals or the American liberals, it was a different form of *neoliberal governmentality* which emanated from their thought: one which sought to mould individuals into actors who would be 'entrepreneurial' and would exercise their freedom in defence of market principles in social life. This form of neoliberalism could accommodate 'stability-inducing' basic welfare provisions and rights, but hung on the idea that individuals should conceive of themselves as active market society citizens. His arguments on neo-liberal governmentality are of particular interest to us here, although as some commentators have noted, governmentality need not entail neoliberal governmentality (see Death, 2011; Joseph, 2012). But how might these thinkers' ideas help us in understanding the trends we've identified in conceptual foundations of democracy support?

Liberalism 'in the air'

The basic theoretical ideas of Gramsci (if not his entire system of thought[1]) are very useful to consider in trying to gain a sense of the 'liberalism in the air' of democracy support today. As in the society, which Gramsci observed, in democracy promotion too apolitical 'common sense' seems to thrive and is indicative of a hegemonic bloc where through ideational controls actors and their causes are co-opted into a consensus ideology, which disenables critical engagement with alternative ideas of democracy.

This common sense in democracy support arguably developed from the more overtly political ideology of liberal internationalism in the 1980s and 1990s but, it seems, has recently evolved into an unquestioned and widely shared set of beliefs, which no longer need to be contested. Thus, liberal democracy, and capitalism as a context of it, share a common-sensical acceptance amongst the actors in democracy support: from the World Bank and the EU Commission to many of the foundations and NGOs.

This is, in many ways, a rather surprising turn of events given the differential backgrounds of some of these actors – political foundations, for example, originate from diverse ideological backgrounds as we have seen. However, this surprising turn can arguably be explained through a Gramscian understanding of the solidification of hegemony of liberal ideas through their dispersion in common sense understandings. Gramsci's thought emphasises that when specific ideological notions achieve a hegemonic role, they also become dispersed. An ideological 'high philosophical idea' becomes fragmented, dispersed and hidden, while retaining a powerful and depoliticised hold in society. Today, such a dispersed common sense belief in core notions of liberal democracy seems to exist in the discourses, practices and management guidelines of democracy support.

What is interesting is that in such a system of thought, the question of interests dissolves. No major intentional trans-nationalist class project seems to exist in democracy support, nor is ideological control exercised through brain-washing or active changing of mentalities. Yet, this does not mean there is not a politico-economic logic to the form of common sense that dominates – even if it is not directly motivated, driven or manipulated.

Again, in framing the interest question, Gramsci helps here. His ideas on hegemony and common sense allow us to realise that there may not be anything accidental about the hidden implicitly liberal confluence of forces in the common sense of democracy support today. Concepts, as Gramsci reminds us, do not arise from nowhere: they are structurally embedded truths, which can and often do come to serve certain interests better than others. We need to keep our eyes open to this: some practicality may arise for some economic and structural forces from the implicitly liberal framings in everyday practices of democracy support. Thus, arguably, the EU's politico-economic interests gain indirect benefits from the system of implicit liberal governance that it enforces in the neighbourhood. This does not mean that EU officials directly intend or plan these policies in an 'interest-driven' way. Strategic selectivity of interests (Hay 2002) and the idea of coincidence of interests (Wedel, 2009) seem more accurate framings of the role of interests in defining values.

Foucault's insights interestingly re-enforce this Gramscian reading of liberalism 'in the air' in democracy support. Governmentality is particularly useful in pushing us to think about technical interventions and techniques as forms of power with hidden ideological content. Foucault's governmentality, and his analysis of neoliberal governmentality in particular, emphasised the way in which specific ideals, visions and plans could be embedded in the most wide-ranging set of innocuous measures, statistics, policy agendas or management structures. One of the key insights of governmentality was to argue that direct control over publics is no longer necessary: governments govern now through shaping the mentalities of the 'free' people in their communities. While Foucault pointed to the dominance of various forms of neoliberal governmentality in Western advanced liberal states, he did not reduce them to a single 'ideological' form but emphasised precisely their context-boundness, flexibility and ability, because of their focus on 'free individuals autonomously shaping their own lives', to accommodate diverse sets of perspectives within an essentially rigid set of basic ideals, management criteria or measures. Thus, Ordo-liberals and American neoliberals, while both differently oriented to neoliberalism, both assumed active individuals self-responsible for the reproduction of market logics and entrepreneurial mentalities. Behind seeming diversity and 'freedom' there are hidden rigidities in governmental systems, which come to define subjects in such ways that they come to conduct themselves in accordance with specific ideological aims rather than others.

It is such trends that we can see in democracy support's implicit liberalism. Not only is there an acceptance of liberal principles, in various contextually different forms, but various technical instruments govern the activities of this supposedly depoliticised realm where the underlying beliefs (or doxa[2]) remain uncontested. In EIDHR's management practices or the technical regulations on trade, it is neoliberal governmentality techniques which target populations are expected to confirm to and internalise. It is governmentality techniques, then, not just ideological shaping of individuals' ideas that do the work in terms of 'regulating' conceptions of democracy.

This Foucauldian reading fits very well with the Gramscian story: the two notions – common sense and governmentality – despite different ontological origins, speak very closely to each other. They both share an interest in ideational control. They also, interestingly, both position understandings of such forms of rule in the context of politico-economic systems of economic and political governance. These frameworks allows us to capture both the move to small-l liberalism and how, even if indirectly, it may benefit some actors more than others. The fact that a liberal, rather than socialist or radical, underlying logic informs the practices is important in enabling the EU and the US to maintain their capital accumulation strategies in relation to other countries, while also protecting their own (paradoxically partly social liberal) markets.

Implicit liberalism in the air of course also justifies democracy support as an agenda. The democracy support community today can say that big-L logic no longer drives what they do. This debilitates a lot of the most obvious criticisms from target states and recipients. It would seem that small-l liberalism works better in a challenging dual crisis context of democracy support, and liberal world order, today. Crucially, it functions in ways that mollifies criticisms and legitimates democracy support. To understand how, let's examine in more detail the 'diversity-accommodating' characteristics of small-l liberalism.

Diversity-accommodating small-l consensus

What we have observed is that small-l liberalism of democracy support today comes together with an interesting 'diversity-accommodating' dynamic. In the rhetoric of most donors and actors it is recognised that diverse paths to democracy exist and that democracy itself can have multiple meanings in different local contexts. No one-size-fits-all model directly emanates from democracy support practice today as it may have done in the 1990s – and on this there is consensus across the actors, from IFIs to NGOs, and EU to United States.

This global consensus on how to proceed with democracy support – through recognition of diversity of ideas on democracy and local ownership of democratic development – is very important to note, for it is a very interesting and surprising consensus, especially given that we have just argued that liberal ideals dominate in democracy support. More interesting still is the impression that even as diversity accommodation is present, political or ideological *disagreements* or *contentions* over democracy's meaning are simultaneously receding into the background. Thus, while the language of alternative models, social democratic and reform liberal ideals, for example, can be accommodated in democracy support discourse, they should not be 'politically contested' or 'debated' vis-à-vis the liberal model. Such debate might be 'destructive' of consensus on core liberal ideals. As soon as ideas veer towards uncomfortably contested and politicised debate on models of democracy, or if democratising actors directly challenge the liberal core (for socialist, social democratic or radical democratic ends), the diversity-accommodating dynamics are under pressure. Too much questioning of the core of democracy support – and its politicisation – is considered dangerous, relativising and consensus-undermining. The diversity-accommodating consensus, then, only goes so far.

This curious consensus can be helpfully read through Gramscian and Foucauldian concepts. As Gramsci argued, one of the key methods of accommodation to a liberal capitalist hegemony is the bringing into a consensual whole a variety of different perspectives, which can 'from within' be mollified and de-radicalised. Part of the power of common sense is that it can hold within it various different perspectives, within limits which define what constitute reasonable limits. This seems to be a key trend in democracy support today.

Diversity-accommodation has another function, however. It enables the self-responsibilisation of diverse actors for a common cause. Foucault anticipated the importance of diversity-accommodation in the rule of societies through governmentality. The semblance of self-control and hence self-determination – the ability to believe in a variety of seemingly different but in the end coherent ideals – is a key aspect of governmentality in a neoliberal context. The governmental logic depends on celebration of difference, of local autonomy, and of self-responsibility. It cannot work if explicitly coercive frameworks of thought are forced on actors. Governmentality arises from self-responsibilisation in the context of a free and multi-choice society where people conduct their own conduct in coherent, ultimately neoliberal ways but fail to realise this. In a Foucauldian frame, we can then see that it is potentially the governmentalisation of democracy support which arguably accounts for its curious 'constrained diversity-accommodating' dynamics.

Here we must also note Mark Duffield's (2007) Foucauldian argument about the role of internal critique as a crucial legitimating device for Western foreign policy activities. As Duffield (2007) and Hardt and Negri (2005) too have argued, there is a significant amount of contestation, at least seemingly, in the liberal world order governance structures – between more liberal and more social egalitarian perspectives, especially. Yet, arguably, what this disagreement does is actually legitimate the order – that is, through 'monotonous critique', which never challenges the foundational assumptions of activities, the order itself is maintained. Arguably, we can see this dynamic at work in democracy support today and its diversity-accommodating consensus. While participatory aims and social democratic language have emerged, little has changed in the core contours of democracy support.

What is crucial to note is that the consensus in democracy support discourses between different actors is of a specific nature and serves specific (if not intentional) purposes. It is strong enough to challenge and accommodate differing perspectives, as long as they accept core commitment to liberal principles, while weak enough to demonstrate disagreements and contestations can also exist within the democracy support discourse. Liberalism in democracy support rules by accommodating, rather than dominating.

This means also that alternative models – social democracy or participatory democracy – today become part of the liberal mainstream. They become deradicalised. As Gramsci argued was the case in his time, social democracy today too is de-radicalised in its meaning through its interpretation within implicitly liberal lenses. In democracy support, as we have seen, there is today concern with basic welfare rights, minimal labour rights and politico-economically aware approach development. Yet, this does not come to entail advocacy of deep corporatism, democratic control of workplaces, dual track democracy, or solidarism-building civil society, as it did for Swedish social democrats in the 1950s (see Chapter 3). Specific understandings of social democracy come to dominate; which de-radicalise this model as an alternative.

Indeed, it could be argued that so much so is this case that what emerges out of social welfare interested democracy support is a form of *embedded neoliberalism* (Apeldoorn, 2001; Joseph, 2012). If liberalism in the post-Second World War period was considered embedded in various international structures and societal structures, it would seem that today a neoliberal model is being embedded within and through the understandings of reform liberalism or social democracy that actors work with. Foucault spoke to these developments in a very powerful way. His interest was precisely in the creation of a new type of liberalism, which was not overtly classically liberal in nature but rather hid its ideological predilictions in a language of rights, welfare and self-determination. The Ordo-liberals were at the forefront of pushing a new adaptation of liberal capitalist governmentality in the European context. It is this form of neoliberal governmentality which seems to rule today; democracy support logics are often neoliberal but in 'socially attuned' ways.

This lesson is important, especially in the current context of the financial crisis: while it may result in more calls for Keynesianism, it may result in calls for Keynesianism which is no longer Keynesian in nature (see e.g. Crouch, 2011). Indeed the work by Hurt, Knio and Ryner (2009) suggests this: in the post-Washington consensus era, a neoliberal agenda seems to come through in democracy promotion with 'compensatory measures' including democracy support, poverty reduction and preventative measures. Here 'there is still faith in liberalisation of the economy but the state is given a complementary role in providing both education and an infrastructure conducive to economic growth' (Hurt et al., 2009: 310). Research from Latin America also indicates the same: 'effective states are important for successful democratic government' it is suggested and hence any thorough-going privatisation is avoided as attention is placed on 'education and healthcare, the policy, the judiciary, regulatory agencies and infrastructure' (Mainwaring and Schully, 2008; see also Levy, 2010; Toledo, 2010; Wollack and Hubli, 2010). Politicisation of politico-economic models – and systematic exploration of reform liberal or social democratic alternatives – is sidestepped while pragmatic shifts to embedded neoliberal post-Washington consensus takes place.

The same it would seem is the case with participatory democracy. The language of participation is adopted and instrumentalised. It is to provide better links with civil society, the state and the economy, while 'radical' interpretations of the idea's meaning are sidelined.

When alternative models are considered in democracy support, they may not be considered in ways that some political enthusiasts might assume but may in fact lend themselves to new forms of governmental neoliberalism.

Autonomy of action – conduct of conduct

Another crucial aspect of the current democracy support system is its reliance on non-coercive forms of control over people and target publics. NGOs and CSOs are key deliverers of democracy aid, even as they work in conjunction with states and to restructure them. While from liberal or constructivist perspectives this move might seem liberating and as a form of power-delegation away from the centre of global liberal order, from Gramscian and Foucauldian perspectives such moves look very different.

Gramsci and Foucault both theorise how delegation of responsibility for management of liberalism and neoliberalism to civil society, NGOs, and citizens themselves is enacted, but also how this delegation of power is embedded in the power of the state, or as Foucault would have it, governmentality. Through delegation, power is diffused but also shared; it is exercised through seemingly autonomous civil society actors. Exercise of power is hidden, and its ideological character is fudged.

Gramscians argue that ideological power is a key aspect of power: subjects thinking that they are not coerced constitutes the most effective form of power, for subjects who do not realise that they are not free are better controlled than those who think they are oppressed. Gramsci placed great emphasis, then, on analysis of ideological power to 'shape preferences' of actors. In such power structures, people will think themselves free and autonomous, while simultaneously being shaped in what they think are 'free actions'. Foucauldian perspective perfects this understanding through its definition of governmental power as 'conduct of conduct'. Foucault (2008) argues that an essential aspect of governmental power of a neoliberal kind is its maintenance and working through of autonomous self-regulating individuals. It is precisely the autonomy and freedom of individuals that makes governmental 'conduct of conduct' so successful. Both perspectives accept that autonomy and freedom of action of civil society are essential to maintenance of hegemony or power.

These logics play out, it seems, in democracy support today. When local ownership and multiple local conceptions of democracy is the name of the game, and when NGOs can 'freely' compete for funds, rather than being directly strategically funded, it is clear that reliance on NGOs is a key process in delivery of democracy. Simultaneously, the political and ideological role of Western donors in democracy facilitation moves to the background.

While it would be foolish to reduce all of democracy support activities to this form of power – clearly also disciplinary and coercive forms of power are present in some facets of democracy support (e.g. some cases of conditionality) – a core form of power that is often missed by analysts is this form of freedom shaping power. Arguably, democracy promotion is most successful when it gets targets of democracy assistance to conduct their own conduct in line with the preferences of funders through their own initiative. Both the United States and the EU have moved to such democracy promotion through governmental perspective. In the United States, private actors and their context-sensitive engagements in local contexts seek to foster the right kind of liberal democratic actors. In the EU too, competitive contest between NGOs for funding funnels these actors towards self-driven, yet essentially (neo)liberal, forms of entrepreneurial freedom-defending attitudes.

It is not just civil society and individuals to which governmentality is attached, however. As Jonathan Joseph (2012) powerfully shows, it is states too that are now governmentalised by global discourses about responsible macro-economic management and business-friendly environments. If correct – and indications here exist that this is plausible (e.g. note the functions of responsibilisation of states in European Neighbourhood Policy or trade discourses) – this means that the role of governmentality as a way of thinking about power is wider than is usually thought. If it relates also to states, as well as individuals, we are provided with a useful way of thinking about the holistic governance of societies through international governance programmes. In such a framework the borders between disciplinary power and governmental power, conditionality and ownership, civil society and state, dialogue and pedagogy of power are intermixed to such an extent that is impossible to separate them. Disciplining of actors into financial regulations or correct business tax policies is at work at the same time as governmental self-responsibilisation of actors is taking place. A holistic form of power projection is at work, and it is decreasingly clearly delineatable into direct, indirect and diffuse forms of power projection.

However, in its 'governmentalisation', democracy support is not unique. As a plurality of writers have noted, many actors (and indeed the world system itself, some would argue), rely on governmental assumptions (Sending and Neumann, 2006, 2010; Abrahamsen and Williams, 2010; Death, 2011; Joseph, 2012). It is in many respects a key aspect of global governance today. Democracy support then slots quite comfortably in with the trends in global governance, development and foreign policy more generally. Crucially, however, it is not as if this form of power were less intrusive, less demanding or less powerful. While different ways of thinking resistance become applicable when governmental power is at work, it cannot be denied that in some regards the very success of world ordering through liberal notions lies in the governmental modes of functioning of core aspects of the current system. This is surely something to be kept in mind by democracy promoters: they need to remain attuned to the implicit and hidden functions and modes of power in their activities.

Strong but limited liberal state

But how does such a perspective fit in with the finding that democracy support today encourages strong rather than weak states? If the democracy promotion industry is liberal, even if in an implicit way, why does it support strong states?

From Gramscian/Foucauldian perspectives, this trend fits rather neatly. Both perspectives emphasise that there is nothing terribly surprising about the fact that a state which is being encouraged in the context of liberal hegemony is *not* a weak *laissez-faire* liberal state. Both approaches recognise that a liberal state always needs to be strong in its institutional, legal and political functions in order to fulfil its key function: supporting a stable governance system, which supports an efficiently-functioning market economy. The kind of liberal democratic state that is needed to do this job is not weak or unstable, but rather a liberal state which is orderly, efficient in administration and, crucially, one which can regulate effectively, so as to produce fair and well-functioning markets where private firms and interests can compete for resources and investment. This is why civil society is, paradoxically, needed: its role is to keep the state in check by prodding it to become more efficient and benign in the eyes of the people.

Arguably, it is precisely because of their interest in such a state that democracy promoters too want to encourage a functioning and orderly democratic political system. What democracy entails is, after all, a business-friendly legal system, with strong protections for private property and intellectual property and efficient business courts for adjudicating between legal and illegal transactions, investments or procurement processes. Liberal democracy also facilitates orderly transitions of leadership and political systems separated from the economic arena. Liberal democracy does not bear down on market freedoms or economic functions but facilitates and regulates such freedoms. There is no contradiction between promotion of democracy, stability, strong state and liberalism.

Caveats to theoretical analysis

The above reading is a theoretical postulation which seeks to account for some of the trends we have identified. Let me, however, clarify the nature of Gramsci–Foucault explanation provided here. Three caveats are in order.

First, my aim is not to build a grand synthesis of Foucault and Gramsci. My interests are purely empirically driven. I wish to understand how we can best make sense of some of the key trends in conceptual foundations of democracy support. What this means is that I remain unsure as to what the reading here means with regard to the compatibility of Gramscian and Foucauldian logics more generally. This reading only suggests that there is potential in exploring synthetic accounts that bring Gramsci and Foucault together (see e.g. Jessop, 2004; Murray Li, 2007; Joseph, 2012).

Second, I should emphasise that while these accounts contribute towards understanding of politico-economic orders in that both of them trace politico-economic assumptions embedded in practices, neither necessarily reduces to, or rather extends to, a singular global systemic account that explains all structural forces at work in global economy and seeks to derive democracy support practices of specific actors from such a system. Because of the much looser and partially Foucauldian nature of the logics identified here, I do not think it is possible to provide a grand synthetic statement on global political economy which explains all the positions of actors in democracy support. Yet, I agree with Jonathan Joseph (2012) that explanations for the contexts of governmentality should be, and can be, developed (see also Dean, 2010: 246). The account here merely points out that certain strategies, interests and ideologies 'fit' within the current discursive parameters of democracy support better than others, and that hence, even if not directly, capital accumulation strategies, market access, and politico-economic controls in democratic states are at stake in the debates reviewed here.

Third, and crucially, it is important to note that while I try to explain the specific trends that I have identified here through these theoretical logics, this does not mean that they explain everything about democracy support. Quite simply, a diverse practice, a whole range of other kinds of decisions, strategies and structures can also inform democracy support. If these implicit liberal trends are what we wish to explain, these theoretical tools help. If other explanatory questions guide the analysis, such as 'why did the EU not push democracy in China?', realist or other theoretical tools may apply. Indeed, even today, strategic and realist decisions are also undertaken on democracy support. Not all decisions are implicitly liberal or non-strategic. My aim here is to argue that if we read democracy support as I have done, we can note new trends which are often not identified through the usual theoretical avenues.

Democracy support and the liberal world order

I have argued above that interesting developments characterise democracy support and that we can make sense of them if we analyse them through a Gramsican–Foucauldian framework. But how does this account speak to current debates on liberal world order? Can the account here provide us with some glimpses of shifts in liberal world order? I examine some of the recent texts on liberal world order and seek to place the findings and arguments advanced here in their context. It seems that democracy support interpreted as suggested in this book can provide an insight into liberal world order practices.

Liberal order and democracy support

When democracy promotion emerged into the world political scene, it did so in the context of an expansion of the so-called liberal internationalist world order in the post-Cold War era. While democracy promotion had played a part in Cold War policies, and was already a part of US foreign policy before this, the major expansion of this policy agenda came in the post-1989 enthusiasm for liberal democratic reform, initially in Eastern and Central Europe and progressively around the globe. The era of liberal internationalism that ensued was premised on belief in the positive consequences for peace of re-invigoration not only of democracy and rule of law within third countries, but also of general liberal internationalist principles of global rule of law, international institutionalisation, and expansion of free, open markets. This liberal international order was to retain its hegemony (based around United States) but was to increasingly open up management of global affairs to multilateral structures of global governance (although not global democracy; see Chapter 5).

The liberal internationalist dream almost came true. Despite the realist reminders that the seeming harmony of interests between key actors in the 1990s was nothing but an illusion hiding much deeper interest calculations by states, there was a step-gear in commitments made to international institutions, in co-operative frameworks between states and multilateral institutionalisation on issues such as climate change and world trade. Yet, by the end of the 1990s the liberal internationalist dream was increasingly challenged, and by late 2000s it is viewed almost nostalgically by many. The liberal world order is, or so it is often stated, now in a crisis (Ikenberry, 2009). Certainly, there is much agreement among commentators now that, even if not in terminal crisis, the liberal world order, challenged from numerous sides by developments in global politics, has developed into quite a different type of global order from that envisaged by classical liberal internationalists.

John Ikenberry is perhaps one of the most prominent analysts of liberal world order and its transformations. In his famous 'Liberal Internationalism 3.0' piece, Ikenberry argued that a new type of global governance system may be emerging in world politics and this, whatever precise form it will take, is likely to be quite different from the classical 1.0 or Cold War 2.0 types of liberal internationalism. Notably, he argues that classical liberal internationalism based on reinforcement of norms of state sovereignty and intervention is under threat as 'liberal order is increasingly defined in terms of the reverse' (Ikenberry, 2009: 71). Liberal internationalism 3.0 'is an evolving order marked by increasingly far-reaching and complex forms of international co-operation that erode state sovereignty and reallocate on a global scale the sites and sources of political authority' (Ikenberry, 2009: 71).

These changes go together with questions being asked about the role of the United States as hegemonic guarantor of the liberal internationalist order. Whereas during the Cold War the 'world "contracted out" to United States to provide global governance' (Ikenberry, 2009: 76) and in so doing provided an essentially social democratic institutional order of stability (2009: 77), now 'liberal internationalism 2.0 is in crisis' (Ikenberry, 2009: 78). An authority crisis exists in the world order. The liberal international order 'will need to become more universal and less hierarchical'; will need to justify its intrusive rules and norms in internal governance of states, and legitimate authority for this; and will have to deal with the clash between global rules and domestic rules (Ikenberry, 2009: 80–1).

Ikenberry is unsure about what will follow: a full reorientation of liberal internationalism into a more network-oriented, rule-bound order, or a United States dominated but adapted hegemony over a system which remains in crucial parts similar to what went before, merely with 'new bargains' (Ikenberry, 2009: 82). He tends to favour the second alternative: the United States might 'in the end, opt for a more fragmented system in which it builds more selective partnerships with key allies', this is despite Europe's preference for a full 3.0 model (Ikenberry, 2009: 83). Ikenberry stops short of envisaging a whole new type of world order in the context of the crisis of authority of liberal internationalism.

Ann Marie Slaughter (1997) disagrees to a degree. In her article 'The real new world order' she pointed to important new trends in the world order, discounted too easily by liberal commentators. Against neo-medievalist arguments that emphasise the shift away 'from hierarchies to networks, from centralised compulsion to voluntary association' (Slaughter, 1997: 184), she notes that the state is likely to remain more important than most enthusiasts realise. Yet, a new world order is emerging, she accepts for: 'the state is not disappearing, it is disaggregating into its separate, functionally distinct parts' (Slaughter, 1997: 184). Different parts of states then increasingly network together 'creating a dense web of relations that constitute a new, transgovernmental order' (Slaughter, 1997: 184), which is rapidly becoming the most effective form of global governance. This transgovern-mentalism, she recognises, is rather 'mundane' in comparison to the high ideals of liberal internationalists (Slaughter, 1997: 185). Yet, it does a lot of work; a lot more than the international institutions proper: 'networks of bureaucrats respond-ing to international crises and planning to prevent future problems are more flex-ible than international institutions' (Slaughter, 1997: 185). They also have a new type of potential in 'spreading democratic accountability', through governmental technical avenues (Slaughter, 1997: 185, 194).

She embraces the informal character of transgovernmentalism: it is more flex-ible and efficient than institutionalised cosmopolitanism (Slaughter, 1997: 193). Yet, it is not aiming to be all-powerful either; there are no plans for world domina-tion here, for most regulators prefer in the end to develop national law and have no particular plans to disenfranchise democratic publics. Transgovernmentalism 'harnesses' the state's power but seeks to 'find and implement solutions to global problems' (Slaughter, 1997: 195). It provides a 'powerful alternative to a liberal internationalism that has reached its limits and to a new medievalism that . . . sees the state slowly fading away' (Slaughter, 1997: 197).

This is an interesting argument which is in interesting ways reminiscent of the themes of recent work by David Chandler. Chandler (2006a, 2009, 2010b), who is a specialist in state-building activities of core Western states, has argued that crucial shifts have been taking place in the global political environment. First, Chandler (2006a) has pointed to the developments towards 'empire in denial': a curious international order in which main 'state-building' actors strangely seek to avoid rather than embrace responsibilities they hold in intervening in deep and persistent ways in the affairs of other states in the name of state-capacity building. He emphasises the depoliticising technical methods through which most state-builders now transform target countries: while actual democratic decision-making is sidestepped, through protectorate-like international administration of countries, anti-corruption, rule of law and governance projects are introduced to bring about the correct type of technical reforms in the states. Through such means the politics or ideology or the interests of state-builders in these states is hidden, but more importantly the lack of real self-government of the target states is concealed.

In his more recent work, Chandler (2009, 2010a, 2010b) extends this argument to the globalisation of politics. He argues that we need new means of understand-ing crucial shifts in the world order. Neither realist, nor liberal, post-realist or post-liberal, understandings of world order do the job (Chandler, 2007; 2010). He argues that the international order is governed by what he calls a 'hollow hegem-ony' 'marked by the lack of instrumental policy-making and the inability to con-struct a clear political project cohering values, frameworks and strategic interests' (Chandler, 2007: 33). Quite contrary to classical realist, Marxist or even liberal commentators then, Chandler emphasises the lack of strategic or even ideologi-cal centre in international system and its projects of governance. These projects rather than being driven by clear interests, strategies or values are, in fact, simply pursued; for no particular purpose, but as a reflection of a bureaucratic mentality of governance.

Interestingly for us, Chandler emphasises the vagueness of many of the international community's calls for action; and crucially emphasises that many of the projects that seem to be driven by the needs of others are in fact driven by the internal needs of the 'helping' states, especially their desire to be needed in the global sphere (Chandler, 2009: 49). Thus, Chandler concludes that 'Western states and international institutions are in a position of international power and authority, yet this power increasingly seems bereft of political purpose' as they increasingly 'institutionali[se] . . . arbitrary and non-strategic policy-making process', while all the time calling for 'a "coherent", "comprehensive" and "holistic" approach to policy-making' (Chandler, 2009: 50). There is a contradictory core to the global political order (Chandler, 2009: 18).

While Chandler points to the waning of 'liberal' world order, given the disappearance of overt ideological agendas, others wish to hold on to the idea of liberal world order. Dunne and Koivisto (2010) have advanced an interesting analysis of liberal world order in the context of less overt ideological framings. They argue that if we take seriously the English School's emphasis on rules and practice theory in general, we come to observe that the talk of crisis of liberal international order is missing a crucial ingredient, namely an analysis of the multiplicity of habitual practices and conventions which still underpin international order, and which then show the durable nature of liberal world order, rather than its shakiness. They hope to argue that when measuring the crisis of liberal world order we need to not only pay attention to the explicit forms of liberalism 'with a large L', but also the far less self-evident everyday practices and assumptions that underpin it. Through such an analysis of 'pre-intentional social institutions and customs of liberal world ordering' (Dunne and Koivisto, 2010: 617) we can re-assess the durability of liberal world order in deep social rules of practice.

These are prescient analytical contributions in analysis of democracy support as well as the liberal world order. They are, moreover, analyses which, while developed in 'mainstream' circles in International Relations, are in large part in agreement with those of 'critical' scholars.

The neo-Gramscian arguments of Stephen Gill (1998) speak to the same trends identified by Ikenberry, Slaughter, Chandler, and Dunne and Koivisto. He also sees a role for liberal ideology today, albeit in changed and depoliticised 'hidden' forms. Rejecting many Marxist analyses as out-dated and empirically mistaken, Gill (1998: 3) analyses the forms which global political economy structures and interests take in constructing a 'hegemony' in economic, political and social spheres of twentieth and twenty-first century societies. A dominant theme is neoliberalism, which is seen as an ideology that has arisen to dominance in global economic discourse and has also become embedded in national as well as international economic – and crucially social and political – discourses. In analysing neoliberalism today, Gill has pointed to what is called new constitutionalism, that is, an attempt to 'confer privileged rights of citizenship and representation to corporate capital and large investors'. 'New constitutionalism', for him, 'requires not simply suppressing, but attenuating, co-opting and channelling democratic forces, so that they do not coalesce to create a political backlash against economic liberalism and build alternatives to this type of socio-economic order' (Gill, 1998: 24). New constitutionalism then requires efforts not only to ideologically redirect political understandings but to 'lock-in' (Gill, 1998: 25) neoliberal governance types through technical regulations and international conventions. What is required is policies which 'make governments operate as facilitators of, and also operate within the context of, market values and market discipline, 'through use of legal guarantees and sanctions to favour private determination of economic policy' (Gill, 1998: 25). What is needed is 'measures to construct markets' (Gill, 1998: 26) in crucial part through 'imposition of internal and external constitutional controls on public institutions'. However, Gill also emphasises the role of attempts to deal with problems of dislocation that arise from the market. There is a need to deal with contradictions and disabling consequences of capital mobility for crucial populaces, including through 'co-optation of opposition' and 'targeting the poorest with real material concessions' (Gill, 1998: 27).

Duffield's analyses point to similar trends. He points to the paradoxes of liberal governance today. In the West social insurance ameliorates life. In developing countries minimal welfare regimes are advocated to take the edge of radicalism. Crucially, social democratic and liberal wings agree; both are concerned to maintain order; in fact policies have often mixed both 'radical' and liberal concerns. So do NGOs, the 'direct heirs of nineteenth century and colonial technologies of development based on community, the small scale ownership of property and self-reliance' (Duffield, 2007: 25). They have been 'absorbed into a web of mutual interests and overlapping objectives that entrepreneurially connect [them] with donor states, recipient government, UN agencies and militaries' (Duffield, 2007: 28). It is through state and NGO development that the 'contingent sovereignty' of the developing is maintained (Duffield, 2007: 28).

Sending and Neumann (2006, 2010), agree. Today, NGOs are wanted as partakers of governance because they have a status 'as actors that possess expertise central to the task of governing and, much more importantly, [because of] the fact that they appear to be autonomous political subjects with a capacity for political will-formation' (Sending and Neumann, 2006: 668). 'Governing', they emphasise, 'is [now] performed *through* autonomous subjects, not *on* passive objects' (Sending and Neumann, 2006: 669, original emphasis).

All these accounts point in powerful ways towards the idea that the nature of the world order and governance within it today is rather different from the image of classical liberal international society: new forms of social interaction but also new forms of power are present in world politics today. How do the insights of the analysis of democracy support fit within this picture of a changing world order? Do democracy support trends indicate similar dynamics or do they challenge or contradict them?

It seems that the analysis here by and large concurs with many of the trends that existing accounts of shifting practices of liberal world ordering bring forward. In the context of the discreet policy-world of democracy promotion, Ikenberry's findings on diffuse internationalism and Slaughter's argument on the new role of regulators and experts in the world order both seem to be confirmed here. Simultaneously, Chandler's argument about shifts towards depoliticised order can also be seen as significant, although he goes too far, perhaps, in suggesting a move away from liberalism. We have found that liberalism is still there, just in more implicit forms. Indeed, Dunne and Koivisto's argument about implicit forms of liberalism in world order seems a close fit with the findings here. So are Gill's findings on disciplinary neoliberalism, although the account here emphasises less disciplinary dynamics in favour of paying attention to more subtle governmental logics. Duffield's argument on order and Sending and Neumann's argument about the new role of NGOs are also confirmed here. We find, then, that the account in this book re-enforces the findings of the existing accounts on trends in liberal order.

Yet, this account also adds specific insights which may be of use in current analyses of liberal order. Notably, it highlights the curious and complex role of democracy support in the facilitation of a curious and shifting kind of liberal world order. Five characteristics are of note about democracy support in such a system, which I will review in concluding this chapter.

Conclusion: understanding democracy promotion in a liberal world order

First, this account emphasises the strangely *un-strategic and unconscious nature of liberalism in today's world order*. Thus, in contrast to the contention that democracy promotion is a strategic national or class ploy, this book finds little evidence of such direct agendas. Certainly, no evidence of a transnational capitalist class directly involved in democracy support emerges. For the most part we find committed development practitioners, working in challenging conditions and within conceptual frameworks which they were sometimes only partially conscious of. A 'will to improve', not will to control or discipline or dominate, is at the heart of democracy support by almost all the actors examined here (Murray Li, 2007). No self-avowed or even plausible representative of a 'transnational capitalist elite' was interviewed, nor were business interests identified as essential in direction of policy decision-making.

This means that intentional strategic instrumentality of democracy support would seem to be limited. This does not mean that at times democracy support systems can be 'played by' interest-driven actors; yet it would seem that on a day-to-day basis, democracy support is not well understood through realist or Marxist frameworks (cf. Murray Li, 2007). As we have seen this does not mean that democracy support does not benefit some interests over others. Certain liberal capitalist strategies for capital accumulation, market access and economic regulation, for example, seem to fit rather neatly within the discursive parameters given for democracy today. This study, then, cannot disconfirm Robinson's claims about politico-economic control of democracy support by capital: merely to state that such a claim also cannot be confirmed. In the absence of such evidence, we should try and capture in more nuanced ways the links between democracy promotion and capital, interests and values. 'Coincidences of interests' (Wedel, 2009) may indeed be present, but this does not entail that democracy support is actively instrumentalised in defence of specific capital or national interests. In Tania Murray Li's (2007: 8–9) words:

> I do not agree that improvement is merely a tactic to maintain the dominance of particular classes; or to assert control by the global North over the South . . . Rather than assume a hidden agenda, I take seriously the proposition that the will to improve can be taken at its word . . . interests are part of the machine, but they are not its master term . . . In my view the rush to identify hidden motives of profit or domination narrows analysis unnecessarily, making much of what happens in the name of improvement obscure. Trustees. . . . must attempt to balance all sorts of relations between 'men and things'. To govern, as Foucault made clear, is to seek not one dogmatic goal, but 'a whole series of specific finalities'.

Second, this analysis highlights the global nature of the democracy support community. The role of states, then, really is rather different in democracy support than many accounts of liberal world order would accept. The democracy promotion industry is now a global community, which shares norms – across the Atlantic and beyond – albeit in 'fuzzy' diversity-accommodating ways. There is now a global discursive hegemony in existence in democracy support, which structures the work of NGOs as much as IFIs. Transnational interests, coincidental interests and flexible ideological confines work within a global system of democracy support. Within such a framework, not only are donors linked and tied to each other in complex ways, but so are donors and recipients. Paying attention to the new formulations of networks as basis of global governance is highlighted by the analysis presented here.

Third, this account highlights the need to analyse in detail the multiple forms of liberalism in world politics. Surprisingly, many analysts, while highlighting shifts in liberal world order, say less about the shifts in liberal thought which frame them. The account here has highlighted the multiplicity and fluid forms of liberal thought today. Liberalism, and liberal democratic thinking in democracy support, is not rigid, singular and unaccommodating. There are classical liberal, reform liberal and neoliberal variations of liberal democratic thinking at work in democracy support. One of the key findings here is that liberalism is plural and can and does manifest itself in a plurality of guises, with important consequences for democracy support. Not only does pluralism emerge quite comfortably as the central ground of current democracy support system – it is only within liberal ideals that the level of pluralism that currently characterises the discourse can exist – but also liberalism in many ways thrives on this pluralism. Not being reduced to a singular position allows liberalism to justify itself as a superior ideological framework and also simultaneously enables the often un-noted hidden forms of liberalism to thrive. The implicit depoliticised forms of liberal thinking identified here only thrive in the context of overt language of freedom, self-determination and diversity (as Gramsci and Foucault affirm so well).

Within the framework presented here social democracy and reform liberalism – much lauded by many democracy promoters today as part of their diversity-accommodating agendas – emerge as particular discursive strategies attached to advancement of (neo)liberalism; not in the sense that they buy-up or co-opt opposition, but in the sense that they provide a wider legitimating edge to an agenda. These agendas 'fudge' the (neo)liberal logics and rationality, and in fact make up a part of it. If this is reflective of wider trends, it means that much indeed needs to be done by critical theorists to dig deeper to the sites where neoliberalism manifests itself and its many contradictory logics.

Fourth, this analysis shows that we need to acknowledge that there are, while similarities and unified logics, also some crucial differences between the actors in today's democracy support and hence liberal world ordering. Many of the existing analyses of liberal world order focus on the United States. I would argue that interesting speculations could be raised on the basis of the analysis presented here about the increasingly adept role of the EU in adjusting itself to an increasingly implicitly liberal world order. The United States, as we have seen, remains the only actor with some ideological commitments in democracy support; the one more closely and religiously tied to core liberal notions. The EU on the other hand, has led the efforts in 'fuzzying the logics' in democracy support; and has as a result successfully silenced critics but also advanced its socially aware form of neoliberalism in its democracy and development aid. The EU, it could be argued, is more suited or adapted to democracy support in today's context than the United States. This is important to note in evaluating the future of world order: perhaps the EU, with all its fuzzy logics, contradictions and confusions is actually the leader in the field of democracy support today.

Finally, and even despite the previous point, we should also note that there are multiple facets, power relations and points of potential resistance in democracy support (cf. Murray Li, 2007). Common sense or governmental logics can have a hard edge, but they can also be resisted and modified, and can have different, often contradictory effects too. This is important to bear in mind in relation to democracy support today. Democracy promotion is politico-economically consequential, but can be so in different ways and to different degrees in different contexts. Room for alternative takes or possibilities also exist in the system. Thus, as we have seen, interestingly, electoral observation – the heart of supposed liberal proceduralism – is not necessarily all that conceptually oppressive but can facilitate alternative economic models to be taken into account. Civil society support too has potential, although openings are often negated by organisational and management demands. Openings towards consideration of alternative models is also helped by the entrapment of democracy promotion in the language of local ownership, even if this ownership is currently interpreted in ways quite antithetical to a radical interpretation of its potential meaning. Room for resistance then exists, which could be used strategically by actors on the ground. Also, relatedly, we cannot assume that just because United States and the EU do what they do, this may not be in the interests of the actors on the ground. Thus, we should not be too dismissive of strategic uses of the system, openings for alternatives within it and resistance within it, despite the system's ideological implicit goals and indeed hegemonic formulations. Opening debate on the meaning of democracy, and especially re-politicising this debate on the meaning of democracy, may do something to open up democracy support practice and room for alternative politico-economic models within it. We will turn to examination of where to go from here in Chapter 12.

12 Policy provocations – from a critical perspective

There is not one question – what is to be done – but hundreds: what should the mineworkers do, what should the abandoned old women do, what should the unemployed do, and on and on.

(Ferguson, 1994: 281)

Consciousness of being part of a particular hegemonic force (that is to say political consciousness) is the first stage towards progressive self-consciousness in which theory and practice will finally be one.

(Gramsci, quoted in Gill, 1998: 37)

What goes without saying and what cannot be said for lack of an available discourse represent the dividing line between the most radical form of misrecognition and the awakening of political consciousness.

(Bourdieu, 1977: 169, 170)

Policy engagement from a critical theoretical perspective is a difficult exercise. There is a tendency in policy circles to dismiss academic research, and especially critical research, as abstract and theoretical, to imply that critical academics are unwilling to 'get their hands dirty'. At the same time, it is often suggested in academia that practitioners tend to work within a limited instrumentalist mind-set, where solving problems of implementation rather than reflecting on conceptual foundations or contradictions is a priority. Because of such perceptions, many academics, especially critical academics, have explicitly resisted taking up the role of acting as the 'prince's advisor'. This would dangerously undermine their academic integrity and also might involve critical theorists inadvertently contributing to social orders that they perceive as oppressive.

What should, then, be a critical academic's relationship to policy? And crucially, what can this critical study contribute to rethinking of democracy promotion practice today?

Clearly, a position which starts from a critical rather than a 'problem-solving' mentality should prioritise critical analysis of states of affairs over practical policy advice. Yet, even so, a critical academic can, I hold, contribute to policy debates and the policy process. I argue here that critical research can be relevant; yet, in different ways from the more positivist or instrumental knowledge perspectives. Crucially, critical theoretical insights may not involve advocacy of specific prescriptive policy measures. While some suggestions are made here as to how democracy promotion practice could be improved by recognition of the conceptual dynamics and contradictions that shape it, I stop short of advocating specific solutions to the problems of democracy support. This is not just because many of the contradictions of democracy promotion may not be 'soluble', but also because it is not 'for me' to solve them.

This is partly because – as Ferguson argues – there is no single question of 'what is to be done' in seeking to reform policy agendas. This is because – in a critical frame of reference – we must recognise that interests and preferences of actors vary depending on their social positions. It is agents in their social and political settings that have to 'read' their preferences and make decisions on the best strategies forward *for them*. I wish *not* to prioritise prescriptive advice to any specific type of actor here, then, although I will point to the kind of openings and potential that can be tapped into in democracy promotion, by policy practitioners, state officials or social movements. I argue that *fostering of critical reflexivity to ideological predispositions and power dynamics can assist, with various sets of actors, in grappling for better ways forward*. Also, I suggest that, while not all alternative visions of democracy are viable for all actors, and while it would be quite unrealistic to expect that many of the democracy promotion actors would suddenly promote radical or cosmopolitan democracy, it is quite possible for us to entertain, that within some limits, extensions to the 'models catalogue' of the different actors more extensive, reflective and open explorations of alternative democratic directions can be inserted. Thus, despite a generally pessimistic view on the possibility of holistic systemic change in international politics, I do not wish to suggest that changes in democracy support are impossible – especially given the many conceptual openings which today exist for a very different type of practice.

The discussion progresses in three sections. In the first I address the problem of critical theory and policy engagement. I then advance the position on policy engagement, based broadly on Frank Fischer's (2003, 2009) work on critical approaches to policy analysis. Finally, I offer tentative suggestions as to where policy changes in democracy support may be forthcoming or desirable for different sets of actors in order to fulfil the open-ended goals advanced here.

Critical theory and practice: the problem

The relationships between theory and practice, and academia and policy-making, are fraught. The problem is relatively simple, but difficult to solve. Theoretical university scholarship of academics is publicly funded; therefore, it should be geared around analysis of problems of relevance to the states and publics which fund it. Yet, universities have also traditionally been seen as the heartlands of critical thinking, of independent autonomous thought, which by its very 'independent' nature seeks to provide avenues for innovation through challenging conventional thinking. Such critical thinking may be undermined by efforts to tie the hands of academics to 'instrumentally' useful agendas or approaches.

That is not all, for an even deeper concern troubles the academia–practitioner relationship. As Ferguson (1994) demonstrates in his excellent analysis of policy practice development in Lesotho: the problem may lie in the nature of the engagement that is to be had between these two communities. Crucially, it is not an equal relationship of power; nor is the knowledge that is produced or sought 'neutral' in nature. Thus, while a practitioner seeks knowledge and turns to academics to provide it, it is also the case that:

> An academic analysis is of no use to a 'development' agency unless it provides a place for the agency to plug itself in, unless it provides a charter for the sort of intervention that the agency is set up to do. An analysis which suggests that the causes of poverty in Lesotho are political and structural (not technical and geographical), that national government is part of the problems (not a neutral instrument for its solution), and that meaningful change can only come through revolutionary social transformation in South Africa, has no place in 'development' discourse simply because 'development' agencies are not in the business of promoting political realignments or supporting revolutionary struggles.
>
> (Ferguson, 1994: 69)

No matter how badly the agencies want it, policy practitioners 'seek only the kind of advice they can take' (Ferguson, 1994: 284).

Another danger resides in such a policy-driven engagement: the danger of feeding into the legitimacy of a specific policy area, simply through critique. As Duffield has warned and as Ferguson too brings to light, there are real dangers in critical scholars seeking to reform policy practices: 'In development, as in criminology, problems and calls for reform are necessary to the functioning of the machine. Pointing out errors and suggesting improvements is an integral part of the process of justifying and legitimating 'development' interventions' (Ferguson, 1994: 285).

How do we deal with these challenges here? What can critical theoretical analysis contribute without undermining critical sensibilities which direct the research itself?

Towards a critical theoretical policy engagement

Policy analysis and policy engagement have been dominated by positivist approaches in the last decades. Indeed, as Frank Fischer (2003) has argued, there is an endemic commitment to positivist ideals and associated technocratic *modi operandi* in current policy work, policy analysis and policy engagement. This creates, he argues, distortions and political biases in policy-making and analysis, which are unjustified and, indeed, undemocratic. Much then remains to be done to bring in a more democratic and open sensibility to policy analysis and engagement.

A crucial starting point for such a process is – in a strikingly complementary manner given the goals of this research project – a critique of positivist assumptions in the underlying philosophy of policy-making and engagement. Frank Fischer (2003) argues that it is essential that we pay attention to and criticise, rather than 'naturalise', a positivist policy-making process. Fischer (2003) argues that the crucial mistake of the positivist approach is to misunderstand the structures of meaning and contestation that are implicit in policy work. The preference for a quantitative approach, where evaluation and policy planning is conducted in reference to a set of 'objective' benchmarks and indicators, misses out the ways in which meaning and concepts structure understandings and background assumptions in policy work.

In seeking a single objective truth about the world 'out there', the positivist framework refuses to engage with the values imbued in any single understanding of the world 'out there' as well as the implicit moral commitments embedded in the advocacy of any specific policy direction. Although positivist policy work is considered as value-neutral, Fischer (2003) shows how all policy frames or suggestions have embedded within them specific ideological and political predilections. There is no such thing, then, as objective value-neutral policy analysis or advice, and the sooner this is recognised, Fischer argues, the better. This is because, in ignoring such hidden ideological dynamics, positivist work becomes distinctly undemocratic in its orientation. Indeed, in dismissing the role of the general public in dealing with complex and technical issues, positivists reproduce a technocratic and hierarchical understanding of policy in 'democratic' states.

Fischer's critique sits comfortably with the critical realist, Gramscian and Foucauldian orientations of research into democracy promotion presented here. It emphasises the importance of paying attention to the underlying conceptual frameworks that policy-makers in democracy promotion work with. It emphasises that critique of positivism in democracy support policy frameworks is not merely a matter of theoretical or abstract nature; it is a key condition of being able to imagine alternative 'realities' and, hence, policy redirections.

Another key starting point for such an imagining is the recognition of pluralism of perspectives: that there is no one point of view from which 'improved policy practice' can be judged. This is not to say that there are no grounds to say that some processes are better than others; but crucially, *processes tend to be better or worse in different ways for different groups of people*. Thus, for example, a policy process which entails incorporation of citizen representation may be costly and cumbersome for a technocratic policy-advisor, while being empowering and productive from the perspective of the citizen (Fischer, 2003). Similarly, in democracy promotion, a perspective which looks productive for radical democratic social movements may not be one that is perceived as efficient or objective-oriented enough by the central administration of donors. *Where one sits affects the perceptions of what works.* In exactly the same way, democracy emerges as a different kind of value system for differently positioned political actors. What exactly 'reforms' should entail in democracy promotion is an issue that can be very differently evaluated by different actors – liberal democratic elites, social democratic agitators, or global democratisers.

Given this need for pluralism of perspective, I separate here different groups of people linked to democracy support and try to advance multiple suggestions with regard to each group. The groups considered here do not, of course, cover all actors in the field of democracy support, but I do seek to speak to most of the groups engaged in this study. These recommendations are focused on not prioritising one or another perspective, but rather on encouraging self-reflection by all practitioners, which in turn is considered as a key condition of seeking adequately pluralism-fostering reforms in concrete policy frameworks. These suggestions draw on concrete practitioner workshops organised with various groups of practitioners during the spring of 2012.

Engaging practitioners: reflections on democracy promotion practice and democratic futures

Democracy promotion actors approach democracy promotion from their own angles, thus reflecting one or a selection of democratic traditions in their democracy promotion. Yet, many of the actors do not fully engage with the possibilities that their work could incorporate, because they fail to systematically engage with alternative conceptualisations of democracy. I argue here that while it is unrealistic to expect that a full range of possible democratic models could be promoted by all actors, there is room for considerably more consideration of conceptual extensions to current democracy support practice. Thus, I suggest that in the US scene, exploration of reform liberalism is possible and in the EU system even more extensive possibilities exist for promotion of multiple visions of democracy: classical, reform liberal and social democratic. International Financial Institutions (IFIs) and non-governmental organisations (NGOs) too can extend and push for more politicised and openly reflective conceptions of democracy. While considerations of how to conceptually reorient policy frameworks must be conditioned by a suitable understanding of the actors themselves and the discursive, political and historical confines they have to work with, implicit liberalism and technocratic practices of democracy promotion are not necessary or inevitable in democracy promotion. In fact, the democracy promotion of various actors might benefit from openings of conceptual horizons.

US State Department representatives

As we observed in Chapter 7, the United States has tended to advocate a liberal democratic conception of democracy, although incipient debate on the exact meaning of this idea seems to be evident, both historically and today in the Obama administration. Yet, the exploration of alternative liberal democratic models today is far from systematic or clearly thought-through and, in fact, ends up contributing towards proliferation of various different liberal democratic leanings in the administration's democracy promotion discourses. While classical liberal ideals are still there, so are Hayekian neoliberal commitments, reform liberal commitments, and what seems like 'embedded neoliberal' ideals.

This research would suggest that systematically building on and clarifying the incipient efforts to rethink the state–economy relationship in democracy support would be fruitful for current US democracy support. At present, in the absence of systematic conceptual reflection and ability to effectively and systematically think about the various meanings of the idea 'liberal democracy', contradictions and confusions abound in US democracy support. Clear thinking on alternative understandings of liberal democracy – through focused conceptual reflection on democratic theory – might help structure and systematise the American understanding of democracy today. This is certainly necessary if Obama's new 'reform liberal' rhetoric is to be made meaningful in the context of democracy support and consistent in US democracy promotion practice. Arguably, more should be done to systematically move away from the neoliberal model promoted during the Bush years. This, however, requires hard thinking about both the contestability of the idea of democracy and the existence of different models of liberal democracy.

At present the efforts to move towards more flexible and pluralistic discourse on democracy support have been severely restricted not only by the continuing background role of Hayekian democracy discourse (in delivery processes as well as specific instruments), but also because there is little knowledge in these circles of the important historical debates within the US scene over the meaning of liberal democracy. Thus, it is surprising that democracy support today is not informed by the thought of Dewey, Thurow or Galbraith. Here were liberals with reform liberal principles guiding their actions. Here were liberals concerned about equality of opportunity, democratic autonomy and control of markets. They noted the clashes between markets and democracy – how the two can undermine each other – and sought to put in place in economics and markets defences which could safeguard meaningful democratisation (Waligorski, 1997). Much can be learned from such thinkers – rather than reproducing focus on Dahl – in today's context where liberalism may have won the day, but continues to be subject to debate within.

Normative and pragmatic reasons exist to rethink the democracy and capitalism relationship in US democracy support today. Not only is US democracy support pragmatically in need of a new direction, and already interested in reformulating the relationship between economy and democracy; but also, normatively, US democracy support should arguably reflect the normative debates in the United States today on the relationship between state and economy. Democracy support is an ideological agenda and for too long has reflected only one side of the ideological spectrum in liberal democratic thought. There is a need and a justification to rebalance the politico-economic orientation of US democracy support – especially as the meaning of democracy is being domestically reconfigured, or at least is being fought over.

This is especially important as, clearly, the hegemony of a single line of thought on democracy is not productive for any democratic society, nor its democracy promotion. Debate about democracy is important for the maintaining of healthy 'democratic' dynamics of dialogue, openness and accommodation. In the US scene, for various ideological and structural reasons, the liberal democratic model has reigned, but not in a singular fashion. Today, there are tentative shifts away from classical liberal and Hayekian ideas. These shifts should be facilitated by greater teaching and guidance on the variations of models within the liberal democratic paradigm, as well as facilitation of awareness about the contested nature of democracy and the relationship between democracy and capitalism historically.

Openness to such learning about alternative notions of liberal democracy – and contestability of the idea of liberal democracy – requires not sacrifice of values, but confidence in one's values. Only with a firm commitment to liberal democracy can one open up for debate and dialogue, and learn from others. A defensive attitude will not facilitate such learning but will simply push out debate as 'irresponsible' or 'dangerous'. Attraction to such defences at the current time must be resisted in the name of more dialogical and listening debate which recognises the contested nature of democracy and the lines on which it can be contested, without necessarily removing from the US framework its unique value commitments.

Indeed, debating liberal democracy's meaning more openly *does not mean that the United States will have to stop promoting democracy or stop promoting liberal democracy*. Nothing in opening up conceptual reflection implies that democracy's promotion is wrong *per se* or that liberal democracy itself is problematic. All that pluralisation of conceptual perspectives does is open up room for debate and create room for more pragmatic and flexible democracy support in action. Nuanced conceptualisation of democracy, then, need not mean the undermining of one's commitments, but rather their sharpening and recharging.

But how can such conceptual reflection and recharging of debate on democracy be achieved? The answer is through various mechanisms such as: (1) inserting systematic flexibility on democracy's meaning into policy discourses on liberal democracy's meaning; (2) facilitating practitioner seminars which facilitate the opening up of democracy's meaning in the activities of practitioners and programme officers; (3) revisitation of democracy handbooks which guide practices and programming at the United States Agency for International Development (USAID), National Endowment for Democracy (NED) and the State Department; (4) rethinking of 'technical' delivery practices, instruments and guidance and their effects on 'models' of democracy which emerge; (5) repoliticisation and de-technicalisation of democracy aid to civil society and state actors; (6) opening up of programming processes to more meaningful dialogue on aims.

Many potential complications arise from such revisitations. Thus, the obsession with measuring democracy projects' 'effects' and 'outputs', for example, may become more problematic if political and ideological debate on democracy's meaning is to be allowed. Dialogical project programming, too, will complicate the process of democracy assistance. Yet, such reforms can also facilitate more meaningful, flexible and democratic democracy support by the United States. It will also address some of the core contradictions at work in US democracy support today, notably the simultaneous advocacy of local ownership of democracy aid and the depoliticised 'fixed' delivery of democratic ideals.

The European Commission and EEAS

In the EU the conceptual problems in democracy promotion are somewhat different from those in the United States. The problem in the EU is not the existence of a hegemonic liberal democratic conceptualisation, but rather the lack of conceptualisation of any clear kind. Such a context requires somewhat different responses in the EU. However, what is fundamentally required here too is a more clear-cut and systematic set of reflections on what is meant by democracy in democracy promotion.

In the EU the context and range of debate on democracy is, as we have seen in Chapter 8, somewhat more open than in the US context. Lacking a clear-cut definitional foundation, and reflecting the influence social democratic traditions of thought, the EU's conceptual approach has been 'fuzzy liberal'. This fuzziness holds promise of more pluralistic practice of facilitation of alternative politico-economic models in EU democracy support. However, at present such pluralism is undermined by lack of systematic thought expended on the meaning of 'pluralist principles' in the EU system as well as the existence of technocratic and neoliberal tendencies in EU practices of delivery of democracy aid. The EU should look to develop, in a serious and concerted way, a more extensive range of models as the reference point for its actions. This would also mean re-engaging political and ideological debate on democracy's meaning within this pluralist political actor.

At the moment the substance of EU democracy support demonstrates a lack of willingness to engage with any clear democratic models and what they would mean in a substantive way: as a result the EU's democracy promotion is characterised by a mixture of effects (Wetzel and Orbie, 2011). While there are some contradictory practices at work in EU democracy support, no systematic pluralism is promoted and, indeed, on the ground democracy promotion seems to veer far away from meaningful social democratic or reform liberal democracy support practice (Reynaerts, 2011; Kurki, 2012a). What I suggest is the development of concrete normative criteria as a reference point for EU action, and debate and mainstreaming of such pluralistic criteria in democracy support activities in an effort to be open and credible about the ideological commitments which the EU advances.

As we have seen, one of the key problems of EU democracy support has been unwieldiness, caused by lack of clear ideological and strategic reference points in action, bureaucratic tendencies towards de-politicisation, and contradictory actions (e.g. between policy areas). All such problems could be addressed through giving up on the EU's current mantra which commits the EU to pluralism of models, while at the same time insisting that the EU is a liberal actor at its core. A fuzzy liberal democracy support structure confuses recipients. They ask: What exactly does the EU stand for? (International IDEA, 2009a).

I suggest that the EU should focus on *clearly defining what it means by liberal democracy, reform liberal democracy, and social democracy* and on this basis develops a properly conceptualised and flexible set of responses to target contexts. It is not the European Endowment for Democracy that is needed (although it may not hurt) but rather a strategic and political rethinking of tools that allow the EU to communicate its (unique) values to the target states in a plausible and credible manner. The current 'EU knows best' discourse mixed in with a 'fuzzy liberal' rhetoric does not assist the EU in finding a role for itself in the Middle East, for example. It has lost credibility and has to rebuild it – policy-wise but also, crucially, conceptually. Indeed, any good new policy thinking must arise from the grounds of adequate conceptual rethinking.

It is in this context, then, that the EU and its European External Action Service (EEAS) – as well as other Commission actors – should be invited to learn about different models of democracy; and especially about the three models listed in italics above. They harbour important similarities but also important differences, the defence and support of which will require hard thought and action on the part of the EU (see for detail, Kurki, 2012a). Debate should be initiated in the Commission and Council on models of democracy – and normative justifications for EU democracy support. The European Parliament (EP) should also play an important role in agitating for such reconfigurations: as the politically pluralist and critical actor in the EU scene it is the EP's responsibility to raise the issue of politics of democracy support and to bring home the need to revisit conceptual foundations and not just instruments and practicalities in EU democracy support (cf. de Keyser, 2011).

Instead of opting for the current bland and depoliticised form of universalism, which depoliticises debate on democracy's meaning, it is my contention that more strategic and direct debate should be conducted on what the EU is willing to support and why. This should also entail reconfiguration of delivery practices. At present, neoliberal governmentality deeply shapes the EU's project delivery process. These dynamics need to be recognised and tackled. New, more politicised and strategic funding instruments, such as the EED, should be formulated and the depoliticising effects of current management demands should be tackled.

These moves might open up, for all to see, the potential contradictions of EU democracy support. The EU might indeed promote contradictory aims: social democracy on the one hand and liberal economics on the other. Yet, this *need not be* a negative attribute of EU democracy support but could be embraced as a strength – if only the language of coherence, complementarity and efficiency were removed from EU discourse. Promoting democracy is after all about promoting differences of viewpoints – clashes of interests and values – and this needs to be recognised.

The EU should – and is uniquely positioned – to take heed of this and be the first promoter of democracy to openly promote clashing as well as complementary values in democracy support. After all, clashing sets of rights and claims were behind the rise of European democracy (Bowles and Gintis, 1987; Armony and Schamis, 2005). The credibility of such an openly contradictory democracy support actor is likely to be double that of a secretly contradictory democracy supporter.

In short, as a starting point before yet another round of institutional and instrumental policy changes, the EU should choose its conceptual mast and nail its colours to it – a fairly pluralistic set of colours indeed. It should move away from technocracy and meaningless pluralism which currently characterises the debate and welcome a more limited but plausible pluralism along with recognition of the potential for clashes and contradictions in democracy support. It should initiate internal debate about the meaning of democracy and foster it in policy reform.

Parliamentarians

As mentioned before, parliamentarians should have an important role in the delivery of democracy support in this new era. They should ensure that debate on democracy's meaning is conducted and maintained in conjunction with democracy support's development (see also Pace, 2009). Their role is important for two reasons. First, they are the political actors who engage daily and directly with democratic publics and democratic processes and their political contestation. They know and defend a political (rather than bureaucratic) process. They have then a unique role in *politicising* debates on democracy.

Second, parliamentarians are an important link between democratic publics in democratising and democracy promoting countries. In the crisis of democracy and capitalism in the West today it is important to foster debate on *democracy's meaning internally as much as externally* and the two processes are inter-linked. The European Street's views on democracy are as important as the Arab Street's views on democracy. It is this debate within the West that parliamentary committees and debates should foster; in a manner which ensures that instrumental logics of state departments and the bureaucratic processes of development agencies do not remove the politics of democracy from democracy support. The parliamentarians' role is to bring to the fore various different perspectives on democracy and its relationship to the market. Their role is to challenge the hegemonic 'there is no alternative' credo through re-politicisation of debate on democracy.

As has been argued in Chapter 8, parliamentary proceduralism is not the main problem in democracy support today; rather, it is the 'wider' forms of democracy support that incapacitate democracy's development in parliamentary or any other directions. Hence refocusing efforts on parliamentary procedural development is likely to be helpful to liberal democratisation – but also, in some regards, to other democratic visions too. Even radical and participatory perspectives are not averse to parliamentary democracy, even if they challenge the idea that democracy consists just in this one institutional procedural level. For this reason, recognition of the procedurally central role of parliaments for democracy should go hand in hand with recognition of the role of parliaments as deeply political and ideological contestation chambers. Parliaments should not be mere 'talking shops' which may end up supporting specific elite interests, but *sites of political contestation, ideological struggles and real debate* – both in the West and the target countries of democracy support.

The development sector: rethinking aid delivery and the development–democracy nexus

One of the key findings of this book is that there is a strong 'market democratic' logic at work in the delivery methods of democracy aid, which in its own way comes to impact on democratisation itself. In the US context there is an open market-driven logic at work in the allocation of delivery aid to private companies over democratic actors 'on the ground'. In the EU's civil society funding streams a more subtle 'calls for proposals' method drives the 'efficient delivery' of funds and projects. In both cases market logic is at the heart of what is understood to constitute democracy-enhancing actions by democracy promotion deliverers. The democracy idea is subjected to the gaze of objectifying positivist knowledge as well as market aims. Here, serious problems arise then for various democracy promoters – if indeed democracy is supposed to be viewed as a value rather than a 'commodified good' (Bridoux, unpublished).

Yet, at the heart of the idea of democracy – if we move away from market liberal ideals of democracy – lies the belief that it is a value in itself which guarantees the freedom and autonomy of individuals while enabling pragmatic decisions to be made in society for the benefit of all. At present, this notion is undermined by the objectification and quantification of democracy as a good which can be delivered by market-driven actors. An anti-democratic logic at the core of democracy promotion's delivery through the European Instrument for Democracy and Human Rights (EIDHR) or the USAID eats away at the heart of the very idea.

With this in mind, then, what should happen in development organisations? In my view the technical expertise, the quantification-requiring frameworks and the emphasis on efficient delivery should be moderated or if possible removed altogether. Instead of relying on objective knowledge and criteria, policy process can and should be attuned to the logic of interpretive, politicised and participatory judgements (see also Crawford, 2003a, 2003b).

A key to achievement of this lies *in fostering self-reflexive critique of positivist assumptions* in development aid work. What this means is concrete reflection on the effects of the current development delivery tools and management practices for development aims. Methods, we are reminded, are not neutral or apolitical but tied up in deep ways in ideological structuring of development work. Politico-economic ideals are embedded in and emerge from methodologies applied. Revealing this is important to redirect development aid practice.

Less market-based, more politicised and more ideologically open development aid projects need to be funded. Instruments of delivery should be de-standardised and adjusted to work of more political, pluralistic and ideological in nature. In the delivery aid of democracy support specifically, the consequences of market logic on democracy's meaning should be counter-acted. *More strategic, more politically driven and more democracy-enhancing* – in various different ways – democracy support should be considered so as to avoid the depoliticising but simultaneously neoliberal logics being pushed through in development aid. What this would mean is more of the kind of aid that the NED provides and less of the kind of aid that EIDHR provides.

Another key focus of development organisations today is to *revisit the democracy–development relationship*. Most development work now seems to accept that democracy and development are mutually constituted. Yet, this connection is rarely properly investigated. Focus is on showing that economic growth depends on democracy or vice versa, but of course a causal relationship is not only difficult to delineate (as research has shown; see Chapter 10), but also, importantly, misses a key aspect of the development–democracy relationship, which the conceptual approach here would highlight: the dependence of specific understandings of democracy on specific understandings of development and vice versa.

Very little consideration exists today in democracy support for the deep ways in which particular ways of understanding the idea of development comes to constrain how democracy can be conceived. If a neoliberal development model is imposed, some democratic ideals are immediately counted out – social democratic, participatory and so on. At the same time, if social democratic ideals are to be promoted, this cannot go hand in hand with a neoliberal ideal of economic development. These important ideational interconnections need to be recognised, for deep contradictions at present exist in the work of development agencies.

NGOs and political foundations

As we have seen in Chapter 9, the NGOs and political foundations are manifold in nature, but united in moving towards a democracy promotion consensus of a more depoliticised and liberal kind. Structural pressures in this direction are great in these times. It is almost impossible for foundations or NGOs to think of themselves outside of the key donor's frameworks, as they are both compelled and encouraged to 'fit in' with their technocratic delivery logics. Challenges for these actors, then, are many and deep. Not to adjust to demands entails possibility of running out of funds, while to adjust to demands requires changes to the nature of the work traditionally conducted. In either case, contradictions in practices are manifold.

While having to play the funding game, I argue, *these actors can and should make a more concerted effort to safeguard the political nature of democracy support* and the political uniqueness of the traditions of democratic thinking that their actions reveal. Not only is too much bland depoliticised 'neutral' democracy support problematic for these more political actors, but also it is likely to undermine their market niche in the democracy promotion industry. Not only do these organisations hold a responsibility to the party affiliations and political interests, which they represent, but they should safeguard the political and dialogical nature of the meaning of democracy as a reminder of the need to provide a different, more political and ideological perspective in democracy promotion. These actors are uniquely well positioned to make this argument; as well as benefiting directly from its acceptance.

The same goes for their responsibility in *highlighting the role of economics in democracy support.* In the context where liberal actors have consistently done so, it is simply unacceptable for social democratic or radical foundations and think-tanks not to bring to the debate the question over democratic controls over the market. It is their responsibility to remind us of the economic consequences of liberal democratic logics and the democratic consequences of liberal economic logics.

Maintaining an effective say in the current agenda under such a brief may be difficult; yet, it is desirable for enabling these organisations to maintain their historical role and maintaining a correct balance in the democracy support industry itself. Organisational changes in donors' agendas might help in this regard – such as relaxation of the log frame or business and reporting demands – but the onus must also be placed on the NGOs and foundations themselves to stick to their guns and fight for such changes in development and donor frameworks. Fighting methods of democracy support as well as democratic discourses matter for their agendas and the shape of the democratic futures they work for.

The IFIs

As we have seen, IFIs have more of a role in democracy support than is often realised; in structuring the field within which other democracy promoters act as well as in taking an active interest in 'indirect' or 'technocratic' forms of democracy support – governance and anti-corruption actions, for example. These policies are highly significant for recipients in structuring their activities. Yet, they also have some important democracy-shaping effects – notably the narrowing down of scope for democratic decision making – and crucially structure democracy to take a (neo)liberal meaning in the target countries, while making impossible social democratic let alone participatory understandings of democracy.

What can be done to reform these institutions? It depends on what one wishes to achieve. If the wish is to achieve more liberal democratisation, these organisations are doing rather well in some regards (in that the structures of states are being slowly moulded into 'liberal' shape). If the aim, however, is some kind of a wider democratisation and stability of target countries, then some problems arise. The neoliberal model has been particularly encouraging of instability, although is today as much as ever also democracy-enhancing in that it tends to get populations angry for change and thus destabilises any government which supports it – eventually (Abrahamsen, 2000). Thus, neoliberalism, certainly in its cruder forms, is simply adverse to adequate democratic change.

This is partly why there has been a shift towards more capacity-facilitating regulatory 'embedded' neoliberal states. As was surveyed in Chapter 10, it has been realised that lack of governance is no solution to fostering of markets, or democracy, and that this is why wider solutions are needed which provide minimal basic social services for citizens as well as participatory avenues, which make them feel as if they can contribute and thus 'own' the reforms conducted. A strong liberal state is needed to effectively open markets and to efficiently manage market exchanges and business transactions.

This movement, it could be argued, has been an improvement in the work of the IFIs. They are now more participatory, equality-sensitive and civil society-interested than ever before. Surely we should embrace this!

Yet, it *must be noted that democratic activists who have in mind non- or extra-liberal economic and political structures within target states have little ability to change the macroeconomic structures and solutions which flow from the IFIs. More room should be made for them; for reconfiguration of participatory projects away from IFI control.* This is possible, for the language of participation is already there for local actors and social movements to 'use' for their own purposes of radical participatory critique (see Bowles and Gintis, 1987; Trommer, 2011).

Also, the hidden politics of IFIs' agendas should be openly embraced and recognised – by others in the democracy field and the IFIs themselves! The IFIs are democracy promoters – of a specific kind – and should take responsibility for this. The IFIs and their hegemonic discourses and logics of democracy would need to engage in some reflection on the limits of their own reflectivity and awareness. This challenge from within to hegemonic consciousness would be a desirable first step to real policy change facilitating more holistically a plurality of possible alternative democratic futures.

This is not to say, however, that radical actors should stop interacting with and trying to change the practices of such organisations.

Radical social movements

Global political developments and donors' interest in grass-roots democratisation have elevated the role of civil society organisations and NGOs. Many have 'gotten with the programme' and devised democracy support projects which fit into the structure and demands of the democracy support system and hence have become part of the democracy support industry. They have become effectively market actors selling their projects on the global market place. Yet, if we remind ourselves of the fact that various committed extra-liberal radical and participatory groups also exist, we need also to think of their role and possibilities in the current system.

Their prospects, it would seem, look poor as things stand. They fail to get money for their global democratic and radical democratic visions within the more conservative and professionalised NGO support industry and at present, given the current structures and aims of democracy support, do not even wish to obtain funds if this would mean depoliticising or changing the nature of their activities.

Conceptually, here you will find the most pluralistic and critical conceptual frameworks for thinking about democracy: the recognition of contestability of the idea of democracy, the rootedness of debates on democracy in global economic structures and awareness of the politico-economic role of democracy in the global system. In terms of challenging hegemonic consciousness in democracy support, here is where an active counter-hegemonic pole exists. But what should it do to be more effective, more influential and more mainstreamed into democracy support? Should these organisations integrate themselves into the democracy support industry?

My advice stops short of advocating such a move. I argue instead that a *set of micro-political strategic resistance actions can and should be undertaken by these actors.* They can, in small ways, insert their logics into the system and should actively seek to do so, despite the difficult working environments. What might such actions look like?

We should probably welcome the kinds of actions that the Network Institute for Global Democratization (NIGD) or the World Social Forum (WSF) are engaged in. They seek to facilitate both independent non-hierarchical actions for democratisation and fora for discussion led by grass-roots movements. These movements aim at global level redirection of development and democratisation discourses.

The actions of the NIGD and the WSF challenge the West-directed assumptions of much of current democracy support and emphasise the need for bottom-up perspectives which cannot be manipulated or bought in to the current democracy support industry. The support these actors provide for non-professionalised openly political civil society actors in countries is crucial, as is their commitment to global democracy, often a key concern of local peasants' and workers' movements in democratising countries.

I also welcome the actions of many critical grass-roots social groups within target and donor countries. In democratising countries many civil society organisations, which are not part of the global democratisation industry continue to advocate for their alternative conceptualisations of democracy. Even in the West important openings are made. Particularly prominent in the last years has been the Occupy movement and its various off-shoots: a non-hierarchical movement seeking in an undirected way 'real democracy' in the West as well as rest, it promises the kind of actions that are both hard to contain by classical liberal democratic means and which push for rethinking of democracy beyond the classical paradigm. This movement in a sense could be seen as a sign of an 'exodus' from democratic life of modern states, as predicted by Hardt and Negri (2005), and maybe something to encourage in the search for a reinvigorated belief in and meaning of democracy globally.

Crucially, such movements have little to do with the current democracy support industry, as they wish to remain autonomous and undirected by other interests and wish to support democratic movement in an open and dialogical manner which is not co-opted by the democracy industry and its discourses and delivery tools. Respecting the autonomy of such movements is one important thing which democracy promoters can do in terms of improving their own stance.

Yet, if changes are forthcoming in democracy aid frameworks and their political objectives and working methods, some sort of co-operation is not unthinkable. If these actors are accepted as having democracy-enhancing qualities and are respected as counter-hegemonic actors from which policy and democratisation can learn, more positive dialogue may be had.

With this in mind, radical *actors should also recognise that room may exist within the current democracy support industry for more strategic entry points.* Labour unions, co-operatives, civil society actors, and peasants' unions can find openings within the project funds and ideas of the hegemonic actors. The EU's EIDHR or civil society dialogues can be used for funds and access. So can participation clauses in trade negotiations (Trommer, 2011). Many more professionalised NGO and civil society organisations also depend, more than is often realised, on local non-professionalised and even radical organisations for knowledge and practical know-how. These organisations, then, may have more of a role, and more power in the democracy industry than is often realised. With adequate safeguards in place (vis-à-vis autonomy of their activities), they can provide crucial locally-rooted democracy-enhancing knowledge and know-how in target countries and regions. Arguably, the donors should do more to encourage such actors or engage these actors directly – as we have seen currently the system is stacked up against radical actors – but simultaneously the radical actors themselves can do more to use the strategic openings for their own benefit. They need to be aware of the slippage 'to justify[ing] and legitimat[ing] the sort of programmes that the bureaucratic establishment is there to execute' (Fergusson, 1994: 70) but with this proviso in mind can do something to also shift the foci of development and democracy promotion actors, for these actors are also dependent on their local roots and access.

General suggestions for redirections in democracy support

Besides these specific suggestions, I have four general suggestions to make for democracy promotion policy work. First, such work should entail detailed, and *broad, engagement with democratic theory and democratic practice from the point of view of pluralist principles*. Democracy promoters have to engage in – and perhaps be required to do so by donors – 'perspective'-changing positioning of themselves in the 'shoes' of other actors in global politics. In International Relations Theory, students are regularly asked to position themselves in the shoes of a realist policy-maker, an anti-globalisation activist, a human rights defender in Russia, a development tycoon in Malaysia – to give just a few examples – in order to appreciate the very different 'world views' (i.e. theoretical positions) that these actors hold in analysing international politics, its core dynamics and its core power relations. This is a process to which democracy promoters – policy-makers and practitioners – should regularly submit themselves. Appreciating how different the world looks through the lenses of different world views and structural positions is essential for democracy promoters too in order to understand how democracy may be perceived from very different viewpoints.

Second, training sessions by pluralist democratic theorists and critical theorists, not just mainstream liberal theorists, are essential today. Thus, reading Dahl and Schumpeter is simply not enough. *Reading Marx, reading Pateman, or reading Galbraith, Hobhouse or Mill, will do much more for the democratic practitioner today than will reproducing a narrow liberal perspective on democracy which fails to perceive its own inadequacies and to appreciate the debate on democracy's meaning historically and today.*

Such a viewpoint will lead to *greater systematisation of thinking on multiple politico-economic models in democracy support*. Thus, the current openings which are unsystematic could actually be followed up in more consistent and systematic ways, meaning that real openings to alternative lines of thought on democracy might actually become possible. Consideration of more meaningful social democracy or participatory democracy might become possible, as might proper engagement with the consequences of reform liberalism for, say, US democracy support. This would be desirable for the 'illusion' of diversity and pluralism in today's democracy support to be broken to the benefit of facilitation of more contestation-centred, real debate on democracy's meaning.

Third, such moves would also *push democracy supporters towards greater reflexivity on their own political and ideological agendas*. All democracy promoters inevitably push for, or support, democracy of one kind or another; they have an ideological agenda; and they engage in 'pedagogy of power' (Teivainen, 2009) in structuring debates and understandings of democracy 'on the ground'. A complex global power system is embedded in democracy support. Given this is the case, surely greater self-reflexivity and awareness is welcome in ensuring that when power is deployed it is at least deployed with realisation of the consequences of power. This also entails that international actors have to *accept responsibility* for their actions – thus, blaming poverty of technical instruments will not wash in explaining away democracy support failures. Rather democracy promoters *need to own up to the politics and ideology* and power of their own work – and accept responsibility for the effects on social relations in recipient countries. Hollow hegemony (Chandler, 2009) in democracy support needs to become more explicit hegemony. Such a move may not benefit donor interest-seeking but it will benefit democratisation. Thus, if commitment to democracy is real, these moves should at least be considered.

Fourth, at the same time the potential for clashing sets of democracy support policies should be accepted. To assume coherence and consistency and complimentarity of the policies of all democracy support actors – NGOs and donors of different kind – is clearly optimistic in the extreme. Instead, *embracing clashing sets of values and contestation over democracy* and democracy support would be preferable. The bureaucratic mentality of simply pushing for technocratic reforms on the basis of world-wide consensus amounts to little more than hegemony-building for the sake of side-lining real democratic debate. This needs to be recognised and real contestation over democracy's meaning – including its essentially clashing sets of rights claims – needs to be embraced. Some donors are in better position than others to do so (e.g. the EU more so than the United States) but this is no excuse for failing to post one's ideological commitments openly and sticking by them, while recognising the possibility that in some instances these commitments may lead to contradictory policies. This is the nature of democracy support, after all: it is a fundamentally contradictory policy agenda.

Conclusion

> Working for social change is not synonymous with working for governments; indeed, it is perhaps not too much to say that the preoccupation of governments and government agencies is more often precisely to forestall and frustrate the processes of popular empowerment.
>
> (Ferguson, 1994: 285)

This goes, I have argued in this book, for many of the actors in the democracy support industry. This is crucial to keep in mind in maintaining a critical perspective on democracy support. A democracy support activity or organisation may not be US- or EU-funded, it may not be liberal democratic, it may not be 'safe' and stability-oriented, it may not be state-focused – yet, it may be democracy-enhancing nevertheless.

In a world of declining room for democracy, but one where democratic aspirations remain strong, it is crucial that more conceptually open debate on democracy is had. This requires, I have suggested here, a few important moves which require self-reflection:

- Democracy promoters – donors, deliverers, recipients – need to explore openly and critically, even if just as an exercise, their own assumptions and how they may reflect a particular hegemonic viewpoint and what they leave out from democracy support.
- They need to think about the structuring of priorities and how they can reflect hierarchies of values or ideological commitments.
- They need to think about the silences that emanate from their assumptions and practices. They need to think about power and how it is embedded in conceptual assumptions as well as in everyday practices.
- They need to think about implicit faces of power in democracy support as well as overt power: the power implicit in agenda setting, discursive power, and conceptual power.
- They need to think about the democracy promotion industry: its global networks, discourses and covert linkages.
- They need to think about empowering not only the grass-roots in target countries, but also in the West to think critically about the nature of democracy and capitalism.
- They need to recognise the historical – and contemporary – contestedness of the relationship between democracy and capitalism, of democracy and economy.
- They need to think seriously about the political and ideological choices of orientation that have to be taken in democracy support if it is to be more open and politicised.
- They need to think about contradictions and clashes that are inherent in democracy support if it is contested – and about the paradoxes that are inherent in democracy support as a foreign policy agenda.
- They need to think about the limits of liberalism when, it turns out, that history has not ended, in an era of shifts in the liberal world order and its structures of power.
- They need to acknowledge the openings that exist today for various models of democracy. Hardt and Negri (2005) argue that one avenue today may spell the 'exodus' of a democratic possibility: an exodus from the assumptions and concepts of hegemonic kind. Such an exodus is, I have suggested here, both desirable and possible in democratic thought and practice, and democracy promotion, today.

Conclusion

Critical theory, democracy and alternative politico-economic futures

In the post-Cold War world, the concept of democracy has been unanchored from its rigid memory and set adrift. . . . Perhaps for that reason, it has some hope of regaining its previous significance.

(Hardt and Negri, 2005: 91, 232)

This book has suggested that the meaning of the concept of democracy can and should be set adrift, and that this would be a good thing for democracy and democratisation. More debate over democracy rather than more 'export' of democracy is needed. Democracy promotion should be able to incorporate and celebrate a 'setting adrift' of democracy's meaning, and focus on facilitation of debate over democracy's future rather than fixing its meaning. Democracy is a value which will continue to have an attraction to most groups of people in most societies and democracy support, then, is bound to continue to have its takers. Yet in all societies – including those in the West – there are *also* endless disagreements, contentions and debates about the meaning of this concept.

Crucially, democracy as a system of social rule *does not* necessarily entail liberal democracy, nor its value-priorities, such as 'stable' government and societal consensus. Indeed, while some traditions of thought – liberal democratic and social democratic traditions, for example – have prioritised social order as a key value of democracy, participatory and radical democratic traditions prioritise other values – facilitation of autonomy and solidarity, for example. For advocates of many alternative traditions of democratic thought and practice, democracies are not about the election of leaders every six years, but should rather facilitate debate, dialogue and contestation in a society, including debate over the meaning of democracy itself.

In the context of multiple crises of democracy and democracy promotion today, the challenge is on for democracy promoters to find constructive ways of revisiting the meaning of democracy in their work. So far efforts have been half-hearted and incomplete, partly as a result of the lack of conceptual tools in analysis of democracy support and the distinct lack of interest in grasping the content of the multiplicity of different liberal and non-liberal democratic visions. In order to assist in the process of moving towards more democratic and dialogical democracy promotion, this book has provided theoretical engagements with alternative democratic traditions which democracy promotion practitioners remain worryingly blind to, and empirical engagements with, and policy provocations towards, understanding how the multiple meanings of democracy are, and could be better, taken into account in democracy support. The focus has been on donors and key Western delivery organisations, partly because this is where the power of democracy industry lies – they are key shapers of democracy's meaning, not just local actors – but also because this is, arguably, where many problems lie in terms of inability to conceptualise democracy beyond 'known' parameters.

The challenge of dealing with normative contestation over democracy in democracy promotion was formulated here through the tools of critical theory. The aim has been to show that critical theory, and a broad selection of critical theoretical approaches, can provide tools – if not definitive problem-solving answers – for policy practitioners and academics to deal with issue areas of concern to them. Critical theory is not abstract then; it is ideally praxaelogical, while at the same time challenging of existing hegemonic structures. Critical thinking is not only pragmatic, it is also politically enabling: it forces us away from instrumental problem-solving perspectives towards a wider framework of pragmatic thought where narrow instrumental goals are overridden by wider normative and political concerns. Thus, it opens horizons, while not seeking to fill them with all the possible and conceivable ready-made answers. The emphasis here is on rejecting analysis of 'surface-level' understandings and actions of social reality – the obvious truths – in favour of deep probing into the inter-subjective and self-defining structures of meaning for the purpose of generating rethinking of subject matters, their causes and their consequences. Such knowledge will be political and normative and, if successful, potentially transformative on a foundational level. It seeks to initiate thought 'outside the box' on the discursive practices that are often taken for granted, or at worst seen as natural and apolitical. In critical theory power resides in structures, in discourses, in understandings, in practices or techniques of acting.

This perspective provides a new and insightful set of provocations for analysis of democracy support. I have argued here that if we adopt this perspective we can see not only the conceptual foundations of democracy support in clearer light but also appreciate the limitations of debate on democracy's meaning today.

We have seen that much more nuance has emerged into the democracy promotion scene in the last few years. From acceptance of multiple models to the language of ownership, shifts have taken place to accommodate the critics of democracy support. Yet, these moves have not resulted in systematic and unquestioned opening up of dialogue over democracy's meaning. A liberal magnetic pole still reverberates through the field of democracy support and in so doing 'redirects' all attempts to formulate alternative visions of democracy back towards a (neo)liberal centre.

I have also argued here that we need to appreciate the increasingly governmental guises that liberalism, democracy promotion and world ordering practices take today. Instead of nailing its principles to the mast, the liberal practice of world ordering, including democracy support within it, happens mostly through assumptions with regard to governance, markets, civil society and their interrelationships. Thus, in an era of post-big-L liberalism, there is no need to be ideological. Instrumental and technical logics suffice. As Hardt and Negri (1999) argue, in a world system of biopolitical orientation there is a move to justification of interventionist action on the basis of 'efficiency' of outcome rather than moral or ideological justification. In such a world order – once ideological agendas are downplayed, de-centred, and depoliticised – democracy support too becomes but a technical tool of governance, of governing life under the principles of freedom and rights.

The democracy promotion system, a global system, is today both seemingly non-coercive, holistic and internally consistent. It aims to perfect power-use which requires minimal coercion of explicit kind, while seeking to control actions and thoughts from the bottom-up. At the same time, it is filled with contradictions, some of which are essential to its very functioning. Thus, while contested-ness of democracy is acknowledged, it is also simultaneously side-stepped, with the contradictions of such moves going unnoticed under a seemingly, although superficially, coherent and consensual discursive framework. This system maintains order, and specifically (it would seem), an effective liberal capitalist order.

Yet, effectiveness in democracy support is not measured on large-scale normative or ideological scales, but through objective indicators of technical progress in specific areas. Democracy becomes reduced to a question of accountability, measured in terms of transparency of reporting, action and delivery efficiency, not of substantive democratic values. At the same time, in a contradictory manner, it is the mixing of liberal and extra-liberal ideals which provides support for such practice, but liberalism is at its core. In the European Union (EU), for example, the invocation of social democracy, far from destabilising support for liberal democracy, actually sustains and legitimates it by fudging the issue of what is supported. Even alternatives today – we must be reminded – become easily sucked into the liberal discourse and come to sustain it.

What is particular notable about the role of implicit liberalism in democracy support is the interconnected nature of the different parts of the liberal order that emerges. Thus, the non-governmental organisations (NGOs) are deeply embedded in the governance agenda of the states, whose agenda is embedded in that of the International Financial Institutions (IFIs). There is a hegemonic structure in place, which reaches from the top to the bottom rather seamlessly – although in a 'diversity-respecting' manner. No longer do NGOs, at least core NGOs, challenge the agenda of the EU or the United States; rather they seek to accommodate themselves to it, changing their own nature and aims as required. All this, while remaining 'autonomous' actors in charge of their 'own agendas'!

It is of course more difficult to resist liberalism in this new form. Indeed, many practitioners or receivers of funding fail to note the dominance of liberal assumptions, or if they do, they sidestep it as insignificant. Yet, ideological assumptions – hidden or otherwise – have consequences for whom is worked with, which actors gain power, how people act and position themselves, and hence how power relations in the target countries may unfold. Herein, then, lies its attraction.

Yet, it is accepted by and large unintentionally, or at least un-strategically. Indeed, what is so notable about 'small-l liberalism' in democracy support today is that it goes almost unnoticed and unremarked on, because it is accepted as a matter of course, as common sense. It may be part of a great conspiracy to mislead and misdirect target populations into subservience to Western capital but if so it is not intentionally fostered for such purposes (Robinson, 1996).

But what of the potential for alternatives to democracy support in such a context where liberalism has gone into hiding? And is there any hope for a different kind of more open democracy support and democratisation?

Is there room for alternatives?

As Chapters 11 and 12 have discussed, it is obvious that at present liberal ideological principles play much more of a role in structuring possible actions and options of democracy promoters and democracy deliverers than is often recognised. It is precisely because of the naturalised nature of the liberal assumptions that many radical perspectives are dismissed straight away as dangerous. At the same time critics are co-opted: while language of participation and social justice abounds, there is little sign of advocacy for workplace democracy or wage-earner democracy in democracy support.

Room for alternative perspectives within such a well-functioning discursive 'Empire' would seem very limited indeed. Yet, from the Gramscian–Foucauldian perspective built in Chapters 11 and 12, some room for resistance and change is also at the same time more apparent. Because in this perspective power is not perceived as 'absolute' or 'overt', is not seen as 'coercive' and as potentially reliant on 'self-responsible activities of agents', power structures are also more challengeable than they might appear to be. Indeed, inherent or latent within the contradictory world order practices are many cracks and inconsistencies which critical perspectives and reflective practitioners can latch on to, affect and open up towards new directions. Indeed, Chapter 12 has pointed out that if democracy promoters are interested in systematising their thought on democracy in democracy support, various alternative models and visions exist to guide their thinking. Liberal principles themselves can be revised and re-debated, and in so doing we may find that within them too exist often ignored radical potential. In Chapter 12 we tackle directly the kinds of methods and strategies that can be adopted to shape democracy promotion practice today, depending on our perspective on global order.

Yet, a condition for all this potential change is acceptance of a conceptual level of debate and some possibility of conceptual change. This in turn requires – as Hardt and Negri (2005) argue so powerfully – willingness to 'exit' from the model and the system as it exists, willingness to think in radically new ways, and to extend the conceptual parameters that exist in new directions. That is the only way of dealing with the problems of democracy promotion today: the undercutting of democracy by democracy promoters themselves; the inability to see new scales and sites of democracy; the intolerance to radical notions of democracy; and the imposition of democracy from above (cf. Hardt and Negri, 2005: 236–7). Just like eighteenth-century radicals, we too should now 'aim higher' in reconceptualising the scale and modes of operation of democracy away from singular corrupted views of democracy's meaning (Hardt and Negri, 2005: 307).

This provocation is important, even if one does not accept the end point of radical democratic pluralism. This is because both the practical credibility and the normative justifications for democracy support today rely on more consistent, and thus more consistently pluralistic, exploration of democracy's meaning. It is to encouraging democratic alternatives in the fullest possible sense that democracy promoters – to have the courage of their convictions – must now turn. Thinking on the alternatives provided here points to but one – relatively unchallenging and moderate – possible avenue, yet it may be the first step we need towards a democratic 'exodus'.

Notes

1 Introduction

1 The terms democracy promotion, support and assistance are often confusing in the literature. The subtle differences of meaning should, however, be clarified. Democracy promotion refers to the overarching idea that democracy should be and can be advanced in other states. Democracy assistance is a subset of democracy promotion but refers to the technical process of concrete democracy 'assistance' provided by donors. Democracy support is a confusing term, which has arisen in the last few years to demonstrate that democracy promotion is now less about coercive promotion of specific ideals and more about 'support' to local forces. However, it should be noted that democracy support, while reflective of the shifts in democracy advocacy (precisely the kinds of trends in democracy promotion identified here), can itself be seen as a rebranding of the generic term democracy promotion in that it still arguably involves advocacy of and assistance to democratic forces in other states The concepts promotion and support will be used interchangably here as generic descriptives for a variety of practices, frameworks and actions in encouraging and advocating democratisation, through whatever means (conditions, support, aid) in other countries.
2 This is not to say, this book is not informed by its own set of theoretical choices and leanings. Indeed, the very assumptions set out below are distinct and in some senses 'narrow' in the way in which they point us in very particular directions in the analysis of democracy support. Nevertheless, I contend that the assumptions set out below provide a broader horizon for analysis than interpretation than a perspective which would start from a very specific set of theoretical orientations.

2 The contested liberal democratic model

1 Can we speak of an 'it', a unitary idea of liberalism? This is by no means self-evident, for liberalism comes in various different phases and forms. For example, many commentators distinguish between economic and political liberalism (Hardin, 1999), others between pre-revolutionary and post-revolutionary liberalism (Manent, 1996). Others yet draw fundamental lines between laissez-faire liberals and welfare liberals (McLean, 1996).
2 We can sustain this argument both in terms of historical record of discussion about 'liberal democracy' and on conceptual grounds, as C.B. Macpherson argues, by pointing out that pre-19th century theories of democracy shared a base in belief in classless or one-class society, an assumption that liberal democracy breaks by accepting explicitly class basis for the democratic system (1977: 9–20).

3 Challenges to liberal democracy

1 Tilton argues that there are four distinct kinds of controls placed on markets: (1) markets would be enlisted to produce for the needs of all, not the rich, (2) government would

seek to provide 'perfect' information on jobs and assist in mobility of the labour market, (3) partially planned market, (4) understanding of property as a 'bundle of rights' (Tilton, 1990: 264–6).

7 Liberal democracy

1 New Nationalism was a call to put national interests before sectional or personal interests, thus arguing that too much decentralization and division of governmental power were nefarious to national activities.
2 While references to bringing freedom to Iraq are made in pre-war speeches, a shift from the WMD threat to democracy promotion gradually took place in justifying the war when it became evident that there were no WMDs to be found in Iraq.
3 NED acknowledges the link between democratisation and economic development but clearly states that its focus is on 'political' democracy, and does not address the politico-economic dimension of democratisation – i.e. the relationship between the political (form of government) and the economic (economic regime).

8 The European Union

1 This is a term used in EU circles for countries which are neither member states nor associated states.

9 Democracy promotion by non-state actors

1 These for-profit organisations also deserve close study, for their work is crucial in understanding the delivery of US democracy promotion especially. This is because, in the US context, delivery of democracy aid has been almost completely privatised to non-profit and for-profit organisations. The private companies, which are specifically designed to deliver projects to USAID or State Department specifications, bid for contracts with the US State Department and then deliver the goods, as any contractor would. The conceptual foundations of these organisations are fascinating for they work on the basis of a pragmatic but also market-led thinking on democracy and quite simply deliver what the donors want.
2 Although are not morally principled about this funding source being their primary aim. Indeed, as Arjens Berkvens, the director of the ENOP stated, the ENoP would happily accept $500 million from Bill Gates, but in the absence of such generous third party donors, relies on partial contributions of the member foundations and the EU's non-state actor project funding.

11 Democracy promotion, implicit liberalism and the liberal world order

1 It is not my aim here to build a grand theoretical edifice on Gramsci's ideas, which were developed in rather fragmentary way anyway.
2 Another interesting way to understand implicit liberalism would be through the idea of 'doxa' developed by Pierre Bourdieu (1977). He distinguished doxa, as background beliefs, from heterodoxy and orthodoxy – conscious contestation of opinion (Bourdieu, 1977: 167–170). Class interests of the dominant, he argues, seek to defend the integrity of doxa, while the dominated seek to challenge it (Bourdieu, 1977: 169). To avoid over-complicating the analysis here, I will not discuss the Bourdieuan avenue of interpretation, which however would have some potential to explain similar trends accounted for here through Gramsci and Foucault.

References

Interviews

Interview with EEAS Official, January 2011, Brussels.
Interview with European Commission Official, January 2011, Brussels.
Interview with EU Trade Official, January 2011, Brussels.
Interview with CSO representative, January 2011, Brussels.
Interview with representative of a political foundation, September 2010, Stockholm.
Interview with representative of a political foundation, January 2011, Brussels/Aberystwyth.
Interview with Arjen Berkvens (ENoP), January 2011, Brussels.
Interview with Heikki Patomäki (NIGD), April 2011, Manchester.
Interview with Barbara Haig (NED), March 2012, Washington DC.
Interview with Senior State Department Official, March 2012, Washington DC.
Interview with representative of a private consulting firm, March 2012, Washington DC.

Bibliography

Abrahamsen, Rita (2000) *Disciplining Democracy: Development Discourse and Good Governance in Africa*. London: Zed Books.
Abrahamsen, Rita (2004) 'The Power of Partnerships in Global Governance', *Third World Quarterly* 25(8): 1453–1467.
Abrahamsen, Rita and Michael Williams (2010) *Security Beyond the State: Private Security in International Politics*. Cambridge: Cambridge University Press.
Adler-Karlsson, Gunnar (1967) *Functional Socialism*. Stockholm: Prisma.
Albert, Michael (2006) *Realizing Hope: Life Beyond Capitalism*. London: Zed Press.
Aggestam, Lisbeth (2008) 'Introduction: Ethical Power Europe?' *International Affairs* 84(1): 1–13.
American Political Foundation (1983) *The Democracy Program*. Washington, DC: American Political Foundation. Available at: http://www.ned.org/docs/democracyProgram.pdf (accessed 20/04/2012).
Apeldoorn, Bastiaan van (2001) 'The Struggle over . . . Embedded Neo-Liberalism', in: A. Bieler and A. David Morton, eds, *Social Forces in the Making of the New Europe: the Restructuring of European Social Relations in the Global Political Economy*. New York: Palgrave.
Apeldoorn, Bastiaan van, Jan Drahokoupil and Laura Horn (2009) *Contradictions and Limits of Neoliberal European Governance: from Lisbon to Lisbon*. Basingstoke, UK; New York: Palgrave Macmillan.
Appleby, J. (1992) 'Recovering America's Historic Diversity: Beyond Exceptionalism', *Journal of American History* 79: 419–431.

Archibugi, Daniele (2008) *The Global Commonwealth of Citizens: Toward Cosmopolitan Democracy*. Princeton, NJ; Oxford: Princeton University Press.

Armony, A.C. and H.E. Schamis (2005) 'Babel in Democratization Studies', *Journal of Democracy* 16(4): 113–128.

Ashford, Nigel (2003) *Principles for a Free Society*. Bromma: Bloomberg & Jason.

Ayers, Alison (2006) 'Demystifying Democratisation: the Global Constitution of (neo)Liberal Polities in Africa', *Third World Quarterly* 27(2): 321–333.

Bachrach, Peter and Aryeh Botwinick (1992) *Power and Empowerment: a Radical Theory of Participatory Democracy*. Philadelphia: Temple University Press.

Barany, Zoltan D. and Robert G. Moser (2009) *Is Democracy Exportable?* Cambridge; New York: Cambridge University Press.

Barbe, Esther and Elisabeth Johansson-Nogues (2008) 'The EU as a Modest "Force for Good": the European Neighbourhood Policy', *International Affairs* 84(1): 81–77.

Barber, Benjamin R. (2003) *Strong Democracy: Participatory Politics for a New Age*. Berkeley, CA; London: University of California Press.

Barro Robert J. and Jong-Wha Lee (2003) 'IMF Programs: Who Is Chosen and What Are the Effects?', Working paper, available at: http://www.economics.harvard.edu/faculty/barro/files/IMF_Programs.pdf

Bell, Daniel (2006) *Beyond Liberal Democracy: Political Thinking for an East Asian Context*. Princeton, NJ; Oxford: Princeton University Press.

Berman, Sheri (2006) *The Primacy of Politics: Social Democracy and the Making of Europe's Twentieth Century*. Cambridge: Cambridge University Press.

Berman, Sheri (2011) 'The Past and Future of Social Democracy and the Consequences for Democracy Promotion', in: C. Hobson and M. Kurki, eds, *Conceptual Politics of Democracy Promotion*. London: Routledge, pp. 68–84.

Bernstein, B.J. (1972) *Politics and Policies of the Truman Administration*. Chicago, IL: Quadrangle Books.

Berry, Christopher J. (1997) *Social Theory of the Scottish Enlightenment*. Edinburgh: Edinburgh University Press.

Bicchi, Federica (2006) '"Our size fits all": normative power Europe and the Mediterranean', *Journal of European Public Policy* 13(2): 286–303.

Bobbio, Norberto (1976) *Which Socialism? Marxism, Socialism and Democracy*. Oxford: Polity Press.

Bouchet, Nicolas (2011) 'Barack Obama's Democracy Promotion at Midterm', *International Journal of Human Rights* 15(4): 572–588.

Bourdieu, Pierre (1977) *An Outline of Theory of Practice*. Cambridge: Cambridge University Press.

Bowen, James D. (2011) 'Multicultural Market Democracy: Elites and Indigenous Movements in Contemporary Ecuador', *Journal of Latin American Studies* 43(3): 451–448.

Bowles, Samuel and Herbert Gintis (1987) *Democracy and Capitalism: Property, Community, and the Contradictions of Modern Social Thought*. London: Routledge.

Bridoux, Jeff (2011a) *American Foreign Policy and Postwar Reconstruction: Comparing Japan and Iraq*. Abingdon, Oxon: Routledge.

Bridoux, Jeff (2011b) 'USAID Forward and the Commodification of Democracy: a Critique'. Paper presented at the BISA US Foreign Policy Working Group Conference, Oxford, UK, 22–23 September 2011.

Bridoux, Jeff and Malcolm Russell (forthcoming) 'Liberal Democracy Promotion in Iraq: A Model for the Middle East and North Africa?', *Foreign Policy Analysis*, in press.

Brown, Wendy (2003) 'Neoliberalism and the end of liberal democracy', *Theory and Event*

7(1). Available at: http://readingrhetoric.wordpress.com/2011/04/07/%E2%80%9Cneo-liberalism-and-the-end-of-liberal-democracy-%E2%80%9D-2/

Burnell, Peter J. (2000) *Democracy Assistance: International Co-operation for Democratization.* London: Frank Cass.

Burnell, Peter (2011) *Promoting Democracy Abroad: Policy and Performance,* Rutgers: Transaction Publishers.

Burnell, Peter J. and Richard Youngs (2010) *New Challenges to Democratization.* London, UK; New York: Routledge.

Callinicos, Alex (2003) *An Anti-capitalist Manifesto.* Oxford: Polity Press.

Carothers, Thomas (1999) *Aiding Democracy Abroad: the Learning Curve.* Washington, DC: Carnegie Endowment for International Peace.

Carothers, Thomas (2000) 'Taking Stock of US Democracy Assistance', in: Michael Cox, John Ikenberry and Takashi Inoguchi, eds, *American Democracy Promotion Impulses, Strategies, and Impacts.* Oxford: Oxford University Press, pp. 181–199.

Carothers, Thomas (2005) *Critical Mission: Essays on Democracy Promotion.* Washington, DC: Carnegie Endowment for International Peace.

Carothers, Thomas (2006a) *Promoting the Rule of Law Abroad: In Search of Knowledge.* Washington, DC: Carnegie Endowment for International Peace.

Carothers, Thomas (2006b) 'The Backlash Against Democracy Promotion', *Foreign Affairs,* March/April, 2006.

Carothers, Thomas (2007) *US Democracy Promotion during and after Bush,* Washington, DC: Carnegie.

Carothers, Thomas (2008) *Does Democracy Promotion have a Future?* Carnegie Endowment for International Peace. Available at: http://www.carnegieendowment.org/publications/index.cfm?fa=view&id=20247 (accessed 01/08/2011).

Carothers, Thomas (2009a) *Revitalizing Democracy Assistance.* Carnegie Endowment for International Peace. Available at: http://www.carnegieendowment.org/files/revitalizing_democracy_assistance.pdf (accessed 01/08/2011).

Carothers, Thomas (2009b) 'Democracy Assistance: Political vs. Developmental', *Journal of Democracy* 20(1): 5–19.

Carothers, Thomas and Marina Ottaway, eds. (2000) *Funding Virtue: Civil Society Aid and Democracy Promotion.* Washington, DC: Carnegie Endowment for International Peace.

Carothers, Thomas and Marina Ottaway (2005) *Uncharted Journey: Promoting Democracy in the Middle East.* Washington, DC: Carnegie Endowment for International Peace.

Carrillo, Santiago (1977) *Dialogue on Spain.* London: Lawrence and Wishart.

Chandler, David (2000) *Bosnia: Faking Democracy after Dayton.* London: Pluto Press.

Chandler, David (2006a) *Empire in Denial: Politics of Statebuilding.* London: Pluto Press.

Chandler, David (2006b) 'Back to the Future: The Limits of Neowilsonian Ideals of Exporting Democracy', *Review of International Studies* 32: 475–494.

Chandler, David (2007) 'Hollow Hegemony: Theorising the Shift from Interest-based to Value-Based International Policy-making', *Millennium* 35(3): 703–723.

Chandler, David (2009) *Hollow Hegemony: Rethinking Global Politics, Power and Resistance.* Pluto Press, London.

Chandler, David (2010a) 'The EU and Southeastern Europe: the rise of post-liberal governance', *Third World Quarterly* 31(1): 69–85.

Chandler, David (2010b) *International Statebuilding: the Rise of Post-Liberal Governance.* London: Routledge.

Chu, Yun-han and Min-hua Huang. (2010) 'Solving an Asian Puzzle', *Journal of Democracy* 21(4): 114–122.

Clary, M.Q. (2009) 'Getting Back on Track: Constructing a Business-Model of American Democracy Promotion,' Paper presented at the annual meeting of the Midwest Political Science Association 67th Annual National Conference (The Palmer House Hilton, Chicago, IL, April). Available at: http://www.allacademic.com//meta/p_mla_apa_research_citation/3/6/0/6/2/pages360629/p360629-1.php

Clinton, H. (2010) 'Civil Society: Supporting Democracy in the 21st Century'. Speech at the Community of Democracies (Warsaw, Poland: 3 July). Available at: http://www.state.gov/secretary/rm/2010/07/143952.htm (accessed 20/03/2012)

Clinton, H. (2011) 'Remarks at the Launch of Strategic Dialogue with Civil Society', Washington DC, 16 February 2011. Available at: http://www.state.gov/secretary/rm/2011/02/156681.htm (accessed 20/03/2012).

Cohen, Theodore (1987) *Remaking Japan: the American Occupation as New Deal.* New York: Free Press.

Cole, G.D.H. (1920) *Guild Socialism.* London: The Fabian Society.

Collier, David and Steven Levitsky (1997) 'Democracy with Adjectives: Conceptual Innovation in Comparative Research', *World Politics* 49: 430–451.

Connolly, William E. (1995) *The Ethos of Pluralization.* Minneapolis, MN; London: University of Minnesota Press.

Cook, Terrence E. and Patrick M. Morgan (1971) *Participatory Democracy.* San Francisco, CA: Canfield Press.

Cooke, Bill and Uma Kothari, eds (2001) *Participation: the New Tyranny.* London: Zed books.

Corcoran, Paul (1983) 'The Limits of Democratic Theory', in: Graeme Duncan. *Democratic Theory and Practice.* Cambridge: CUP.

Council of the European Union (2007) 'The Africa–EU Strategic Partnership; A Joint Africa–EU Strategy', 16344/07 (Presse 291) Lisbon, 9 December 2007. Available at: http://www.consilium.europa.eu/uedocs/cms_data/docs/pressdata/en/er/97496.pdf (accessed 20/03/2012).

Council of the European Union (2009) 'Council Conclusions on Democracy Support in the EU's External Relations', 2974th External Relations Council meeting Brussels, 17 November 2009. Available at: http://www.consilium.europa.eu/uedocs/cms_data/docs/pressdata/en/gena/111250.pdf (accessed 20/03/2012).

Cox, Michael G., John Ikenberry and Takashi Inoguchi (2000) *American Democracy Promotion: Impulses, Strategies, and Impacts.* Oxford; New York: Oxford University Press.

Cox, Robert (1981) 'Social Forces, States and World Orders: Beyond International Relations Theory', *Millennium: Journal of International Studies* 10, 2: 126–155.

Coyne, C.J. and T. Cofman Wittes (2008) 'Can We Export Democracy?', *Cato Policy Report* 30(1): 11–13.

CPA [Coalition Provisional Authority] (2003) *Achieving the Vision to Restore Full Sovereignty to the Iraqi People.* Baghdad, Iraq. Available at: http://www.globalsecurity.org/military/library/congress/2003_hr/03-10-08strategicplan.pdf (accessed 03/08/2011).

Crawford, Gordon (2003a) 'Promoting Democracy from Without – Learning from Within (Part I)', *Democratization* 10(1): 77–98.

Crawford, Gordon (2003b) 'Promoting Democracy From Without – Learning From Within (Part II)', *Democratization* 10(2): 1–20.

Crawford, Gordon (2006) 'The World Bank and Good Governance: Rethinking the State or Consolidating Neo-Liberalism?', in: A. Paloni and M. Zanardi, eds, *The IMF, World Bank and Policy Reform*. London: Routledge, pp. 115–141.

Crawford, Gordon (2008) 'EU Human Rights and Democracy Promotion in Central Asia: From Lofty Principles to Lowly Self-interests', *Perspectives on European Politics and Society* 9(2): 172–191.

Crouch, Colin (2004) *Post-Democracy*. Cambridge: Polity.

Crouch, Colin (2011) *The Strange Non-Death of Neo-Liberalism*. Oxford: Polity.

Dahl, Robert (2000) *A Preface to Economic Democracy*. Berkeley, CA: University of California Press.

Dean, Mitchell (2010) *Governmentality: Power and Rule in Modern Society*. London: Sage.

Death, Carl (2011) 'Foucault and Africa: Governmentality, IR theory, and the Limits of Advanced Liberalism', paper presented at panel entitled 'Africa and Theory II: Reimagining relations international' at BISA Annual Conference 2011, Manchester, 27–29 April.

Diamond, Larry Jay (2008a) *The Spirit of Democracy: the Struggle to Build Free Societies Throughout the World*. New York: Times Books/Henry Holt and Company.

Diamond, L. (2008b) 'Democracy in Retreat', *Real Clear Politics*. Available at: http://www.realclearpolitics.com/articles/2008/03/democracy_in_retreat.html(accessed01/08/2011).

Diamond L. (2008c), 'How to Save Democracy?', *Newsweek* (31 December, 2008). Available at: http://www.newsweek.com/2008/12/30/how-to-save-democracy.html (accessed 01/08/2011).

Diamond, L. (2008d) 'The Democratic Rollback: the Resurgence of Predatory State', *Foreign Affairs* 87(2): 36–48.

Diamond, Larry (2010) 'Introduction to Forum on Meanings Of Democracy', *Journal of Democracy* 21(4): 102–103.

Doorenspleet, Renske (2004) 'Structural Context of Recent Transitions to Democracy', *European Journal of Political Research* 43: 309–335.

Dower, John W. (1999) *The Showa Emperor and Japan's Postwar Imperial Democracy*. Cardiff, CA: Japan Policy Research Institute.

Downs, Anthony (1957) *An Economic Theory of Democracy*. New York: Harper & Row.

DRL (2010a) – Bureau of Democracy, Human Rights and Labor, *Advancing Freedom and Democracy Reports, Russia*. Washington DC: U.S. Department of State. Available at: http://www.state.gov/g/drl/rls/afdr/2010/eur/129785.htm (accessed 20/03/2012).

DRL (2010b) 'August 2010 Proposal Submission Instructions (PSI)'. Available at: http://www.state.gov/g/drl/p/august_2010/index.htm 2009 (accessed 20/03/2012).

DRL (2010c) 'DRL Monitoring and Evaluation Primer and Sample M&E Plan'. Available at: http://www.state.gov/documents/organization/138430.pdf (accessed 20/03/2012).

DRL (2011) – Bureau of Democracy, Human Rights and Labor, 'DRL Programs, Including Human Rights Democracy Funds (HRDF)'. Available at: http://www.state.gov/g/drl/p/index.htm (accessed 20/03/2012).

Dryzek, John S. (1996) *Democracy in Capitalist Times: Ideals, Limits, and Struggles*. New York; Oxford: Oxford University Press.

Dryzek, John S. (2006) *Deliberative Global Politics: Discourse and Democracy in a Divided World*. Cambridge: Polity Press.

Duffield, Mark (2007) *Development, Security and Unending War: Governing the World of Peoples*. Oxford: Polity Press.

Dunne, Tim and Marjo Koivisto (2010) 'Crisis, What Crisis? Liberal Order Building and World Order Conventions', *Millennium* 38(3): 615–640.

EEAS/European Commission (2011) *A New Response to a Changing Neighbourhood: a Review of European Neighbourhood Policy*. Available at: http://ec.europa.eu/world/enp/pdf/com_11_303_en.pdf (accessed 20/03/2012).

Eklund, Klas (2001) 'Gosta Rehn and the Swedish Model: Did We Follow the Rehn-Meidner Model Too Little Rather than Too Much?', in: Henry Milner and Eskil Wadensjo, eds, *Gosta Rehn, the Swedish Model and Labour Market Policies: International and National Perspectives*. Farnham, Surrey: Ashgate.

Enterline, Andrew J. and J. Michael Greig (2008) 'Against All Odds? The History of Imposed Democracy and the Future of Iraq and Afghanistan', *Foreign Policy Analysis* 4(4): 321–347.

EPD (2009) Report from the Conference 'Building Consensus about EU Policies on Democracy Support' March 9 and 10, 2009, Prague, Czech Republic. Available at: http://www.epd.eu/uploads/68f92bc22fcba0184b90bbb2e6e73b62.pdf (accessed 20/03/2012).

Eschle, Catherine (2001) *Global Democracy, Social Movements, and Feminism*. Boulder, CO; Oxford: Westview Press.

Eschle, Catherine and Bice Maiguashca (2005) *Critical Theories, International Relations, and 'The Anti-Globalisation Movement': The Politics Of Global Resistance*. London: Routledge.

European Commission (1995) *The Inclusion of Respect for Democratic Principles and Human Rights in Agreements between the Community and Third Countries. Communication from the Commission*, COM (95) 216 final, 23 May, 1995 (http://aei.pitt.edu/4097/1/4097.pdf).

European Commission (1998) *Democratisation, the Rule of Law, Respect for Human Rights and Good Governance: The Challenges of the Partnership between the European Union and the ACP States, Communication from the Commission to the Council and the European Parliament*, COM (98) 146 final, 12 March 1998 (http://eur-lex.europa.eu/LexUriServ/LexUriServ.do?uri=COM:1998:0146:FIN:EN:PDF).

European Commission (2001) *The European Union's Role in Promoting Human Rights and Democratisation in Third Countries, Communication from the Commission to the Council and the European Parliament*, COM(2001) 252 final, 8 May 2001 (http://eur-lex.europa.eu/LexUriServ/LexUriServ.do?uri=COM:2001:0252:FIN:EN:PDF).

European Commission (2003) *Governance and Development, Communication from the Commission to the Council, the European Parliament and the European Economic and Social Committee*, COM(2003) 615 final, 20 October 2003 (http://eur-lex.europa.eu/LexUriServ/LexUriServ.do?uri=COM:2003:0615:FIN:EN:PDF).

European Commission (2004a) *European Neighbourhood Policy (Strategy Paper), Communication from the Commission*, COM (2004) 373 final, 12 May 2004 (http://ec.europa.eu/world/enp/pdf/strategy/strategy_paper_en.pdf)

European Commission (2004b) *Implementation of the Commission Communication on the EU's Role in Promoting Human Rights and Democratisation in Third Countries, Commission Staff Working Document* (COM (2001) 252 final), SEC(2004) 1041, 30 July, 2004 (http://www.europarl.europa.eu/RegData/docs_autres_institutions/commission_europeenne/sec/2004/1041/COM_SEC(2004)1041_EN.pdf)

European Commission (2005a) *Ukraine Action Plan*. Available at: http://ec.europa.eu/world/enp/pdf/actionplans/Ukraine_enp_ap.final_en.pdf.

European Commission (2005b) *European Initiative for Democracy and Human Rights*

(EIDHR) Programming Update for 2005 (http://ec.europa.eu/europeaid/what/human-rights/documents/eidhr_programming_update_2005_50211_en.pdf).

European Commission, DG RELEX (2006a) *European Instrument for Democracy and Human Rights (EIDHR) Strategy Paper 2007–2010*, DG RELEX/B/1 JVK 70618 (http://ec.europa.eu/europeaid/what/human-rights/documents/eidhr_strategy_paper_2007-2010_en.pdf).

European Commission (2006b) *Thematic Programme for the Promotion of Democracy and Human Rights Worldwide Under the Future Financial Perspective 2007–2013, Communication from the Commission to the Council and the European Parliament*, COM (2006) 23 final, 25 January 2006 (http://eur-lex.europa.eu/LexUriServ/LexUriServ.do?uri=COM:2006:0023:FIN:EN:PDF).

European Commission (2006c) Regulation (EC) No 1889/2006 of the European Parliament and of the Council of 20 December, 2006 on establishing a financing instrument for the promotion of democracy and human rights worldwide (http://eur-lex.europa.eu/LexUriServ/LexUriServ.do?uri=OJ:L:2006:386:0001:0011:en:PDF).

European Commission (2006d) *Methodological Guide on Electoral Assistance*, October, 2006, Brussels: European Communities (http://ec.europa.eu/europeaid/multimedia/publications/documents/thematic/ec_methodological_guide_on_electoral_assistance_en.pdf)

European Commission (2006e) *Staff Working Document on 'Strengthening the European Neighbourhood Policy: ENP Progress Report, Ukraine.* COM (2006) 726 final. Brussels: EC.

European Commission, (2007a) *The European Union: Furthering Human Rights and Democracy across the Globe, 2008.* Available at: http://eeas.europa.eu/human_rights/docs/brochure07_en.pdf (accessed 20/03/2012).

The European Commission (2007b) *European Neighbourhood and Partnership Instrument: Ukraine National Indicative Plan 2007–2010.* Brussels: European Commission.

European Commission (2008) *Democracy and Human Rights, Programming Guide for Strategy Papers.* Available at: http://www.developmentportal.eu/snv1/dmdocuments/F20_human_rights_en.pdf (accessed 20/03/2012).

European Commission (2009) *Supporting Democratic Governance through the Governance Initiative: A Review and the Way Forward, Commission Staff Working Paper.* Available at: http://ec.europa.eu/development/icenter/repository/CSWP_SEC_2009_0058_governance_en.pdf (accessed 20/03/2012).

European Commission (2010a) *Annual Report 2010 on the European Community's Development and External Assistance Policies and their Implementation in 2009.* Available at: http://ec.europa.eu/europeaid/multimedia/publications/publications/annual-reports/2010_en.htm (accessed 20/03/2012).

European Commission (2010b) *Engaging and Supporting Parliaments Worldwide: Strategies and Methodologies for EC Action in Support to Parliaments, Reference Document No. 8..* Available at: http://capacity4dev.ec.europa.eu/sites/default/files/file/23/04/2012_-_1754/support_to_parliaments-final-low-res_web.pdf (accessed 20/03/2012).

European Commission (2010c) *The Future of EU Budget Support to Third Countries, Green Paper from the Commission to the Council, the European Parliament, the European Economic and Social Committee and the Committee of the Regions*, Brussels, 19.10.2010, COM (2010) 586 final. Available at: http://ec.europa.eu/development/icenter/repository/green_paper_budget_support_third_countries_en.pdf (accessed 20/03/2012).

European Commission (2010d) *European Instrument for Democracy and Human Rights (EIDHR) Strategy Paper 2011 – 2013*, C(2010)2432. Available at: http://ec.europa.

eu/europeaid/what/human-rights/documents/eidhr_strategy_paper_2011_2013_com_decision_21_april_2011_text_published_on_internet_en.pdf (accessed 20/03/2012).

European Commission (2011a) *Equal in Rights Worldwide, European Instrument for Democracy and Human Rights, Compendium 2007–2010.* Available at: http://www.eidhr.eu/files/dmfile/EUAID_EIDHR_Compendium_LR_20110609.pdf (accessed 20/03/2012).

European Commission (2011b) *Annual Report 2011 on the European Community's Development and External Assistance Policies and their Implementation in 2010.* Available at: http://ec.europa.eu/europeaid/multimedia/publications/publications/annual-reports/2011_en.htm (accessed 20/03/2012).

European Community (2006) Joint statement by the Council and the representatives of the governments of the Member States meeting within the Council, the European Parliament and the Commission on European Union Development Policy: 'The European Consensus', *Official Journal of the European Communities*, 24.02.2006. C 46/01. Available at: http://ec.europa.eu/development/icenter/repository/european_consensus_2005_en.pdf (accessed 20/03/2012).

European Community (2000) Charter of fundamental rights of the European Union, *Official Journal of the European Communities*, 18.12. 2000. C364/1. Available at: http://www.europarl.europa.eu/charter/pdf/text_en.pdf (accessed 20/03/2012).

Fairclough, Norman (1995) *Critical Discourse Analysis: the Critical Study of Language.* Harlow, UK: Longman.

Femia, Joseph V. (1993) *Marxism and Democracy.* Oxford: Oxford University Press.

Ferguson, James (1994) *The Anti-politics Machine: Development, Depoliticisation and Bureaucratic Power in Lesotho.* Minneapolis, MN: University of Minnesota Press.

FES [Friedrich Ebert Stiftung] (2012) 'Global Policy and Development'. Available at: http://www.fes.de/GPol/en/democracy.htm (accessed 25/04/2012).

Fischer, Frank (2003) *Reframing Public Policy Discursive Politics and Deliberative Practices.* Oxford: Oxford University Press.

Fischer, Frank (2009) *Democracy and Expertise.* Oxford: Oxford University Press.

Fishkin, James S. (1991) *Democracy and Deliberation: New Directions for Democratic Reform.* New Haven, CT; London: Yale University Press.

Foley, Michael (2007) *American Credo: the Place of Ideas in US Politics.* Oxford: Oxford University Press.

Foucault, Michel (2008) *The Birth of Biopolitics Lectures at the College de France, 1978–79*, Edited by Michel Senellart and Graham Burchell. Basingstoke, UK: Palgrave Macmillan.

Freeden, Michael (1998) *Ideologies and Political Theory: A Conceptual Approach.* Oxford: Oxford University Press.

Freeden, Michael (2008) 'European Liberalisms: an Essay in Comparative Political Thought', *European Journal of Political Theory* 7(1): 9–30.

Friedman, Milton (1980) *Free to Choose: a Personal Statement.* New York; London: Harcourt Brace Jovanovich.

Friedman, Milton (2002 [1962]) *Capitalism and Freedom.* Chicago, IL: University of Chicago Press.

Friedrich Naumann Stiftung (2002) 'The role of democracy foundations'. Available at: http://www.fnf.org.ph/liberallibrary/role-of-democracy-foundations.htm (accessed 25/04/2012).

Fukuyama, Francis (1992) *The End of History and the Last Man.* London: Hamish Hamilton.

Fukuyama, Francis and Michael McFaul (2007) 'Should Democracy be Promoted or Demoted?', *The Washington Quarterly* 31(1): 1–25.

Gabardi, Wayne (2001) 'Contemporary Models of Democracy' *Polity* XXXIII(4): 547–568.

GAO (2009) 'US Agencies Take Steps to Coordinate International Programs but Lack Information on Some US-funded Activities'. Washington, DC: Government Accountability Office. Available at: http://www.gao.gov/assets/300/296097.pdf

Gasirowski, Mark J. and T.J. Power (1998) 'The Structural Determinants of Democratic Consolidation: Evidence from the Third World', *Comparative Political Studies* 31(6): 747–771.

Gebel, Anja (unpublished PhD thesis) 'The ideal within: conceptions of politics, economics and civil society in the international anticorruption discourse'. Aberystwyth University.

Gebel, Anja (2012a) 'Human nature and morality in the anti-corruption discourse of Transparency International', *Public Administration and Development* 32(1): 109–128.

Gebel, Anja (2012b) 'Dealing with Dislocations: International Anticorruption Discourse and Neoliberal Hegemony'. Paper presented at International Studies Association Annual Convention, San Diego, CA, 1–4 April, 2012.

Gershman, Carl and Michael Allen (2006) 'Assault on Democracy Assistance', *Journal of Democracy* 17(2): 36–51.

Giddens, Anthony (1998) *The Third Way: The Renewal of Social Democracy*. Cambridge: Polity.

Gill, Stephen (1998) 'European Governance and New Constitutionalism: Economic Monetary Union and Alternatives to Disciplinary Neoliberalism in Europe', *New Political Economy* 3(1): 5–26.

Gills, Barry K., Joel Rocamora and Richard Wilson (1993) *Low Intensity Democracy: Political Power in the New World Order*. London: Pluto.

Goldsmith, Arthur A. (2008) 'Making the World Safe for Partial Democracy?: Questioning the Premises of Democracy Promotion', *International Security* 33(2): 120–147.

Gramsci, Antonio (1998 [1971]) *Prison Notebooks: Selections*. London: Lawrence & Wishart.

Gray, John (1977) 'On the contestability of social and political concepts', *Political Theory* 5(3): 331–348.

Haggard, Stephan and Robert R. Kaufman (1995) *The Political Economy of Democratic Transitions*. Princeton, NJ: Princeton University Press.

Hahnel, Robin (2005) *Economic Justice and Democracy: from Competition to Cooperation*. New York, NY: Routledge.

Hardin, Russell (1999) *Liberalism, Constitutionalism, and Democracy*. Oxford: Oxford University Press.

Hardt, Michael and Antonio Negri (2000) *Empire*. Cambridge, MA; London: Harvard University Press.

Hardt, Michael and Antonio Negri (2005) *Multitude: War and Democracy in the Age of Empire*. London: Penguin.

Harrington, Michael (1981) 'Marxism and Democracy', *Praxis International* 1(1).

Harvey, David (2005) *A Brief History of Neoliberalism*. Oxford: Oxford University Press.

Hay, Colin (2002) *Political Analysis: A Critical Introduction*. Basingstoke, UK: Palgrave.

Hayek, Friedrich A. von (1973) *Law, Legislation and Liberty: a New Statement of the Liberal Principles of Justice and Political Economy*. London: Routledge & Kegan Paul.

Hayek, Friedrich A. von (2001) *The Road to Serfdom*. London: Routledge.

Hearn, Julie (2000) 'Aiding democracy? Donors and Civil Society in Africa', *Third World Quarterly* 21(5): 815–830.

Held, David (1995) *Democracy and the Global Order: from the Modern State to Cosmopolitan Governance*. Cambridge: Polity.

Held, David (1996) *Models of Democracy*, 2nd edn. Cambridge: Polity.

Held, David (2004) *Global Covenant: the Social Democratic Alternative to the Washington Consensus*. Cambridge: Polity.

Helgesen, Vidar (2010) Interview recorded on Video. Available at: http://www.idea.int/eudd_video.cfm

Hobson, Christopher and Milja Kurki (2011) *The Conceptual Politics of Democracy Promotion*. London: Routledge.

Hobson, J.A. (1909) *The Crisis of Liberalism: New Issues of Democracy*. London: P.S. King & Son.

Hout, Wil (2010) 'Governance and Development: changing EU policies', *Third World Quarterly*, 31(1): 1–12.

Howard, Marc Morje (2002) 'The Weakness of Postcommunist Civil Society', *Journal of Democracy* 13(1): 157–169.

Huber, Daniela (2008) 'Democracy Assistance in the Middle East and North Africa: A Comparison of US and EU Policies', *Mediterranean Politics* 13(1): 43–62.

Hulme and Edwards, eds (1997) *NGOs, States and Donors: Too Close for Comfort*. London: Save the Children / Macmillan Press.

Hunold, Christian (2005) 'Green Political Theory and the European Union: The Case for a Non-Integrated Civil Society', *Environmental Politics*, 14(3): 324–344.

Hurt, Stephen R., Karim Knio and J. Magnus Ryner (2009) 'Social Forces and the Effects of (Post)-Washington Consensus Policy in Africa: Comparing Tunisia and South Africa', *The Round Table: the Commonwealth Journal of International Affairs*, 98(402): 301–317.

Hyde-Price, Adrian (2008) 'A "Tragic Actor"? A Realist Perspective on "Ethical Power Europe"', *International Affairs* [Royal Institute of International Affairs] 84(1): 29–44.

Ikenberry, G. John (2000) 'America Liberal Grand Strategy: Democracy and National Security in the Post-War Era', in: Michael Cox, G. John Ikenberry and Takashi Inoguchi, eds, *American Democracy Promotion. Impulses, Strategies, and Impacts*. Oxford: Oxford University Press, pp. 103–126.

Ikenberry, G. John (2001) *After Victory: Institutions, Strategic Restraint, and the Rebuilding of Order after Major Wars*. Princeton, NJ; Oxford: Princeton University Press.

Ikenberry, G. John (2009) 'Liberal Internationalism 3.0: America and the Dilemmas of Liberal World Order', *Perspectives on Politics* 7(1): 71–87.

International IDEA (2008) *Assessing the Quality of Democracy: A Practical Guide*. Stockholm: IDEA. Available at: http://www.idea.int/publications/aqd/upload/aqd_practical_guide.pdf (accessed 25/04/2012).

International IDEA (2009a) *Democracy and Development: Global Consultations on the EU's Role in Democracy Building*. Stockholm: International IDEA.

International IDEA (2009b) 'At a Glance'. Available at: http://www.idea.int/about/upload/idea_ataglance_eng_web2.pdf. (accessed 25/04/2012).

International IDEA (2012) Front page. Available at: http://www.idea.int/ (accessed 25/04/2012).

IRI (2009) The International Republican Institute 2009 Brochure. Washington, DC: IRI. Available at: http://www.iri.org/sites/default/files/2009%20IRI%20Brochure.pdf (accessed 01/08/2011).

Iriye, A. (1993) *The Cambridge History of American Foreign Relations. Volume III. The Globalizing America.* Cambridge: Cambridge University Press.

Jacoby, Wade and Sophier Meunier (2010) 'Europe and the Management of Globalisation', *Journal of European Public Policy* 17(3): 299–317.

Jessop, Bob (2004) 'Critical Semiotic Analysis and the Critique of Political Economy', *Critical Discourse Studies* 1(1): 1–16.

Joseph, Jonathan (2012) *The Social in the Global.* Cambridge: Cambridge University Press.

Keane, John (2009) *The Life and Death of Democracy.* New York; London: W.W. Norton & Co.

Kelegama, Saman (2010) *EU Trade Policy and Democracy Building in South Asia,* Stockholm: International IDEA.

Kelley, Judith (2006) 'New Wine in Old Wineskins: Promoting Political Reforms through the New European Neighbourhood Policy', *JCMS: Journal of Common Market Studies* 44(1): 29–55.

Keyser, Veronique de (2011) 'Democracy Support: Seizing the Moment, Shifting the Paradigm', *OPPD News,* June 2011. Available at: http://www.europarl.europa.eu/pdf/oppd/Page_1/newsletter2011-06.pdf (accessed 24/10/2012).

Kochenov, Dimitry (2007) *EU Enlargment and the Failure of Conditionality: Pre-accession Conditionality in the Fields of Democracy and Rule of Law.* Dordrecht, Netherlands: Wolters Kluwer.

Kopstein, Jeffrey (2006) 'The Transatlantic Divide over Democracy Promotion', *The Washington Quarterly* 29(2): 85–98.

Korosteleva, Elena, ed. (2011) *The Eastern Partnership: a New Opportunity for the Neighbours?* London: Routledge.

Krugman, Paul (2007) 'Introduction', in: John Maynard Keynes, *The General Theory of Employment, Interest and Money.* Basingstoke, UK: Palgrave Macmillan for the Royal Economic Society.

Kumar, Krishna (2005) 'Reflections on international political party assistance', *Democratization,* 12(4): 505–527.

Kurki, Milja (2008) *Causation in International Relations: Reclaiming Causal Analysis.* Cambridge; New York: Cambridge University Press.

Kurki, Milja (2010), 'Democracy and Conceptual Contestability: Reconsidering Conceptions of Democracy in Democracy Promotion', *International Studies Review* 12(3): 362–386.

Kurki, Milja (2011a) 'The Limitations of the Critical Edge: Reflections on Critical and Philosophical IR Scholarship Today', *Millennium: Journal of International Studies* 40(1): 129–146.

Kurki, Milja (2011b) 'Governmentality and EU Democracy Promotion: The European Instrument for Democracy and Human Rights and the Construction of Democratic Civil Societies', *International Political Sociology* 5(4): 349–366.

Kurki, Milja (2012a) 'How the EU Can Adopt a New Type of Democracy Support', FRIDE working paper. Madrid: Fride. Available at: http://www.fride.org/publication-newsletter/998/how-the-eu-can-adopt-a-new-type-of-democracy-support (accessed 24/10/2012).

Kurki, Milja (2012b) 'Revisiting Politico-Economic Models of Democracy in Democracy Promotion', *International Studies Perspectives,* in press. [update?]

Lacey, Michael James (1989) *The Truman Presidency.* Cambridge: Cambridge University Press.

Laclau, Ernesto and Chantal Mouffe (2001) *Hegemony and Socialist Strategy: Towards a Radical Democratic Politics*. London: Verso.

Landman, Todd (2009) 'Concepts Matter: Delineating Democracy, Governance and Human Rights' Stockholm: International IDEA. Available at: http://www.idea.int/resources/analysis/delineating_democracy.cfm (accessed 25/04/2012).

Latham, Robert (1997) *The Liberal Moment: Modernity, Security, and the Making of Postwar International Order*. New York; Chichester: Columbia University Press.

Lavenex, Sandra and Frank Schimmelfennig (2009) 'EU Rules Beyond EU Borders: Theorizing External Governance in European politics', *Journal of European Public Policy* 16(6): 791–812.

Lavenex, Sandra and Frank Schimmelfennig (2010) *EU External Governance: Projecting EU Rules Beyond Membership*. London: Routledge.

Leftwich, Adrian (1996) 'On the Primacy of Politics in Development', in: A. Leftwich, ed., *Democracy and Development: Theory and Practice*. Oxford: Polity Press, pp. 1–18.

Lenin, Vladimir (1918) 'The Proletarian Revolution and the Renegade Kautsky', Available at: www.marxists.org/archive/lenin/works/1918/prrk/democracy.htm (accessed 24/10/2012)

Lenin, Vladimir Ilyich (1933) *State and Revolution*. London: Martin Lawrence.

Levy, Brian (2007) *Governance Reform: Bridging Monitoring and Action*. Washington, DC: World Bank.

Limbach and Michaelowa (2010) 'The Impact of World Bank and IMF Programs on Democratization in Developing Countries'. *CIS Working Paper No. 62*. Available at: http://papers.ssrn.com/sol3/papers.cfm?abstract_id=1678463 (accessed 28/04/2012).

Linklater, Andrew (1998) *The Transformation of Political Community*. Oxford: Polity Press.

Linklater, Andrew (2000) *International Relations: Critical Concepts in Political Science*. London: Routledge.

Lipset, Seymour Martin (1960) *Political Man: the Social Bases of Politics*. London: Heinemann.

Locke, John (1960 [1689]) *Two Treatises of Government*. Cambridge: Cambridge University Press.

Luckham, Robin (1998) 'Are There Alternatives to Liberal Democracy?', in: Mark Robinson and Gordon White, eds, *The Democratic Developmental State*. Oxford: Oxford University Press.

Lukes, Stephen (1974) *Power: A Radical View*. London: Macmillan Press.

Macpherson, C.B. (1977) *The Life and Times of Liberal Democracy*. Oxford: Oxford University Press.

McCann, Dermot (2010) *The Political Economy of the European Union*. Cambridge: Polity Press.

McFaul, Michael (2004/5) 'Democracy Promotion as a World Value', *Washington Quarterly* 28(1): 147–163.

McFaul, Michael (2010) *Advancing Democracy Abroad: Why We Should and How We Can*. Lanham, MD: Rowman & Littlefield.

Magen, Amichai A., Thomas Risse-Kappen and Michael McFaul, eds (2009) *Promoting Democracy and the Rule of Law: American and European Strategies*. Basingstoke, UK: Palgrave Macmillan.

Maiguascha, Bice and Catherine Eschle (2005) *Critical Theories, International Relations, and 'The Anti-Globalisation Movement': The Politics of Global Resistance*. London: Routledge.

Mainwaring, Scott and Timothy R. Scully (2008) 'Latin America: Eight Lessons for Governance', *Journal of Democracy* 19(3): 113–227.

Mair, Stefan (2000) 'Germany's Stiftungen and Democracy Assistance: Comparative Advantages, New Challenges', in: Peter Burnell, ed., *Democracy Assistance*. London: Frank Cass, pp. 128–149.

Mandelbaum, Michael (2007) *Democracy's Good Name: the Rise and Risks of World's Most Popular Form of Government*. New York: Public Affairs.

Manent, Pierre (1996) *An Intellectual History of Liberalism*. Princeton, NJ: Princeton University Press.

Manners, Ian (2006) 'The Constitutive Nature of Values, Images and Principles in the European Union', in: Sonia Lucarelli and Ian Manners, eds, *Values and Principles in European Foreign Policy*. London: Taylor and Francis, pp. 19–42.

Manners, Ian (2008) 'The Normative Ethics of the European Union', *International Affairs* 84(1): 45–71.

Marcuse, Herbert (1964) *One-dimensional Man: Studies in the Ideology of Advanced Industrial Society*. Boston: Beacon Press.

Marx, Karl and Friedrich Engels [Robert C. Tucker, ed.] (1978) *The Marx–Engels Reader*. New York; London: WW Norton.

Mayo, H. B. (1955) *Democracy and Marxism*. New York: Oxford University Press.

MCC (2007) *MCC and the Long Term Goal of Deepening Democracy*. Washington, DC: MCC. Available at: http://www.mcc.gov/documents/reports/mcc-112007-paper-democracy.pdf (accessed 20/03/2012).

MCC (2011) *Report on the Criteria and Methodology for Determining the Eligibility of Candidate Countries for Millenium Challenge Account Assistance for Fiscal Year 2011*. Washington, DC: MCC. Available at: http://www.mcc.gov/documents/reports/report-2010001039502-selection-criteria-and-methodology.pdf (accessed 20/03/2012).

Meernik, J. (1996) 'United States Military Intervention and the Promotion of Democracy', *Journal of Peace Research* 33(4): 391–402.

Merrill, Dennis (2006) 'The Truman Doctrine: Containing Communism and Modernity', *Presidential Studies Quarterly*, 36. Available at: http://www.questia.com/PM.qst?a=o&d=5015817872 (accessed 06/08/2011).

Miliband, Ralph (1977) *Marxism and Politics*. Oxford: Oxford University Press.

Moore, Barrington (1966) *Social Origins of Dictatorship and Democracy: Lord and Peasant in the Making of the Modern World*. Boston: Beacon Press.

Moyo, Sam (2001) 'The Land Occupation Movement and Democratisation in Zimbabwe: Contradictions of Neoliberalism', *Millennium: Journal of International Studies* 30(2): 311–330.

Murray Li, Tania (2007) *The Will to Improve: Governmentality, Development, and the Practice of Politics*. Durham: Duke University Press.

Nau, Henry R. (2002) *At Home Abroad: Identity and Power in American Foreign Policy*. Ithaca, NY: Cornell University Press.

NED (undated) *Statement of Principles*. Available at: http://www.ned.org/publications/statement-of-principles-and-objectives (accessed 20/03/2012).

NED (2006) The Backlash Against Democracy Assistance. Washington, DC: National Endowment for Democracy. Available at: http://www.ned.org/docs/backlash06.pdf (accessed 20/03/2012).

NED (2010) *2010 Annual Report*. Washington, DC: National Endowment for Democracy. Available at: http://www.ned.org/publications/annual-reports/2010-annual-report (accessed 20/03/2012).

NED (2012) *2012 Strategy Document*. Washington, DC: National Endowment for Democracy. Available at: http://www.ned.org/docs/strategy/2012StrategyDocument.pdf (accessed 20/03/2012).

Nelson, Stephen and Geoffrey Wallace (2005) 'Conditional Credibility: Explaining the Impact of the IMF on Democratization', conference paper for *American Political Science Association Meeting, September 1–5, Washington, D.C.* Available at: http://government.arts.cornell.edu/assets/psac/fa05/nelson_wallace_PSAC.pdf (accessed 20/03/2012).

NIGD (2012) 'About'. Available at: http://nigdwp.kaapeli.fi/?page_id=2 (accessed 20/03/2012).

Novitz, Tonia (2008) 'Legal Power and Normative Sources in the Field of Social Policy: Normative Power Europe at Work?', in: Jan Orbie, ed., *Europe's Global Role: External Policies of the European Union*. Farnham, UK: Ashgate, pp. 139–156.

Nylen, William R. (2003) *Participatory Democracy versus Elitist Democracy: Lessons from Brazil*. New York; Basingstoke, UK: Palgrave Macmillan.

Obama, B. (2007) Remarks of Senator Barak Obama to the Chicago Council on Foreign Affairs, 23 April. Available at: http://www.cfr.org/us-election-2008/remarks-senator-barack-obama-chicago-council-global-affairs/p13172 (accessed 20/03/2012).

Obama, B. (2011a) 'Remarks by the President on the Economy'. Osawatomie, KA: 6 December, 2011. Available at: http://www.whitehouse.gov/the-press-office/2011/12/06/remarks-president-economy-osawatomie-kansas (accessed 20/03/2012).

Obama, B. (2011b) 'Joint Statement by President Rousseff and President Obama'. Washington, DC: The White House, 19 March, 2011. Available at: http://www.whitehouse.gov/the-press-office/2011/03/19/joint-statement-president-rousseff-and-president-obama (accessed 20/03/2012).

Obama, B. (2012a) 'Remarks by the President at the Consumer Financial Protection Bureau'. Washington, DC: The White House, 6 January, 2012. Available at: http://www.whitehouse.gov/the-press-office/2012/01/06/remarks-president-consumer-financial-protection-bureau (accessed 20/03/2012).

Obama, B. (2012b) 'State of the Union Address'. Washington, DC: United States Capitol, 24 January, 2012. Available at: http://www.presidentialrhetoric.com/speeches/01.24.12.html (accessed 20/03/2012).

O'Donnell, Guillermo (2007) 'The Perpetual Crises of Democracy', *Journal of Democracy* 18(1): 5–11.

OPPD [Office for the Promotion of Parliamentary Democracy] (2009) *Democracy Revisited; Which Notion of Democracy for the EU's External Relations?* Brussels: European Parliament.

Orbie, Jan (2008) 'European Union's Role in World Trade: Harnessing Globalisation', in: Jan Orbie, ed., *Europe's Global Role: External Policies of the European Union*. Farnham, UK: Ashgate, pp. 35–66.

Orbie, Jan and Lisa Tortell (2009) 'From Social Clause to the Social Dimension of Globalisation', in: Jan Orbie and Lisa Tortell, eds, *European Union and the Social Dimension of Globalisation: How the EU Influences the World*. London: Routledge, pp. 1–26.

Pace, Michelle (2009) 'Liberal or Social Democracy? Aspects of the EU's Democracy Promotion Agenda in the Middle East'. Stockholm: International IDEA. Available at: http://www.idea.int/resources/analysis/upload/Pace-2.pdf (accessed 25 April, 2012).

Pace, Michelle (2010) 'Interrogating the European Union's Democracy Promotion Agenda: Discursive Configurations of "Democracy" from the Middle East', *European Foreign Affairs Review* 15: 611–630.

Pateman, Carole (1970) *Participation and Democratic Theory.* Cambridge: Cambridge University Press.

Patomäki, Heikki and Teivo Teivainen (2004) *A Possible World: Democratic Transformation of Global Institutions.* London: Zed.

Peceny, M. (1999) 'Forcing Them to Be Free', *Political Research Quarterly* 52(3): 549–582.

Perkins, B. (1993) *The Cambridge History of American Foreign Relations. Volume I. The Creation of a Republican Empire, 1777–1865.* Cambridge: Cambridge University Press.

Philp, Mark (1997) 'Defining Political Corruption', *Political Studies* 45(3): 436–462.

Pridham, Geoffrey (2005) *Designing Democracy: EU Enlargement and Regime Change in Post-Communist Europe.* Basingstoke, UK: Palgrave Macmillan.

Przeworski, Adam (1991) *Democracy and the Market: Political and Economic Reforms in Eastern Europe and Latin America.* Cambridge: Cambridge University Press.

Przeworski, Adam, Michael Alvarez, José Antonio Cheibub and Fernando Limongi (2000) *Democracy and Development.* Cambridge: Cambridge University Press.

Raik, Kristi (2004) 'EU Accession of Central and Eastern European Countries: Democracy and Integration as Conflicting Logics', *East European Politics and Societies* 18(4): 567–595.

Rawls, John (1971) *A Theory of Justice.* Cambridge, MA: Belknap Press of Harvard University Press.

Rawls, John (1993) *Political Liberalism.* New York: Columbia University Press.

Rawls, John (2004) *Justice as Fairness: a Restatement.* Delhi: Universal.

Reagan, Ronald (1982) 'Address to the British Parliament', Royal Gallery at the Palace of Westminster, London, 8 June, 1982. Available at: http://www.reagan.utexas.edu/archives/speeches/1982/60882a.htm (accessed 20/03/2012).

Reynaerts, Vicky (2011) 'Preoccupied with the Market: the EU as a Promoter of 'Shallow' Democracy in the Mediterranean', *European Foreign Affairs Review* 16: 623–638.

Riley, Jonathan (1994) 'Editors' Introduction', in: *Principles of Political Economy: and Chapters on Socialism* by J.S. Mill, ed. by Jonathan Riley. Oxford: Oxford University Press.

Robinson, William I. (1996) *Promoting Polyarchy: Globalization, US Intervention, and Hegemony.* Cambridge: Cambridge University Press.

Roosevelt, Theodore (1910) The New Nationalism, Speech at Osawatomie, Kansas, 31 August. Available at: http://www.theodore-roosevelt.com/images/research/speeches/trnationalismspeech.pdf (accessed 20/03/2012).

Roosevelt, F.D. (1941) *The Four Freedoms*, Speech at the US Congress. Washington, DC: 6 January. Available at: http://www.americanrhetoric.com/speeches/fdrthefourfreedoms.htm (accessed 20/03/2012).

Rosanvallon, Pierre (2008) 'Democratic Universalism as a Historical Problem'. Available at: http://www.booksandideas.net/Democratic-Universalism-as-a.html?lang=fr (accessed 20/03/2012).

Rupnik, Jacques (2007) 'From Democracy Fatigue to Populist Backlash', *Journal of Democracy* 18(4): 17–25.

Rupnik, Jacques (2010) 'Twenty Years of Postcommunism: in Search of a New Model', *Journal of Democracy* 21(1): 105–112.

Ryner, Magnus (2002) *Capitalist Restructuring, Globalisation, and the Third Way: Lessons from the Swedish model.* London: Routledge.

Sabine, George H. (1961) *A History of Political Theory.* Edinburgh: Harrap.

Sadiki, Larbi (2000) 'Popular Uprisings and Arab Democratization', *International Journal of Middle East Studies* 32: 71–95.

Sadiki, Larbi (2004) *The Search for Arab Democracy: Discourses and Counter-Discourses.* London: Hurst & Company.

Santiso, Carlos (2003) 'Sisyphus in the Castle: Improving European Union Strategies for Democracy Promotion and Governance Conditionality', *European Journal of Development Research* 15(1): 1–1?.

Sayer, Andrew (1992) *Method in Social Science: A Realist Approach.* London: Routledge.

Sayer, R. Andrew (2000) *Realism and Social Science.* London: Sage.

Schimmelfennig, Frank and Hanno Scholtz (2008) 'EU Democracy Promotion in the European Neighbourhood: Political Conditionality, Economic Development and Transnational Exchange', *European Union Politics* 9(2): 187–215.

Schumpeter, Joseph Alois (1976) *Capitalism, Socialism, and Democracy.* London: Allen and Unwin.

Sen, Amartya (1999) 'Democracy as a Universal Value', *Journal of Democracy* 10(3): 3–17.

Sending, Ole Jacob and Iver Neumann (2006) 'Governance to Governmentality: Analyzing NGOs, States, and Power', *International Studies Quarterly* 50(3): 651–672.

Sending, Ole Jacob and Iver Neumann (2010) *Governing the Global Polity Practice, Mentality, Rationality.* Minneapolis, MN: University of Minnesota Press.

Shah, R. (2011) '2011 Annual Letter'. Washington, DC: USAID. Available at: http://50. usaid.gov/2011-annual-letter/introduction (accessed 20/03/2012).

SIGIR (2007) *15th Quarterly Report to The United States Congress.* 30 October, 2007.

SIGIR (2008) *16th Quarterly Report to The United States Congress.* 31 January, 2008.

Sjursen, Helene (2006) 'The EU as a 'Normative' Power: How Can This Be?' *Journal of European Public Policy* 13(2): 235–251.

Sklar, Richard L. (1987) 'Developmental Democracy' *Comparative Studies in Society and History* 29(4): 686–714.

Slaughter, Ann Marie (1997) 'The Real New World Order', *Foreign Affairs* 76(5): 183–197.

Smith, Adam (1970 [1776]) *The Wealth of Nations.* Books I–III [Introduction by Andrew S. Skinner]. Harmondsworth, UK: Penguin.

Smith, Karen E (2008) *European Union Foreign Policy in a Changing World.* 2nd edn. Cambridge: Polity Press.

Smith, Tony (1994) *America's Mission: the United States and the Worldwide Struggle for Democracy in the Twentieth Century.* Princeton, NJ: Princeton University Press.

Smith, Tony (2011) 'From "Fortunate Vagueness" to "Democratic Globalism": American Democracy Promotion as Imperialism', in: C. Hobson and M. Kurki, eds, *Conceptual Politics of Democracy Promotion.* London: Routledge, 201–214

Spanger, Hans-Joachim and Jonas Wolff (2003) 'Poverty Reduction through Democratisation? PRSP: Challenges of a New Development Strategy', PRIF Report, No. 66, Frankfurt: Peace Research Institute.

Swedberg. Richard (1986) 'Doctrine of Economic Neutrality of the IMF and the WB', *Journal of Peace Research* 23(4): 177–189.

Szymanski, Marcela and Michael Smith (2005) 'Coherence and Conditionality in European Foreign Policy: Negotiating the EU-Mexico Global Agreement'. *JCMS: Journal of Common Market Studies* 43(1): 171–192.

Teivainen, Teivo (2002) *Enter Economism, Exit Politics: Experts, Economic Policy and the Damage to Democracy.* London: Zed.

Teivainen, Teivo (2009) 'The Pedagogy of Global Development: the Promotion of Electoral Democracy and the Latin Americanisation of Europe', *Third World Quarterly* 30(1): 163–179.

Teixeira, Nuno Severiano, ed. (2008) *The International Politics of Democratization: Comparative Perspectives.* London: Routledge.

Thayer, Bradley A. (2010) 'The Continued Relevance of Realism in the Age of Obama: *Plus Ça Change plus C'est La Même Chose'. American Foreign Policy Interests* 32(1): 1–4.

Thirkell-White (2005) *The IMF and the Politics of Financial Globalization.* Basingstoke: Palgrave Macmillan.

Tilton, Timothy Alan (1990) *The Political Theory of Swedish Social Democracy: Through the Welfare State to Socialism.* Oxford: Clarendon Press.

Toledo, Alexandro (2010) 'Latin America: Democracy with Development', *Journal of Democracy* 21(4): 5–12

Trommer, Silke (2011) 'Activists Beyond Brussels: Transnational NGO Strategies on EU–West African Trade Negotiations', *Globalizations* 8(1): 113–126.

Tsoukalis, Loukas (2003) *What Kind of Europe?* Oxford: Oxford University Press.

US Department of State (2010a) *Advancing Freedom and Democracy Reports* (Washington, DC: US Department of State). Available at: http://www.state.gov/g/drl/rls/afdr/2010/frontmatter/129719.htm (accessed 20 October 2010).

US Department of State (2010b) *Leading through Civilian Power. The First Quadrennial Diplomacy and Development Review.* Washington, DC: US Department of State.

USAID (1998) *Handbook of Democracy and Governance Program Indicators* (Washington, DC: United States Agency for International Development).

USAID DCHA/DG (2010) *User's Guide to DG Programming* Washington, DC: United States Agency for International Development.

USAID (2007) *Iraq PRTs.* Washington, DC: United States Agency for International Development.

USAID (2010) *Building Local Development Leadership. USAID's Operational and Procurement Improvement Plan.* Washington, DC: United States Agency for International Development. Available at: http://forward.usaid.gov/sites/default/files/Building%20local%20development%20leadership%20PA.pdf (accessed 20/03/2012).

USAID (2011a) *USAID Policy Framework 2011–2015.* Washington, DC: United States Agency for International Development. Available at: http://www.usaid.gov/policy/USAID_PolicyFramework.PDF (accessed 20/03/2012).

USAID (2011b) *Partnering with USAID. Building Alliances for Sustainable Solutions.* Washington, DC: United States Agency for International Development. Available at: http://pdf.usaid.gov/pdf_docs/PNADW238.pdf (accessed 20/03/2012).

USAID (2011c) *USAID Partner Compliance and Oversight.* Washington, DC: United States Agency for International Development. Available at: http://www.usaid.gov/compliance/ (accessed 20/03/2012).

Vazquez-Arroyo, Antonio Y. (2008) 'Liberal Democracy and Neoliberalism: a Critical Juxtaposition' *New Political Science* 32(2): 127–159.

Waligorski, Conrad (1997) *Liberal Economics and Democracy: Keynes, Galbraith, Thurow, and Reich.* Lawrence, KS: University Press of Kansas.

Wedel, Janine R (2009) *Shadow Elite: How the World's New Power Brokers Undermine Democracy, Government, and the Free Market.* New York: Basic Books.

Wetzel, Anne and Jan Orbie (2011) 'Promoting Embedded Democracy? Researching the Substance of EU Democracy Promotion', *European Foreign Affairs Review* 16: 565–587.

Whitehead, Laurence (2002) *Democratization: Theory and Experience.* Oxford: Oxford University Press.

Whitehead, Laurence (2009) 'Losing "the Force"? The "Dark Side" of democratization after Iraq', *Democratization* 16(2): 215–242.

Whitehead, Laurence (2010) 'The Crash of '08', *Journal of Democracy* 21(1): 45–56.

Williams, A. (1998) *Failed Imagination? New World Orders and the Twentieth Century.* Manchester: Manchester University Press.

Williams, Andrew (2006) *Liberalism and War: the Victors and the Vanquished.* Abingdon, UK: Routledge.

Williams, David (1999) 'Constructing the Economic Space: the World Bank and the Making of Homo Oeconomicus', *Millennium* 28(1): 79–99.

Williams, David (2011) *The World Bank and Social Transformation in International Politics: Liberalism, Governance and Sovereignty.* London: Routledge.

Williams, Michelle (2008) *The Roots of Participatory Democracy: Democratic Communists in South Africa and Kerala, India.* New York: Palgrave Macmillan.

Wolfe, Robert (1984) *Americans as Proconsuls: United States Military Government in Germany and Japan, 1944–1952.* Carbondale: Southern Illinois University Press.

Wolff, Jonas (2009) 'De-Idealizing the Democratic Civil Peace: On the Political Economy of Democratic Stabilisation and Pacification in Argentina and Ecuador', *Democratization* 16(5): 998–1026.

Wolff, Jonas (2011) 'Challenges to Democracy Promotion: the Case of Bolivia'. Carnegie Paper. Available at: http://carnegieendowment.org/2011/03/30/challenges-to-democracy-promotion-case-of-bolivia/1mfi (accessed 13/08/2012).

Wolin, Sheldon S. (2008) *Democracy Incorporated: Managed Democracy and the Specter of Inverted Totalitarianism.* Princeton, NJ; Oxford: Princeton University Press.

Wollack, K. (2010) 'Assisting Democracy Abroad. American Values, American Interests', *Harvard International Review.* Fall 2010. Available at: http://www.ndi.org/files/Harvard_International_Review_Wollack_Fall2010.pdf (accessed 20/03/2012).

Wollack, Kenneth and Scott Hubli (2010) 'Getting Convergence Right'. *Journal of Democracy* 21(4): 35–42 (accessed 20/03/2012).

World Bank (1997) *A State in a Changing World.* Washington, DC: World Bank.

World Bank (2002) *Building Institutions for Markets.* Washington, DC: World Bank.

World Bank Institute (2012a) 'Supporting Open Governance', Available at: http://wbi.worldbank.org/wbi/content/supporting-open-governance (accessed 28/04/2012).

World Bank Institute (2012b) 'Collaborative Governance', Available at: http://wbi.worldbank.org/wbi/about/topics/governance (accessed 28/04/2012).

Youngs, Richard (2001) *The European Union and the Promotion of Democracy.* Oxford: Oxford University Press.

Youngs, Richard (2003) 'European Approaches to Democracy Assistance: Learning the Right Lessons?' *Third World Quarterly* 24(1): 127–138.

Youngs, Richard (2008a) Is European Democracy Promotion on the Wane? CEPS Working Document No. 292. Available at: http://ssrn.com/abstract=1337603 or http://dx.doi.org/10.2139/ssrn.1337603 (accessed 20/03/2012).

Youngs, Richard (2008b) *Is the European Union Supporting Democracy in its Neighbourhood?* Madrid: FRIDE. Available at: http://www.fride.org/download/librofride.pdf (accessed 20/03/2012).

Youngs, Richard (2009) Democracy promotion as external governance? *Journal of European Public Policy* 16(6): 895–915.

Youngs, Richard (2010) *The European Union and Democracy Promotion: a Critical Global Assessment.* Baltimore, MD: Johns Hopkins University Press.

Youngs, Richard (2011a) 'Misunderstanding the Maladies of Liberal Democracy Promotion', in: C. Hobson and M. Kurki, eds, *Conceptual Politics of Democracy Promotion.* London: Routledge, pp. 100–116.

Youngs, Richard (2011b) *The EU's Role in World Politics: A Retreat from Liberal Internationalism.* London: Routledge.

Zakaria, Farid (1997) 'The Rise of Illiberal Democracy', *Foreign Affairs* 76(6): 22–43.

Zeeuw, Jeroen de (2005) 'Projects Do Not Create Institutions: The Record of Democracy Assistance in Post-Conflict Societies', *Democratization* 12(4): 481–504.

Zielonka, Jan and Peter Mair (2002) *The Enlarged European Union: Diversity and Adaptation.* London: Frank Cass.

Zinn, Howard (2003) *A People's History of the United States: 1492–present.* London: Pearson Longman.

Zittel, Thomas and Dieter Fuchs (2007) *Participatory Democracy and Political Participation.* London: Routledge.

Index